KU-078-876

To the victims and the survivors
of the Holocaust
and to those who preserve and tell their story

'Remember the days of yore,
Learn the lessons of the generation that came before you.'

– Deuteronomy 32:7

Contents

Preface to the Paperback Edition

In April 1993, in conjunction with the opening of the United States Holocaust Memorial Museum, the Roper Organization conducted a poll to determine the extent of Americans' knowledge of the Holocaust. Neither the Roper Organization nor the American Jewish Committee, which sponsored the poll, expected any startling results. But they were surprised by the response to one of the questions. When asked 'Do you think it possible or impossible that the Holocaust did not happen?' 22 percent of American adults and 20 percent of American high school students answered, yes, it was possible.* The response shocked many people who had long dismissed Holocaust denial as a wacky phenomenon of no more validity than the claim that the earth is regularly visited by alien beings. The poll's results, coupled with the deniers' recent forays onto college campuses in order to publish ads in campus newspapers denying the Holocaust, convinced many people that Holocaust denial constituted a clear and present danger. When *Denying the Holocaust* appeared but a few weeks after the Roper poll, many of these former skeptics hailed me for having realized long before virtually anyone else that this was a serious threat.

Some reviews of the book made particular note of the fact that when I began investigating the Holocaust denial phenomenon in 1987 I had been subjected by colleagues and friends to some friendly and – not so friendly – skepticism for 'taking these kooks seriously.' Among the most contrite were those who had been most vigorous in their

---

* Ironically, those who conceived of the poll originally considered omitting this question because they assumed that the affirmative responses would be negligible.

assaults on me for believing the deniers worthy of serious scholarship. In a public *mea maxima culpa*, one reviewer identified himself as one who had taken me to task for wasting my time on this topic. Admitting his mistake, he declared the book a work of 'stunning relevance.'

Ironically, I counseled and continue to counsel a more cautious, certainly not benign, reaction to the Roper statistic. It is true that when a similar question was asked in Britain and France, doubters numbered less than 7 percent. But the 22 percent response must be considered within the American social context. A significant number of Americans, when asked if the most outlandish situation is possible or impossible, are prone to answer yes, 'possible'.* Second, the question was awkwardly constructed, with a double negative embedded within it. Even the Roper organization acknowledged that it could have been worded more clearly. (The same double negative did not, however, appear to confuse those who were polled in other countries.) There is also the possibility that respondents interpreted the question in a more colloquial sense and that it was simply hard for them to believe that the Holocaust might have happened.

My suspicions about the Roper poll were confirmed recently by a Gallup poll which posed the same question but without the double negative. The results were markedly different: 83% said the Holocaust definitely happened, 13% said it probably happened and 4% said it did not or had no opinion. These results indicate that the deniers have not made great inroads into public opinion.

When this particular question is analyzed together with the responses to the sixteen other questions on the poll there is cause for alarm, but not about the deniers. The other responses indicate an appalling American ignorance of the most basic facts of the Holocaust. Thirty-eight percent of adults and 53 percent of high school students either 'don't know' or incorrectly explain what is meant by 'the Holocaust.' Twenty-two percent of adults and 24 percent of students do not know that it occurred after the Nazis came to power in Germany. The poll demonstrates what will be possible in years to

---

* According to certain surveys the number who believe Elvis Presley is alive is in the double digits.

come if the deniers' methodology and agenda are not exposed now and, more important, if basic education about the Holocaust is not improved. It was this fear and not prescience that prompted me to address this subject years ago. And it is this fear about the potential impact of the deniers that prompts my continued interest in this topic.

The deniers' window of opportunity will be enhanced in years to come. The public, particularly the uneducated public, will be increasingly susceptible to Holocaust denial as survivors die. The dramatic difference between hearing a story directly from one who has experienced it and hearing it second- or third-hand has long been illustrated for me by my cousins' experience. Approximately fifteen years older than I, they grew up in Cincinnati. Their father employed an elderly African American gentleman, Charlie Washington, who had been born a slave on a plantation. My cousins heard stories of slavery from him and some of his friends who had also been slaves. For my cousins the Civil War and slavery are not events of the distant American past. They occupy primary places in the storehouse of their childhood memories. In contrast, though I recognize them as exceptionally important aspects of our nation's history, they are for me part of nineteenth-century America. So too with the Holocaust. Future generations will not hear the story from people who can say 'this is what happened to *me*. This is *my* story.' For them it will be part of the distant past and, consequently, more susceptible to revision and denial.

The results of the Roper poll have also elicited challenges to my steadfast refusal to debate deniers. Since the book's appearance I have received numerous invitations to appear on television talk shows aired nationally in the United States. Whenever the plans include inviting a denier I categorically decline to appear. As I make clear in these pages the deniers want to be thought of as the 'other side.' Simply appearing with them on the same stage accords them that status. Those who have challenged me to reconsider this policy fear that when I refuse, the deniers are left free to posit their claims with no one to challenge them. In fact, whenever I refused an invitation to appear on such a show, the producers abandoned the idea for the show shortly thereafter. Refusal to debate the deniers thwarts their desire to enter the conversation as a legitimate point of view.

The deniers have painted my refusal to debate them and my resistance to the publication of Holocaust denial ads in campus newspapers as a reflection of my lack of tolerance for the First Amendment and my opposition to free intellectual inquiry. In an ad they began to circulate in the fall of 1993, they have labeled me an 'intellectual fascist.' However, their claim that the Holocaust is treated as a sacrosanct subject that is not open to debate is ludicrous. There is little about the Holocaust that is *not* debated and discussed. Among the questions continually being debated in any conference or class on the Holocaust are:

> Was the Final Solution a product of Hitler's evil machinations alone, or was it devised and proposed by lower-level officials in response to war-related developments?

> Is the Holocaust the same as a variety of other acts of persecution and genocide, e.g., the massacre of Native Americans or the 'ethnic cleansing' in Bosnia?

> Could Jews have resisted the Nazis more forcefully?

> Were the actions of the non-Jewish rescuers heroic or the minimum one might have expected from any person who professed to be God-fearing and decent?

> Were the *Judenräte*, the Jewish councils installed by the Nazis in every ghetto in order to supervise ghetto life, too compliant with Nazi demands? Was a *Judenrat*'s refusal to alert the ghetto population to the fate awaiting it an act of collaboration or an attempt to ease the victims' mental anguish during their final days?

> Could American Jewish organizations have had a significant impact on the course of the Holocaust if they had been more organized and less engaged in internecine warfare?

There is a categorical difference between debating these types of questions and debating the very fact of the Holocaust.

This is not to suggest that students who ask how we evaluate the veracity of certain testimony should be shunted aside. It is crucial that they be shown *how* we know what we know, e.g., how oral testimony is correlated with written documentation; how testimony is evaluated for its historical accuracy; and how artifacts are determined to be genuine. Some conclusions we once thought to be true we now know are not. The intellectual process is rooted in the constant reevaluation of previous findings based on new information. So too with the Holocaust. We will debate much about it but not whether it happened. That would be the equivalent of the scholar of ancient Rome debating whether the Roman empire ever existed or the French historian proving that there really was a French Revolution.

In the academic arena there have been those who have interpreted this stance as inconsistent with the free pursuit of ideas for which the academy stands. This reflects a failure to understand both the ludicrousness of Holocaust denial and the nature of the academy. It reflects the moral relativism prevalent on many campuses and in society at large. The misguided notion that everyone's view is of equal stature has created an atmosphere that allows Holocaust denial to flourish.

This kind of confusion surfaced on a number of college campuses in the fall of 1993 in response to an advertisement attacking me and the United States Holocaust Memorial Museum. The ad, which makes the wild accusation that the museum contains no proof of homicidal gassing chambers, also claims that 'the Deborah Lipstadts – and there is a clique of them on every campus – work to suppress revisionist research and demand that students and faculty ape their fascist behavior.'

The New York State University College at Buffalo ran the ad. In a column explaining his decision, the editor dismissed Holocaust denial as lacking all validity.

> There is enough undeniable proof for the existence of the Nazi atrocity for the educated to understand why it shouldn't happen again. The real question is not whether it happened, but how many people don't know that it happened?

Despite this he ran the ad because, he claimed, 'there are two sides to every issue and both have a place on the pages of any open-minded paper's editorial page.' The *Georgetown Record* offered the same justification. According to its editor-in-chief 'the issue of freedom of expression outweighed the issue of the offensive nature of the advertisement.' The editors discussed running a disclaimer next to the ad but rejected it because it 'didn't seem like the true spirit of freedom of expression.' Given this position one should logically expect to find op-ed columns, letters to the editor, and advertisements claiming that women should be kept barefoot and pregnant, that individuals of African descent should be physically separated from America's 'European' population, that the moon landing was staged in Nevada, and a variety of other nonsensical positions that are held by some portion of the population.

Those who take this position fail to understand that which Hannah Arendt observed in an essay called 'Truth and Politics.' Opinion must be grounded in fact.

> Facts inform opinions and opinions, inspired by different interests and passions, can differ widely and still be legitimate as long as they respect factual truth. Freedom of opinion is a farce unless factual information is guaranteed and the facts themselves are not in dispute.

One can believe that Elvis Presley is alive and well and living in Moscow. However sincere one's conviction, that does not make it a legitimate opinion or 'other side' of a debate. In the name of free inquiry we must not succumb to the silly view, as these editors did, that every idea is of equal validity and worth. Although the academy must remain a place where ideas can be freely and vigorously explored it must first be a place that differentiates between ideas with lasting quality and those with none.*

---

* The University of Michigan editors displayed the same confused thinking that typified their colleagues' behavior two years earlier. While explicitly rejecting the notion that the Holocaust was a hoax, the editors ran the ad as an op-ed piece in the paper's Viewpoint section. They claimed that because the first time they ran the ad there had been such a strong reaction on campus, this new ad was 'relevant' to the community. (One could argue that if there had been a homophobic incident on the campus, *everything* homophobes wrote would be relevant to the university community.) The editors' primary reason for running the ad was that if it was 'suppress[ed]' the notions it expounded 'would fester and grow.' The editors con-

Finally, in the wake of the publication of my book, I have been asked whether I believe that the threat posed by the deniers has been mitigated. Given the attention accorded the Holocaust deniers and their methodology, I would like to believe that it has been. I would like to imagine that my study of people and material with 'no redeeming social value' had denied the deniers future success. But ultimately I recognize that though Holocaust denial is totally irrational, in some strange fashion it appeals to the quixotic side in us. We would prefer the deniers to be right. Moreover, there is a part in everyone – including survivors – that simply finds the Holocaust beyond belief. This may explain why some of the 22 percent who answered Roper in the affirmative did so. They found it hard to believe the Holocaust happened. Given that the Holocaust itself beggars the imagination, it is predictable that the deniers will find good-hearted but uneducated people who will succumb to these mental gyrations.

More important, we must remember that we are dealing with an

---

tended that it was their responsibility to make sure that such claims received the 'scrutiny they deserve.' While they did not fall prey to a mistaken notion that this was a First Amendment issue, the wisdom of their tactic is open to question. They could have published an analytical article that used segments of the ad to explain Holocaust denial's tactics and nonsensical nature. Rather they gave this nonsense the status of a 'viewpoint,' something the deniers are quick to exploit. (*Michigan Daily*, October 6, 1993)

The editors of Brandeis University's *Justice* took a similar approach and proclaimed that they ran the ad so readers would 'know that such thinking existed.' When they were castigated by other students on campus for their actions, the editors condemned the students for their lack of 'empathy.' (*The Justice*, December 7, 1993; *New York Times*, December 12, 1993)

The editor of the *Stanford Daily* published an eloquent and impassioned editorial attacking Holocaust deniers and ran the ad, with the address for additional information obscured, as a sidebar to the editorial. Students and faculty protested that he could have accomplished the same ends with the editorial but without the ad. (*Stanford Daily*, October 26, 1993)

When the Notre Dame *Observer* ran the ad as a result of an 'oversight,' it received a long letter from a student who compared the deniers' claims to other historical assumptions that have been altered as a result of scholarly inquiry including the Ptolemaic view that the earth is the center of the solar system. This student granted the deniers exactly what they wished: they became a legitimate other side that would eventually be vindicated by the evidence. (*The Observer*, November 18, 19, 23, 1993) irrational phenomenon that is rooted in one of the oldest hatreds, antisemitism. Antisemitism, like every other form of prejudice, is not responsive to logic. We may battle against contemporary manifestations of it and hope that we are successful, but none of us should be deluded into thinking that any particular battle will be the last. Deniers may have been dealt a blow by major developments such as the opening of the United States Holocaust Memorial Museum and the film *Schindler's List*. But a museum and film alone will not vanquish them. Either the deniers or the next genre of antisemites will eventually surface in some other form. As Albert Camus reminds us in the final paragraphs of *The Plague*:

> He knew that the tale he had to tell could not be one of a final victory. It could be only the record of what had had to be done and what assuredly would have to be done again in the never-ending fight against terror and its relentless onslaughts ... And indeed, as he listened to the cries of joy rising from the town Rieux remembered that such joy is always imperilled. He knew what those jubilant crowds did not know but could have learned from books: that the plague bacillus never dies or disappears for good; that it can lie dormant for years and years in furniture and linen-chests; that it bides its time in bedrooms, cellars, trunks and bookshelves; and that perhaps the day would come when ... it roused up its rats again and sent them forth to die in a happy city.

In the 1930s Nazi rats spread a virulent form of antisemitism that resulted in the destruction of millions. Today the bacillus carried by these rats threatens to 'kill' those who already died at the hands of the Nazis for a second time by destroying the world's memory of them. One can only speculate about the form of the bacillus' next mutation. All those who value truth, particularly truths that are subject to attack by the plague of hatred, must remain ever vigilant. The bacillus of prejudice is exceedingly tenacious and truth and memory exceedingly fragile.

– Deborah E. Lipstadt
Atlanta, Ga.
January, 1994

Preface

When I first began studying Holocaust denial, people would stare at me strangely. Incredulous, they would ask, 'You take those guys seriously?' Invariably I would be challenged with the query, 'Why are you wasting your time on those kooks?' My intention to write a book on this topic would have evoked no stronger a reaction if I were to write about flat-earth theorists.

That situation has changed dramatically. Regrettably, I no longer have to convince others of the relevance of this work. In fact, those who once questioned my choice of a topic now ask when the book will be available. The deniers' recent activity has fostered enhanced interest that gives my work unanticipated relevance. But rather than be delighted at no longer having to convince people that this is a legitimate topic, I wish we could still afford the luxury of wondering whether we should take these people seriously. Given the terrible harm they can cause, I would have much preferred to pursue something obscure than an issue that is now so relevant.

This has been a difficult project because at times I have felt compelled to prove something I knew to be true. I had constantly to avoid being inadvertently sucked into a debate that is no debate and an argument that is no argument. It has been a disconcerting and, at times, painful task that would have been impossible without the aid and support of a variety of people. Without them I would have never emerged from this morass. A number of friends and colleagues carefully read and commented on portions of this manuscript. Their observations and criticisms enhanced my work immeasurably. My profound thanks to Arnold Band, Yisrael Gutman, Manuel Prutschi,

Michael Nutkiewicz, Regina Morantz-Sanchez, David Ellenson, Michael Berenbaum, David Blumenthal, and Grace Grossman. In addition, I received important assistance from Gail Gans and the research department of the Anti-Defamation League. Adaire Klein, chief librarian of the Simon Wiesenthal Center, graciously made the Center's resources available to me, as did Elizabeth Koenig of the United States Holocaust Memorial Museum. Tony Lehrman of the Institute for Jewish Affairs in London generously helped with research. Manuel Prutschi of the Canadian Jewish Congress provided me with important background information on the activities of Ernst Zundel. Michael Maroko and Jeff Mausner shared important aspects of the Mel Mermelstein case with me. Shelly Z. Shapiro was particularly generous with her time and energy.

I would like to thank Yehuda Bauer, the chairman of the Vidal Sassoon Center for the Study of Antisemitism, The Hebrew University of Jerusalem, who was a patient and valuable colleague throughout.

Elliot Dorff, Peter Hayes, Elinor Langer, Laurie Levenson, Doug Mirell, Larry Powell, Claudia Koonz, Jason Berry, Alex Heard, Terry Pristin, Paul Kessler, Joyce Appelby, Riki Heilik, Rutty Gross, Mark Saperstein, Glenda B. Minkin, and Sherry Woocher all gave their time and insights. Kenneth Stern of the American Jewish Committee provided important data on the deniers' recent activities.

At The Free Press, Erwin Glikes recognized the importance of this work from the outset. At a time when others were looking at me strangely and wondering why I was bothering with this project, he urged me to move forward with it. Adam Bellow was a precise and demanding editor, exactly what I needed and wanted. His support of this project and his sensitivity to the broader dangers of Holocaust denial were crucial in helping me reach this stage. Susan Llewellyn copy edited with careful attention. Edith Lewis helped ensure speedy production of the final manuscript.

I complete this book as one chapter of my life has closed and a new one is opening. Finishing the book would have been impossible if not for the support of a close circle of friends. They were like family: loving, dependable – particularly at times of crisis – and supportive of me even when it was difficult to be so. Though I am now physically distant from most of them, they remain quite near, having taught me that God's presence can be found in many different places and made manifest in a variety of ways (Genesis 28:16).

Deborah E. Lipstadt
Atlanta, Georgia
January 14, 1993

I
Canaries in the Mine

*Holocaust Denial and the Limited
Power of Reason*

We are not afraid to follow truth wherever it may lead,
nor to tolerate any error so long as reason is left free to
combat it.

– *Thomas Jefferson*[1]

You are mistaken if you believe that anything at all can be
achieved by reason. In years past I thought so myself and
kept protesting against the monstrous infamy that is antisemitism. But it is useless, completely useless.

– *Theodor Mommsen*[2]

The producer was incredulous. She found it hard to believe that I
was turning down an opportunity to appear on her nationally tele-
vised show: 'But you are writing a book on this topic. It will be great
publicity.' I explained repeatedly that I would not participate in a
debate with a Holocaust denier. The existence of the Holocaust was
not a matter of debate. I would analyze and illustrate who they were
and what they tried to do, but I would not appear with them. (To do
so would give them a legitimacy and a stature they in no way deserve.
It would elevate their antisemitic ideology – which is what Holocaust
denial is – to the level of responsible historiography – which it is not.)
Unwilling to accept my no as final, she vigorously condemned Holocaust denial and all it represented. Then, in one last attempt to get

me to change my mind, she asked me a question: 'I certainly don't agree with them, but don't you think our viewers should hear the *other side*?'

I soon discovered that this was not to be an isolated incident. Indeed, in the months before I completed this manuscript, I had one form or another of this conversation too many times. A plethora of television and radio shows have discovered Holocaust denial. Recently the producer of a nationally syndicated television talk show was astounded when I turned down the opportunity to appear because it would entail 'discussing' the issue with two deniers. She was even more taken aback when she learned that hers was not the first invitation I had rejected. Ironically – or perhaps frighteningly – she had turned to me because she read my work while taking a course on the Holocaust. When the show aired, in April 1992 deniers were given the bulk of the time to speak their piece. Then Holocaust survivors were brought on to try to 'refute' their comments. Before the commercial break the host, Montel Williams, urged viewers to stay tuned so that they could learn whether the Holocaust is a 'myth or is it truth.'

My refusal to appear on such shows with deniers is inevitably met by producers with some variation on the following challenge: Shouldn't we hear their *ideas*, *opinions*, or *point of view*? Their willingness to ascribe to the deniers and their myths the legitimacy of a point of view is of as great, if not greater, concern than are the activities of the deniers themselves. What is wrong, I am repeatedly asked, with people hearing a 'different perspective'? Unable to make the distinction between genuine historiography and the deniers' purely ideological exercise, those who see the issue in this light are important assets in the deniers' attempts to spread their claims. This is precisely the deniers' goal: They aim to confuse the matter by making it appear as if they are engaged in a genuine scholarly effort when, of course, they are not.

The attempt to deny the Holocaust enlists a basic strategy of distortion. Truth is mixed with absolute lies, confusing readers who are unfamiliar with the tactics of the deniers. Half-truths and story segments, which conveniently avoid critical information, leave the listener with a distorted impression of what really happened. The abundance of documents and testimonies that confirm the Holocaust are dismissed as contrived, coerced, or forgeries and falsehoods.[3] This book is an effort to illuminate and demonstrate how the deniers use this methodology to shroud their true objectives.

My previous book on the Holocaust dealt with the American press's coverage – or lack thereof – of the persecution of the Jews from 1933 to 1945. Much of the story that I told justly deserved the title *Beyond Belief*. For most editors and reporters this story was literally beyond belief, and the press either missed or dismissed this news story, burying specific news of gas chambers, death camps, and mass killings in tiny articles deep inside the papers.

When I turned to the topic of Holocaust denial, I knew that I was dealing with extremist antisemites who have increasingly managed, under the guise of scholarship, to camouflage their hateful ideology. However, I did not then fully grasp the degree to which I would be dealing with a phenomenon far more unbelievable than was my previous topic. On some level it is as unbelievable as the Holocaust itself and, though no one is being killed as a result of the deniers' lies, it constitutes abuse of the survivors. It is intimately connected to a neofascist political agenda. Denial of the Holocaust is not the only thing I find beyond belief. What has also shocked me is the success deniers have in convincing good-hearted people that Holocaust denial *is* an 'other side' of history – ugly, reprehensible, and extremist – but an other side nonetheless. As time passes and fewer people can personally challenge these assertions, their campaign will only grow in intensity.

The impact of Holocaust denial on high school and college students cannot be precisely assessed. At the moment it is probably quite limited. Revisionist incidents have occurred on a number of college campuses, including at a midwestern university when a history instructor used a class on the Napoleonic Wars to argue that the Holocaust was a propaganda hoax designed to vilify the Germans, that the 'worst thing about Hitler is that without him there would not be an Israel,' and that the whole Holocaust story was a ploy to allow Jews to accumulate vast amounts of wealth. The instructor defended himself by arguing that he was just trying to present 'two sides' of the issue because the students' books only presented the 'orthodox view.'[4] When the school dismissed him for teaching material that was neither relevant to the course nor of any 'scholarly substance,' some students complained that he had been unfairly treated.[5] During my visit to that campus in the aftermath of the incident, a number of his students argued that the instructor had brought articles to class that 'proved his point.' Others asserted, 'He let us think.'[6] Few of the students seemed to have been genuinely convinced by him, but even among those who were not, there was a feeling that somehow firing him violated the basic American ideal of fairness – that is, everyone has a right to speak his or her piece. These students seemed not to grasp that a teacher has a responsibility to maintain some fidelity to the notion of truth.

High school teachers have complained to the United States Holocaust Memorial Council that when they teach the Holocaust in their classes, they increasingly find students who have heard about Holocaust denial and assume it must have some legitimacy. I have encountered high school and college students who feel that the deniers' view should at least be mentioned as a 'controversial' but somewhat valid view of the Holocaust. Colleagues have related that their students' questions are increasingly informed by Holocaust denial: 'How do we know that there really were gas chambers?' 'What proof do we have that the survivors are telling the truth?' 'Are we going to hear the German side?' This unconscious incorporation of the deniers' argument into the students' thinking is particularly troublesome. It is an indication of the deniers' success in shaping the way coming generations will approach study of the Holocaust.

One of the tactics deniers use to achieve their ends is to camouflage their goals. In an attempt to hide the fact that they are fascists and antisemites with a specific ideological and political agenda, they state that their objective is to uncover historical falsehoods, *all* historical falsehoods. Thus they have been able to sow confusion among even the products of the highest echelons of the American educational establishment. A history major at Yale University submitted his senior essay on the Luftwaffe in the Spanish Civil War to the *Journal of Historical Review*, the leading Holocaust denial journal, which in format and tone mimics serious, legitimate social science journals. The student acknowledged that he had not closely examined the *Journal* before submitting his essay. He selected it from an annotated bibliography where it was listed along with respected historical and social science journals. Based on its description, title, and, most significantly, its proximity to familiar journals, he assumed it was a legitimate enterprise dedicated to the reevaluation of historical events.

Deniers have found a ready acceptance among increasingly radical elements, including neo-Nazis and skinheads, in both North America and Europe. Holocaust denial has become part of a mélange of extremist, racist, and nativist sentiments. Neo-Nazis who once argued that the Holocaust, however horrible, was justified now contend that it was a hoax. As long as extremists espouse Holocaust denial, the danger is a limited one. But that danger increases when the proponents of these views clean up their act and gain entry into legitimate circles. Though they may look and act like 'your uncle from Peoria,' they do so without having abandoned any of their radical ideas.[7] David Duke's political achievements are evidence of this. The neo-Nazi Duke, a former Imperial Wizard of the Ku Klux Klan and a Holocaust denier, was elected to the Louisiana state legislature in the late 1980s. Two years later he won 40 percent of the vote in the race for the U.S. Senate. In his November 1991 race for governor, he received close to seven hundred thousand votes. He subsequently entered the 1992 presidential campaign. Despite the fact that his efforts were soon eclipsed, he managed to attract a significant number of followers. Duke, who celebrated Adolf Hitler's birthday until late in the 1980s, has been quite candid about his views on the Holocaust.[8] In a letter accompanying the *Crusader*, the publication of the National Association for the Advancement of White People (NAAWP) – an organization Duke created – he not only described the Holocaust as a 'historical hoax' but wrote that the 'greatest' Holocaust was 'perpetrated on Christians by Jews.'[9] Jews fostered the myth of the Holocaust, he claimed, because it generates 'tremendous financial aid' for Israel and renders organized Jewry 'almost immune from criticism.'[10] In 1986 Duke declared that Jews 'deserve to go into the ashbin of history' and denied that the gas chambers were erected to murder Jews but rather were intended to kill the vermin infesting them.[11] Under Duke the NAAWP advocated the segregation of all racial minorities in different sections of the United States. (Jews were to be confined to 'West Israel,' which would be composed of Manhattan and Long Island.)

In order most effectively to spread their lies, deniers such as Duke must rewrite not only the history of World War II but also their own past lives. In order to forge his way in the political arena, David Duke had to reformulate his personal history. His efforts to distance himself from his more extremist past are reflective of deniers' tactics. They increasingly avoid being linked with identifiable bigots. When Duke was identified as a Klansman his access to the public arena was limited. When he decided to run for office he shed his sheet and donned a three-piece suit, winning him, if not adherents, at least a respectable audience. He gained political respectability despite the fact that but a short time earlier he had sold racist, antisemitic, and denial literature, including *The Hitler We Loved and Why* and *The Holy Book of Adolf Hitler*, from his legislative offices.[12]

But it is not only former members of extremist groups who serve as vehicles for disseminating Holocaust denial. More mainstream individuals have assisted in this effort as well. Patrick Buchanan, one of the foremost right-wing conservative columnists in the country, used his widely syndicated column to express views that come straight from the scripts of Holocaust deniers. He argued that it was physically impossible for the gas chamber at Treblinka to have functioned as a killing apparatus because the diesel engines that powered it could not produce enough carbon monoxide to be lethal. Buchanan's 'proof' was a 1988 incident in which ninety-seven passengers on a train in Washington, D.C., were stuck in a tunnel as the train emitted carbon monoxide fumes. Because the passengers were not harmed, Buchanan extrapolated that the victims in a gas chamber using carbon monoxide from diesel engines would also not have been harmed.[13] He ignored the fact that the gassings at Treblinka took as long as half an hour and that the conditions created when people are jammed by the hundreds into small enclosures, as they were at Treblinka, are dramatically different from those experienced by a group of people sitting on a train. Asked where he obtained this information, Buchanan responded, 'Somebody sent it to me.'[14] Buchanan has also referred to the 'so-called Holocaust Survivor Syndrome.' According to him, this involves 'group fantasies of martyrdom and heroics.'[15]* I am not suggesting that Patrick Buchanan is a Holocaust denier. He has never publicly claimed that the Holocaust is a hoax. However, his attacks on the credibility of survivors' testimony are standard elements of Holocaust denial. Buchanan's ready acceptance of this information and reliance on it to make his argument are disturbing,† for this is how elements of Holocaust denial find their way into the general culture. During the 1992 presidential campaign, when Buchanan was seeking the Republican nomination, he refused to retract these contentions. Nonetheless few of his fellow journalists were willing to challenge him on the matter. As troubling as Buchanan's easy acceptance of these charges was the latitude given him by his colleagues.[16]

Denial arguments have been voiced not only by politicians in the United States but by those in other countries as well. Extremist nationalist groups in those Central and Eastern Europe countries with a tradition of populist antisemitism have a particular attraction to Holocaust denial. Many of the precursors of these movements collaborated with the Nazis. Holocaust denial offers them a means of both wiping out that historical black mark – if there was no Holocaust then cooperating with the Nazis becomes less inexcusable – and

* Buchanan's statements were made as part of his defense of John Demjanjuk, a retired Cleveland auto worker accused of being Ivan the Terrible, notorious camp guard and a mass murderer at Treblinka. It is not Buchanan's defense of Demjanjuk with which I take issue – it is his use of denial arguments to do so. Buchanan has consistently opposed any prosecution of Nazi war criminals.

† It is ironic that Duke's efforts to win the Republican presidential nomination were overshadowed by Buchanan, who had earlier advocated that the Republicans stop feeling guilty about their 'exploitation' of the Willie Horton issue and instead take a 'hard look at Duke's portfolio of winning issues' (*New Republic*, October 15, 1990, p. 19).

rehabilitating those who were punished by Communists for collaborating. Since the fall of communism, deniers in North America and Western Europe have worked with like-minded groups in Eastern European countries to establish 'mini' Institutes for Historical Review (referring to the California-based pseudo-academic institution that is the bastion of denial activities and publications). Their objective is to attract people, particularly intellectuals, who are seeking an extremist nationalism cleansed of taints of Nazism.[17] Former Communist bloc countries are particularly susceptible to this strain of pseudo-history because postwar generations have learned virtually nothing about the specifically Jewish nature of Nazi atrocities. The Communists, engaging in their own form of revisionism, taught that it was the fascists (not Germans) who killed Communists (not Jews). The specifically Jewish facet of the tragedy was excised.

While no politician has based his or her entire campaign on Holocaust denial, a number have used it when it was in their interest to do so. Croatian president Franjo Tudjman wrote of the 'biased testimonies and exaggerated data' used to estimate the number of Holocaust victims. And in his book *Wastelands – Historical Truth*, he always places the word Holocaust in quotation marks.[18] Tudjman has good historical reasons for doing so: Croatia was an ardent Nazi ally, and the vast majority of Croatian Jews and non-Jews were murdered by their fellow Croatians, not by Germans.[19] Tudjman obviously believes that one of the ways for his country to win public sympathy is to diminish the importance of the Holocaust.

It is likely that as Eastern Europe is increasingly beset by nationalist and internal rivalries, ethnic and political groups that collaborated in the annihilation of the Jews will fall back on Tudjman's strategy of minimization. In Slovakia crowds of protesters at political gatherings have chanted antisemitic and anti-Czech slogans and waved portraits of Nazi war criminal Josef Tiso, who was directly involved in the deportation of Slovakian Jews to Auschwitz. In an effort to whitewash Tiso's antisemitism during World War II and to resurrect him as a national hero, his speeches have been broadcast at these rallies. For Slovakian separatists Tiso's regime constitutes the legal and moral precedent for a sovereign Slovakia.

Neither Tudjman nor the Tiso protesters are engaged in overt denial. However, their efforts to diminish the magnitude of the deeds and roles of the central players are critically important aspects of Holocaust denial.[20] There is a psychological dimension to the deniers' and minimizers' objectives: The general public tends to accord victims of genocide a certain moral authority. If you devictimize a people you strip them of their moral authority, and if you can in turn claim to be a victim, as the Poles and the Austrians often try to do, that moral authority is conferred on or restored to you.

Holocaust denial, which has well-established roots in Western and Central Europe, has in recent years manifested itself throughout the world. The following brief survey demonstrates the breadth of the deniers' activities, many of which shall be explored in greater depth in the chapters that follow.

In 1992 a Belgian publisher of neo-Nazi material distributed thousands of pamphlets purporting to offer scientific proof that the gas chambers were a hoax. In 1988 in Britain over thirty thousand copies of *Holocaust News*, a newsletter which maintains that the Holocaust was a myth, were sent to Jewish communities in London, Glasgow, Newcastle, Birmingham, Cardiff, Norwich, and Leicester as well as to lawyers, schools, and members of Parliament throughout the country. (According to the *Sunday Times*, *Holocaust News* is published by the overtly racist British National party – which is composed of those who find the extremist National Front too mild. It campaigns for the repatriation of Jews and non-whites.)[21]

In recent years Holocaust denial in England has undergone a disturbing new development. David Irving, the writer of popular historical works attempting to show that Britain made a tactical error in going to war against Germany and that the Allies and the Nazis were equally at fault for the war and its atrocities, has joined the ranks of the deniers, arguing that the gas chambers were a 'propaganda exercise.'[22] Irving, long considered a guru by the far right, does not limit his activities to England. He has been particularly active in Germany, where he has regularly participated in the annual meetings of the extremist German political party Deutsche Volks Union.[23] In addition, he has frequently appeared at extremist-sponsored rallies, meetings, and beer hall gatherings. Irving's self-described mission in Germany is to point 'promising young men' throughout the country in the 'right direction.' (Irving believes women were built for a 'certain task, which is producing us [men],' and that they should be 'subservient to men.'[24] Apparently, therefore, he has no interest in pointing young women in the right direction.*) Ironically, young Germans who are dedicated German nationalists find Irving and other non-German deniers particularly credible because they are not themselves Germans.[25]

In France, Holocaust denial activities have centered around Robert Faurisson, a former professor of literature at the University of Lyons-2 whose work is often reprinted verbatim, both with and without attribution, by deniers worldwide. According to Faurisson the 'so-called gassings' of Jews were a 'gigantic politico-financial swindle whose beneficiaries are the state of Israel and international Zionism.' Its chief victims were the German people and the Palestinians.[26] Faurisson's area of specialization is the rather unique field of the 'criticism of texts and documents, investigation of meaning and counter-meaning, of the true and the false.'[27] There is a definite irony in his choice of field because Faurisson, whose methodologies have been adopted by virtually all other deniers, regularly creates facts where none exist and dismisses as false any information inconsistent with his preconceived conclusions. He asserts, for example, that the German army was given 'Draconian orders' not to participate in 'excesses' against civilians including the Jews; consequently, the massive killings of Jews could not have happened. In making this argument Faurisson simply ignores the activities of the *Einsatzgruppen*, the units responsible for killing vast numbers of Jews. Pierre Vidal-Naquet, one of Faurisson's prime adversaries in France and someone who has studied him closely, observed that Faurisson is particularly adept at finding 'an answer for everything' when encountering information that contradicts his claims. Faurisson interprets the Nazi decree which mandated that Jews wear a yellow star on

---

* His solution to unemployment would be to declare the employment of a female a 'criminal offense.'

pain of death as a measure to ensure the safety of German soldiers, because Jews, he argues, engaged in espionage, terrorism, black market operations, and arms trafficking. German soldiers needed a means to protect themselves against this formidable enemy. He even had an explanation as to why Jewish children were required to start wearing the star at age six: They too were engaged in 'all sorts of illicit or resistance activities against the Germans' against which the soldiers had to be protected. Documents containing information that Faurisson cannot explain away or reinterpret, he falsifies. Regarding the brutal German destruction of the Warsaw ghetto, Faurisson wrote that in April 1943, 'suddenly, right behind the front,' the Jews started an insurrection. The ghetto revolt, for which the Jews built seven hundred bunkers, was proof of the quite serious threat the Jews posed to German military security. Although it is true that the Jews started an insurrection, it was not right behind the front but hundreds of miles from it. Faurisson's source for the information regarding the insurrection and the bunkers was a speech delivered in Posen in October 1943 by the Nazi leader Heinrich Himmler. But even Himmler was more honest than Faurisson: He described the uprisings as taking place in Warsaw and in 'territories in the rear.'[28]

Faurisson has not worked alone in France. In June 1985 the University of Nantes awarded a doctoral degree to a Faurisson protégé, Henri Roques, for a dissertation accusing Kurt Gerstein, one of those who transmitted the news of the gas chambers to the Allies, of being a 'master magician' who created an illusion that the world accepted as fact.[29] Implicitly denying the existence of the gas chambers, Roques tried to prove that Gerstein's reports were so laden with inconsistencies that he could not possibly have witnessed gassings at Belzec, as he maintained. There exist a variety of official documents and testimonies attesting to Gerstein's presence at these gassings, Roques, adhering to his mentor's pattern of ignoring any document that contradicts his preexisting conclusions, simply excluded this material from his dissertation.[30] (After a public uproar Roques' doctoral degree was revoked by the French minister of higher education in 1986.[31])

Though Faurisson and most of his admirers are on the political

right, they and their activities have been abetted by an extreme
left-wing revolutionary group, La Vieille Taupe (The Old Mole).[32]
Originally a bookstore, it has become a publishing house that shel-
ters an informal coterie of revolutionary types. Under the direction
of its proprietor, Pierre Guillaume, it has distributed periodicals, cassettes, comic books, journals, and broadsheets all attesting to the
Holocaust hoax. Guillaume is France's leading publisher of neo-Nazi
material. Twenty-four hours after the Klaus Barbie trial began in
France, the first issue of *Annals of Historical Revisionism*, a journal
edited by Guillaume and containing articles by Faurisson, was distributed for sale to Paris bookstores and kiosks.[33]

Suggestions of Holocaust denial have come from French political
figures as well. The leader of the far right National Front, Jean Marie
Le Pen, declared in 1987 that the gas chambers were a mere 'detail'
of World War II. In a radio interview he asserted that he had never
seen any gas chambers and that historians had doubts about their
existence. 'Are you trying to tell me [the existence of gas chambers]
is a revealed truth that everyone has to believe?' Le Pen asked rhe-
torically. 'There are historians who are debating such questions.'[34]
Le Pen, who has complained that there are too many Jews in the
French media, is considered the leader of Europe's extreme right. A
charismatic speaker, he has exploited French fears about the immigration of Arabs from North Africa and has espoused the kind of
right-wing antisemitism associated with the Dreyfus affair. Popular
support for Le Pen in France has been as high as 17 percent. In the
1988 presidential election he received 14.4 percent of the popular
vote, coming in fourth overall.[35]

Shades of Holocaust denial were evident at the Klaus Barbie trial
when defense attorneys, attempting to diminish the significance of
the Holocaust, argued that forcing people into gas chambers was no
different from killing people in a war, and that it was no more of a
crime to murder millions of Jews because they were Jews than it was
to fight against Algerians, Vietnamese, Africans, or Palestinians who
were attempting to free themselves from foreign rule.[36] These
slight-of-hand attempts at moral equivalence constitute a basic tactic

of those who hover on the periphery of Holocaust denial. (See chapter 11 for an analysis of Holocaust relativism in Germany.)

In 1978 Louis Darquier de Pellepoix, Vichy France's commissioner of Jewish affairs and the person responsible for coordinating the deportation of Vichy Jews to death camps, told the French weekly *L'Express* that the Nazi genocide was a typical Jewish hoax. 'There was no genocide – you must get that out of your head.' Expressing the standard denier's explanation for this hoax, he charged that the Jews' aim was to 'make Jerusalem the capital of the world.' The rather ambiguous headline of the article, which ran without any editorial comments, was 'Only Lice Were Gassed in Auschwitz.'[37] Leon Degrelle, the leader of the World War II fascist movement in Belgium and a Nazi collaborator, called on the European right to accept neo-Nazis as honorable allies. He also wrote an 'Open Letter to the Pope about Auschwitz,' informing the Polish-born cleric, who had witnessed the war at close range, that there were no gas chambers or mass annihilation in Hitler's Third Reich and that Jews who had been killed were actually murdered by American and British bombings.[38]

But one does not have to be a committed neo-Nazi to be receptive to deniers' arguments. In Paris, in an interview with the leftist monthly *Le Globe*, Claude Autant-Lara, one of France's most acclaimed film directors and at the time a member of the European parliament, described the Holocaust as a legend 'stuffed' with lies and claimed that France was in the hands of a left-wing cabal dominated by Jewish internationalists and cosmopolitans.[39]

In Austria, where the Kurt Waldheim affair uncovered hidden antisemitism, Holocaust denial has been centered around a number of neo-Nazi publications including the newspaper *Sieg*, which states that the number of Jews who died under Nazi rule was less than two hundred thousand.[40] The publisher, Walter Ochensberger, has been repeatedly convicted by Austrian courts for the crime of 'incitement.' During lecture tours in various countries including the United States, he has preached the doctrine of denial.[41] The publisher of another neo-Nazi denial magazine, *Halt*, was indicted for Holocaust denial activities.[42] In addition to *Sieg* and *Halt*, denial publications targeted at schoolchildren have appeared in Austria.[43] Since the late 1980s the American Ku Klux Klan has established groups in both Germany and Austria. These groups have added Holocaust denial to their traditional racist extremism.[44]

In certain parts of Europe, Holocaust denial has found its way into the general population. In the fall of 1992 a public opinion poll in Italy, where a wide array of denial publications have appeared, revealed that close to 10 percent of the Italian population believe the Holocaust never happened.[45]

Denial arguments have permeated the work of those who would not describe themselves as deniers. An English play entitled *Perdition* charged that Zionist leaders both during and after the war were a separate class of rich capitalists who betrayed the Jewish masses to the Nazis. The playwright described the Holocaust as a 'cozy set of family secrets, skeletons in closets.' In a key passage, the leading character charges that Jews who died in Auschwitz 'were murdered, not just by the force of German arms but by calculated treachery of their own Jewish leaders.'[46] Though the play did not deny the Holocaust, the result was the same: The perpetrators were absolved and the victims held responsible.

But it has not only been Europe that has witnessed this phenomenon. Since 1965, Holocaust denial material has been available throughout Latin America. In Brazil, much of it has been released by a publishing house specializing in Portuguese-language antisemitic materials. This publisher recently claimed that within four years of publication, one of its denial books had appeared in twenty-eight editions and was read by two hundred thousand people. (Though the figures may be highly inflated, the publisher did boost sales by offering bookstore owners extremely generous terms, allowing them to keep half the cover price as opposed to the usual 30 percent, and giving them 120 days to pay, a major benefit in a country with a 40 percent monthly inflation rate. Obviously, profit was not the publisher's primary motive.[47]) Holocaust deniers have also been active in Argentina, Mexico, Chile, and Peru.

In Australia and New Zealand, Holocaust denial has adopted a particularly deceptive guise. The Australian Civil Liberties Union, camouflaging its intentions behind a facade of defending civil liberties, is in fact an ardently antisemitic organization. Its bookstore sells an array of traditional antisemitic works, including denial tracts and its leader, John Bennett, has called the Holocaust a 'gigantic lie' designed to foster support for Israel. Under him the Union has distributed denial and neo-Nazi material and arranged for radio interviews by Fred Leuchter, the self-described 'engineer' and gas chamber expert who claims to have conducted scientific tests at Auschwitz and Majdanek proving that the gas chambers there could not have functioned as homicidal killing units. (For an analysis of Leuchter's report see chapter 9 and the Appendix). The league's meetings have been addressed by an assortment of Holocaust deniers, including hard core Nazis and representatives of the California-based Institute for Historical Review. When Leuchter was in Australia, he was interviewed on the radio and given other significant media coverage. The league, which uses conspiracy theories to attract economically vulnerable members of the working class, informed unemployed timber workers that their jobs had been lost because Jewish bankers had taken over their forests and lands.[48] The Australian Human Rights and Equal Opportunities Commission describes the league as the most 'influential and effective as well as the best-organized and most substantially financed racist organization in Australia.'[49]

New Zealand has its own League of Rights whose activities approximate those of its Australian counterpart. Because these leagues do not have the same offensive public image that some of the more blatantly antisemitic and neo-Nazi groups do, they have been more successful at winning popular support. By projecting an image of being committed to the defense of free speech, these pseudo–human rights organizations have attracted followers who would normally shun neo-Nazi and overtly antisemitic organizations and activities. The manner in which they obfuscate and camouflage their agenda is the tactic Holocaust deniers will increasingly adopt in the future. It is part of the movement's strategy to infiltrate the mainstream.

In Japan, an array of antisemitic books have reached the best-seller list in recent years. Masami Uno, the author of some of the most popular of these books, asserts that Jews form a 'behind-the-scenes nation' controlling American corporations. His books link Jews to Japan's deepest economic fears, declaring America a 'Jewish nation' and proclaming Jews responsible for Japan bashing. Uno, whose books have sold millions of copies, has told Japanese audiences that the Holocaust is a hoax and the *Diary of Anne Frank* full of 'lies.'[50] Holocaust denial in Japan must be seen as part of the country's revisionist attitude toward World War II in general. Japan has ignored those aspects of the war that focus on its own wrongdoings. Japanese textbooks distort the historical reality of the Japanese 'rape of Nanking,' calling it the 'Nanking Incident.' No mention either is made of the medical experiments conducted by the Japanese on prisoners of war, or the army's exploitation of Korean 'comfort women.' Even the attack on Pearl Harbor is presented as a defense tactic which the Japanese were compelled to take because of America's refusal to acquiesce to reasonable Japanese demands. The use of Koreans as slave labor is also left unmentioned in official war histories.[51] Since the Holocaust deniers try to prove that it was the Allies, not the Axis, who committed atrocities during World War II, Holocaust denial may find an increasingly receptive audience in Japan, particularly if the economic situation there worsens and a scapegoat is needed.

Not surprisingly, given deniers' objective of delegitimizing Israel, Arab countries have proven particularly receptive. During the 1970s, when Holocaust denial was first trying to present itself as a credible academic enterprise, Saudi Arabia financed the publication of a number of books accusing Jews of creating the Holocaust hoax in order to win support for Israel. These books were distributed worldwide.[52] Articles denying the genocide against the Jews have appeared in publications of the Palestine Liberation Organization and the Palestinian Red Crescent Society, an affiliate of the International Red Cross. The latter published an article charging that 'the lie concerning the existence of gas chambers enabled the Jews to establish the State of Israel.'[53] Another article in a Palestinian journal chided Jews for complaining about gestapo treatment when they were really 'served healthy food' by the Germans.[54] Arabs have long argued that Israel was created by the United Nations because the world felt guilty over Jewish suffering during the Holocaust. The deniers' claims add fuel to these charges. Not only did the world, as Robert Faurisson said to me, displace one people 'from its land so another could acquire it,' but Holocaust denial proves that it was deceived into doing so.[55]

The confluence between anti-Israel, antisemitic, and Holocaust denial forces was exemplified by a world anti-Zionist conference scheduled for Sweden in November 1992. Though canceled at the last minute by the Swedish government, scheduled speakers included Black Muslim leader Louis Farrakhan, Faurisson, Irving, and Leuchter. Also scheduled to participate were representatives of a variety of antisemitic and anti-Israel organizations, including the Russian group Pamyat, the Iranian-backed Hezbollah, and the fundamentalist Islamic organization Hamas.[56]

Echoes of Holocaust denial have also been heard from individuals who are not associated with extremist or overtly antisemitic groups. In an interview with *Esquire* magazine in February 1983, Robert Mitchum, who played a leading role in the television production of Herman Wouk's World War II saga, *Winds of War* and *War and Remembrance*, suggested that there was doubt about the Holocaust. Asked about the slaughter of six million Jews, he replied, 'so the Jews say.' The interviewer, incredulous, repeated Mitchum's comment verbatim, 'So the Jews say?' and Mitchum responded, 'I don't know. People dispute that.'[57]

The editor of *The Progressive*, a socialist monthly, recently observed that while he is used to receiving a significant amount of 'crackpot mail,' the material he receives from Holocaust deniers is a 'more subtly packed, slicker' form of hate propaganda. Despite its restrained and objective tone, he wondered who if anyone might be convinced by such 'pernicious rot.' His question was answered when he received a letter from a high school senior who described himself as eager for articles that grappled with difficult ideas. He complimented the editor for the wide variety of topics covered in the magazine but urged that he also address 'controversial ideas about the Holocaust' such as the existence of gas chambers. The editor, himself a survivor of the Holocaust, wrote the young student assuring him that if he meant to suggest that there were no gas chambers he was wrong. The student sent back a strongly worded challenge asking the editor to reveal precisely how many gas chambers he had actually seen and how he had managed to survive.[58]

In Illinois, two parents have conducted an extremely focused letter campaign against the state law that mandates teaching of the Holocaust in all schools in the state. Though many of their arguments are the standard charges repeated *ad infinitum* in denial publications, these parents have added a new element, threatening to withdraw their children from classes that taught the history of the Holocaust to protect them from 'this highly questionable and vulgar hate material.'[59] Their letter, sent to thousands of people including elected officials, educators, academicians, and parents, asked recipients to ponder how it was that a small minority was able to use the school systems and to 'manipulate our children for their political and national purposes.'[60]

The inroads deniers have been able to make into the American educational establishment are most disconcerting. Defenders – Noam Chomsky probably the best known among them – have turned up in a variety of quarters. The MIT professor of linguistics wrote the introduction to a book by Faurisson. Faurisson, whom the *New York Times* described as having 'no particular prominence on the French intellectual or academic scene,' has argued that one of the reasons he does not believe that homicidal gas chambers existed is that no death-camp victim has given eyewitness testimony of actual gassings.[61] This argument contradicts accepted standards of evidence. It is as if a jury refused to convict a serial killer until one of his victims came back to say, 'Yes, he is the one who killed me.' Such reasoning is so soft that it makes one wonder who could possibly take him seriously. Moreover, it ignores the extensive testimony of the Sonderkommandos who dragged the bodies from the gas chambers.

Chomsky contended that, based on what he had read of Faurisson's work, he saw 'no proof' that would lead him to conclude that the Frenchman was an antisemite.[62] According to Chomsky, not even Faurisson's claims that the Holocaust is a 'Zionist lie' are proof of his antisemitism. 'Is it antisemitic to speak of Zionist lies? Is Zionism the first nationalist movement in history not to have concocted lies in its own interest?'[63] That students editing a college newspaper or television producers interested in winning viewers should prove unable to make such distinctions is disturbing. That someone of Chomsky's stature should confuse the issue is appalling. Indeed, it was this kind of reasoning that led Alfred Kazin to describe Chomsky as a 'dupe of intellectual pride so overweening that he is incapable of making distinctions between totalitarian and democratic societies, between oppressors and victims.'[64] Though Chomsky is his own unique case, his spirited defense of the deniers shocked many people including those who thought they were inured to his antics.

In his essay Chomsky argued that scholars' ideas cannot be censored irrespective of how distasteful they may be.* Throughout this imbroglio Chomsky claimed that his interest was Faurisson's civil rights and freedom to make his views known.[65] During the past few years, as deniers have intensified their efforts to insinuate themselves into the university world by placing ads denying the Holocaust in campus newspapers, echoes of Chomsky's arguments have been voiced by students, professors, and even university presidents. (See chapter 10 for additional information about denial on campus.) In response to student and faculty protests about the decision of the *Duke Chronicle* to run an ad denying the Holocaust, the president of Duke University, Keith Brodie, said that to have done otherwise would have 'violated our commitment to free speech and

---

* It is ironic that this internationally known professor should have become such a defender of Faurisson's right to speak when he would have denied those same rights to proponents of America's involvement in Vietnam. In *American Power and the New Mandarins* he wrote, 'By accepting the presumption of legitimacy of debate on certain issues, one has already lost one's humanity.' Though written long before the Faurisson affair, his comments constitute the most accurate assessment of his own behavior.

contradicted Duke's long tradition of supporting First Amendment rights.'[66] Brodie failed to note that the paper had recently rejected an ad it deemed offensive to women. No one had complained about possible violations of the First Amendment.

Let this point not be misunderstood. The deniers have the absolute right to stand on any street corner and spread their calumnies. They have the right to publish their articles and books and hold their gatherings. But free speech does not guarantee them the right to be treated as the 'other' side of a legitimate debate. Nor does it guarantee them space on op-ed pages or time on television and radio shows. Most important, it does not call for people such as Chomsky to stand by them and thereby commend their views to the public.*

We have only witnessed the beginning of this movement's efforts to permeate cultural, historical, and educational orbits. They must be taken seriously: Far more than the history of the Holocaust is at stake.

While Holocaust denial is not a new phenomenon, it has increased in scope and intensity since the mid-1970s. It is important to understand that the deniers do not work in a vacuum. Part of their success can be traced to an intellectual climate that has made its mark in the scholarly world during the past two decades. The deniers are plying their trade at a time when much of history seems to be up for

---

* Chomsky's behavior can be contrasted with that of thirty-four of France's leading historians who, in response to Faurisson's efforts, issued a declaration protesting his attempt to deny the Holocaust. The declaration read in part: 'Everyone is free to interpret a phenomenon like the Hitlerite genocide according to his own philosophy. Everyone is free to compare it with other enterprises of murder committed earlier, at the same time, later. Everyone is free to offer such or such kind of explanations; everyone is free, to the limit, to imagine or to dream that these monstrous deeds did not take place. Unfortunately, they did take place and no one can deny their existence without committing an outrage on the truth. It is not necessary to ask how *technically* such mass murder was possible. It was technically possible, seeing that it took place. That is the required point of departure of every historical inquiry on this subject. This truth it behooves us to remember in simple terms: there is not and there cannot be a debate about the existence of the gas chambers.' The full text of the declaration appeared in *Le Monde*, February 21, 1979.

grabs and attacks on the Western rationalist tradition have become commonplace.

This tendency can be traced, at least in part, to intellectual currents that began to emerge in the late 1960s. Various scholars began to argue that texts had no fixed meaning. The reader's interpretation, not the author's intention, determined meaning. Duke University professor Stanley Fish is most closely associated with this approach in the literary field.[67] It became more difficult to talk about the objective truth of a text, legal concept, or even an event. In academic circles some scholars spoke of relative truths, rejecting the notion that there was one version of the world that was necessarily right while another was wrong.[68] Proponents of this methodology, such as the prominent and widely read philosopher Richard Rorty, denied the allegation that they believed that two incompatible views on a significant issue were of equal worth.[69] But others disagreed. Hilary Putnam, one of the most influential contemporary academic philosophers, thought it particularly dangerous because it seemed to suggest that every conceptual system was 'just as good as the other.'[70] Still others rightfully worried that it opened the doors of the academy, and of society at large, to an array of farfetched notions that could no longer be dismissed out of hand simply because they were absurd.

Nonetheless, as a methodology this approach to texts had something to recommend it. It placed an important, though possibly overstated, emphasis on the role played by the reader's perspective in assigning meaning to a text. It was also a reminder that the interpretations of the less powerful groups in society have generally been ignored. But it also fostered an atmosphere in which it became harder to say that an idea was beyond the pale of rational thought. At its most radical it contended that there was no bedrock thing such as experience. Experience was mediated through one's language. The scholars who supported this deconstructionist approach were neither deniers themselves nor sympathetic to the deniers' attitudes; most had no trouble identifying Holocaust denial as disingenuous. But because deconstructionism argued that experience was relative and nothing was fixed, it created an atmosphere of permissiveness toward questioning the meaning of historical events and made it hard for its proponents to assert that there was anything 'off limits' for this skeptical approach. The legacy of this kind of thinking was evident when students had to confront the issue. Far too many of them found it impossible to recognize Holocaust denial as a movement with no scholarly, intellectual, or rational validity. A sentiment had been generated in society – not just on campus – that made it difficult to say: 'This has nothing to do with ideas. This is bigotry.'

This relativistic approach to the truth has permeated the arena of popular culture, where there is an increasing fascination with, and acceptance of, the irrational. One area in which this has been evident is in the recurring debate regarding the assassination of President Kennedy. While there is reason to question some of the conclusions of the Warren Commission, the theories regarding the killing that have increasingly gained acceptance border on the irrational. Notions of a conspiracy within the highest echelons of American government are readily accepted as plausible. According to Oliver Stone's 1991 movie *JFK*, a coup d'état was underway in the United States, with the collusion of the vice president, Joint Chiefs of Staff, chief justice of the United States, FBI, CIA, members of Congress, and the Mafia. Stone's film imposed a neat coherence on a mass of confusing information, providing a self-contained explanation for what still seemed to be an unbelievable event. Many reviewers and moviegoers alike pondered these charges with great seriousness.

In another debasing of history, serious credence has been given to reverse racist charges about white scholarship. Some extremist Afrocentrists, who rightfully assert that Africa's role in shaping Western civilization is too often ignored, would have us believe that the basis of *all* intellectual and scientific thought as we know it originated on that continent. Leonard Jeffries, professor of Afro-American studies at New York's City College, has declared blacks to be 'sun people' and whites 'ice people.' All that is warm, communal, and full of hope comes from the former; all that is oppressive, cold, and rigid from the latter.[71] In these instances, history is rewritten for political ends and scientific historiography is replaced, in the words of Henry Louis Gates, Jr., professor of Afro-American studies at Harvard, with 'ideological conformity.'[72] Scholars who might once have dismissed these outlandish views feel compelled to treat them as having some validity.

These attacks on history and knowledge have the potential to alter dramatically the way established truth is transmitted from generation to generation. Ultimately the climate they create is of no less importance than the specific truth they attack – be it the Holocaust or the assassination of President Kennedy. It is a climate that fosters deconstructionist history at its worst. No fact, no event, and no aspect of history has any fixed meaning or content. Any truth can be retold. Any fact can be recast. There is no ultimate historical reality.

Holocaust denial is part of this phenomenon. It is not an assault on the history of one particular group. Though denial of the Holocaust may be an attack on the history of the annihilation of the Jews, at its core it poses a threat to all who believe that knowledge and memory are among the keystones of our civilization. Just as the Holocaust was not a tragedy of the Jews but a tragedy of civilization in which the victims were Jews, so too denial of the Holocaust is not a threat just to Jewish history but a threat to all who believe in the ultimate power of reason. It repudiates reasoned discussion the way the Holocaust repudiated civilized values. It is undeniably a form of antisemitism, and as such it constitutes an attack on the most basic values of a reasoned society. Like any form of prejudice, it is an irrational animus that cannot be countered with the normal forces of investigation, argument, and debate. The deniers' arguments are at their roots not only antisemitic and anti-intellectual but, in the words of historian Charles Maier, 'blatantly racist anthropology.'[73] Holocaust denial is the apotheosis of irrationalism.

Because the movement to disseminate these myths is neither scholarship nor historiography, I have chosen to eschew the term *revisionism* whenever possible and instead to use the term *denial* to describe it. The deniers' selection of the name *revisionist* to describe themselves is indicative of their basic strategy of deceit and distortion and of their attempt to portray themselves as legitimate historians engaged in the traditional practice of illuminating the past. For historians, in fact, the name *revisionism* has a resonance that is perfectly legitimate – it recalls the controversial historical school known as World War I 'revisionists,' who argued that the Germans were unjustly held responsible for the war and that consequently the Versailles treaty was a politically misguided document based on a false premise. Thus the deniers link themselves to a specific historiographic tradition of reevaluating the past. Claiming the mantle of the World War I revisionists and denying they have any objective other than the dissemination of the truth constitute a tactical attempt to acquire an intellectual credibility that would otherwise elude them.

Revisionism is also the name given to a more contemporary approach to historical research. Associated with the noted historian William Appleman Williams, a past president of the Organization of American Historians, it addresses itself to questions of American foreign policy particularly as they relate to the origins of the Cold War and the conflict between the West and the Communist world. Because this form of revisionism is critical of American foreign policy, which it sees as motivated by a desire for hegemony via open-door imperialism, it is a useful model for the deniers.[74] While many historians strongly disagree with its particular bias, all agree that for the 'Wisconsin school,' as Williams's followers came to be known, and its descendants, the canons of evidence are as incontrovertible as they are for all other historians. In contrast, evidence plays no role for deniers.

Finally I abjure the term *revisionist* because on some level revisionism is what all legitimate historians engage in. Historians are not just chroniclers – they do not simply retell the tale. Each one tries to glean some new insight or understanding from a story already known, seeking some new way of interpreting the past to help us better understand the present. That interpretation always involves some constant 're-visioning' of the past. By its very nature the business of interpretation cannot be purely objective. But it is built on a certain body of irrefutable evidence: Slavery happened; so did the Black Plague and the Holocaust.

In order to maintain their facade as a group whose only objective is the pursuit of truth, the deniers have filled their publications with articles that ostensibly have nothing to do with World War II but are designed to demonstrate that theirs is a global effort to attack and revise historical falsehoods. Articles on the Civil War, World War I, and Pearl Harbor are included in their journals as a means of illustrating how establishment historians, with ulterior political motives, have repeatedly put forward distorted views of history. The deniers aim to undermine readers' faith in 'orthodox' historians' commitment to transmitting the truth. They argue that this tactic of distortion by 'court historians' for political means reached its zenith in the Holocaust 'myth.'

What claims do the deniers make? The Holocaust – the attempt to annihilate the Jewish people – never happened. Typical of the deniers' attempt to obfuscate is their claim that they do not deny that there was a Holocaust, only that there was a plan or an attempt to annihilate the Jewish people.[75] They have distorted and deconstructed the definition of the term *Holocaust*. But this and all the ancillary claims that accompany it are embedded in a series of other arguments. They begin with a relatively innocuous supposition: War is evil. Assigning blame to one side is ultimately a meaningless enterprise. Since the central crime of which the Nazis are accused never happened, there really is no difference in this war, as in any other, between victor and vanquished.[76] Still, they assert, if guilt is to be assigned, it is not the Germans who were guilty of aggression and atrocities during the war. The real crimes against civilization were committed by the Americans, Russians, Britons, and French against the Germans. The atrocities inflicted on the Germans by the Allies were – in the words of Harry Elmer Barnes, a once-prominent historian and one of the seminal figures in the history of North American Holocaust denial – 'more brutal and painful than the alleged exterminations in the gas chambers.'[77] Once we recognize that the Allies were the aggressors, we must turn to the Germans and, in the words of Austin App, a professor of English literature who became one of the major 'theoreticians' of Holocaust denial, implore them 'to forgive us the awful atrocities our policy caused to be inflicted upon them.'[78]

For some deniers Hitler was a man of peace, pushed into war by the aggressive Allies.[79] According to them, the Germans suffered the bombing of Dresden, wartime starvation, invasions, postwar population transfers from areas of Germany incorporated into post-war Poland, victors' vengeance at Nuremberg, and brutal mistreatment by Soviet and Allied occupiers. Portrayed as a criminal nation that had committed outrageous atrocities, Germany became and remains a victim of the world's emotional and scholarly aggression.

But it is showing the Holocaust to have been a myth that is the deniers' real agenda. They contend that the ultimate injustice is the false accusation that Germans committed the most heinous crime in human history. The postwar venom toward Germany has been so extreme that Germans have found it impossible to defend themselves. Consequently, rather than fight this ignominious accusation, they decided to acknowledge their complicity. This seeming contradiction – namely that the perpetrators admit they committed a crime while those who were not present exonerate them – presents a potential problem for the deniers. How can a group that did not witness what happened claim that the perpetrators are innocent while the perpetrators acknowledge their guilt? The deniers explain this problem away by arguing that in the aftermath of World War II the Germans faced a strategic conflict. In order to be readmitted to the 'family of nations,' they had to confess their wrongdoing, even though they knew that these charges were false. They were in the same situation as a defendant who has been falsely convicted of committing horrendous crimes. He knows he will be more likely to receive a lenient sentence if he admits his guilt, shows contrition, and makes amends. So too the innocent Germans admitted their guilt and made (and continue to make) financial amends.

The defendants at the war crimes trials adopted a similar strategy. They admitted that the Holocaust happened but tried to vindicate themselves by claiming they were not *personally* guilty. Arthur Butz, a professor of electrical engineering at Northwestern University, is the denier who has most fully developed this theory of what I call incrimination to avoid self-incrimination. (For a fuller treatment of this see chapter 7.)

Deniers acknowledge that some Jews were incarcerated in places such as Auschwitz, but, they maintain, as they did at the trial of a Holocaust denier in Canada, it was equipped with 'all the luxuries of a country club,' including a swimming pool, dance hall, and recreational facilities.[80] Some Jews may have died, they said, but this was the natural consequence of wartime deprivations.*

The central assertion for the deniers is that Jews are not victims but victimizers. They 'stole' billions in reparations, destroyed Germany's good name by spreading the 'myth' of the Holocaust, and won international sympathy because of what they claimed had been done to them. In the paramount miscarriage of injustice, they used the world's sympathy to 'displace' another people so that the state of Israel could be established.[81] This contention relating to the establishment of Israel is a linchpin of their argument. It constitutes a motive for the creation of the Holocaust 'legend' by the Jews. Once the deniers add this to the equation, the essential elements of their argument are in place.

Some have a distinct political objective: If there was no Holocaust, what is so wrong with national socialism? It is the Holocaust that gives fascism a bad name. Extremist groups know that every time they extol the virtues of national socialism they must contend with the question: If it was so benign, how was the Holocaust possible? Before fascism can be resurrected, this blot must be removed. At first they attempted to justify it; now they deny it. This is the means by which those who still advocate the principles of fascism attempt to reintroduce it as a viable political system (see chapter 6). For many falsifiers this, not antisemitism, is their primary agenda. It

---

* A small group of Americans has used tactics, similar to those of the deniers, in their claims about the World War II Japanese detention camps in the United States. They make the argument that Manzanar, the infamous camp for Japanese Americans, contained only 'voluntary visitors.' According to these historical revisionists, the camp inmates were treated well and had 'all they could eat at our government's expense.' This group asserts that the contemporary Japanese Americans who foster the notion that the Japanese Americans in the camps were mistreated have a rationale for doing so – to divert attention from their community's complicity with Japan during the war (*Los Angeles Times*, August 28 and December 6, 1991).

is certainly a central theme for the European deniers on the emerging far right.

When one first encounters them it is easy to wonder who could or would take them seriously. Given the preponderance of evidence from victims, bystanders, and perpetrators, and given the fact that the deniers' arguments lie so far beyond the pale of scholarly argument, it appears to be ludicrous to devote much, if any, mental energy to them. They are a group motivated by a strange conglomeration of conspiracy theories, delusions, and neo-Nazi tendencies. The natural inclination of many rational people, including historians and social scientists, is to dismiss them as an irrelevant fringe group. Some have equated them with the flat-earth theorists, worthy at best of bemused attention but not of serious analysis or concern. They regard Holocaust denial as quirky and malicious but do not believe it poses a clear and present danger.

There are a number of compelling reasons not to dismiss the deniers and their beliefs so lightly. First, their methodology has changed in the past decade. Initially Holocaust denial was an enterprise engaged in by a small group of political extremists. Their arguments tended to appear in poorly printed pamphlets and in right-wing newspapers such as the *Spotlight*, *Thunderbolt*, or the Ku Klux Klan's *Crusader*. In recent years, however, their productivity has increased, their style has changed, and, consequently, their impact has been enhanced. They disguise their political and ideological agendas.[82] Their subterfuge enhances the danger they pose. Their publications, including the *Journal of Historical Review* – the leading denial journal – mimic legitimate scholarly works, generating confusion among those who (like the Yale history student) do not immediately recognize the *Journal*'s intention. Their books and journals have been given an academic format, and they have worked hard to find ways to insinuate themselves into the arena of historical deliberation. One of the primary loci of their activities is the college campus, where they have tried to stimulate a debate on the existence of the Holocaust. It is here that they may find their most fertile field, as is evident from the success they have had in placing advertisements that deny the Holocaust in college newspapers (see chapter

10). They have also begun to make active use of computer bulletin boards, where they post their familiar arguments. Certain computer networks have been flooded with their materials. Their objective is to plant seeds of doubt that will bear fruit in coming years, when there are no more survivors or eyewitnesses alive to attest to the truth.

There is an obvious danger in assuming that because Holocaust denial is so outlandish it can be ignored. The deniers' worldview is no more bizarre than that enshrined in the *Protocols of the Elders of Zion*, a report purporting to be the text of a secret plan to establish Jewish world supremacy.[83] The deniers draw inspiration from the *Protocols*, which has enjoyed a sustained and vibrant life despite the fact it has long been proved a forgery.

Many years ago the prominent German historian Theodor Mommsen warned that it would be a mistake to believe that reason alone was enough to keep people from believing such falsehoods. If this were the case, he said, then racism, antisemitism, and other forms of prejudice would find no home. To expect rational dialogue to constitute the sole barriers against the attempts to deny the Nazi annihilation of European Jewry would be to ignore one of the ultimate lessons of the event itself: Reasoned dialogue has a limited ability to withstand an assault by the mythic power of falsehood, especially when that falsehood is rooted in an age-old social and cultural phenomenon. There was no rational basis to the Nazi atrocities. There was, however, the mythic appeal of antisemitism. Hitler and the Nazis understood this. Mythical thinking and the force of the irrational have a strange and compelling allure for the educated and uneducated alike. Intellectuals in Nazi Germany were not immune from irrational, mystical thinking. So, too, among the deniers.

The vast majority of intellectuals in the Western world have not fallen prey to these falsehoods. But some have succumbed in another fashion, supporting Holocaust denial in the name of free speech, free inquiry, or intellectual freedom. An absolutist commitment to the liberal idea of dialogue may cause its proponents to fail to recognize that there is a significant difference between reasoned dialogue and anti-intellectual pseudoscientific arguments. They have failed to

make the critical distinction between a conclusion, however outrageous it may be, that has been reached through reasonable inquiry
and the use of standards of evidence, on the one hand, and ideological extremism that rejects anything that contradicts its preset
conclusions, on the other. Thomas Jefferson long ago argued that in
a setting committed to the pursuit of truth all ideas and opinions
must be tolerated. But he added a caveat that is particularly applic-
able to this investigation: Reason must be left free to combat error.[84]
One of the ways of combating errors is by making the distinctions
between scholarship and myth. In the case of Holocaust denial, we
are dealing with people who consciously confuse these categories. As
a result reason becomes hostage to a particularly odious ideology.

Reasoned dialogue, particularly as it applies to the understanding
of history, is rooted in the notion that there exists a historical reality
that – though it may be subjected by the historian to a multiplicity of
interpretations – is ultimately found and not made.[85] The historian
does not create, the historian uncovers. The validity of a historical
interpretation is determined by how well it accounts for the facts.
Though the historian's role is to act as a neutral observer trying to
follow the facts, there is increasing recognition that the historian
brings to this enterprise his or her own values and biases. Consequently there is no such thing as value-free history. However, even
the historian with a particular bias is dramatically different from the
proponents of these pseudoreasoned ideologies. The latter freely
shape or create information to buttress their convictions and reject as
implausible any evidence that counters them. They use the language
of scientific inquiry, but theirs is a purely ideological enterprise.

This absolutist commitment to free inquiry and the power of irrational mythical thinking at least partially explain how the deniers
have managed to find defenders among various establishment figures
and institutions. Even the supposed protectors of Western liberal
ideals of reasoned dialogue can fall prey to the absolutist notion that
all arguments are equally legitimate arenas of debate. By arguing that
the deniers' views, however ugly, must be given a fair hearing, they
take a positive Western value to an extremist end. They fail to recognize that the deniers' contentions are a composite of claims founded

on racism, extremism, and virulent antisemitism. The issue is not interpretation: The challenge presented by the deniers is whether disinformation should be granted the same status and intellectual privileges as real history.

I reiterate that I am not advocating the muzzling of the deniers. They have the right to free speech, however abhorrent. However, they are using that right not as a shield, as it was intended by the Constitution, but as a sword. There is a qualitative difference between barring someone's right to speech and providing him or her with a platform from which to deliver a message. Quick to exploit this situation, the deniers have engaged in a calculated manipulation of two principles dear to Americans: free speech and the search for historical truth.

In the pages that follow I shall examine both the *modus operandi* of Holocaust denial and the impact it has had on contemporary culture. I undertake this task with some hesitation, since readers might wonder how marginal the deniers can be if historians do not simply dismiss them. Does scholars' attention suggest that they are not merely falsifiers? Does research on them give them the publicity they crave?* Indeed, deniers are quick to pounce joyfully on *any* discussion of their work as evidence of the serious consideration their views are receiving. In 1981 President Reagan, speaking at the official commemoration of the Days of Remembrance of the Holocaust, related how 'horrified' he was to learn that there were people who claimed that the Holocaust was an invention. In its newsletter the Institute for Historical Review, the leading disseminator of Holocaust denial material, cited the president's comments to demonstrate Holocaust denial's 'vibrancy' and 'just how far Revisionism has come since our founding'[86] – a response reminiscent of the witticism: I don't care what they say about me as long as they say something.

The deniers understand how to gain respectability for outrageous

---

* Robert Lifton expressed similar ambivalences about the potential impact of his research on doctors who participated in the Nazi killing system. He feared that his explanation would sound as if he were condoning or rationalizing their actions (Lifton, *The Nazi Doctors: Medical Killing and the Psychology of Genocide* [New York, 1986], pp. xi–xii).

and absolutely false ideas. The anthropologist Marshall Sahlins has described how this process operates in the academic arena. Professor X publishes a theory despite the fact that reams of documented information contradict his conclusions. In the 'highest moral tones' he expresses his disregard for all evidence that sheds doubt on his findings. He engages in *ad hominem* attacks on those who have authored the critical works in this field and on the people silly enough to believe them. The scholars who have come under attack by this professor are provoked to respond. Before long he has become 'the controversial Prof. X' and his theory is discussed seriously by non-professionals, that is, journalists. He soon becomes a familiar figure on television and radio, where he 'explains' his ideas to interviewers who cannot challenge him or demonstrate the fallaciousness of his argument.[87]

While we have not yet descended to the point at which respectful reviews of denial literature appear in *Time*, *Newsweek*, or *The New Yorker*, virtually all else has evolved as Sahlins described. Normal and accepted standards of scholarship, including the proper use of evidence, are discarded. What remains, in the word of this eminent anthropologist, is a 'scandal.'

The danger that my research might inadvertently give the deniers a certain stature is not my only cause for trepidation. Another more serious problem is inherent in the process of refuting the deniers. It is possible, as the French historian Pierre Vidal-Naquet has observed, that in the course of answering the deniers an 'exterminationist' school will be created in opposition to the 'revisionist' one.[88] Such was the case when radio and television producers wondered why I wouldn't talk to the 'other side.' Deniers have, in fact, already taken to calling those who do research on the Holocaust 'exterminationists.'

Despite these dangers I have undertaken this work for a number of reasons. First, denial of an individual's or a group's persecution, degradation, and suffering is the ultimate cruelty – on some level worse than the persecution itself. Those who have not experienced the Holocaust or the sting of antisemitism may find it difficult to understand the vulnerability it engenders in the victim. So, too, those who have never experienced racism cannot fully grasp the pain and anger it causes. This book is, in part, an attempt to convey the pain the deniers inflict. In writing it I have often found myself angry with them despite the facts that they live in a strange mental wonderland and that neither they nor the nonsense they spread are worthy of my anger. Although we do not take their conclusions seriously, contradictory as it may sound, we must make their method the subject of study. We must do so not because of the inherent value of their ideas but because of the fragility of reason and society's susceptibility to such farfetched notions. Many powerful movements have been founded by people living in similar irrational wonderlands, national socialism foremost among them.

I have also delved into this distasteful topic because of my conviction that only when society – particularly that portion of society committed to intellectual inquiry – comprehends the full import of this group's intentions will there be any hope that history will not be reshaped to fit a variety of pernicious motives. Time need not be wasted in answering each and every one of the deniers' contentions. It would be a never-ending effort to respond to arguments posed by those who falsify findings, quote out of context, and dismiss reams of testimony because it counters their arguments. It is the speciousness of their arguments, not the arguments themselves, that demands a response. The way they confuse and distort is what I wish to demonstrate; *above all, it is essential to expose the illusion of reasoned inquiry that conceals their extremist views.*

It is also crucial to understand that this is not an arcane controversy. The past and, more important, our perception of it have a powerful impact on the way we respond to contemporary problems. Deniers are well aware of history's significance. Not by chance did Harry Elmer Barnes believe that history could serve as a 'means for a deliberate and conscious instrument of social transformation.'[89] History matters. Whether the focus be the Middle East, Vietnam, the Balkans, the Cold War, or slavery in this country, the public's perception of past events and their meaning has a tremendous influence on how it views and responds to the present. Adolf Hitler's rise to power was facilitated by the artful way in which he advanced views of recent German history that appealed to the masses. It did not matter if his was a distorted version – it appealed to the German people because it laid the blame for their current problems elsewhere. Although history will always be at a disadvantage when contending with the mythic power of irrational prejudices, it must contend nonetheless.

I was reminded of the potency of history when, on the eve of the Louisiana gubernatorial election in 1991, one of David Duke's followers remarked in a television interview that there was all this talk about Duke's past views on Jews and blacks and his Ku Klux Klan activities. That, the follower observed, was the past; what relevance he wondered, did it have for this election? The answer was obvious: His past had everything to do with his quest for election; it shaped who he was and who he remained. It has never been more clearly illustrated that history matters. (Neither was it pure happenstance that the late Paul de Man, one of the founders of deconstructionism, also falsified his past and reworked his personal history.[90])

And if history matters, its practitioners matter even more. The historian's role has been compared to that of the canary in the coal mine whose death warned the miners that dangerous fumes were in the air – 'any poisonous nonsense and the canary expires.'[91] There is much poisonous nonsense in the atmosphere these days. The deniers hope to achieve their goals by winning recognition as a legitimate scholarly cadre and by planting seeds of doubt in the younger generation. Only by recognizing the threat denial poses to both the past and the future will we ultimately thwart their efforts.

2

The Antecedents

History, Conspiracy, and Fantasy

Modern Holocaust denial draws inspiration from a variety of sources. Among them are a legitimate historical tradition that was highly critical of government policies and believed that history was being used to justify those policies; an age-old nexus of conspiratorial scenarios that place a neat coherence on widely diverse developments; and hyperbolic critiques of government policies which, despite an initial connection to reality, became so extreme as to assume a quality of fantasy. The aforementioned historical tradition was taken over and co-opted by the Holocaust deniers. In the other two cases, denial was their logical successor.

The deniers consider themselves heirs of a group of influential American historians who were deeply disturbed by American involvement in World War I. These respected scholars, who called themselves revisionists, would have been appalled to learn of the purposes to which their arguments were put. In contrast to the Holocaust deniers, who make no distinction between fact and fiction, the World War I revisionists engaged in serious research and relied upon established canons of evidence. Despite these differences, deniers have tried to link the two traditions, arguing that each has sought to create an alternative history for major events of the twentieth century. However, one of these schools used traditional historiographic methodology to do so, whereas denial relies on pseudoscience.

The opening salvo in this fight was fired in 1920, when Sidney B. Fay, a professor at Smith College, published a series of articles in the *American Historical Review* on the origins of World War I. In these articles and in his subsequent book, Fay used archival material released after the war to argue that, contrary to prevailing American opinion, the Germans had not sought to go to war. Americans, Fay protested, had been fed a great deal of 'silly propaganda' about who was really responsible for the war.[1] He insisted that Germany had neither plotted nor wanted a war and had made real efforts to avoid one. On the eve of World War I, according to Fay, German statesmen were the last leaders in Europe to abandon the quest for peace and mobilize their army, doing so only when all other options had been closed.[2]

Thus was born American World War I revisionism. One of Fay's earliest associates in this effort was Harry Elmer Barnes, who in 1923 became his colleague at Smith College. Barnes, a prolific writer and a full professor by the age of thirty, quickly joined the battle. Soon he surpassed Fay and virtually every other revisionist in his vehement criticism of American foreign policy. His relentless attacks on the 'orthodox' presentation of the war made him a hero in Germany. In American historical circles, he was infamous for his *ad hominem* assaults on those whom he believed advocated the traditional historiography of World War I.[3] While Barnes played a seminal role in the post–World War I revisionist debate, his importance for us is as the 'father' of American Holocaust denial: He became one of Holocaust denial's earliest proponents and wrote some of the first attacks on the history of the destruction of European Jewry. As we shall see in chapter 5, his method in both contexts was remarkably similar.

Prominent among the other academics who joined Fay and Barnes was Charles A. Beard.[4] Beard derisively dismissed the 'Sunday-school theory' of the war: namely that Russia, France, and England, 'three pure and innocent boys,' were assailed by two villains, Germany and Austria, who had been conspiring to commit 'cruel deeds in the dark.'[5] Not only did they reject the idea of German responsibility, but they were distressed by the Versailles treaty's use of the notion of war guilt in order to impose severely punitive conditions on Germany. The revisionists considered Article 231 of the treaty, which held German aggression responsible for imposing a war on the Allies, 'historically incorrect and morally unjustifiable.'[6]

But these revisionists did not just exonerate Germany; they excoriated the Allies, accusing them of behaving duplicitously before and after the war. In their view, the British and French, anxious to lure the United States into the war, prevented it from learning about the very real German desire for peace and the 'reasonable and statesmanlike' proposals offered by the Germans in order to avert war.[7] France's aggressive and combative policy repeatedly closed off options for peace. Britain falsely accused Germany of committing horrible atrocities. According to the revisionists, even when World War I ended the Allies continued to behave in a deceptive fashion and refused to consider evidence that contradicted the notion of sole German war guilt.[8] The British, French, and American acts of postwar deception were particularly odious to the revisionists because, as victors, the Allies knew that Germany was not really guilty. Using their power to keep the truth from emerging, the Allies engaged in a calculated refashioning of fact and forced the dregs of defeat down German throats even though the Germans did not deserve it.

Some of the more extreme revisionists, Barnes prominent among them, specifically castigated President Woodrow Wilson as responsible for the expense, losses, and miseries of the war and for the 'arrogant and atrocious policies of France and England.'[9] They claimed that Wilson's initial support of American neutrality was disingenuous. According to their account, Wilson had long been convinced that England could not defeat Germany without American aid. Consequently he decided to enter the war on England's side as soon as possible and simply waited for the proper provocation to do so.[10] World War II revisionists would voice virtually the same arguments about President Roosevelt. They contended that, just like his predecessor Wilson, Roosevelt had long intended for the United States to enter the European fray and was only waiting for the right opportunity to make it happen. According to these critics, both men were less than honest with the American people and both led the United States down a disastrous foreign policy path.

In fact, much of the revisionist argument was historically quite sound. Germany was *not* solely culpable for the war. The Versailles treaty contained harsh and vindictive elements that placed so onerous a financial burden on Germany as to virtually guarantee the collapse of the Weimar regime. The French did have ulterior motives. The American munitions industry and bankers did benefit greatly from the war. The war did not bring peace to Europe or resolve any of its long-simmering disputes. The revisionist cause was strengthened by the fact that during the war the British propagated all sorts of false horror stories about German atrocities against civilians, including that the Germans used homicidal gas to kill noncombatants, employed babies for target practice, and mutilated Belgian women. The American public, unaware that a hoax was being perpetrated, proved particularly susceptible to these stories.[11] (This effort was so successful that an entire industry was born as a result: The field of public relations traces its origins directly to British and, to a lesser degree, American propaganda regarding the war.) Twenty years later, when reports reached Americans about Nazi Germany's use of gas to kill Jews, the lingering impact of these false atrocity tales was evident. Americans dismissed the second spate of stories as yet another set of tall tales about the Germans. The problem, of course, was that this time the stories were true.

One of the reasons many Americans were intrigued by revisionism and supported the noninterventionism of the interwar period was that although the war had ended in victory, the outcome was far less than had been anticipated. During the war politicians such as Wilson nourished the notion that this was a crusade for democracy, when in fact it was more often a matter of distasteful national interest.[12] For many people, including World War I revisionists, these efforts to cast the war in grandiose, hyperbolic terms backfired. They were bitterly disappointed that the war had been neither the democratic crusade nor the war to end all wars Wilson had promised.

Neither did it establish peace among the war-weary peoples of the earth. As the situation in Europe became increasingly volatile in the interwar years, growing numbers of Americans, the revisionists and isolationists foremost among them, became embittered and disillusioned.[13] They were convinced that an unsuspecting American public had been duped and that American intervention in the war had been an unmitigated disaster not only for the United States but for the world.[14] Their ex post facto attacks were bitter and unwavering. During the interwar period the debate over World War I's origins provided a framework for the passionate discussion of American foreign policy. The revisionists' aim was to alter public opinion.[15] Revisionism became the prism through which future policies were refracted.[16]

Harry Elmer Barnes is the only link between these revisionists and Holocaust denial. But the revisionists' arguments were nonetheless a perfect foil for the deniers. Their contentions about government chicanery, mistreatment of Germany, and atrocity reports and their desire to change public attitudes were too tempting to be ignored. The deniers would hijack this movement and use it for their own purposes.

On both the home and international fronts the interwar period was a turbulent time. Critics of American foreign policy were to be found at all points of the political spectrum.[17] On Capitol Hill, liberals, conservatives, and progressives faulted Roosevelt and the direction of his overseas policies.[18] In certain quarters there was a conviction that there existed a conspiracy or a series of conspiracies to do America harm. Red scares took on the character of a witch-hunt. A deep-seated xenophobia tinged with significant antisemitism emerged in the United States. As the impact of the depression intensified, there was also a growing sentiment in various quarters that someone – a group, ideology, financial interest – was to blame. The ramifications of these fears could be seen in a variety of arenas.

The passage of the Immigration Act of 1924 was motivated by a desire to limit the number of people not of Anglo-Saxon Protestant background who could enter the country. Opponents of the new type of immigrants charged that they were changing the face of America. Passed when Americans felt financially secure, the act won even stronger support as the economic and international situation deteriorated. The depression fostered a deep distrust of business and banking interests. For many people the culprits responsible for this steadily deteriorating situation were easily identifiable.

In 1935, Sen. Gerald P. Nye (R-ND) convened hearings on the role of shipbuilders, munitions manufacturers, and international bankers in World War I. The premise of the hearings was that it was not only political leaders who bore the blame for getting the country into this war. 'Wicked' Wall Street bankers aided and abetted by 'sinister' arms merchants were part of an insidious self-enriching effort to lure the United States into the conflagration.[19] The Nye committee hearings aroused intense isolationist sentiment in the United States and had profound implications for American foreign policy.[20] Though they found no evidence to prove Wall Street responsible for precipitating American involvement, some senators believed the hearings the most effective medium for fostering American isolationism during this period.[21] When Sen. Homer T. Bone (D-WA), a vehement isolationist, observed in 1935 that the war had been 'utter social insanity,' and that America had 'no business' being in it, his view resonated with millions of people.[22]

In certain quarters there was little doubt as to the identity of those responsible for the dire situation facing the United States. Roosevelt was accused of pandering to 'Jewish interests' with his foreign policy. Sen. Hiram W. Johnson (R-CA), echoing a view harbored by a growing number of antisemites, complained in February 1939 that all the Jews were 'on one side, wildly enthusiastic for the President and willing to fight to the last American.' He charged that Jews' loyalties were to their group and not to their nation. Arrayed against this powerful entity, Johnson continued, were 'those of us – a very considerable number who are thinking in terms of our own country, and that alone.' Johnson argued that though Germany's treatment of its Jewish population was at the heart of the struggle over American policy in Europe, no one was brave enough to say so because they were afraid of 'offending the Jews.' He accused Roosevelt, whom he believed had a 'dictator complex,' of having found the Jews powerful supporters who vociferously demanded that he provide aid for 'their people, who neither live here, nor have anything in common with our country.'[23]

Father Charles C. Coughlin's antisemitic diatribes on CBS radio had a nationwide listening audience in the millions, and his journal,

Social Justice, reprinted antisemitica that came directly from the propaganda machine of Joseph Goebbels (without, of course, identifying the source). In 1941 Democratic congressman John E. Rankin of Mississippi, a known antisemite, accused 'Wall Street and a little group of our international Jewish brethren' of trying to precipitate a war and complained that 'white Gentiles' were being persecuted in the United States.[24] In 1941 isolationist senators investigated the movie industry's use of propaganda to 'influence public sentiment in the direction of participation by the United States in the present European war.'[25] The hearings took on an antisemitic tone because virtually all those named by the investigation were Jewish. Charles A. Lindbergh believed that Jews constituted a separate, distinct, and cohesive unit committed to a policy of interventionism and possessed of the political power to realize their goal.* His public expression of these views attracted tremendous controversy.[26]

In the wake of Germany's absorption of Czechoslovakia in March 1939, even such a respected scholar as Charles Beard attacked two 'major pressure groups' for thwarting a realistic American 'foreign policy based on geographical position and its democratic ideals.' The two groups were the idealistic internationalists and the 'boarders,' ethnic groups and communists whose 'hopes and passion are linked with the fate of foreign governments and nationalities.'[27]

The age-old inclination to find a Jewish conspirator behind a country's problems was deeply ingrained. Jews had been blamed for poisoning wells, killing Christian children, spreading the Black Plague, and causing famines, earthquakes, and droughts. In twentieth-century America this kind of conspiratorial delusion was given a major boost when Henry Ford, whose name was synonymous with American ingenuity and industriousness, blamed a Jewish conspiracy

---

* Lindbergh's best-known and most controversial statement during this period was made in September 1941 at an America First rally in Des Moines, Iowa. In a speech entitled 'Who Are the War Agitators?' he told eight thousand people that the 'three most important groups who have been pressing this country toward war are the British, the Jewish and the Roosevelt Administration . . . If any one of these groups – the British, the Jewish, or the Administration – stops agitating for war . . . [there would] be little danger of our involvement.'

for social and economic upheavals. Between 1920 and 1927, Ford's *Dearborn Independent*, which had a circulation of 600,000, published the *Protocols* in English and ran a series of articles accusing Jews of utilizing communism, banking, labor unions, alcohol, gambling, jazz music, newspapers, and the movies to attack and weaken America, its culture and people. The Jews' objective was to absorb the country into the 'All-Judan,' a putative world government. Published in book form, *The International Jew: The World's Foremost Problem* sold over a half a million copies in the United States and was translated into sixteen foreign languages.[28]

The *Protocols* were often cited as 'evidence' of a Jewish conspiracy. An article in the *Chicago Tribune* contended that communism was intimately linked to the Jewish conspiracy to dominate the world. On the same day that this article appeared, the *Christian Science Monitor*'s lead editorial, entitled 'The Jewish Peril,' argued that the *Protocols* bore a striking similarity to the conspiracy of the Order of the Illuminati.[29] Conspiracy theorists had long identified the Illuminati as Lucifer's modern successors. They supposedly used reason to undermine religion and the political order and establish world government. Not only were they said to be the force behind the French revolution but they were also held responsible for Karl Marx's *Communist Manifesto* and facilitated the rise of communism. According to this nexus of conspiratorial delusions, which the *Dearborn Independent* repeated, Jews, and Jewish bankers in particular, were responsible for the Illuminati's nefarious deeds. Those who unearthed this conspiracy were able to impose a logical coherence on the seemingly irrational nature of their charges – bankers aiding communists – by arguing that the bankers anticipated that the communists would create a world government that they would then appropriate and control.[30]

Ford, facing a lawsuit, eventually apologized for fostering this fantasy. But the damage had already been done. The image of a Jewish conspiracy that connected communist and capitalist forces in an attempt to dominate the world had taken root in the minds of many Americans, particularly those from the extremist right.

Many of these Jewish-conspiracy theories, including Holocaust denial, share common features. Behind each conspiracy is a collective that has targeted another group. Though the victims are more numerous than the conspirators, because they remain unaware of the conspiracy they are highly vulnerable. It is the responsibility of those who have uncovered the scheme to bring it to the victims' attention. The conspirators are thought to pursue their goals with a diabolical skill that far exceeds that of their enemies. Endowed with almost mystical powers, they control the stock exchange, world banks, and the media. Having successfully carried out such conspiracies in the past, these conspirators are so adept that, unless they are stopped, they will surely triumph in the future.[31]

These delusions impose orderly consistency on situations that seem inexplicable – worldwide depressions, famines, and the death of millions – and draw on familiar stereotypes. The Holocaust deniers have built on this tradition. Some among them may actually be convinced of the truth of their charges. The conviction that they are right does not, of course, make their claims any more rational or true than the earlier claims of those who accused the Jews of poisoning wells, killing Christian children for ritual purposes, and fomenting world revolution.

In the immediate aftermath of World War II a number of isolationists again took up the cudgels on behalf of Germany. Among the post–World War II revisionists were extremists who shared a belief that a military and political conspiracy of major proportions had again been perpetrated to drag the United States into war. According to them, Roosevelt had been intent on U.S. participation from the outbreak of the war in 1939. With a select cadre of advisers and the support of certain ethnic and interest groups, he sought a 'back door' into World War II. In order to achieve his objective he concealed information indicating that an attack on Pearl Harbor was forthcoming. Convinced of Roosevelt's complicity in allowing the attack to occur, the *Chicago Tribune* accused him of deliberately sacrificing the lives of thousands of American soldiers. Led by journalists, pacifists, and politicians, critics argued further that Pearl Harbor was part of a bigger and more complex picture. They believed that the Roosevelt administration needed a war to divert public attention from the failures of the New Deal.

Criticism came from those who were bitterly disappointed that the war had taken place and unhappy with its outcome. Bitterness was reflected in their rhetoric. In his book *The Roosevelt Myth*, America First leader John T. Flynn accused Roosevelt of finding war a 'glorious, magnificent escape from all the insoluble problems of America.' Flynn argued that nothing had been accomplished by the war except to 'put into Stalin's hands the means of seizing a great slab of the continent of Europe.' Flynn's book, which was rejected by all major publishers because of its inflammatory rhetoric, was eventually released by Devin-Adair, which would in turn become one of the leading publishers of Holocaust denial material. Its rhetoric notwithstanding, it reached the number two position on the *New York Times* best-seller list.[32]

Charles Beard also argued that the defeat of one totalitarian entity resulted in the rise of an equally despotic regime. Nazism had been replaced by another despotism, consequently there was no justifiable reason for going to war. Juxtaposing the outrages committed by the Nazis with those committed by the Soviets, Beard wondered how it could be argued 'that the "end" justified the means employed to involve the United States in the war?'[33] Citing Beard for a purpose that would have appalled him, Holocaust deniers' journals and publications argue that the war against Hitler was not just folly but counterproductive to American interests. Consequently, the deniers contend, there must have been some interest group that wanted the war to occur.

These critics had various objectives. Some, possibly prompted by their German American heritage, wished to win more lenient economic and political terms for a defeated Germany. Others may have been motivated by their conservative midwestern roots and were wary of foreign entanglements. Many among them were anticommunists who believed that a strong postwar Germany provided the best defense against the spread of Communism. Others, such as

Barnes, were World War I revisionists who did not distinguish between one conflagration and the other. While the idea of a strong Germany became the linchpin of American postwar policy, some of the more extreme post–World War II revisionists took it a step further and, echoing a prewar argument, contended that Nazi Germany had also been an excellent defense against Communism but that the Allies had been blind – or blinded – to this fact.

The most extreme revisionist account of America's entry into World War II, *Back Door to War*, by Charles C. Tansill, a professor of American diplomatic history at Georgetown University, was published in 1952. Tansill had previously addressed the issue of distorted accounts of American history when he accused Lincoln, whom he called a ' "do-nothing" soldier, invincible in peace and invisible in war,' of having tricked the South into attacking Fort Sumter and thereby precipitating the Civil War.[34] Tansill's book made a strong impression on Holocaust deniers who energetically promote it and use his arguments as a foundation for their own. Tansill declared that the 'main objective' of American foreign policy during the first half of the twentieth century was 'the preservation of the British Empire.' He linked U.S. entry into World War I with the rise of Nazism in Europe, the former having resulted in the latter: 'Our intervention completely shattered the old balance of power and sowed the seeds of inevitable future conflict.' According to him this sordid set of affairs did not end with World War I, and in his view America's entry into World War II was thus an attempt to preserve, irrespective of the cost, the 'bungling handiwork of 1919.'[35]

Tansill set out a number of arguments that would become essential elements of Holocaust denial. Most have no basis in fact; for example, Tansill and other revisionists contended that Hitler did not want to go to war with Poland but planned for Germany and Poland to dominate Europe together. If Poland had agreed to Hitler's scheme that it become the chief satellite in the Nazi orbit, its security would have been guaranteed.[36] It was the Poles' refusal – prompted by promises they had received from the British and made at America's urging – to accede to the Nazi plan that was responsible for the outbreak of the war. Therefore it was American machinations that were ultimately responsible for pushing Poland into war and precipitating World War II.[37] Roosevelt, according to this extreme revisionist point of view, played a 'grotesque role' in the entire episode by pressing British Prime Minister Neville Chamberlain to make promises to the Poles that could not be fulfilled.[38] These extreme arguments, which are rejected by virtually all historians, ignore the fact that Hitler did not intend to make Poland a satellite but to decimate it and that he regarded the Poles as *Untermenschen*, less than complete human beings. These arguments also exaggerate Roosevelt's role in convincing the British and the Poles to go to war. Stretching existing historical evidence to distorted limits, these arguments exonerated Nazi Germany and placed responsibility for the war on the Allies. Not surprisingly, deniers would make them a critical component of the nexus of arguments that together constitute their world view.

Among the extremists who, within months of the end of the war, were engaged in an attempt to lessen Germany's burden of responsibility were the vanguard of the deniers. They generally agreed that the United States should not have allowed itself to be drawn into the war. But their primary objective was to help Germany regain moral standing in the world. They believed that a strong, revived Germany was the key to the future of Western Europe. They recognized that the Allies in general and Americans in particular were likely to balk at aiding a country that was perceived as vicious, if not genocidal. It was necessary, therefore, to mitigate, if not totally dissipate, the uniqueness of Germany's wartime behavior. They did so in a number of ways: by portraying Nazi Germany in a positive light, by minimizing the severity of its hostile actions, and by engaging in immoral equivalencies – that is, by citing what they claimed were comparable Allied wrongs.

Some of them were quite sympathetic to Hitler and portrayed him as a leader whose only motivation was the good of his own country. In addition to demonstrating a conciliatory attitude toward Poland, he had sought to avoid war. He was, according to Austin App, a 'man of architecture and art, not of armaments and war.' He did not want to go to war and was reluctant to mobilize the German people.[39] Hitler's Germany had been a society with many positive features that were overlooked because of disproportionate focus on some of its less appealing domestic policies.[40] The war could not be defined as a moral struggle: All sides had been equally devious and, consequently, were equally guilty. In order to free Germany of its particular burden of guilt those engaged in this effort had to address directly the issue of the atrocities committed under the Nazis. The most extreme among them tried to neutralize German actions by directly comparing the Nazis' annihilation of the Jews and murder of millions of others with Allied actions. They contended that the United States had committed wrongdoings of the same magnitude. The ardent isolationist Freda Utley made the same point in *The High Cost of Vengeance*:

> If imitation is the sincerest form of flattery no one ever paid a higher compliment to the Nazis than their conquerors ... We reaffirmed the Nazi doctrine that 'might makes right.' Instead of showing the Germans that Hitler's racial theories were both wrong and ridiculous, we ourselves assumed the role of a master race.[41]

The argument that the United States committed atrocities as great, if not greater, than those committed by Germany has become a fulcrum of contemporary Holocaust denial and a theme repeated continually in their literature. But the deniers do not stop with this. In order to achieve their goals, one of which is the historical rehabilitation of Germany, they must 'eliminate' the Holocaust. Once they do so, this equation – everyone is equally guilty – becomes even easier to make. If there was no Holocaust and the Allies committed terrible atrocities, then what was so bad about Nazi Germany?

It is also a central argument for those who relativize the Holocaust – that is, those who say the Nazis were no worse than anyone else. For the relativizer, these charges serve as immoral equivalents that mitigate the uniqueness of German wrongs. George Morgenstern, an editor of the *Chicago Tribune*, offered a mild example of American postwar equalizing, or relativizing, wrongdoings when he argued that none of the Allies had 'clean hands' or were real 'exemplar[s] of justice.' While the fascist 'slave states' were abhorrent to decent people, the British Empire, whose existence was dependent on the 'exploitation' of millions of natives, was equally abhorrent.[42] William Neumann, who had been one of the first to attack prewar U.S. foreign policy, believed that Allied atrocities were the 'point by point' equivalent of the Nazis'.[43] Stalin had invaded Poland in 1939, England and France had declared war on Germany, and the United States had committed acts of aggression against Germany *before* Pearl Harbor in the form of lend-lease. Frederick Libby of the National Council for the Prevention of War tried to lessen Germany's burden by stating that 'no nation has a monopoly on atrocities. War itself is the supreme atrocity.'[44]

There were also those who, not satisfied with attacking Roosevelt or equating German and American wrongdoing, went a step further and portrayed Germany as the much-maligned victim of Allied aggression. Such arguments served as the model for those who would eventually seek not just to exculpate Germany for the Holocaust but to deny its existence altogether. According to these postwar revisionists, the bombing of Dresden and Cologne as well as Allied postwar policy toward Germany were equivalent to Nazi atrocities. They assailed Allied acquiescence in allowing the bifurcation of Germany and Soviet hegemony in Eastern Europe, ignoring the fact that the West had no alternative short of armed conflict with the Soviets. They demanded, and succeeded in getting, special American immigration permits for Germans.[45] Ignoring similar conditions in other parts of Europe, they accused the United States of allowing the German people to starve and insisted that special relief plans be instituted to help Germany. Isolationist forces in the Senate persuaded a total of thirty-four senators to inform the president jointly that Germany and Austria were 'facing starvation on a scale never before experienced in Western Civilization.'[46] Utley and other revisionists falsely claimed that, for three years after their unconditional surrender, the Allies had kept the Germans on rations that were less than or, at best, the same as those in a concentration camp.

Many of these isolationists seemed – according to Justus Doenecke, who has written a sympathetic portrait of them – to draw righteous justification from the fact that they had found a way to portray Germany as the victim and the United States as the victimizer and 'malicious power.'[47] Some World War II revisionists found it hard to exonerate the German political and military leaders who led the nation in war. Instead they attempted to distinguish between the behavior of the 'people' as opposed to their 'leaders,' depicting the Germans as a people who had themselves been persecuted and victimized. While there may have been elements of truth in their charges, these extremists carried them to a point where fantasy subsumed reality.[48]

Relativists and German apologists cited the Allies' mass transfer of German citizens from Czechoslovakia and Poland in the immediate aftermath of the war as the ultimate example of Allied brutality. Sen. William Langer (R-ND), who had vigorously opposed Roosevelt's foreign policy, spoke of a 'savage and fanatical plot' to destroy fifteen million German women and children.[49] Senator Langer claimed that three million of the German refugees had died en route.[50] Freda Utley described these population transfers as 'crimes against humanity.' Her choice of this particular phrase, which had already gained wide currency as a result of the Nuremberg indictments, was telling. (Eventually Utley would become one of the most vocal of Sen. Joseph McCarthy's supporters, branding one of those he accused of being a Communist spy as a 'Judas cow,' an animal who led others to be slaughtered).[51] Using a tactic that typified the actions of those who, in their quest to defend Nazi Germany, stopped short of denying the atrocities, she compared these transfers with what had been done to the Jews. According to her the expulsion of millions of people from their homes for the sole 'crime' of being part of the German 'race' was an 'atrocity' equivalent to 'the extermination of the Jews and the massacres of the Poles and Russians by the Nazis.' Utley continued: 'The women and children who died of hunger and cold on the long trek from Silesia and the Sudetenland to what remained of the German Reich, *may have thought that a quick death in a gas chamber would have been comparatively merciful.*'[52]

She exonerated the German war criminals who were tried at Nuremberg because what they did was 'minor in extent if not in degree' compared with the postwar behavior of the Russian armies and the 'genocide' committed by Poles and Czechs against

Germans.[53] Taking the tactic of immoral equivalencies to its ultimate extreme, she argued that 'there was no crime the Nazis had committed which we or our allies had not also committed.'[54] Although Utley was an extremist who did not abandon her political beliefs even after the war, such charges were not only made by extremists. The *Chicago Tribune* accused the French of not permitting more than half a million German prisoners of war to return home. According to the paper they were being kept as 'slaves,' denied food sufficient to allow them to work, and beaten by 'Moroccan savages.'[55]

Many of the critics focused on a plan proposed toward the end of the war by Secretary of the Treasury Henry Morgenthau, which would have prevented the economic rehabilitation of Germany. Though the plan was never put into effect, World War II revisionists and Holocaust deniers claim it was and cite it as an example of the Allies' diabolical attitude toward Germany and of the way Germany was to be made the victim of Allied postwar retribution. Henry Regnery, who published much of the World War II revisionist material, issued a pamphlet comparing Morgenthau's proposal with the Nazi plan to destroy millions of Jews through starvation.[56] The fact that Morgenthau was not only a member of Roosevelt's cabinet but an identifying Jew was something these critics were quick to exploit.*

These postwar isolationists and World War II revisionists also cast Germany as the victim by stressing the 'inhumanity' and 'injustice' of the Allied war crimes trials and de-Nazification programs. (Lindbergh accused the Allies of imposing an 'eye for an eye' punishment.) They questioned the legality of the Nuremberg trials and accused the Allies of hypocrisy in holding them, arguing that had the outcome of the war been reversed the Allied leaders would have

---

* In 1977, denier James Martin described Morgenthau's plan as an example of running postwar Germany 'according to the Old Testament instead of the New.' He claimed the plan had been implemented and resulted in the German population transfers, which he called the 'most barbarous event of the history of Europe . . . It is rare that one ever sees an animal forced to endure under such degraded and forlorn circumstances.' Martin, a member of the *Journal of Historical Review*'s editorial board, is listed as a contributor to the 1970 *Encyclopedia Britannica*. James J. Martin, *The Saga of Hog Island and Other Essays in Inconvenient History* (Colorado Springs, 1977), p. 193.

found themselves in the dock. Beard also attacked the trials.[57] Sen. Robert Taft (R-OH) argued that the trials were marked by a 'spirit of vengeance,' and the *Chicago Tribune* declared that Russia's participation transformed them into a 'kangaroo court.'[58] Congressman Rankin accused the court at Nuremberg of having 'perpetrated more outrages than any other organization of its kind.' He found it particularly appalling that Soviet Communist Jews, who, he argued, bore responsibility for the murder of tens of millions of Christians, should be able to sit in judgment of 'German soldiers, civilians and doctors, five or six years after the war closed.'[59] Robert McCormick, probably America's most influential isolationist, refused to have dinner with former Attorney General Francis Biddle because, as a result of his role in the Nuremberg trials, McCormick considered him a 'murderer.'[60] The *New York Daily News* declared that the defendants' 'real crime was that they did not win.'[61]

Allied behavior in the immediate aftermath of the war was not without fault. There had been insufficient planning for this period, and there were many shortcomings in Allied policies. The de-Nazification program was applied unequally, and inequities in punishment resulted from it. But the critics ignored the circumstances that had produced this situation. Furthermore there was no starvation program in Germany, and the rations Germans received far surpassed anything concentration camp inmates were ever given by the Nazis. The vigor of the isolationists' attacks on the de-Nazification program did not abate even when it became clear that Washington wished to change, if not totally abandon it.

(The degree to which Germans could be singled out for having committed atrocities was a matter of debate from the moment the war ended. The concentration camps had barely been liberated when some critics and commentators began to argue that the reports, official photographs, and films of the camps were being released in order to implant in American minds a feeling of vengeance. James Agee, writing in the *Nation* of May 19, 1945, attacked the Signal Corps films of concentration camp victims even though he had not seen them. He did not believe it 'necessary' to show them: 'Such propaganda' – even if true – was designed to make Americans equate all Germans with the few who had perpetrated these crimes.[62] Milton Mayer, in an article in the *Progressive*, went a step further than Agee. He not only argued against vengeance but questioned whether the films and reports could really be true. 'There are, to be sure, fantastic discrepancies in the reports.'[63] Despite overwhelming evidence, doubts persisted.[64])

Respected Americans voiced concern about a spirit of vengeance. They sometimes did so by casting doubt on the veracity of the stories and by defending the perpetrators. Robert Maynard Hutchins, president of the University of Chicago, a vigorous isolationist who had been an adviser to America First, wrote in 1945 that 'the wildest atrocity stories' could not change the 'simple truth' that 'no men are beasts.' (The implicit message in Hutchins's juxtaposition of the terms 'wild atrocity stories' with 'simple truth' may have been unintended, but it must have had an impact on his readers.) An article in the *Progressive* by William B. Hesseltine, a historian at the University of Wisconsin, compared the false atrocity stories that had been circulated in the aftermath of the Civil War with those that emerged from Germany after the end of hostilities there.[65]

Years later, in an example of how deniers pervert historical arguments, a virtually identical argument was made by Austin App:

> The top U.S. media, possibly because they are dominated by Jews . . . have no tradition of fairness to anyone they hate . . . They have also in wartime subverted much of the public to a frenzy of prejudice. Even in our Civil War, where Americans fought against Americans, Americans of the North were told and came to believe that Choctaw County stunk with dead bodies of murdered slaves and that Southern belles had worn necklaces strung of Yankee eyeballs! . . . If Yankees could believe that Southern girls wore necklaces of Yankee eyeballs, would they not even more readily believe that Germans made lampshades out of the skins of prisoners, or that they boiled Jews into soap?[66]

Two decades later this argument would be reiterated in an essay in the Holocaust revisionist publication the *Journal of Historical Review*.[67] (See chapter 9 for a discussion of the Civil War analogy.)

By finding what they deemed to be historical parallels, deniers hoped to demonstrate that the Holocaust was not the only time the public had been tricked by historical orthodoxies.

During the early years after the war, Germans also tried to minimize Nazi wrongdoings and place the blame elsewhere. Some German neo-Nazis maintained that German crimes were not as immense as the Allies had charged.[68] Others sought to clear Hitler of any responsibility. In 1952 the Institute for German Post-War History was organized in Tübingen by Dr. Herbert Grabert, who had known connections to extreme-right-wing and neo-Nazi groups. Grabert denounced those who claimed that Hitler had any ambitions to dominate the world,[69] despite the fact that in order to do so he had to ignore the clear statements to the contrary in *Mein Kampf* (see chapter 5). In 1960 the Committee for the Restoration of Historical Truth – which argued that World War II had been caused by the Versailles treaty, that Britain had long sought a war against Germany, and that Roosevelt had helped push Britain into the war – was founded in Hanover. The committee's organizers denounced the Jews as a 'cancerous growth' on the body politic. When dealing with such an adversary, 'human considerations do not enter.'[70] In 1962 *Nation Europa*, Germany's foremost neo-Nazi paper, claimed there was no 'evidence that Hitler knew of the mad doings of a small clique of criminals.' And in 1963 the *Deutsche Hochschullehrer-Zeitung*, a newspaper for German teachers of higher education, argued that the Holocaust had been a legitimate 'retaliatory action' against Jews, in response to Jewish 'business methods' and the murder by Jewish Bolsheviks of German patriots.[71]

By 1950 the foundation had been laid for those who would not simply seek to relativize or mitigate Germany's actions – the arguments they needed to buttress their charges of a Holocaust 'hoax' had been made, some voiced by legitimate historians and others expressed by extremist politicians and journalists. Virtually all the revisionists' charges were adopted by the deniers, including Germany's lack of culpability, chicanery by both Presidents Wilson and Roosevelt, suppression of the truth after both wars, and use of propaganda – falsified atrocity stories in particular – to whip up public support. These arguments would become crucial elements in the deniers' attempt to prove that the Holocaust 'hoax' is not a unique phenomenon but a link in a chain of tradition whose hallmarks were chicanery, conspiracy, and deception. The French writer Nadine Fresco noted in her analysis of Holocaust denier Robert Faurisson, 'One cannot establish a science whose only ethic is suspicion.'[72] Yet that is what the more extreme World War II revisionists were attempting to do.

Nonetheless, there was one thing these defenders of Nazi Germany and critics of American involvement and postwar Allied policy never suggested: namely that the atrocities in question had not happened. Irrespective of which side of the ocean they were on, they stopped short of this denial. They may have claimed that they were not as bad as had been reported. They may have argued that the Soviets or the Allies had committed similar acts or that Hitler knew nothing about them. They may have also ignored the moral implications of such behavior in order to argue that Allied and Axis behavior were virtually equal. But they did not deny that they were factual. Accusations to that effect were not long in coming, however, gaining currency within a few years after the war.

3
In the Shadow of World War II

Denial's Initial Steps

The end of World War II meant the defeat of Adolf Hitler's dream of a Third Reich. Most rational people assumed it also meant the end of fascism as an ideology. As long as fascism could be linked with Nazism, and Nazism, in turn, could be linked with the horrors of the Final Solution, then both would remain thoroughly discredited. There were those, however, who were not willing to abandon these political systems. They knew that the only means of trying to revive them would be to separate them from the Holocaust and the multitude of atrocities that accompanied it. Nowhere would this effort be more evident in the immediate aftermath of the war than in France, where Holocaust denial found some of its earliest proponents.

Within a few years after the liberation of Europe the effort to minimize the scope and intensity of the Nazi atrocities was overtaken by claims that the death of six million Jews was not only greatly exaggerated but a fabrication. Though the earliest deniers did not become part of a larger group, their tactics and arguments have since become integral elements of contemporary Holocaust denial. They made little, if any, effort to disguise their antisemitism.

In 1947 Maurice Bardèche, a prominent French fascist, began a concerted attack on Allied war propaganda. He also engaged in a vigorous defense of the Nazis. In his first book, *Letter to François Mauriac*, Bardèche strongly defended the politics of collaboration. In his second, *Nuremberg or the Promised Land*, he contended that at least a portion of the evidence regarding the concentration camps had been falsified and that the deaths that had occurred there were primarily the result of war-related privations, including starvation and illness. Bardèche claimed that since the end of the war the world had been 'duped by history.'[1] According to Bardèche, Nazi documents that spoke of the 'final solution of the Jewish problem' were really referring to the proposed transfer of Jews to ghettos in the east.

His fundamental argument was not only that the Nazis were not guilty of atrocities, but that the true culprits were the Jews themselves. Jews, both those who died and those who survived, deserved no sympathy because they had helped to instigate the war by supporting the Treaty of Versailles. He argued that it was morally wrong to hold German soldiers or officers of any rank culpable for following orders. Nazi Germany had to defeat the Communists in order to survive. A strong state with a strong and loyal army were absolute necessities for it to do so. The Nuremberg trials were both morally and legally wrong because they punished Germany for having done what was needed in order to defeat Stalin. For Bardèche the Allies' bombing policy constituted a war crime.

While some of these notions, particularly those regarding the Versailles treaty and the Allied bombing policy, were being articulated by others, including isolationists in the United States, Bardèche was the first to contend that the pictorial and documentary evidence of the murder process in the camps had actually been falsified. He was also the first to argue that the gas chambers were used for disinfection – not annihilation.

Bardèche's dubious credentials – he remained a committed fascist all his life – made him a controversial figure in denial circles. Despite his contentions that the Holocaust was a myth and that the Nazis were wrongly implicated, Bardèche has never been openly embraced by contemporary deniers. That has not kept them from adopting his ideas. Though they use his arguments, they rarely mention him by name because of his political views, about which he was always quite explicit. Indeed, he began his book *What Is Fascism?* with the unequivocal declaration: 'I am a fascist writer.'

In Bardèche's second book he laid out his objectives, which remain, almost verbatim, the credo of contemporary deniers: 'I am not defending Germany. I am defending the truth . . . I know a lie has been put about, I know a systematic distortion of facts exists . . . We have been living with a falsification: it captures the imagination.'[2] Today deniers protest that they are neither for Germany nor against Jews. They are not out to defend Hitler or castigate the Allies. They are interested only in revising history so that it will convey the truth. But such claims notwithstanding, examination of their methods and arguments reveals that since Bardèche's work, truth has been the antithesis of their enterprise.

The next assault on the history of the war also emanated from France. In 1948 Paul Rassinier, a former Communist and a Socialist who had been interned in the concentration camps of Buchenwald and Dora, published *Le Passage de la Ligne* (Crossing the line). This was the first in a series of books he would write during the next two decades intended to show that survivors' claims about the behavior of the Nazis, particularly in relation to the atrocities, could not be trusted. Rassinier, who became a member of the Communist party in 1922 when he was sixteen, left the Communists in the mid-1930s and joined the Socialists. When the war broke out he became part of the resistance. Eventually he was captured and sent to Buchenwald. On liberation in 1945, he returned to France and was elected a Socialist member of the National Assembly, where he served for a year. Shortly thereafter he began a prolific publishing career, the bulk of which was devoted to vindicating the Nazis by proving that the atrocity accusations against them were inflated and unfair. Given his earlier role in the French resistance, his arguments have the flavor of the utterances of a repentant sinner.

His books are a mixture of blatant falsehoods, half-truths, quotations out of context, and attacks on the 'Zionist establishment.' In 1977 Rassinier's major books concerning the Holocaust were reissued in one volume, *Debunking the Genocide Myth*, by the Noontide Press, which publishes neo-Nazi material and is connected with the California-based headquarters of the contemporary deniers, the Institute for Historical Review. The first part of this composite volume is made up of his first two works, *Crossing the Line* and *The Lie of Ulysses*, in which he focused on the concentration camps and the behavior of both inmates and Nazis administrators. He set out two propositions: Survivors exaggerate what happened to them, and it was not the SS that was responsible for the terrors of the camps but the inmates to whom they entrusted the running of the camps. He dismissed as gossip the testimony of survivors who claimed they had witnessed atrocities and denigrated the credibility of their assertions regarding the number of Jews who had been killed. 'Concerning figures the "witnesses" have said and written the most improbable things. Concerning the implementation of the means of killing, also.'[3] He described concentration camp literature as 'a collection of contradictory pieces of ill-natured gossip.'[4]

Rassinier initially limited his argument regarding the killing process to denying that there was a policy of annihilation. People may have been killed, he declared, but those who conducted such 'exterminations' were acting on their own and not in the name of 'a state order in the name of a political doctrine.'[5] Rassinier sought to absolve the National Socialist leadership from responsibility for the gas chambers, claiming there appeared to have been no official Nazi policy of gas exterminations. Though Rassinier would eventually deny the existence of gas chambers altogether, in these early works he stopped short of doing so and posited that there probably had been exterminations by gas, but not as many as had been claimed. At this time even the most extreme neo-Nazi groups were not denying that gas chambers had been used to murder Jews. Instead of denying Nazi atrocities, however, they defended them – one of the major distinctions between the earliest deniers and more recent ones. Bardèche, Rassinier, Barnes, App, and others among the first generation of deniers differ from those who followed them. The first group sought to vindicate the Nazis by justifying their antisemitism. While they argued that the atrocities were exaggerated or even falsified, they also contended that whatever was done to the Jews had been deserved because the Jews were Germany's enemy. Distorting the truth, they blamed Jews for Germany's financial and political plight and made the wildly exaggerated claim that Jews had been the prime beneficiaries of the chaos of Weimar. Jews were disloyal citizens, likely to be subversives and spies.

Only in the 1970s, when they finally began to recognize the futility of trying to justify Nazi antisemitism, did deniers change their methods. They saw that, from a tactical perspective, the proof of Nazi antisemitism was so clear that trying to deny or justify it undermined their efforts to appear credible. As deniers became more sophisticated in the subtleties of spreading their argument, they began to 'concede' that the Nazis were antisemitic. They even claimed to deplore antisemitism, all the while engaging in it themselves. They acknowledged that some Jews may have died as a result of Nazi mistreatment but continued to argue that there was no Holocaust.

In *Crossing the Line* Rassinier chose an interesting tactic to express his most radical contentions regarding the inmates and their experiences. Instead of arguing in his own voice, he quoted a fellow inmate, whom he described as a Czech, a lawyer who had been the assistant mayor of Prague before the war.[6] It is not clear whether this Czech really existed or whether Rassinier created him as a foil for his own controversial notions. What is clear is that the Czech voiced ideas that became part of Rassinier's litany of claims regarding the Holocaust. Rassinier may have put this argument in the Czech's voice for a practical reason. In the early 1950s, when he was arguing that the Nazi leadership bore little, if any, responsibility for atrocities, war wounds were still quite fresh. This was particularly so in France, which had been occupied by the Nazis. Rassinier may have been reluctant to express his views about the innocence of the Nazi leadership, the inmates' culpability in their own suffering, and the trustworthiness, or lack thereof, of survivors' testimony. Such views would have been particularly odious in the 1950s.

In truth, whether this Czech existed or was a literary creation is immaterial, since Rassinier not only articulated no reservations about his views but in fact acknowledged that he was convinced that this Czech was right. Even when Rassinier challenged the Czech's views, in the end he always conceded that his friend's ideas vanquished his own.

In these early works Rassinier set out to do three things: First he had to demolish the credibility of his fellow prisoners' testimony. As long as one could trust what they said, any attempt to absolve the Nazis would be futile. But given the sympathy toward the inmates that existed particularly during the years immediately after the war, he could not ascribe to them diabolical or even devious motives. Instead he explained their supposed behavior in psychological terms:

> Human beings need to exaggerate the bad as well as the good and the ugly as well as the beautiful. Everyone hopes and wants to come out of this business with the halo of a saint, a hero, or a martyr and each one embroiders his own Odyssey without realizing that the reality is quite enough in itself.[7]

Had Rassinier or his Czech argued that *some* concentration camp inmates were wont to exaggerate certain aspects of the treatment they endured, few would have questioned their conclusions. For a variety of reasons, some inmates did and still do embellish their experiences. Others sometimes adopt the experiences of fellow survivors as their own. Historians of the Holocaust recognize this and do not build a historical case on the oral history of an individual survivor, engaging instead in what anthropologists call triangulation, matching a survivor's testimony with other forms of proof, including documents and additional historical data. But Rassinier blatantly dismissed all survivors' testimony. Nor did he stop there in his attack on the survivors. He not only cast doubt on the testimony of victims but he exonerated the perpetrators – the Nazi leadership in general and the SS in particular. According to Rassinier, the 'SS never meddled with the camp life.' If there were any excesses in the camps it was the responsibility of the inmates. Outrages in the camps were always made 'still worse' by the prisoners.[8]

In response to those who argued that the camps constituted a peculiarly Nazi form of punishment and incarceration, Rassinier asserted that the camps were not uniquely German institutions. Incarceration in concentration camps was a 'classic method of coercion' practiced by all countries, including France. Once again we see a harbinger of what would become a familiar method for absolving the Nazis: Whatever they did was not as severe as that of which they were accused. Moreover, all nations did the same.

Finally, in one of his most extreme arguments, Rassinier attempted to transform the Nazis from perpetrators into benefactors. He claimed that they had benign, if not positive, motives when they put people in concentration camps. Initially the National Socialists' incarceration of people in concentration camps was a 'gesture of compassion.' Their objective was to protect their adversaries by putting them 'where they could not hurt the new regime and where they could be protected from the public anger.' Not only did they want to shield them, they also wanted to 'rehabilitate the strayed sheep and to bring them back to a healthier concept of the German community, [and] . . . its destiny.'[9] This latter claim evoked memories of some of the explanations and justifications offered by Goebbels's propaganda bureau during the early years of the regime. When people were placed in camps or in ghettos, the Nazis claimed they were doing so for educational or rehabilitative purposes. They were 'helping' them become more productive members of society by incarcerating them. Rassinier ignored two essential elements: This 'rehabilitation' was conducted in the harshest of fashions and, according to Nazi philosophy, there was no way Jews could be 'rehabilitated.'

Given his own experiences and those of a myriad of others in the camps, Rassinier could not very well argue that they had been character-building institutions. He had to acknowledge that the Nazis' supposedly benign intentions notwithstanding, life in the camps was quite difficult. Intent on rendering the Nazi leadership blameless, he shifted responsibility from their shoulders by explaining that the escalating severity was not the intention of those at the helm but of those in the lower echelons of the SS who disobeyed their orders. According to Rassinier, when the authorities in Berlin discovered something 'awry in the way the camps were being administered, the SS staffs were called to account.'[10] Even the SS decision to select criminals, murderers, and rapists to serve as *Lagerältester* (camp elder) and *Kapos* was justifiable, despite the fact that these people were particularly ruthless to other inmates. The SS did not select such individuals to run the camps out of 'sadism' but to 'economize personnel.' The *Kapos* were brutal but that was not the fault of the SS. In fact, Rassinier preferred dealing with the SS because they were 'in principle . . . better and . . . more humane.'[11]

In the 1960s Rassinier began to change the focus of his attacks. No longer did he devote his primary energies to defending the SS or casting doubt on the stories told by concentration camp survivors. His preoccupation became the 'genocide myth.' In *The Drama of European Jewry* (1964) he argued that the accusation that the Nazis committed mass murder through the use of gas chambers was an invention of the 'Zionist establishment.' Moreover, he contended, the charge about gas chambers was a fabrication, as was the claim that six million Jews died. In his attempt to explain who was responsible for the hoax, Rassinier did not blame the survivors. Though they may have 'exaggerated' their experiences, Rassinier forgave them that: 'They are victims who are fired by a resentment in proportion to what they suffered.' As did other deniers, he had to explain away the perpetrators' confessions. Those who falsely admitted that they had committed atrocities had little choice but to tell Allied officials the story they wanted to hear. 'In order to get into the good graces of his captors, some poor SS private attached to an *Einsatzgruppe* reports that his unit exterminated . . . tens of thousands of Jews.'[12]* The testimonies of Nazi leaders who were tried at the war crimes trials also had to be discounted because they were 'testifying under threat of death' and they confessed what they thought would 'be most likely to save [their] . . . life.' For Rassinier such behavior was 'easily understood,' and consequently the credibility of such testimony could be summarily dismissed.[13]

But if the survivors and the perpetrators were not responsible, who then perpetrated the hoax? For Rassinier the culprits in the dissemination of this fraud were easily identifiable. The 'Zionists,' abetted in their conspiracy by a select number of Jewish historians and institutions that conduct research on the Holocaust, were the responsible parties. Rassinier unleashed his most acerbic comments and unrelenting attacks on them. Unlike the survivors who lied because of all they had suffered, and the Nazis, who fabricated confessions to please their captors and protect their lives, the perpetrators

---

* The *Einsatzgruppen* were the special mobile killing units that conducted the massacres of Soviet Jewry immediately after the Germans declared war on the USSR.

of this hoax did not have motives that were either psychologically understandable or morally justifiable. The only reason these historians and the institutions that backed them spread this calumny about Germany was to reap institutional, communal, and personal gain.

Regarding the prominent historian of the Holocaust Raul Hilberg, Rassinier wrote that only 'dishonesty' could 'excuse' his actions. Rassinier informed readers that Hilberg was associated with a Jewish publication: 'As I . . . read his biographical note, I find that he is a collaborator in the *Jewish Encyclopedia Handbooks*.' This, in Rassinier's opinion, explained 'everything.' But Hilberg was not alone in his culpability for spreading this myth on behalf of a Jewish institution. Hannah Arendt's 'intellectual outlook' and writings on the Holocaust were not trustworthy, according to Rassinier, because of her position as research director with the Conference on Jewish Relations.[14] The testimony at the Eichmann trial by the renowned historian Salo Baron, the first occupant of the chair in Jewish history at Columbia University, was clearly open to question because of Baron's Jewish identity. Lest readers be unaware of Baron's background, Rassinier made a practice of referring to him throughout his book as 'Mr. *Shalom* Baron.'[15]

Their dishonesty and that of the Jewish institutions with which they were formally or informally associated was motivated by what Rassinier considered a traditional Jewish vice: the love of money. Their motive for concocting the genocide myth, Rassinier bluntly stated, 'is purely and very basely, a material problem.'[16] They wished to 'make Germany an ever-lasting milk cow for Israel.'[17] They devised the hoax and then demanded that 'Germany pay to Israel sums calculated on the basis of about 6,000,000 dead.' Rassinier contended that the amount of reparations Germany paid to Israel was calculated on the basis of the number of dead; the higher the death toll, the greater the financial reward.[18] Israel, with the aid of cooperative Jewish historians and the 'Zionist establishment,' had inflated the number of dead in order to 'swindle' the Germans out of millions of marks. They claimed that six million died, but, in truth, at least four-fifths of those six million 'were very much alive at the end of the war.'[19] Rassinier offers no evidence to prove this or most of his other claims. Their existence had been kept a secret in order to inflate the amount of money Israel was able to extract from the Germans.

Rassinier based his argument on a completely false premise. One must assume that he did so knowingly, given the documents he cites. The reparations Germany paid to Israel were not based on the death toll but on the cost to Israel of absorbing and resettling both Jews who fled Germany and German-controlled countries during the pre-war period and survivors of the Holocaust who came to Israel during the postwar years.

Israeli officials detailed their claims against Germany in their communiqué of March 1951 to the Four Powers, and this document became the official basis for the reparations agreement. It contained an explanation of Israel's means of calculating the size of the reparations claim. In the communiqué Israeli officials explained that Nazi persecution had stimulated a 'second Jewish exodus' of close to five hundred thousand. Based on the size of this exodus, Israel determined the amount of the reparations it would request:

> The government of Israel is not in a position to obtain and present a complete statement of all Jewish property taken or looted by the Germans, and said to total more than $6 thousand million. It can only compute its claim on the basis of total expenditures already made and the expenditure still needed for the integration of Jewish immigrants from Nazi-dominated countries. The number of these immigrants is estimated at some 500,000, which means a total expenditure of $1.5 thousand million.[20]

It seems hardly necessary to point out that since the money the state received was based on the cost of resettling *survivors*, had Israel wanted to increase the amount of reparations it obtained from Germany it would have been in its interest to argue that fewer than six million had been killed and that more had managed to flee to Israel.

The contention that Israel is the main financial beneficiary of the 'genocide myth' has become a critical element of Holocaust denial for a number of reasons. This explanation is particularly important for the deniers because it provides a rationale for the 'hoax.'

Moreover, it harks back to traditional antisemitic imagery: Jews' association with money, particularly ill-gotten gains. For those with an inclination to believe antisemitic charges and to accept the stereotypes associated with them as true, this is a charge that feels familiar and makes sense. This is but one of many instances in which the deniers have woven a web that deftly combines pseudohistorical research with traditional antisemitism. The depiction of Israel as the beneficiary of a worldwide Jewish conspiracy also plays on preexisting hostilities toward the Jewish state. Those who are opposed to its existence and believe it came into being through nefarious means find this myth compelling. In fact, the vast majority of reparations went to individual survivors, not to Israel.

But it was for Raul Hilberg that Rassinier reserved his greatest contempt. Hilberg's internationally acclaimed study of the German death machine in *The Destruction of the European Jews*, which was first published in 1961, made him an obvious target for Rassinier and subsequent generations of deniers. Because of his extensive research on the German bureaucracy during the Third Reich, specifically as it was used in the killing process, deniers have long felt obligated to try to destroy his credibility. In *The Drama of European Jewry* Rassinier branded Hilberg 'dishonest' and accused him of being a falsifier of information particularly in regard to the number of Jews killed by the Nazis. Revealingly, on the same page that Rassinier made those accusations, he engaged in the very same tactics of which he had accused Hilberg.

One of the methods Rassinier used to convince his readers that the Holocaust was a fraud was his use of the numbers game. Among the first to engage in this practice, he established a pattern followed by all deniers who try to prove that the death tolls are not valid. Rassinier argued that Jewish historians have fraudulent intentions and manipulate the data accordingly. For Rassinier the proof of this dishonesty is that they each interpret the data in a dramatically different fashion. Consequently their findings cannot be relied on, and they cannot be personally trusted.

In trying to make his case, Rassinier fabricated data, misquoted, and used quotations out of context. He first tried to demonstrate that

Arendt and Hilberg were in disagreement about the number of Jews who were killed in Poland. According to Rassinier, in her February 23, 1963, *New Yorker* article Arendt 'coolly inform[ed] us that "three million Polish Jews were massacred during the first day of the war."' He then wrote: 'Mr. Raul Hilberg found that "about 2,000,000 *Polish* Jews ... were transported to their deaths in 1942 and 1943.' Rassinier complained about this apparent contradiction between the findings of these two historians and added: 'It would be a good thing to come to an understanding: were there in Poland 3 to 3.3 million Jews during the war, as all statisticians unanimously claim, including those who are Jewish, or were there 5.7 million as Mme. Hannah Arendt is obliged to claim, since here are 5 million exterminated.'[21]

Rassinier simply falsified Arendt's statement. In addition, he made minor but strategically important changes in Hilberg's quote and then quoted it out of context in order to make it appear as if there were some contradiction between the two scholars. In *The Destruction of the European Jews*, Hilberg analyzed the role of the railways in the annihilation process. He observed that the 'railway network managed to carry about 2,000,000 Polish Jews to their deaths in 1942 and 1943.' Rassinier ignored the references to the railway network. He makes it appear as if Hilberg is citing the total number of Polish Jews who were annihilated and not just those transported by rail. (Hilberg does not include in this total Jews deported by other means and those who were killed in ghettoes or in areas immediately adjacent to their homes.[22] When those Polish victims are included, Hilberg's total comes to three million Polish Jews.)

But Rassinier committed an even more egregious falsehood in connection with Arendt's quote. Arendt did *not* write that three million Polish Jews were killed on the first day. Discussing German estimates of the number of Jews left in Europe in 1940, Arendt observed that one particular estimate 'did not include three million Polish Jews, who, as everybody knew, had been in the process of being massacred even since the first days of the war.'[23] By changing Arendt's quote to say three million had been killed *on the first day*, Rassinier manages to make Arendt sound not only in total contradiction to other historians but quite out of touch with reality. Deniers would repeatedly rely on this tactic to try to make the findings of Holocaust historians seem particularly fantastic.

While Rassinier wished to cast doubt on the findings and motives of as many Jewish scholars as possible, he was particularly intent – as we have seen – on destroying Hilberg's status. Ironically, after attacking Hilberg's credibility, he used Hilberg's standing as the premier historian in this field to cast doubt on the finding, of other Jewish historians and institutions. In an obvious attempt to throw into question the findings of the World Jewish Congress, he wrote that while the congress 'gives the figure of 1,000,000 (dead in the USSR) Mr. Raul Hilberg finds only 420,000.'[24] Once again Rassinier misrepresented Hilberg's findings. In one of his tables delineating the number of victims according to their countries of origin, Hilberg lists the prewar and postwar populations of the USSR. The difference between the two figures is 420,000. But the two figures represent dramatically different categories, as Hilberg clearly acknowledges at the bottom of the table, where he notes that the first column was based on prewar and the second on postwar boundaries. The postwar boundaries of the USSR were significantly larger than those of the prewar period, and Hilberg's list reflects this. Since the Baltic republics were independent when the war began they are listed as separate countries in the prewar table. Because they became part of the USSR as a result of an agreement between Germany and the Soviet Union in 1940, in postwar totals Hilberg treats their Jewish victims as part of the toll for the entire USSR. Moreover, Hilberg's postwar total must also be adjusted because it includes, as again he clearly notes, three hundred thousand refugees, deportees, and survivors from other regions.* With these adjustments Hilberg's total

* The section on the USSR appears as follows:

	Prewar Jewish Population, 1939	Postwar Jewish Population, 1945
USSR	3,020,000	2,600,000
Estonia	4,500	
Latvia	95,000	
Lithuania	145,000	
Total:	3,264,500	2,600,000

was one million, precisely that of the World Jewish Congress. By ignoring these critical and obvious pieces of information, Rassinier makes it sound as if Hilberg is not only contradicting other historians but himself as well, since elsewhere in the book he cites the total dead in the USSR as approximately one million.[25]

Rassinier devised this alleged contradiction in order to depict these historians as willfully creating farfetched facts and figures. 'One would like to invite all of these people – [Arendt, Baron, and Hilberg] and the multitude of others in the same boat – to please get together and agree on their figures before undertaking to explain us to ourselves.'[26] The fact is that while there are differences in totals, there are no fundamental contradictions between the findings of these or any other major historians. Virtually all agree that of the total killed approximately three million were Polish Jews. There is some variation of opinion on the number of Soviet Jews killed. The estimates range between 1 million and 1.3 million. The total death toll is somewhere between five and six million.[27]

Rassinier's thesis, built on falsified data, is that the discrepancies between these historians invalidate their findings. Rassinier is correct in one regard, however: There are variances in each of their findings. Few agree on precisely the same number. But rather than invalidating their credibility, these discrepancies support it. According to Rassinier, if Hilberg has one toll for the victims and Baron another, it is proof that both are creating fictionalized accounts. Since both use official documents and testimonies to reach their conclusions, the contradictions in their findings supposedly illustrate that neither they nor the documents can be trusted. But in making this argument Rassinier ignores a critically important historical fact. Complete unanimity among historians regarding an event of such magnitude would itself be highly suspicious. A death toll on which all historians unequivocally agreed would raise legitimate suspicions about the independent nature of their historical research. It is

---

Note: The postwar USSR total includes 300,000 deportees, refugees, and survivors from other territories.

When the three hundred thousand deportees, refugees, and survivors are deducted from the 2.6 million the total corresponds to a loss of 1 million Jews in the USSR.

precisely these differences that show that these are not 'court-appointed' historians but independent researchers, each trying to assemble a myriad of details regarding one of the most brutal and chaotic chapters in recent history.

Despite having 'discovered' the ones who are responsible for generating this myth, Rassinier still faced, as do all deniers, a fundamental obstacle – one he could not manipulate as easily as he had the misinformation regarding the reparations. Hitler and those around him had explicitly stated many times the Nazi intention to destroy the Jews. Hitler's best-known diatribe in this regard was made on January 30, 1939:

Today I want to be a prophet once more: If international finance Jewry inside and outside of Europe should succeed once more in plunging nations into another world war, the consequence will not be the Bolshevization of the earth and thereby the victory of Jewry, but the annihilation of the Jewish race in Europe.[28]

This was not his only public threat to annihilate the Jews. In September 1942, six months after the gas chambers began to operate, he recalled his speech of 1939 and reiterated his predictions about the Jews' fate. This time he was even more specific about the outcome:

In my Reichstag speech of September 1, 1939,* I have spoken of two things: first, that now that the war has been forced upon us, no array of weapons and no passage of time will bring us to defeat, and second, that if Jewry should plot another world war in order to exterminate the Aryan peoples in Europe, it would not be the Aryan peoples which would be exterminated but Jewry . . .

At one time, the Jews of Germany laughed about my prophecies. I do not know whether they are still laughing or whether they have already lost all desire to laugh. But right now I can only repeat: they will stop laughing everywhere and I shall be right also in that prophecy.[29]

Rassinier had to explain away such statements – which had to be interpreted as meaning something other than what they clearly

---

* Author's note: Hitler changed the date of his original speech threatening the Jews with annihilation from January 30, 1939, to September 1, 1939.

say – in order to maintain that genocide was a myth. Rassinier dismissed the 1939 statement as irrelevant hyperbole, typical of the 'kind of defiance that was hurled by the ancient heroes' and consequently of 'little significance.'[30] Here too – as in the case of the total number of victims – Rassinier positioned himself on both sides of the argument. He repeatedly demanded explicit proof specifically indicating that it was the Nazis' objective to murder the Jews. The absence of such proof, he argued, invalidated all conclusions regarding mass murder. But when a document or statement explicitly indicating an intention to annihilate was cited as proof, Rassinier dismissed it as euphemistic, hyperbolic, or irrelevant. These tactics were later adopted by deniers in their treatment of historical documents that, they argued, proved that the genocide of the Jews was not a myth. (If the documents are specific they are dismissed as euphemistic. If they are euphemistic they are interpreted at face value.)

Rassinier used a slightly different approach for the 1942 speech. Rather than simply dismissing this as hyperbole, Rassinier contended that the fact that this threat against European Jewry was not cited at the Nuremberg war crimes trials proved that it was not considered to be serious evidence. Had the Allies considered it a serious document, they would have introduced it as evidence. But Rassinier failed to note that Hitler was not on trial at Nuremberg and that, consequently, many of his statements and speeches, including those with specific antisemitic themes, were not cited. Moreover, it is both ironic and revealing that Rassinier, who had such contempt for all that went on at Nuremberg, should have used the trial as a standard for determining what does and does not constitute serious evidence.

Rassinier's attempt to explain how the Holocaust hoax has been perpetrated and spread worldwide is even more clumsy, and it revealed the true objective of his Holocaust denial. His explanation relied on traditional antisemitic imagery in order to explain the Jews' intentions. It can be briefly summarized:

> The Jews have been able to dupe the world by relying on their mythic powers and conspiratorial abilities. As they have so often done in the past, world Jewry has once again employed its inordinate powers to

harness the world's financial resources, media and political interests for their own purposes.

In isolating the source of this huge conspiracy against Germany, Rassinier rooted it in the actions of one Polish Jew.

After some fifteen years of historical research, I have come to the following conclusion: it was in 1943 that National Socialist Germany was accused for the first time of the systematic mass extermination of the Jews in the gas chambers. The author of this first, horrible and infamous accusation was a Polish Jew, . . . Rafael Lemkin.[31]

Lemkin, who in 1944 introduced both the word and concept of genocide into international law, served as counsel to Supreme Court Justice Robert Jackson when Jackson was the United States chief counsel for the prosecution at the Nuremberg trials.[32] Rassinier was wrong about this, as he was on so many other things. Nazi Germany was first accused of mass murder of Jews in 1942, not 1943. Lemkin had nothing to do with this accusation. Rassinier attributed Lemkin's success in making such an accusation take hold and stick to the fact that he was supposedly aided and abetted in his efforts by falsified documents and an amenable world press, which took its marching orders from Jews:

With the release of this information by a Polish Jew and the 'discovery' during the Nuremberg trials of documents detailing the existence of gas chambers at Auschwitz, in the world press, the gas chambers mythology began its dance to every tune and diabolical rhythm; that unrestrained saraband full of missteps has not stopped since.[33]

The media were one of the primary instruments the Jews used to spread this calumny. Here again Rassinier relied on traditional anti-semitic imagery. The media had to help Jews because they were dominated by them. Consequently the media 'publicize[d], with remarkable consistency,' the thesis that six million Jews had been victims of the Nazis.[34]

According to Rassinier the real culprits behind Lemkin, the historians, Jewish institutions, and all others who participated in the hoax were the 'Zionists,' who used their remarkable powers to prevent the truth from emerging, including thwarting a census of world Jewry from being taken so that they could subject the Holocaust death toll 'to all kinds of manipulation.'[35] (His source for this claim was the *American Mercury*, which from 1952 until its demise in the 1970s was a publication whose most distinguishing feature was its antisemitism.)[36] Their ultimate objective was financial: Once they had rendered Germany a 'cash cow' for Israel and its supporters, they could turn to their larger and more monstrous objective: control of world finances. Rassinier, who had already relied on an almost unbroken chain of traditional antisemitic images – Jews' nefarious use of their inordinate international political powers, control of the press, and financial chicanery – now slipped into a purely antisemitic diatribe in his description of what would happen when the Jews consolidated their power:

> Today, speaking metaphorically, the aim [of the Zionists] is the gold of Fort Knox. If the plan should succeed – and all that is needed is for the American branch of international Zionism to get its hand on Wall Street – the Israeli home-port of the Diaspora would become . . . the command post of all the world's industry. 'You will earn bread by the sweat of your brow,' the Eternal One said to Adam and to Eve, 'You will give birth in pain,' as he chased the couple from the earthly Paradise he had created for them . . . The women of Israel would, to be sure, continue to bear their children in pain, but their men would earn their bread and that of their children by the sweat of other's [*sic*] brows. Then at the very least, it could be said that the designation 'Chosen People,' which the Jews claim for themselves, would assume it [*sic*] full significance.[37]

Ultimately it was arguments such as these that conclusively demonstrated that Rassinier's Holocaust denial was no more than a guise for the expression of a classic form of antisemitism. Though Rassinier's work may be 'distinguished' by its Holocaust denial, it is in fact no different from the myriad of antisemitic tirades that have been published over the centuries. His invective about Jewish power and influence and his conviction that Jews have the most sinister intentions qualify him for the company of a host of antisemites.

His are the observations of a man whose work is cited by all subsequent deniers as the formative influence in their thinking. Rassinier's and Bardèche's contributions to the evolution of Holocaust denial in France would eventually be magnified by the work of their protégé Robert Faurisson, a former professor at the University of Lyons, who today is one of the leading Holocaust deniers. But shades of French fascism and Holocaust denial would also be found in the political arena, as exemplified by the policies and statements of Jean-Marie Le Pen and his political party, the National Front. They constitute Bardèche's and Rassinier's most important legacies and demonstrate that both fascism and Holocaust denial have found a sympathetic environment in contemporary France.

4
The First Stirrings of Denial in America

Holocaust denial found a receptive welcome in the United States during the 1950s and 1960s – particularly among individuals known to have strong connections with antisemitic publications and extremist groups. Their Holocaust denial was preceded by their antisemitism.[1] Until the beginning of the 1970s Holocaust denial in the United States was primarily the province of these fringe, extremist, and racist groups, though they found unexpected support in a number of seemingly respectable circles.

The earliest deniers in the United States were extremely receptive to Paul Rassinier's arguments that the Holocaust had been created by Jewish leaders in order to control the world's finances and increase support for Israel. Like Rassinier they tried to demonstrate that it was statistically impossible for millions of Jews to have died. Their arguments were unsophisticated, crude, and often lacking in any attempt to prove their point. In 1952 W. D. Herrstrom, and American antisemite, declared in *Bible News Flashes* that there were five million illegal aliens in the United States, most of whom were Jews. These were the Jews who were supposed to have died in the Holocaust. 'No use looking in Shickelgruber's [Hitler's] ovens for them. Walk down the streets of any American city. There they are.'[2] In 1959 James Madole, who published the racist *National Renaissance Bulletin*, wrote: 'Although the World Almanac attests to the fact that fewer than 600,000 Jews ever lived in Germany the Jews persisted in their monstrous lie that Nazi Germany had cremated six million of their co-racials.'[3] Madole's chicanery is easily exposed. While it is true that Germany's Jewish population was less than six hundred thousand in 1933, most of the Jewish victims of the Holocaust were not German Jews. Benjamin H. Freedman, who provided the financial support for the antisemitic publication *Common Sense*, argued in 1959 that there were many million more Jews in the United States than Jews were willing to admit. These were the six million 'allegedly put to death in furnaces and in gas chambers between 1939 and 1945.'[4] Offering an argument that would be echoed in the 1970s by a number of Holocaust deniers, including Arthur Butz of Northwestern University, Freedman contended that the American Jewish community was opposed to a question about religious affiliation on the census because it would reveal that the Jews who had 'allegedly' died were actually in the United States.*

The well-known American Nazi leader George Lincoln Rockwell called the Holocaust 'a monstrous and profitable fraud.' He echoed Freedman's notion that the six million 'later died happily and richly in the Bronx, New York.' In June 1959, in an article entitled 'Into the Valley of Death Rode the Six Million. Or Did They?' American antisemite Gerald L. K. Smith's *Cross and the Flag* informed its readers that the six million Jews were in the United States.[5]

Such blatant attempts to confuse readers were typical of deniers' behavior during the first two decades after the war. Ultimately most of these people had little impact because they could so easily be dismissed as extremists and right-wingers. Nonetheless their arguments eventually worked their way into the mainstream of Holocaust denial. In subsequent years their statistical claims would become if not more sophisticated then certainly more complicated.[6] Flagrant falsehoods would be entwined in complex arguments, confusing those who did not know the facts.

Not all the early deniers had overt associations with extremist groups. Consequently they were able to make some of their accusations in more mainstream publications. In the June 14, 1959, issue of the widely circulated Catholic weekly *Our Sunday Visitor* a letter writer claimed: 'I was able to determine during six post-war years in

* American Jewish organizations have traditionally opposed such a question because they believe it would violate the constitutional guarantee of the separation of church and state.

Germany and Austria, there were a number of Jews killed, but the figure of a million was certainly never reached.'[7] Newspaper editors who received denial material from Boniface Press, the publishing outlet run by App, turned to the Anti-Defamation League to ask for clarification. One editor requested documentation demonstrating that Jews had really died.[8]

Harry Elmer Barnes was the most direct link between the two generations of American revisionists and the Holocaust deniers.[9] Some of his numerous books and articles, particularly those on Western civilization, were used as required texts through the 1960s at prestigious American universities, including Harvard and Columbia. Barnes also lectured widely at other universities throughout the United States, his arguments about needless American participation in World War I winning the admiration of many people in the United States and abroad, including the publisher of the *Nation*, Oswald Garrison Villard; the Socialist leader Norman Thomas; the journalist H. L. Mencken; and the historian Charles Beard. At one time he served as bibliographic editor of *Foreign Affairs*.[10]

But from the outset Barnes's career was not without controversy. During World War I he had been an ardent advocate of the Allied cause. The material he submitted to the National Board for Historical Service, the principal vehicle for dissemination of pro-Allied propaganda by historians, was deemed 'too violent to be acceptable,' and those involved in the effort described him as 'one of the most violent sort of shoot-them-at-sunrise Chauvinists.'[11] But his views changed dramatically after the war. With the zeal of a convert, he moved to the isolationist, pro-German end of the political spectrum and stayed there for the rest of his life. Much of his work relied on polemics and flamboyant tactics. He so savaged advocates of the 'orthodox' view of the war that even those who agreed with him recoiled from his reliance on *ad hominem* attacks.[12] When he publicly accused Bernadotte Schmitt, a prominent and well-respected historian at the University of Chicago, of adjusting his historical conclusions in order to advance his academic career, he evoked the ire of numerous academics, including revisionists. According to Barnes, Schmitt concluded that Germany was responsible for precipitating the war in order to obtain his prestigious university post. This kind of attack typified Barnes's subsequent attacks on those who disagreed with him. He was convinced that his beliefs constituted objective truth; consequently anyone who took a different view was neither objective nor honest.

Barnes's work won a broad popular audience in the United States and abroad. In 1926 he visited Germany to deliver a series of lectures that argued that Germany was not guilty for World War I. Barnes waxed euphoric about his reception there, which he described as a 'fairy tale.' He was particularly impressed by the 'great interest and energy' shown by Weimar scholars and officials in 'seeking to clear Germany of the dishonor and fraud of the war-guilt clause of the Treaty of Versailles.'[13] While in Europe he even met with the exiled kaiser, Wilhelm II, a considerable honor for a relatively young scholar. According to Barnes the kaiser 'was happy to know that I did not blame him for starting the war in 1914.' But, Barnes recalled, they were not in complete accord: 'He disagreed with my view that Russia and France were chiefly responsible. He held that the villains of 1914 were the international Jews and Free Masons, who, he alleged, desired to destroy national states and the Christian religion.'[14] Barnes did not fully agree with the kaiser on this point, preferring to point at England and France as the primary perpetrators.

During the interwar years Barnes used his World War I revisionism to propound the isolationist cause. Even before World War II had ended he was challenging the official version of its history. He was part of a small group of isolationists who tried to resurrect the movement's reputation and to sully Roosevelt's. They were funded by prewar isolationists, including Charles Lindbergh and Henry Ford. Barnes repeated his World War I arguments and attacked politicians, journalists, and historians who failed to acknowledge Allied responsibility for the war. He assaulted Roosevelt's policies and defended Hitler's, contending that virtually all Hitler's political and military moves, including the invasion of Czechoslovakia, were necessary to 'rectify' the injustices of the Versailles treaty.[15] But it was not just the Versailles treaty that was at fault; the real problem was the Allies' fundamental failure to understand Hitler himself. In a 1950 letter to fellow revisionist Charles Tansill, Barnes described Hitler's demands in 1939 as the 'most reasonable of all,' and in his articles and essays he continuously sought to exonerate Hitler.[16] Barnes did not perceive Hitler as a megalomanic leader who was defeated because he was intent on controlling Europe. It was not the German führer's ferocity but his humanity that caused his military demise. According to Barnes Hitler's downfall resulted from his 'unwillingness to use his full military power' against innocent English civilians.[17] Contrary to the prevailing consensus, Hitler did not 'precipitously launch' an aggressive attack on Poland. In fact, Barnes argued, Hitler made a greater effort to avoid war in 1939 than the kaiser had in 1914. Barnes not only vindicated Hitler but held the British 'almost solely responsible' for the outbreak of war on both the Eastern and Western fronts. Hitler did not wantonly stick 'a dagger in the back of France' in June 1940 but was 'forced' into war by British 'acts of economic strangulation.'[18]

In 1952 in a letter to Harvard historian William Langer, who had authored a two-volume defense of America's prewar policies, Barnes wrote that he considered Roosevelt's foreign policy 'the greatest public crime in human history.'[19] Barnes pursued this argument throughout his career, arguing in 1958 that Roosevelt 'lied the United States into war,' and, had he not been able 'to incite the Japanese' to attack Pearl Harbor, the tragedies of the war and the even 'greater calamities' that resulted from it could well have been avoided.[20] (Barnes had made precisely the same arguments about Wilson and World War I.) Barnes not only believed Hitler 'reasonable' and Britain, France, and the United States responsible for the war, he also argued that a pervasive historical 'blackout' silenced anyone who might question the notion of German guilt. The blackout was the keystone of a plan to prevent the truth about World War II from emerging. Barnes's initial assault on this 'conspiracy' was contained in a lengthy pamphlet, *The Struggle Against Historical Blackout*, which appeared in 1947 and which had gone through nine printings by 1952. According to Barnes Western liberals allowed their hatred of Hitler and Mussolini to blind them to France's aggressiveness, Britain's duplicity, and Roosevelt's deception. 'Court historians' kept the truth from emerging by quashing any information that might tarnish Roosevelt's image and silencing critics who questioned American 'intervention' in World War II. Scholars suspected of revisionist views were denied access to public documents. Publishers who wished to issue books or periodicals dealing with the topic were intimidated. Material that embodied revisionist facts or arguments was ignored or obscured. Revisionist authors were smeared.[21] This was not simply a case of obtuseness; this was willful deceit. The 'court historians' were not just blind or unaware of the facts; they lied, ignored contradictory information, and created new truths. In subsequent years Holocaust deniers would claim that they faced precisely the same situation.[22] According to Barnes, politicians', diplomats', and historians' vindictiveness toward Germany was completely out of proportion to reality, *and they knew it*. Consequently they needed a rationale to justify their enmity. Thus they accused Germany of starting the war and of unparalleled atrocities.

Barnes claimed that only ten years after the war had he concluded that Germany was not responsible for the outbreak of war or for the atrocities of which it was accused. He wrote in 1962: 'For a decade following 1945 I was convinced that the best thing which could have happened to Germany and the world in pre-war days would have been the assassination of Hitler, say around 1938 or early 1939, if not much earlier.'[23] He claimed that it was only with great reluctance that he was weaned from this view of an evil Nazi Germany and forced by the evidence to accept a new truth. This assertion is disingenuous in light of what he wrote in 1947, in *The Struggle Against the Historical Blackout*, as well as the opinions he expressed in private correspondence. Indeed, the war had barely ended when Barnes began to blame the Allies and exonerate Hitler.

More significantly his protestations that he reluctantly revised his notion of the truth when he came into contact with revisionist literature are reminiscent of the tactics adopted by many conspiracy theorists and by Holocaust deniers in particular. Virtually all of them claim to have been enlightened only after being forced by the evidence to abandon their previously mistaken beliefs. On being confronted with a preponderance of 'information' contradicting their original conclusion that there was a Holocaust, they ashamedly acknowledge that they have been victims of a hoax. They apparently think that this contention adds plausibility to their new beliefs. It also prevents them from being accused of having harbored hostile attitudes toward Jews or having had fascist sympathies.

The fact is, however, that Barnes did not have to be convinced to adopt this view, nor did he wait ten years to espouse it. In a letter to Villard dated June 1948, Barnes said that Roosevelt and Churchill, 'backed by certain pressure groups,' were more responsible than Hitler for the war. That same year he argued that throughout history France had repeatedly invaded Germany without provocation. 'Offhand,' he wrote in a private communiqué, 'I cannot recall a really unprovoked German invasion of France in modern times.'[24] To buttress his point he prepared a list of all the French invasions of Germany, beginning in 1552 and concluding his list with two twentieth-century entries:

> 1918 – French invade Germany with American aid
> 1944–45 – French again ride into Germany on backs of
> Americans[25]

He failed to acknowledge that both of these 'invasions' were in response to massive German attacks.

Despite this evidence to the contrary, Barnes continued to assert that it was only in 1955, when he came upon a dissertation completed at Harvard by David Leslie Hoggan, that he realized that 'Hitler had not desired war' and that Britain was almost 'exclusively responsible.'[26] Hoggan, then teaching in the History Department of the University of California at Berkeley, convinced Barnes that Hitler had not desired war in 1939. Hoggan argued that Hitler 'had made more moderate demands on Poland than many leading American and British publicists had recommended in the years after Versailles. Moreover, Hitler had offered in return an amazing concession to Poland that the Weimar Republic would never even remotely countenance.'[27]

Barnes was instrumental in helping Hoggan publish his book – *The Forced War* (*Der erzwungene Krieg*) – which is based on, but quite different from, the dissertation. According to one of Hoggan's advisers at Harvard, his dissertation had been 'a solid, conscientious piece of work, critical of Polish and British policies in 1939, but not beyond what the evidence would tolerate.' But when it was published in Germany in 1961 by Herbert Grabert, it was a very different book.[28] Hoggan portrayed the English and the Poles as having willfully provoked the war and the Germans as innocent victims who tried every means to avert a confrontation. This was a war that had been imposed on Hitler.

Though it was not his main focus, Hoggan also addressed the question of Germany's treatment of the Jews. In an attempt to rehabilitate Germany's reputation and relieve Hitler and the Nazis of any particular onus, he argued that Poland's treatment of its Jewish population was far more brutal than Germany's. In fact, he asserted, most of Germany's antisemitic measures were taken in order to preempt Poland from expelling its Jewish population into the Reich.[29] Hoggan continually represented Nazi Germany's Jewish policies as benign or, at the very least, as better than Poland's. Hoggan suggested that the fine levied on German Jews in the wake of Kristallnacht was simply an equitable way to keep Jews from getting rich from the destruction by 'pocket[ing] vast amounts of money from the German insurance companies.'[30] He failed to note that the moneys were payments reimbursing Jews for property that had been destroyed. In fact the fine was designed not to keep Jews from obtaining insurance payments but to confiscate virtually all of the Jewish population's remaining liquid assets.[31] And contrary to all reports, Hoggan also claimed that no Jews had been killed either during the pogrom or in its immediate aftermath.

In an attempt to demonstrate that the Jews had not really been discriminated against and were in quite a secure position as late as 1938, Hoggan noted that in early 1938 Jewish doctors and dentists were still participating in the German national compulsory insurance program. This 'guaranteed them a sufficient number of patients.'[32] Hoggan failed to cite the many obstacles that were put in the way of Jewish medical personnel, including that by 1938 it had become a radical if not illegal act for a German to use a Jewish doctor. Furthermore, in July 1938 a decree was enacted withdrawing licenses from Jewish physicians. Again, ignoring the host of laws and regulations that severely limited Jews' ability to function in German society, he argued that Jewish lawyers had been free to practice as late as 1938. Citing information contained in a letter to the State Department from the American ambassador in Germany, Hoggan noted that, as of 1938, 10 percent of German attorneys were Jews. If this was indeed correct, how could it be argued that they were being persecuted? The ambassador did mention that 10 percent of the lawyers were Jews, but in a context quite different from the one in which Hoggan presented it. The ambassador had written to Washington to report that the situation of Jewish lawyers, which had been deplorable for a long time, was growing worse. 'As early as 1933 pressure was exerted to oust Jews from the legal profession,' the ambassador told the State Department. Jews faced exceptional obstacles in seeking admission to the bar, and Jewish attorneys were prevented from serving as notaries – a measure, according to the ambassador, which, 'in view of the wide requirements and high charges for notarial services in Germany,' constituted a considerable handicap to the Jewish legal profession.'[33] Thus, although as late as 1938, 10 percent of all lawyers may well have been Jews, since they were barely able to function they were lawyers in name only. They were barred from court and prevented from performing an array of tasks fundamental to their profession. Moreover, Hoggan neglected to say why the ambassador was reporting on the situation of Jewish lawyers. On September 27, 1938, Nazi Germany completely banned Jews from the practice of law.

Hoggan also totally distorted the implications of the Nazi decision to end the Jewish community's status as an officially sanctioned religious body. For many years the German government had collected a religion tax, which was turned over to the individual's designated religious community, from every German resident. Essentially the government served as a transfer agency, collecting funds from German citizens and transmitting them to their religious community. The American ambassador reported that because the Jewish community was no longer an officially sanctioned entity, it would no longer receive the 'taxes levied upon [its] members by the State for the meeting of community expenses.' In other words, Jews would continue to pay the tax, but the government would not give it to their community. Hoggan gave an entirely different – and dishonest – slant to this decision. Making it sound as though the Jewish community was supported by the state, he wrote that the new law 'meant that German public tax receipts would go no longer to the Jewish church.' Then, in an effort to diminish further the impact of the decree, Hoggan falsely claimed that it had simply brought German practice into 'conformity with current English practice.'[34] He failed to note that the same was not done to other religious communities and ignored the ambassador's comment that the new law constituted 'discriminatory' legislation that would greatly hamper 'the social and welfare world of the already seriously harassed Jewish Gemeinde [community].'[35]

Hoggan's book, on which Barnes heaped accolades, is full of such misrepresentations in relation to British and Polish foreign policy and concerning Germany's treatment of the Jews. His dissertation contains few such observations. Barnes read the dissertation before it was turned into a book and was in contact with Hoggan for a full six years before the book was published. Barnes helped get it published and provided a blurb for its jacket, obviously playing a significant role in turning this 'solid conscientious piece of work' into a Nazi apologia. One German historian observed that 'rarely have so many inane and unwarranted theses, allegations and "conclusions" ... been crammed into a volume written under the guise of history.'[36] Gerhard Weinberg, in his review of the book in the *American Historical Review*, described it as full of fabrications, twisted evidence, and transpositions of the sequence of events. All public statements by Hitler that substantiated Hoggan's thesis were taken at face value, as when Hitler professed that he only wanted peace. All statements, public or private, which did not agree, were ignored.[37] Hoggan's contribution to Holocaust denial is significant. He buttressed the bogus notion that Germany was the victim, the

Allies the victimizers, and the war easily preventable. In addition his Harvard credentials and his association with Berkeley, however tenuous, provided a measure of credibility to a movement that had thus far been relegated to the scholarly fringes.

Beginning in the 1960s Barnes began to pay increasing attention to the issue of German atrocities. He did not explicitly state that the atrocity stories were fabricated. Instead he suggested that they were inaccurate and politically motivated. In a 1962 publication, *Revisionism and Brainwashing*, he condemned the 'lack of any serious opposition or concerted challenge to the atrocity stories and other modes of defamation of German national character and conduct.' Attempting to deflect the charges of German atrocities, Barnes relied on immoral equivalencies arguing that there was a 'failure to point out that the atrocities of the Allies were more brutal, painful, mortal and numerous than the most extreme allegations made against the Germans.'[38] This form of relativism was becoming a fundamental component of Holocaust denial.

During this period Barnes was exposed to Paul Rassinier's claims that the Holocaust was a hoax. Apparently it was Rassinier's work that prompted Barnes to contend that the atrocity stories were fabrications. Barnes described Rassinier as a 'distinguished French historian' and applauded him for questioning the existence of gas chambers in concentration camps in Germany and for exposing the 'exaggerations of the atrocity stories.'[39] (See chapter 8.) In an essay entitled 'Zionist Fraud,' which originally appeared in the *American Mercury*, Barnes heaped lavish praise on Rassinier and expressed support for many of the Frenchman's accusations:

> The courageous author [Rassinier] lays the chief blame for misrepresentation on those whom we must call the swindlers of the crematoria, the Israeli politicians who derive billions of marks from nonexistent, mythical and imaginary cadavers, whose numbers have been reckoned in an unusually distorted and dishonest manner.[40]

Still engaged in fighting both world wars, Barnes found that Rassinier's defense of Germany and his attempt to remove from its shoulders the blame for atrocities validated his most precious historical conviction: the Allies were the real culprits. For Barnes, Rassinier's denial constituted important historical ammunition and intellectual proof that World War II was just like World War I. Germany was the wonderful nation it had always been, and America had once again needlessly entered the conflagration. Why was this fact not generally known by most Americans? Barnes had a simple answer. There was a conspiracy to blame Germany for terrible atrocities and wildly exaggerate the wrongs it had committed.

These 'allegations' and 'exaggerations' against Germany were not just capricious, Barnes argued, but served an important purpose for historians and political leaders from the Allied nations. They were essential to protect the reputation of prominent American, English, and French leaders who had supported appeasement during the 1930s. The leaders displayed a benign attitude to Hitler and other Nazi leaders even after the 'worst aspects of the Hitler regime had been in operation for some years,' including the persecution of the Jews under the Nuremberg Laws.[41] In light of their positive assessments of Hitler and National Socialism during the prewar period, it was difficult for them to justify their subsequent condemnations of Hitler as a 'pathological demon.' How could he have been a reasonable leader in the 1930s and the epitome of evil ten years later? Something 'different and dramatic' was needed to 'make the thesis of diabolism sink in and stick.' Without it these 'eminent [prewar] eulogists' would appear to be 'silly dupes.' The allegations regarding the atrocities committed by the Nazis *during* the war were thus part of the plan to protect the reputations of Allied leaders who had previously sought to appease Hitler. Now they could portray him as a 'madman,' whose potential for evil was not known until the war itself.

But it was not only the prewar 'eulogists' who needed to justify their war with Hitler. The postwar legacy of the 'attempt to check "the Nazi madman"' was 'even more ominous than the war.' From Barnes's isolationist perspective, the war had been a disaster for the Allies. Germany was divided. Stalin was stronger than before. The Soviet Union controlled much of Eastern Europe, including portions of Germany, and the United States had to spend billions to rebuild and arm Western Europe. All this resulted from an attempt to stop Hitler, who, Barnes contended, had no interest in going to war against the Allies. In order to justify the 'horrors and evil results of the Second World War,' those who had led the Allies into war also needed to justify their efforts.[42] There were two false dogmas that 'met the need perfectly': Germany's diabolism in provoking the war and committing massive atrocities. Hitler and national socialism became the Allies' 'scapegoat.'[43] According to Barnes these two accusations were linked in a pernicious fashion:

> Hitler's setting off the war was also deemed responsible for the wholesale extermination of Jews, for it was admitted that this did not begin until a considerable time after war broke out.

Though not yet willing to deny the Holocaust, he did cast doubt on it by declaring it a theory at best:

> The size of the German reparations to Israel has been based on the *theory* that vast numbers of Jews were exterminated *at the express order of Hitler*, some six million being the most usually accepted number.[44]

A few years later Barnes again raised questions about the veracity of the Holocaust in his article, 'Revisionism: A Key to Peace.' Apparently reluctant explicitly to deny the Holocaust, Barnes relativized the 'alleged' atrocities of the Germans as he had previously done:

> Even if one were to accept the most extreme and exaggerated indictment of Hitler and the National Socialists for their activities after 1939 made by anybody fit to remain outside a mental hospital, it is almost alarmingly easy to demonstrate that the atrocities of the Allies in the same period were more numerous as to victims and were carried out for the most part *by methods more brutal and painful than alleged extermination in gas ovens.*[45]

In 1967, in 'The Public Stake in Revisionism,' Barnes charged that what had begun as a 'blackout' had now become a 'smotherout' as a result of the Eichmann trial. It provided an 'unexpected but remarkably opportune moment and an effective springboard for stopping

World War II revisionism dead in its track.' Moving close to explicit denial, Barnes argued that the trial revealed

> an almost adolescent gullibility and excitability on the part of Americans relative to German wartime crimes, real or *alleged*.[46]

The charges against Eichmann and Nazi Germany were based on

> fundamental but *unproved assumptions* that what Hitler and the National Socialists did in the years *after* Britain and the United States entered the war revealed that they were ... vile, debased, brutal and bloodthirsty gangsters.[47]

Barnes attacked popular American weekly and monthly journals for their 'sensational articles' about 'exaggerated National Socialist savagery.'[48] He repeated what had become a consistent refrain in his articles: Allied atrocities surpassed those of the Germans. The Allied atrocities, to which Barnes made repeated reference, included the bombing of Hamburg, Tokyo, and Dresden and the postwar expulsion of the Sudeten Germans during which, he charged, 'at least four millions of them perish[ed] in the process from butchery, starvation and disease.' Using language that was purposely chosen to evoke a comparison to what the Jews 'claimed' was done to them, Barnes described the population transfer as 'the final solution' for defeated Germans.

In 'The Public Stake in Revisionism,' Barnes again stopped short of explicitly denying the existence of gas chambers:

> The number of civilians exterminated by the Allies, before, during and after the second World War, equalled, if it did not far exceed those liquidated by the Germans and the Allied liquidation program was often carried out by methods which were far more brutal and painful than *whatever extermination actually took place* in German gas ovens.*[49]

---

* The editor of the *Journal of Historical Review* was clearly distressed by the ambiguity of this statement, which could be interpreted to suggest that Barnes believed that there might have actually been 'gas ovens' in Auschwitz. When the *Journal* reprinted the article in 1980 the editor added a footnote to Barnes's comment about

Once again coming close to, but not quite crossing the boundary into denial, he complained in the same article that Allied atrocities are never 'cogently and frankly placed over against the doings, *real or alleged*, at Auschwitz.'[50]

Barnes tried to argue that the gas chambers were postwar inventions. Ignoring the fact that information on gas chambers in various death camps had been publicized long before the war ended, he falsely claimed that the charges had only been made afterward, when it was necessary to justify the war and its outcome. According to Barnes, when the 'court historians' were forced by 'revisionists' to admit reluctantly that there were only concentration camps and not death camps in Germany, they needed something else to maintain the evil image of the Nazi empire. It was then, he argued, that they contrived the existence of gas chambers at other camps. Once this allegation was placed in the public domain, the 'smotherout' historians changed the focus of their attacks on Nazi Germany. No longer did they emphasize the Japanese attack on Pearl Harbor or Hitler's precipitation of the war. They found something far more potent:

> What is deemed important today is not whether Hitler started war in 1939 or whether Roosevelt was responsible for Pearl Harbor but the number of prisoners who were *allegedly* done to death in the concentration camps operated by Germany during the war. These camps were first presented as those in Germany, such as Dachau, Belsen, Buchenwald, Sachsenhausen, and Dora, but it was demonstrated that there had been no systematic extermination in those camps. Attention was then moved on to Auschwitz, Treblinka, Belzec, Chelmno, Jonowska [*sic*], Tarnow, Ravensbrück, Mauthausen, Brezeznia [*sic*], and Birkenau, which does not exhaust the list that appears to have been extended as needed.[51]

These new charges kept the public from becoming 'bored' by hearing the same stories. To ensure public interest the details were

---

the gas ovens: 'Of course Barnes is confused here by the difference between a "gas chamber" and a "gas oven." Shortly after writing this article, he came to reject the entire holocaust myth, not just part of it.'

'made more unceasing, exaggerated and inflammatory.'[52] Once again Barnes totally distorted the truth and reshaped the historical record. Information about Chelmno, Auschwitz, Birkenau, and other camps was well known long before the war ended; details about them had been published in the Western press on repeated occasions.

Moreover it was precisely those whom Barnes accused of being 'court historians' who, in fact, were responsible for demonstrating that there had been no homicidal gas chambers in German concentration camps. After the war there had been persistent confusion about the difference between concentration camps and death camps. The latter, located outside Germany, had facilities for the express purpose of murdering people, primarily Jews. While there were no death camps in Germany, there were many concentration camps, in which multitudes died from overwork, disease, starvation, beatings, and severe mistreatment. Much of the confusion centered around the idea that there was a functioning homicidal gas chamber in Dachau. This was what historians were trying to clarify in 1962, when Professor Martin Broszat, who served for many years as the director of Munich's Institute for Contemporary History, wrote to the newspaper *Die Zeit* to 'hammer home, once more, the persistently ignored or denied difference between concentration and extermination camps.' Contrary to deniers' claims, he said, his letter did not constitute an 'admission' on his part but an effort to 'set the record straight.'[53] This remains a consistent tactic of the deniers. Every time historians who study the Holocaust correct a mistake in the record, deniers immediately claim that they do so because their previous lies were about to be exposed.*

Barnes also tried to recast history by changing the nature of the assignment of the *Einsatzgruppen* that functioned as the mobile killing units. The *Einsatzgruppen* entered Soviet territory in July 1941. Between that date and the beginning of the retreat of German forces in the spring of 1943, it is estimated that they murdered well over one

---

* This is what they have done in relation to the charge that Nazis used Jewish cadavers for the production of soap. When scholars of the Holocaust corrected this notion, the deniers were quick to charge they did so in order to avoid being exposed as willful liars. (See chapter 10.)

million Jews and hundreds of thousands of other Soviet nationals. Their brutal methods were eventually replaced by the more 'efficient' gas chambers. Barnes transformed them from groups whose express task was to murder Jews in Soviet territory into units that were 'battling guerrilla warfare behind the lines.' This profile is totally contradicted by reams of documents and the testimony of *Einsatzgruppen* leaders and members, as well as that of those who saw them massacre Jews. Barnes's transformation of their role was his means of trying to work around the truth. He did not have to deny that they may in fact have killed some Jews, but, according to his explanation, their actions were justified because their victims were anti-German guerrillas.

But even with all these attempts to twist information and misrepresent established historical fact, Barnes and other revisionists faced a fundamental challenge in their effort to exculpate Nazi Germany. It was difficult to argue that Germany had not committed these outrages when the postwar West German government accepted responsibility for the war and the atrocities.[54] Barnes castigated both the government and the academic community of the Federal Republic of Germany for failing to challenge this 'unfair' verdict and the 'false dogma[s]' propagated by the Allies and accepted by the Bonn government.[55] The government's approach to history prevented 'the restoration of Germany to its proper position of unity, power and respect among the nations of the world.'[56]

Barnes's ire at the Adenauer government for its 'masochistic' behavior was heightened by his comparison of it with the Weimar government's attitude toward World War I. Barnes complained that none of the open-mindedness he had discovered during his trip to Germany in the Weimar period was evident in the Federal Republic. The Bonn government had 'brainwashed' or 'indoctrinated' the German people into accepting an 'indictment of German responsibility for the war. According to Barnes the postwar German leadership did more than acquiesce in the charges brought against it. It furthered the 'smotherout' by 'oppos[ing] the discovery and publication of the truth.'[57] Barnes claimed to be 'deeply puzzled' about the Adenauer government's acceptance of responsibility for German precipitation of the war and its 'downright disinclination to seek to refute the most outrageous charges of cruelty and barbarism levelled against Germany by conscienceless atrocity mongers [and] the continuation to this very day of not-so-little Nuremberg trials.'[58] Barnes did not, of course, consider the possibility that West Germany did not contest the accusations because they were true and West Germans, from Chancellor Konrad Adenauer on down, knew it. Instead he condemned German leaders for 'smearing' people like Rassinier and for the 'sheer lunacy' of paying reparations 'based on atrocity stories.'[59] This was a precise repetition of Barnes's behavior in relation to World War I revisionism. Convinced that his view constituted objective truth, he dismissed any information that challenged his conclusion, treating it as the work of perverted minds.

Barnes found West Germany's relationship with the State of Israel particularly galling. He was nonplussed by a speech given by the president of the West German Bundestag in Israel in 1962 in which he acknowledged Germany's wrongdoings and asked for forgiveness for the Holocaust. Barnes characterized the speech as 'subserviency' and 'almost incredible grovelling.'[60] He was appalled by the German decision to send a group of volunteers to work in Israel as a form of penance. Barnes's disgust, as a non-German, at the German leader's request from Israel for forgiveness and at German citizens' desire to work on Israeli *kibbutzim*, is noteworthy. Barnes and Rassinier helped set the tone for subsequent Holocaust denial with their particular contempt for the Jewish state, its supporters, and Jews in general.

The roots of Barnes's views about the Holocaust and his attitudes toward Israel go beyond his deep-seated Germanophilia and revisionist approach to history: They can be found in his antisemitism. While this animus did not generally pervade his articles until the late 1960s, privately he had given voice to it as early as the 1940s. In an article published immediately after the war he suggested that Lord Vansittart (Robert Gilbert Vansittart), who served as Britain's permanent under-secretary of the British Foreign Office until the beginning of 1938 and after that as chief diplomatic adviser to His Majesty's Government, should be tried along with the Nazis for having helped precipitate the war. Vansittart, who was an anti-Nazi, is often singled out by revisionists and deniers as one of those chiefly responsible for pushing England to adopt anti-German policies. In response to Barnes's attacks, Vansittart decided to sue for libel and asked the prominent American lawyer, Louis Nizer, to represent him. When the suit was announced in the *Washington Post*, Barnes complained to Oswald Garrison Villard. Both staunch isolationists, Villard and Barnes had regularly exchanged letters regarding America's 'misguided' foreign policy. (However, despite his ardent conviction that American policy had been wrong, Villard did not share Barnes's views regarding atrocities or the victimization of Germany.) Barnes described the suit as a 'plot of the Jews and the Anti-Defamation League to intimidate any American historians who propose to tell the truth about the causes of the war.' He attacked Louis Nizer as an 'Anti-Defamation League stooge,' who had 'needled [Vansittart] into action,' and bemoaned his inability to counter the inordinate power and financial resources of the other side:*

> If I could raise money enough for a real defense we could make this an international cause celebre, but I cannot fight the thirty million dollars now in the coffers of the Anti-Defamation League to be used for character assassination on empty pockets. If we let them get away with this, we are licked from the start.[61†]

Barnes's blaming his problems on a Jewish lawyer and a Jewish organization's success in needling a prominent British official into action is another indication of his antipathy toward Jews and the

* The Anti-Defamation League (ADL) was a favorite target of the revisionists. In a confidential report written in 1944 John Flynn cited the ADL as one of the groups responsible for a program to silence isolationists and 'destroy the[ir] reputations' by intimidating them and anyone who might be influenced by them. In 1947 the *Chicago Tribune* ran a series of five articles by Flynn making these allegations (Wayne S. Cole, *Roosevelt and the Isolationists, 1932–1945* [Lincoln, Nebr, 1983]).

† Villard admonished Barnes about making these claims: 'I do not think for a moment that you need lay this to the Jews. [Vansittart] is a hard, aggressive fighter as his books have shown and when he chose Nizer as his counsel he picked the man who got a $100,000 verdict against Victor Ridder, which the judge cut to $50,000. Englishmen are very sensitive about libels . . . I don't believe he needed the slightest prodding from anybody.'

degree to which he subscribed to antisemitic stereotypes. It is also an example of Barnes's pattern of accusing others of conspiring against him. Peter Novick of the University of Chicago, who has closely examined Barnes's correspondence, describes it as constituting a 'full clinical record' of his abusiveness toward those who disagreed with him and his conviction that he was the target of innumerable conspirators. When the *New York World-Telegram* dropped his column in 1940, he blamed British intelligence, the Morgan bank, and Jewish department store owners in New York City, who, Barnes claimed, threatened the publisher with 'loss of all advertising if he kept me on any longer.'[62]

Yet Barnes apparently also understood that, like all deniers, he faced a fundamental obstacle. As long as they could be dismissed as antisemitic extremists, they would never make headway with the general public. If their work was perceived as simply a reworked expression of an age-old animus, it would have no credibility. Barnes tried to preempt this accusation by turning it back on those who made it: He accused those who charged that the deniers were antisemites of using this label as a means of silencing anyone who questioned the 'official' version of history. According to Barnes, the keystone of this effort was the claim that Jews had been subjected to unique persecution and atrocities. This aspect of the hoax was ingenious in that it enabled its architects to muzzle critics. Anyone who dared to question the official version of history was labeled an antisemite. Employing tactics that again reflected his personal hostility towards Jews, Barnes charged those behind the 'smotherout' with believing that 'it [was] far worse to exterminate Jews, even at the ratio of two Gentiles to one Jew, than to liquidate Gentiles.' When Barnes or like-minded people challenged this assertion in the name of 'non-racial humanitarianism,' they were accused of being antisemitic, which was considered 'worse than parricide or necrophilia.'[63]

Barnes's standing as a historian is a matter of some dispute. His early works on World War I won positive reviews, and for many years his was considered to be a serious though extreme historical voice. His personal attacks on those who disagreed with him and his writings about World War II alienated many of his earlier followers but did not totally cost him his credibility as a historian. In his later years, while he was writing pamphlets about a 'smotherout' and a 'theory' of the Holocaust, his books were being used as required texts in university-level Western Civilization courses.* When 'The Public Stake in Revisionism' – in which he referred to the 'doings real or alleged, at Auschwitz' and described the *Einsatzgruppen* as 'battling guerrillas' – appeared in the journal of Rampart College, Robert LeFevre, the college dean, writing in the journal, demonstrated the academic community's willingness to regard Barnes's behavior as excusable excesses: 'There are places where Dr. Barnes' understandable frustration is indicated by the use of emotive words and that may be unfortunate although it can be forgiven.'[64]

Today Barnes's work is generally dismissed by scholars because of his obsession with a conspiracy theory related to America's entry into World War II. However, he remains something of a cult historian for some members of the Libertarian party, who subscribe to Barnes's style of revisionist scholarship. As Paul Berman noted in an article in *The Village Voice*, bookstores specializing in Libertarian works have carried extensive offerings for books by Barnes and James Martin, who also subscribes to denial views.[65] While the Libertarians can still be considered a fringe group, more disturbing was the 1975 edition of *History Teacher*, a publication of the Society for History Education, which at the time was housed at California State University at Long Beach. *History Teacher* is designed to aid teachers in finding interesting ways to present historical information to their students. This edition, entitled 'Harry Elmer Barnes: Prophet of a "Usable" Past,' identified Barnes as someone who practiced the 'scholarship of commitment.' Thus, notwithstanding his notions regarding the Holocaust and other aspects of World War II, Barnes's legacy was still at least somewhat intact. According to Justus Doenecke, author of the profile on Barnes, the causes Barnes 'heralded resemble our own and the dilemmas he faced are hauntingly familiar.' Barnes's views regarding Hitler, the power of the Jews, atrocities

---

* Students at Harvard and Columbia have told me that they had no idea he was writing in this fashion when they were using his books.

committed by the Allies, or the Holocaust were never mentioned in this lengthy essay. Instead Barnes was portrayed as a useful model for those who believed in the relevance of history. His conviction that Allied atrocities overshadowed those of the Germans was also ignored, although there is a passing reference to his tendency to present views that are only 'partially digested.' Having chosen to rely on Barnes's work, any teacher who came upon his views about the Holocaust might take them seriously. After all, would *History Teacher* have suggested Barnes as a role model if they were not valid?[66]

5
Austin J. App

The World of Immoral Equivalencies

Harry Elmer Barnes was not the only American academic who attempted to exonerate Germany by denying the Holocaust. Austin
J. App, a professor of English at the University of Scranton and
LaSalle College, also played a central role in the development of
Holocaust denial, especially in the United States. Though not as
prominent as Barnes, he was far more virulent and began explicitly
denying the Holocaust within a few years after the war. By the late
1950s he was not only writing to the Catholic *Brooklyn Tablet* offering 'proof' that the figure of six million was 'a bloated libel,' but was
appearing before varied audiences accusing Jews of perpetrating a
massive hoax.[1]

Like Barnes, App was mainly concerned to lift the moral burden
of the atrocities charge from the shoulders of a defeated and divided
Germany. In contrast to Barnes, App had no independent standing in
the academic world. An active member of various German American
groups, App was an ardent defender of Germans and Nazi Germany.
He served for several years as president of the five-thousand-member
Federation of American Citizens of German Descent, founded in
1945. Though it never reached its membership goal of three million,
it was part of a successful postwar congressional lobbying effort to
allocate a substantial number of the immigration slots that had been
intended for Holocaust survivors to Germans and Austrians.[2]

Born in Milwaukee in 1902 to German immigrant parents,
App attended Catholic University in Washington, D.C., where he
obtained his M.A. and Ph.D. degrees in English literature. At the

University of Scranton, where he taught from 1934 to 1942, he received its faculty medal as an outstanding educator. He served for a brief period in the army in 1942 but for unknown reasons was released within a short time after his induction. He subsequently joined the faculty of LaSalle College, where he remained throughout the rest of his teaching career. At LaSalle, where he taught medieval English literature and was known for pronouncing *Beowulf*, *The Canterbury Tales*, and other Old and Middle English works in the original, some of his students regarded him as a sort of 'dry arrangement' the college kept on its staff to achieve accreditation. They had no idea of his other activities.[3]

But, completely unknown to his students, App had a far more dubious side. He inundated newspapers, magazines, politicians, and journalists with letters attacking U.S. intervention in World War II, Allied demands for unconditional surrender, and the imposition of 'Morgenthauism' on Germany. The latter was App's way of placing responsibility for all of Germany's postwar problems on President Roosevelt's secretary of the treasury, Henry Morgenthau. Of course, Morgenthau's plan was never put into effect. In fact, Allied treatment of Germany was the exact opposite of the plan. The letters were also App's self-described attempt to explode the 'lies and calumnies' that had been spread about Germany since the war and to prevent Roosevelt and Morgenthau from selling out 'Christian Europe to the Red barbarians.' The letters bristled with overt antisemitism and racism. Talmudists, Bolsheviks, and Zionists, all of whom were intimately connected in App's mind with one another, were blamed for the evils that beset the world after the end of the war.[4] Though few of his letters were actually published by the newspapers or magazines that received them, App kept up a steady stream of communiqués.

Though much of what App wrote can be relegated to traditional, almost gutter-level antisemitism, he is nonetheless an important figure in the development and evolution of Holocaust denial. His major contribution was to formulate eight axioms that have come to serve as the founding principles of the California-based Institute for Historical Review and as the basic postulates of Holocaust denial. Since

App posited them in 1973, virtually all deniers have built their arguments on them. The deniers' tactics may have changed over time, but their arguments have remained the same.

Though App echoed many of Barnes's views – he stated, for example, that 'Hitler was a man of architecture and art, not of armaments and war'[5] and that Germany was the victim, not the victimizer – App was a more extreme figure than Barnes. Barnes was avidly pro-German but was not a fascist. He wished to defend Germany against all claims of wrongdoing but did not look for a resurrection of a totalitarian regime, a notion to which App was attracted. His Holocaust denial was more fully developed and explicit far earlier than Barnes's. As we have seen, Barnes had initially been reluctant to assert openly that the Holocaust was a fraud. Instead he found various ways to suggest it was 'theory,' a 'doing, real or imagined,' or only an 'alleged atrocity.' During the war itself Barnes refrained from overt criticisms of Allied policies. In contrast, Austin App showed no such reluctance. He did not wait for the war to be over to begin building a case in defense of German actions. In 1942, while the Allies were being defeated on all fronts, App sent a steady stream of letters to newspapers, periodicals, and individual journalists expressing a strong sympathy for Germany and its political objectives. Echoing World War I revisionists, he vigorously contested the notion that Germany could be held responsible for starting the war and sought to justify Germany's prewar behavior.

In May 1942, barely six months after Pearl Harbor, in a letter to CBS radio commentator Elmer Davis, App challenged the notion that Germany desired to 'dominate' Europe. According to App, Germany's territorial conquests did not represent naked aggression but rather the Reich's aspiration to secure the raw materials and power it needed and, in his view, deserved. At a time when the Allies were being pushed back by the Axis in both Europe and the Pacific, App proclaimed that the 'Anglo-Saxon block' would have to give Germany both raw materials and power 'commensurate with its talents' or inevitably the Allies would be 'terribly mangled and defeated.' App maintained that Germany had gone to war because this was the only way she could obtain what justifiably belonged to her. He argued that the means to end the war and win the peace was to give Germany 'precisely the things, which, if we had given them in 1939, would have prevented the war.'[6] But App did not stop there. His defense of Germany and his critique of Allied policy continued unabated through the war. In 1943, in the wake of the Casablanca Conference, at which Roosevelt and Churchill agreed that peace could only come to the world by the 'total elimination' of Germany and Japan as war powers, he complained to the *Columbus Evening Dispatch* that to demand unconditional surrender from Germany was 'grossly unethical.'[7] In 1944, as it became increasingly clear that Germany would be defeated and speculation had begun as to what a postwar Germany would look like, App argued that the Allies perpetrated a war on Germany because of the latter's legitimate desire to reunite with Danzig (now Gdansk). According to App, the prospect of a reunited Germany had frightened the Allies, and that is why they started the war. In this and numerous other letters App reiterated his central arguments. On the eve of World War II, Germany was emerging as a stronger nation than Britain. This the British and their ally the United States could not abide. According to App the only reason the United States was at war with Germany was that it did not want 'anybody in Europe so civilized and so efficient that our kith and kin, Britain, can't kick them around and tell them what they may or may not do.'[8]

App maintained this pro-Nazi line – Germany was innocent and the Allies guilty of starting the war – throughout the conflict. Once the war ended, App expanded the parameters of his defense of Germany's political demands and wartime behaviors. Taking his cue from the World War I revisionists like Beard and Barnes, he argued that Germany had not been responsible for the outbreak of the war. But he did not limit himself to vindicating Germany's territorial aspirations or attacking supposed Allied political machinations. He now commenced a far more serious endeavor: defending and justifying German atrocities. In May 1945, a week after the end of the war in Europe and while news of the liberation of the concentration camps filled the pages of American newspapers, App argued that what Germany had done was legally justified in the context of the rules of warfare.

Initially he focused on a few limited atrocities, such as the German massacre of the inhabitants of the Czechoslovakian town of Lidice. When Nazi leader Reinhard Heydrich was assassinated in May 1942, the Germans claimed that the villagers of Lidice had helped his assassin. They killed all the men in the village, 192 in all, as well as 71 women. The remaining 198 women were incarcerated in Ravensbrück, where many of them died. Of the 98 children who were 'put into educational institutions,' no more than 16 survived. Lidice was razed to the ground.[9] The annihilation of this town elicited an intense reaction from the American public. But, App contended, according to international law the killings were justified because the Germans had executed everybody who aided political murders,[10] and American law would have supported such action. He offered no evidence of how he concluded that the entire village had aided the assassins. Nor did he explain how murdering all the males and one third of the women, incarcerating the rest, including the children, and razing the entire town could be regarded as applications of international or American law.

Two weeks after vindicating German actions in Lidice, App addressed the killing of the Jews. Having not yet reached the point of overt denial, he simply exonerated the Germans' actions, basing his argument on two premises. Acknowledging that the Germans had committed 'crimes and mistakes,' he insisted that whatever they did any other nation would have done under similar circumstances. In fact, he argued, the United States had acted similarly during the war: Just as Germany had imprisoned Jews, America had arbitrarily imprisoned Japanese Americans.

But that was not App's only means of exculpating Germany for its persecution of Jews. The truculent behavior of Germany's victims justified their annihilation. Had the Japanese been as 'obstinate' as the German Jews, he argued, 'we conceivably would have killed them the same way.'[11] App's exoneration of Germany's annihilation of the Jews is particularly striking because at this point he was not yet denying that millions had been murdered. Obstinacy was just cause for the killing of millions.

Five months later App changed tactics and moved closer to denial.

In an attempt to downplay the severity of Nazi atrocities, he began to obfuscate the existence of gas chambers. In 1945, in a letter to the author of an article on the war crimes trials, App insisted that the German 'so-called offenders' be quickly tried. It was, App noted, 'in the interest of impartiality and justice' that 'all war criminals of both sides be so tried.' He then proceeded to define what constituted a war criminal:

Just as the Germans who put Germans of Jewish descent into concentration camps because of their race should be tried so Americans who put Americans of Japanese descent into concentration (relocation) camps because of their race must be tried; just as Hitler was to have been tried for attacking Poland (to rectify the self-determination principle violated at Versailles regarding Danzig) so Stalin must be tried for invading Finland (without any justification at all); just as Germans who raped and looted must be tried so the troops under General Eisenhower who raped 2000 Stuttgart girls in one weekend and hundreds of others since and the Russians, who ... raped ... looted and pillaged ... must be tried and if found guilty treated just as you say, according to the Golden Rule and impartial justice, Germans must be treated.[12]

For obvious reasons App avoided any mention of the German use of gas chambers to murder Jews and other victims. In order to engage in these immoral equivalences – everybody did something wrong and all should be equally punished – App had to eliminate the Holocaust and the murder of multitudes of others in death and concentration camps from the list of atrocities. Some of the atrocities listed by App have never been proven, for example, the Stuttgart rapes. Including the Holocaust and the gas chambers would have spoiled his equation. The Holocaust made it impossible to relativize the behavior of the warring parties, since nothing the Allies had done could compare to the number of people killed by the Germans or the primary method used to kill them. App had to turn the Allies and the Nazis into traditional adversaries embroiled in the horrors of war. Reducing the numbers and deleting this unique technological means from the equation were thus a *sine qua non* for deniers – one of the reasonable facades behind which they hide: War is an unmitigated evil, all sides are equally responsible, and there is no moral distinction between combatants.

Initially App simply omitted the mass murders and the gas chambers from his account of the war. He shortly recognized, however, that in order to achieve his objective he could no longer just ignore them and commenced an effort to convince the public that they were being fooled. It was an effort he would not abandon for more than three and a half decades.

In 1946, intensifying his campaign to justify German behavior, App began to play the 'numbers game,' something all deniers engage in with great fervor. They attempt to demonstrate that it is statistically impossible for six million to have died. Along with their questioning the scientific plausibility of the gas chambers, it is the most critical component of their enterprise. The deniers consciously fix on those aspects of the Holocaust that are the hardest to believe precisely because they demand the greatest leap of the imagination. The use of advanced technology for the purposes of mass murder, and the sheer scope of the endeavor – particularly the number of its victims – help to render this event beyond belief.

App, who engaged in this numerical chicanery even before Paul Rassinier, began in quite a clumsy fashion. First he tried to disprove the Jewish 'claim' about the Holocaust by demonstrating that most of Germany's Jews had survived the war. In a letter to *Time* magazine in 1946, he declared that Germany never had a Jewish population greater than seven hundred thousand and that when Germany surrendered 'there still seemed to be about a half million there.'[13]

Here App indulged in some of the tactical maneuvers that have come to typify Holocaust denial. First, in his attempt to prove that the numbers were inflated, he more than doubled the actual number of Jewish survivors without offering any proof of how he reached that figure.[14] In addition to exaggerating the number of Jewish survivors in Germany after the war, he also gave them a new identity as *German* Jews. In fact these survivors were not from Germany but came instead from many occupied countries. Many of them had been in concentration camps in the East and, in the latter months of the war, as the Soviet army advanced, had been transferred to Germany on brutal death marches that were part of the Nazis' effort to prevent camp inmates from falling into Soviet hands. Many died en route, and those who survived found themselves in Germany at the end of the war. Their numbers were augmented by Jews who immediately on liberation began to head west to avoid falling into Soviet hands.

By official Allied policy, all displaced persons (DPs) were to be returned to their homes as rapidly as possible. But a significant number adamantly refused to be repatriated to Poland, the Soviet Union, and other Communist bloc countries and petitioned to be allowed to enter Palestine or the United States. The British were firmly opposed to their entry into Palestine, and the Americans would only allow a very limited number to immigrate into the United States. As a result of the controversy over these DPs, the fact that practically all the Jews then in Germany were not actually German Jews was widely publicized and would have been well known to someone like App, who followed events so closely.

In the same letter, App suggested that among the putative Jewish victims of Nazi atrocities were many who had died of 'legitimate' causes and many who were not really dead at all but were living in comfort in the Western Hemisphere. He wrote to *Time* magazine demanding that it investigate

> just how many Jews were executed and for what; how many died of abuse in concentration camps and for what; how many were said to have been killed when they simply died of old age. And how many were in one way or another brought into the United States, Mexico and Canada. An AP dispatch ... states that the United States had rescued 3,000,000 refugees. Most of them appear to have been Jews, yet Judge Símon F. [*sic*] Rifkind recently stated that the Nazis *slew* 6,000,000 Jews. What are the facts?[15]

The facts were quite simple: The United States *had* rescued many European refugees. But it had not allowed three million refugees, Jewish displaced persons, survivors, or refugees of *any* ethnic group to immigrate. In fact, App was using a crafty but obvious ploy. The AP dispatch he cited was based on the report of the military governor of the American Zone on the *repatriation* – not the immigration into America – of the approximately three million DPs who were in the American zones in Germany and Austria at the end of the war. The report and the dispatch clearly indicated that the vast majority of the DPs had been returned to their homes by December 1945. Moreover, nowhere in the governor's report was there any indication that the refugees in question were Jews.[16] Most of the Jews who were allowed into the United States after the war did not begin arriving until the early 1950s.

But App was not just trying to cast doubt on the number of Jews that had been killed. He was also suggesting, none too subtly, that a major deception was being perpetrated by Jewish leaders who claimed that millions had been killed despite the fact that many of those millions were still alive. App would repeatedly return to this theme – supposedly dead Jews were really hiding in America – and in the future he would do so more directly. Indeed, in 1973 he cited a 1947 statement by Rabbi Philip S. Bernstein, an adviser on Jewish affairs to the U.S. army commanders in Germany and Austria. Bernstein believed that the 'only realistic solution' for the DP problem in Germany was resettlement in either the United States or Palestine. As App put it, 'That may explain why since 1945 New York [has been] a Jewish Sodom and Gomorrah and Washington, D.C., a half Jewish and half Negro employment agency!' falsely implying that sending DPs to the United States was exactly how the issue had been resolved.[17]

In 1949 App sent another of his periodic letters to *Time*, again urging it to investigate the matter of the number of Jewish dead 'thoroughly.' He also made one of the most radical calculations to date of the actual number of victims involved in the Holocaust 'hoax.'

> When I came to Europe in June I had calculated from the best sources then available to me that about 1,500,000 Jews had lost their lives through the Nazis, some because they were partisans and spies, killed as America did or would have killed persons guilty of similar offenses. After being here a month, evidences are accumulating that even that estimate is too high.[18]

App provided no evidence to substantiate his claim. App's efforts resonated with those who were interested in resurrecting the Nazis' image. (In 1952 a former member of the German Foreign Office under the Nazis pared the figure down to 1,277,212.[19]) But at this point App was breaking new ground. None of the other deniers, including Bardèche, Rassinier, or Barnes, had made such extreme suggestions.

Years later App described this visit to Europe. His account reveals the tremendous antipathy he felt toward the Jews he found there. 'When I visited Germany and Austria in 1949 I found them deluged with uncouth-looking Eastern Jews.' These Jews were 'arrogant to all Germans,' App wrote. 'They all seemed to engage in black marketeering, and the German police seemed forbidden to touch them. They lied, cheated and stole from Germans, almost at will.'[20] (App obviously knew that the Jews remaining in Germany at the end of the war were not German Jews.) App's description relies on all the traditional stereotypes used by antisemites – financial knavery, the power of the Jewish minority over the innocent majority, arrogance, and deception – a mendacious refrain that would be a constant theme in his work. In addition, he continued to dispute the number of dead and urged other deniers to do likewise throughout his career.

In 1965 App escalated his attack on the Holocaust by denouncing the figure of six million as a 'smear terrorizing myth,' and, despite the mass of evidence to the contrary, claiming that there was not a 'single document, order, blue-print' that proved that the Nazis intended to annihilate the Jews. He offered a strange argument to prove his point: The fact that some survived now constituted proof that none were killed. App tautologically maintained it was 'obvious' that the accusation was false *'from the fact that they did not exterminate them. Every Jew who survived the German occupation is proof of this.'* He argued that Nazi Germany was so efficient that 'not a calf was born without their record nor a pig slaughtered.' Had the Nazis decided to kill all Jews, 'They would have done so – they had five years to do it in.'[21]

The notions that the Third Reich was too efficient for any Jews to have escaped, and that it could have killed them all if it wanted to, became standard components of deniers' arguments.[22] The fallacious logic of App's argument was obvious, however. Nazi Germany was a relatively efficient society, but this efficiency was not unlimited nor was every goal the regime set for itself realized: Nazi Germany lost the war. Neither was it realized with regard to the Jews: Denmark and Bulgaria saved their Jews. And many Jews fought in partisan units, and thousands were held in concentration camps throughout the war.

But there is something even more disturbing about App's argument than its sublime illogic and cruelty. The horrific implications of his claim become evident when we locate the assumptions of his argument. Scholars often focus on the scientific and technological aspects of the horror and on its unimagined and unimaginable scale. These, as we have seen, are the things that strain credibility and so require the largest leap of faith. But, as the theologian Richard Rubenstein has observed, the greatest horror of Nazi Germany was its breaching of a moral barrier of social organization. It was this inhuman social organization that enabled the Nazis to realize their goal of annihilating masses of Jews with such technologically advanced instruments.[23] Thus, because they made the latter possible the bureaucratic achievements of the Nazis were more frightening than the technological ones.

Max Weber, writing long before the evolution of Nazism, understood the potential power of bureaucracy in social organization. According to Weber bureaucracy is valued the more it is absolutely dehumanized. The more successfully it eliminated emotions from its official business the more 'perfect' it became. The absolute bureaucratic organization demanded optimum precision, unity, unambiguity, knowledge of the files, and strict subordination.[24] Weber also understood that bureaucracies rarely, if ever, achieve this level of efficiency although that is their aim. The Nazis were keenly aware of the critical role the bureaucratic mechanism could play in allowing them to realize their plans. They knew that just as Weber taught, they had to demand complete 'dehumanization' from their system if they were to realize their goals. They may not have achieved an ideally operating bureaucratic system but not for lack of trying. Consequently some Jews may have survived. Ironically, then, in App's attempt to defend

Nazi Germany from the standpoint of its bureaucratic efficiency, he pinpointed its essential horror.

By 1973 App's fully evolved Holocaust denial was laid out in his pamphlet, *The Six Million Swindle: Blackmailing the German People for Hard Marks with Fabricated Corpses.* His use of the term *swindle* in the title is another of his not so subtle attempts to link his Holocaust hoax arguments to traditional antisemitic imagery. In the pamphlet App explained that the Holocaust hoax was a plot jointly inspired and nurtured by Communists and Jews. In the late 1950s he had argued that the 'utterly unsubstantiated' claims of six million dead worked only to benefit the Reds.[25] According to App the Soviets had a very good motive for participating in this hoax: They wished to hide the grim fact that more Jews had come to 'grief' in Stalin-controlled territory than in Nazi-occupied lands. Whatever atrocities had occurred were committed by the Soviets themselves, not the Nazis. The Holocaust hoax conveniently allowed them to shift the blame onto the Germans.

But the Soviets were not in this alone. App charged that 'Talmudic' leaders were well aware of the 'horrid truth' that the atrocity charges had been fabricated and the Germans innocent. But if the Jews knew this why did (and do) they go along with it? What was (and is) their motive for blaming Germany if they know the USSR was really responsible? App offered a simple and, for those inclined toward antisemitism, completely logical answer. These Jews knew the truth but did not publicize it for a practical reason: The Bolsheviks could not be successfully blackmailed for reparations for 'either real or fabricated corpses.'[26] As long as money was their ultimate objective, blaming the USSR served no purpose. Germany, on the other hand, had both the financial ability and the political inclination to pay in order to remove the stain from its reputation. In an article in *American Mercury* entitled 'The Elusive "Six Million,"' App elaborated on this point and accused Zionists of wanting to 'use the figure of six million vindictively as an eternal club for pressuring indemnities out of West Germany and for wringing financial contributions out of American Jews.'[27] The Zionists – who were, according to App, identical with the Bolsheviks in terms of their propensity for evil – thus emerge as the main force behind the Holocaust myth.* In *The Six Million Swindle*, written shortly after the Yom Kippur War, App left no doubt as to the Jews' rationale. 'The Talmudists have from the beginning used the six million swindle to blackmail West Germany into "atoning" with the twenty billion dollars of indemnities to Israel.'[28] (App exaggerated wildly. The actual sum Germany paid to Israel was $735 million. Far larger sums were paid to individuals.[29]) Moreover, he claimed, Israel and its supporters continued to use the 'fraudulent six million casualty' figure to achieve their political and military objectives.

It was 'secret unacknowlege [*sic*] guilt' that caused the United States to side with Israel in the Arab-Israeli War of 1973. Here too is another basic flaw in App's reasoning. According to him the U.S. government played a pivotal role in fostering the notion of the hoax. Why would the government be motivated to act by unacknowledged guilt when it knew the charges were a hoax? For App all claims of Israel's importance to American security were nothing but 'hogwash and hypocrisy.' For him Israel was a 'millstone about America's neck and we and Germany are its feedtrough.'[30] Israel manipulated public opinion in America and Germany by exploiting the myth of the Nazi Holocaust. In 1974 App returned to this theme, tying together its essential elements. He argued that at least five hundred thousand of the Jews who were supposedly gassed in German concentration camps were actually in Israel, where they received 'huge' reparations from Germany. Other putative victims were really in New York, where they had helped precipitate the 1973 energy crisis by 'blackmailing' Nixon into rushing several billion dollars' worth of weaponry to Israel so it could 'clobber' the Arabs. The 'Talmudists' had a secret ally in their efforts to manipulate foreign policy: the media. Jews used '*their* media,' which for App included, among others, the *New York Times*, *Washington Post*, and *Newsweek*, to cry themselves 'hoarse' because the Arabs refused to sell oil to the West.[31] App was not the first to link Jewish control of the media to

---

* This argument was used by the deniers until the Soviets adopted a sharp anti-Zionist policy. It then became difficult to claim the existence of a Zionist-Soviet plot, and the deniers stopped repeating this argument.

the Holocaust hoax – Rassinier had done so previously – but App made it a central element of his argument. He repeatedly returned to the theme of Jewish domination of the media.[32] It was through their domination of the press that Jews had been able not only to perpetrate this hoax but subsequently to control the foreign and domestic policies of nations around the world. This theme of Jewish control of the media was a traditional component of modern antisemitism. At the core of antisemitism from the far-right end of the political spectrum was the image of the Jews as a permanent source of unrest and revolutionary zeal in society.[33] According to these antisemites the media was one of the primary tools Jews used to foster that unrest. They ignored the paradox inherent in this accusation. If Jews controlled the media why did it treat Nazi Germany's persecution of the Jews in such a lackadaisical fashion during the 1930s and 1940s.

Though App identified the main force behind the Holocaust hoax as the 'Talmudists and Bolsheviks,' he believed there was another participant in the spread of this slander. At the end of the war, when the Americans and British 'invaded' Germany, they saw the results of their indiscriminate bombing. The Allies knew, App wrote, that they had been responsible for more destruction than any 'vandals of history except the Bolsheviks.' Recognizing that their people would not understand or condone the 'unnecessary barbarism,' Allied leaders needed something that would save them from the condemnation that was sure to come. It was then, according to App, that they discovered that their only 'salvation' was to 'manufacture' and 'harp on a mountain of atrocities,' particularly those against the Jews. Harping on Jews as victims was particularly efficacious for the Allied leaders because, App explained, Jews controlled the media and the media would play a critically important role in disseminating the hoax. And their plan worked. They exaggerated real and phony Third Reich atrocities to such monstrous proportions that Allied crimes were totally ignored. They then took matters a step further by instilling such a guilt complex in Germany that the Germans felt compelled to pay unprecedented sums of reparations to Jews and Israel.[34]

But even when he linked the Holocaust hoax to the Allies' need for a camouflage in which to hide their own outrages, App did not absolve the 'Talmudist leaders.' In fact, he maintained that the Jews were ultimately responsible for Allied actions and actually controlled Allied policy. This leap enabled him to argue that Soviet and American atrocities against the German people were the result of Jewish influence. App focused on the two people he considered responsible for these atrocities. Not surprisingly, both of them were Jews. American Secretary of the Treasury Henry Morgenthau and Ilya Ehrenburg, a member of the Soviet Antifascist Committee, were to blame for the Soviet soldiers' rape of German women and plunder of German property. App argued, without offering a shred of proof, that Ehrenburg personally urged Soviet soldiers to commit rape, against the German people. (Ehrenburg did call for vengeance but not for rape.) This vindictive Jewish Communist supposedly gave the most 'beastly directive in history: Rape the German women as booty!' Similarly, App blamed virtually every American action against the Germans on Henry Morgenthau. It is true that Morgenthau, after learning of the horrors of the German annihilation of the Jews, proposed that in the postwar period Germany be converted into a country that was primarily agricultural and pastoral in character.[35] As we have seen, the plan was never seriously considered and was subsequently completely abandoned by President Truman. But App claimed that the plan had been put into effect, at least in part. He contended that Morgenthau not only bribed Churchill to stiffen the treatment of German prisoners of war but also inspired the Allies to starve and 'abuse-unto-death' several million of these prisoners. This was obviously a Jewish plot, App argued, because 'Christians at their worst are not as barbarous as Communists and Jews at their average.'[36] Thus, when the Jews saw that the Allies were going to deal leniently with the Germans in the postwar period, they went into action. According to App the American army was planning to allow the German prisoners to be repatriated as soon as possible after the war. But this did not happen despite the fact that it was what the army leadership and 'our Christian citizens' wanted. App had a simple explanation as to how the 'tribalists' were able to prevent it. They kept 'screeching the lie that the Germans "gassed"

6,000,000 of them. It was the Jews who kept screaming for abusing German prisoners of war, for keeping them from home, for slave-laboring them ... This is the voice of the Talmudists, the barbarians of the Morgenthau Plan!'[37]

As his rhetoric about the Jewish role in directing Allied policy escalated, the two became fused in his mind. No longer did he even speak of the Jews' ability to direct Allied policy. For App, Allied tactics and the Jews' objectives became one: Allied policy, at its worst, was Jewish policy. This is most evident at the end of *A Straight Look at the Third Reich*. Immediately after discussing Allied atrocities, without any indication that the subject of his diatribe had changed, App wrote:

> Not finding the Nazis guilty of real war crimes at all commensurate with the monstrous ones of the victors, they resorted to the only alternative open to hypocrites and liars namely to fabricate a mass atrocity. This they did with the legend of the six million Jews 'gassed.' ... This is a fabrication and swindle.[38]

Allied policymakers and Jewish leaders had become one and the same to App. He then fell back on the same approach that Harry Elmer Barnes had utilized, accusing those behind the hoax of 'smear terroriz[ing]' and branding as an antisemite anyone who tried to investigate this myth in a scholarly fashion.[39]

It was not by chance that App relied on the New Testament phrase 'hypocrites and liars' to describe Jews. In fact it served two purposes for him: It was a means of drawing on antisemitic imagery that would resonate with many non-Jews. Moreover, for him the Jews of the twentieth century who perpetrated this hoax were essentially the same as the New Testament Jews who were depicted as crucifiers of Jesus. In the foreword to the 1975 edition of his collected letters, App noted that just as his letters failed to ease Germany's fate and prevent the atrocity stories from gaining currency, so too Jesus of Nazareth was unable to prevent his crucifixion. But that did not mean that either Jesus' or App's struggle was wrong. Both these martyrs were defeated by the same adversaries. App implied that the ancestors of the 'World War Talmudists' had crucified Jesus, and now their descendants thwarted those who wished to tell the truth.*

By the end of *The Six Million Swindle* App had fully formulated his Holocaust denial, offering readers what he described as eight 'incontrovertible assertions' that demonstrate the fallaciousness of the figure of six million, which the media kept repeating *'ad nauseam* without any evidence.' These basic assertions – which were eventually adopted by the Institute for Historical Review as well as other revisionist groups as the fundamental tenets of Holocaust denial – fall into three distinct categories. First they absolve the Nazis by arguing that they never had any plan for annihilating Jews and that the means supposedly used for annihilation were technologically impossible. They only wanted Jews to emigrate, and if any Jews did die it was the USSR that was ultimately responsible. Second, they legitimate the killing of those Jews who died by contending that they were killed for justifiable reasons. Third, they blame the perpetuation of this hoax on Israel and Jewish leaders and scholars, all of whom have material and political interests in its dissemination.

The eight assertions were:

1. Emigration, never annihilation, was the Reich's plan for solving Germany's Jewish problem. Had Germany intended to annihilate all the Jews, a half million concentration camp inmates would not have survived and managed to come to Israel, where they collect 'fancy indemnities from West Germany.'

2. 'Absolutely no Jews were gassed in any concentration camps in Germany, and evidence is piling up that none were gassed in Auschwitz.' The Hitler gas chambers never existed. The gassing installations found in Auschwitz were really crematoria for cremating corpses of those who had died

---

* This was not the only time App relied on biblical themes to depict Jews. In 1948 he called for the reeducation of Jews 'away from their eye for an eyeism.' (App, *Morgenthau Era Letters*, p. 73.)

from a variety of causes, including the 'genocidic'
Anglo-American bombing raids.

3. The majority of Jews who disappeared and remain un-
accounted for did so in territories under Soviet, not German,
control.

4. The majority of Jews who supposedly died while in German
hands were, in fact, subversives, partisans, spies, saboteurs,
and criminals or victims of unfortunate but internationally
legal reprisals.

5. If there existed the slightest likelihood that the Nazis had
really murdered six million Jews, 'World Jewry' would
demand subsidies to conduct research on the topic and Israel
would open its archives to historians. They have not done
so. Instead they have persecuted and branded as an antisemite anyone who wished to publicize the hoax. This
persecution constitutes the most conclusive evidence that the
six million figure is a 'swindle.'*

6. The Jews and the media who exploit this figure have failed
to offer even a shred of evidence to prove it. The Jews
misquote Eichmann and other Nazis in order to try to
substantiate their claims.

7. It is the accusers, not the accused, who must provide the
burden of proof to substantiate the six million figure. The
Talmudists and Bolsheviks have so browbeaten the Germans
that they pay billions and do not dare to demand proof.

8. The fact that Jewish scholars themselves have 'ridiculous'
discrepancies in their calculations of the number of victims
constitutes firm evidence that there is no scientific proof to
this accusation.[40]

While all these assertions are easily controverted by evidence and
documentation, some are based on such faulty reasoning that their
fallaciousness can be exposed without even turning to the evidence.

---

* All these assertions are absolutely false. Israel has opened its archives to all credible scholars and students working in this field.

As was the case with Rassinier, App ignored a fundamental flaw in his eighth assertion. If the Holocaust was truly a fraud perpetrated by the Jews, one could legitimately expect a powerful force like 'World Jewry' to have seen to it that no discrepancies were allowed to creep into research by Jewish scholars. All their findings should neatly dovetail with and confirm one another. And if the 'Talmudists' were crafty enough to recognize that precise conformity might arouse suspicion, they would have ensured that there was only the slightest variation among scholars' findings.

But this, of course, is not the only inconsistency in App's arguments. At the same time that he described Israeli archives as playing a pivotal role in the 'swindle,' he also used their findings to validate his own. In an attempt to prove that even Israeli institutions have been unable to document the number of dead, App cited a statement by Yad Vashem, the national memorial to the victims in Israel, that it has been able to gather only 2.5 million pages of testimony.* App argued that if in the years since the end of the war Yad Vashem had been unable to document even 4 million, it was because there had not been that many. Even the 2.5 million figures they supplied were nothing but 'a lie and a swindle.'[41] But if Yad Vashem was as App depicted it – an Israeli institution at the heart of the hoax – it should have had no difficulty forging the additional documentation needed to fill the quotient of six million.[42]

More recently the Institute for Historical Review published a report from the *Jerusalem Post* in which the director of Yad Vashem's archives reported that more than half of its testimonies from Holocaust survivors are 'unreliable.' According to Yad Vashem officials, these testimonies have never been used as evidence in Nazi war crimes trials because survivors who wanted to be 'part of history' may, in fact, have allowed their imaginations to 'run away with them.'[43] For the deniers this was further evidence of a 'hoax.'

---

* A 'page of testimony' at Yad Vashem consists of the name and birthdate of the victim as well as additional biographical information. It is usually filled out by a surviving relative, friend, or neighbor. Obviously many people died and did not leave behind any relatives or neighbors who could perform this task of memorializing their name.

What the Institute for Historical Review could not ask, given its ideological predilections, was the question of why Yad Vashem would acknowledge that some of its archival holdings are incorrect if its objective was to perpetuate the Holocaust 'myth.' Why did it not simply replace these testimonies with 'correct' ones? Why did it not have its researchers further 'falsify' the data? If Jews were able to forge documents sufficient to convict Nazi war criminals within a few months after the war, they should certainly have been able to deposit reliable and historically accurate testimonies in Yad Vashem in the decades since then. This simplistic and yet deceptive claim is but another example of the deniers' use of tactics that conveniently either ignore proof of the Holocaust or twist it in a way that substantiates their conspiracy theory.

App's faulty arguments regarding the scholarly dispute about the number of victims and his use of statements and figures from Yad Vashem to prove his point were not the only occasions when he became ensnared in his own attempts to manipulate the evidence. In *The Six Million Swindle* he also attacked a journalist who had written that the Nazis wished to kill 'as many Jews as possible' before the end of the war. In order to substantiate his charge that this journalist was lying, App cited Himmler's fall 1944 order prohibiting any further execution of Jews.[44] This evidence, he argued, proved two things: First the Nazis did not wish to kill as many Jews as possible, for if so Himmler would not have halted the killings. Second, he argued, it showed that Himmler, not Hitler, was in charge of Jewish policy.[45] In his attempt to exonerate both the Nazis in general and Hitler in particular by laying the blame for this policy at Himmler's doorstep, App ignores a basic contradiction in his argument: If there *was* not a policy to kill the Jews, what then was Himmler ordering stopped?

Here and elsewhere App's approach to evidence is reminiscent of Rassinier's arguments regarding eyewitness accounts. It is the standard method by which deniers dismiss evidence which contradicts their conclusions. All affidavits by Nazis admitting the existence of a Final Solution are declared 'outright frauds,' and all testimony by Jews regarding mass murder is 'in part or whole perjured, often well rewarded and altogether unreliable.'[46] This blanket denial of the validity of any evidence attesting to the Holocaust, including that of eyewitnesses, has become a centerpiece of the deniers' methodology. Simply put, anything that disagrees with their foregone conclusion is dismissed. Because of the sheer number of affidavits by survivors, perpetrators, and eyewitnesses, unless the deniers categorically dismiss this mass of evidence they cannot perpetrate their own hoax.

Ultimately App's arguments are a composite of faulty assertions, manipulation of data, and above all, outright antisemitism. He has done more than just draw on preexisting antisemitic imagery. He has made a significant contribution to contemporary anti-Jewish propaganda in the United States and abroad. His distillation of Holocaust denial into these eight assertions, each of which plays on an antisemitic theme, has proven extremely useful to individuals and groups which not only deny the Holocaust but wish to portray the Jews as able to control American foreign policy for their own diabolical ends. It has also proved extremely efficacious for those who would delegitimize the existence of Israel.

Together App, Barnes, Rassinier, Bardèche, and Hoggan constitute the most significant figures in the evolution of the denial hoax. Those who followed them discarded some of their more blatant and vulgar arguments, learning how to render them in a slightly more oblique fashion. But with the fundamental text established, virtually all the rest would be commentary.

6

Denial: A Tool of the Radical Right

In the late 1960s and 1970s, neofascist organizations and political parties in Western Europe, especially in England, grew in number and strength. These groups – which vehemently opposed the presence in their countries of blacks, Asians, Arabs, Jews, and all non-Caucasian immigrants – were responsible for launching a series of violent attacks on immigrants, minority groups, and Jewish institutions. In England the neofascist National Front built its political agenda on opposition to the immigration of Africans and East Asians from Commonwealth countries. By 1977 it was polling close to a quarter of a million votes in national elections.

These groups, whose ideology embraced racism, ethnocentrism, and nationalism, faced a dilemma. Since World War II, Nazism in general and the Holocaust in particular had given fascism a bad name. Those who continued to argue after the war that Hitler was a hero and national socialism a viable political system, as these groups tended to do, were looked upon with revulsion. Consequently Holocaust denial became an important element in the fabric of their ideology. If the public could be convinced that the Holocaust was a myth, then the revival of national socialism could be a feasible option.

This effort to deny the Holocaust was materially assisted by the publication in 1974 of a twenty-eight-page booklet, *Did Six Million Really Die? The Truth at Last*, by Richard Harwood. Sent to all members of Parliament, a broad spectrum of journalists and academics, leading members of the Jewish community, and a wide array of public figures, for close to ten years it was the preeminent British work on Holocaust denial.[1] Within less than a decade, more than a million copies had been distributed in more than forty countries.[2] Because at first glance it seemed to be a sober scholarly effort, many outside the circle of deniers were confused by the claims it made. Deniers continually cite it as an authoritative source.

Given the pamphlet's wide distribution, there was significant public curiosity about the identity of both the author and publisher. Richard E. Harwood was described as a writer who specialized in the political and diplomatic aspects of World War II and who was 'at present with the University of London.' It did not take the British press long to discover that this was false. The University of London told the *Sunday Times* that Harwood was neither a staff member nor a student and was totally unknown to it; it returned all mail to Harwood marked 'Addressee Unknown.'[3] In fact Richard Harwood was a pseudonym for Richard Verrall, the editor of *Spearhead*, the publication of the British right-wing neofascist organization the National Front. *Did Six Million Really Die?* is identical in format, layout, and printing with *Spearhead*.[4] Neither the National Front nor Verrall denied that he was the editor of the pamphlet.[5] In 1979, in a letter to the *New Statesman*, Verrall, who had a degree in history from the University of London, responding to articles on the Holocaust, reiterated the pamphlet's basic arguments and defended its conclusions against attacks that had appeared in the British press. He did so despite the fact that most of his conclusions had already been shown to be false.[6] He made no attempt to challenge the assertion that he was the author, even though the article in the *New Statesman* specifically identified him as such. His letter to the magazine was described by the editors as one of 'numerous mock-scholarly letters' it regularly received from Verrall and his cohorts.

In addition to concealing the author's true identity, the publishers also attempted to camouflage their identity. Though the booklet listed the address of its publisher, Historical Review Press, the address was that of a vacant building whose landlord, the British press discovered, was Robin Beauclair, a farmer with established connections to the National Front and various other organizations all of which were dedicated to defending 'racial purity.'[7] Asked by the press about the publication, he declared the Holocaust part of a network of 'Jewish propaganda' and revealed his own deep-rooted antisemitism. 'Don't you know that we live under Jewish domination? The entire mass media is Jewish controlled. It is time that we as British people dictated our own destiny.'[8]

Not an original creation, this work was largely based on a small American book, *The Myth of the Six Million*, published in 1969 by Noontide Press, a subsidiary of the antisemitic Liberty Lobby. The American publication contained both an unsigned publisher's foreword and an introduction by an E. L. Anderson, identified as a contributing editor to *American Mercury*, which by that time had become unabashedly antisemitic. The anonymous publisher was apparently Willis Carto, founder of the Liberty Lobby, Noontide Press, and the Institute for Historical Review. Carto had, as we shall see in a subsequent chapter, long-standing ties to a mélange of extremist right-wing political groups in the United States. (According to Carto's former associates, E. L. Anderson was a pseudonym of his.[9]) The *Myth of the Six Million* also contained an appendix consisting of five articles that had originally appeared in the Carto-controlled *American Mercury* in 1967–68. They included App's 'The Elusive "Six Million," ' Barnes's 'Zionist Fraud,' Teressa Hendry's 'Was Anne Frank's Diary a Hoax?', 'The Jews That Aren't,' by Leo Heiman, 'Paul Rassinier: Historical Revisionist,' by Herbert C. Roseman, and a review of Rassinier's book by Harry Elmer Barnes.

The American publication was apparently written by David Hoggan, the Harvard Ph.D. whose work had influenced Harry Elmer Barnes. In 1969 he sued Noontide Press for damages, claiming authorship of *The Myth of the Six Million*.[10] (The book's introduction described the author as a college professor who had written this booklet in 1960 but had been unable to obtain a publisher daring enough to take the risks involved. It claimed that he could not reveal his identity because he wanted 'one day [to] retire on a well-earned pension.'[11])

Both these publications consistently mixed truth with fiction, accurate with fabricated quotes, and outright lies with partially correct information. The manner in which the British work liberally paraphrased the American publication indicates that in many instances Harwood may not have gone back to the original sources but simply repeated what the Americans had already said.* The Americans, in turn, had done their own borrowing from other deniers. This liberal borrowing was not something out of the ordinary for deniers, who make it a practice to draw on other deniers not only for their sources but for verification. They have long engaged in what has been described as an 'incestuous merry-go-round [of] cross-fertilizing and compounding [of] falsehood.'[12] The basic arguments cited in both works are based on material gleaned from Rassinier, though in certain instances they go even further in their extremism.[13]

These publications constitute vivid examples of the relationship between Holocaust denial, racist nationalism, and antisemitism. Harwood complained that the 'big lie' of the Holocaust stymied the growth of nationalism, and that whenever Britain or any other European nation attempted to preserve its 'national integrity,' it was immediately branded as neo-Nazi.[14] Preservation of a nation's national integrity had a specific meaning for both publications. The Holocaust myth threatened the 'survival of the Race itself.' Harwood echoed the familiar extremist charge that the Anglo-Saxon world faced the gravest danger in its history: the presence of 'alien races' in its midst. Linking Holocaust denial and the defense of the 'race,' he argued that unless something was done to halt the immigration and assimilation of non-Caucasians, Anglo-Saxons were certain to experience not only 'biological alteration' but the 'destruction' of their European culture and racial heritage.[15]

---

* For example, both the American and the British authors describe Eichmann's assistant as 'a nervous wreck and addicted to uncontrollable fits of sobbing for hours' (pp. 46, 11). In addition, Dr. M. Nyiszli, the author of *Doctor at Auschwitz*, is described in the American and the British versions as 'apparently a mythical and invented figure' (pp. 118, 20). Nyiszli was a Jewish doctor who worked under the infamous Dr. Josef Mengele as a pathologist. His role is well established in documents and testimonies. There are numerous other examples of 'shared' citations and paraphrasing. See, for example, the section on the International Committee of the Red Cross, 'Letters of thanks which came pouring in from Jewish internees' (pp. 99, 25). Compare also p. 98 with p. 24 and p. 101 with p. 25.

This argument – a standard element in National Front ideology – blamed Jews for engineering the racial and national degeneration of England as well as Europe as a whole. Shortly after the publication of Harwood's pamphlet, a National Front leader accused Jews of pouring 'billions' into promoting 'race mixing' in order to weaken nationalist identity throughout the world, thereby enhancing the possibility of their own world domination.[16] According to Harwood, Jews have used the Holocaust myth to preserve their heritage and, at the same time, render other peoples 'impotent' in their attempts at self-preservation.[17] In his view, Jews, who have relied on their formidable powers of manipulation, have reaped personal and communal gains at a substantial cost to the well-being and security of other nations. (There was no doubt, of course, that the nations Harwood was referring to were white ones.) Harwood complained that any time a person dared to speak of the race problem, he or she was branded a racist, a code word for *Nazi*, and that *Nazi* was, of course, synonymous with a perpetrator of the Holocaust.[18]

The introduction to the American book made the same connection, arguing that the Holocaust myth made it impossible for America to deal with its 'overwhelming race problem.' The Holocaust had caused Nazism to fall into disrepute, consequently the problems that emanated from 'Negro-White contact' in the same society could not be addressed for what they really were: biological and political. Anyone who dared to do so was accused of advocating '*racism*, the very hallmark of the Nazi!'[19] Since the 1960s and the increased immigration of non-Caucasians into Europe, particularly to Britain and France, the extreme right in each of these countries has articulated this strange mélange of arguments that knit together racism, the revival of fascism, and Holocaust denial. In North America they have been espoused by an array of right-wing extremist groups. Given the connection between these two ideologies, it is logical to expect the Holocaust 'hoax' to remain a fixed component of the litany of arguments posed by these extremist fringes of society.

In order to rehabilitate the reputation of National Socialism, these two publications tried to prove that the Nazis' intention was emigration, not annihilation. First they argued that the Final

Solution was nothing but a plan to evacuate all Jews from the Reich. Then they tried to give this evacuation plan historical legitimacy by linking it with the name of the founder of the modern Zionist movement, Theodor Herzl. They claimed that the Nazis were simply trying to realize Herzl's original goal of transferring all the Jews to Madagascar. In fact Herzl never addressed the issue of Madagascar. At one point he briefly considered Uganda as an alternative to the land of Israel but dropped the idea when it met with furious opposition from other Zionists.

This is not the only way Harwood used revised history to transform the Nazis into supporters of emigration. Attempting to prove that the Nazis were primarily interested in a benign population transfer, he wrote that a main plank of the National Socialist party platform before 1933 was Jewish emigration to Madagascar. In fact emigration of the Jews was never included by the Nazis in their party platform prior to 1933, let alone used as a main plank.[20] The Madagascar Plan was never mentioned as a possibility until the late 1930s. The Nazi slogan was *Juda Verrecke*, 'perish Judah,' not 'emigrate Judah.' The full meaning of *Juda Verrecke* is lost in English translation. It is akin to perishing like a 'lice-ridden cur.'[21] Nazi leaders, among them Josef Goebbels, Julius Streicher, and Hans Frank, frequently described Jews as vermin in need of extermination. In 1929 Goebbels wrote: 'Certainly the Jew is a human being. But then the flea is a living thing too – only not a pleasant one. Since the flea is not a pleasant thing, we are not obliged to keep it and let it prosper . . . but our duty is rather to exterminate it. Likewise with the Jews.'[22] In an article in the *Völkischer Beobachter* in 1921 Hitler described the Jews as 'lice and bugs sucking the German people's blood out of its veins.'[23]

The claim that the Nazis were interested in Jewish emigration exemplifies how deniers draw falsehoods from truth. Emigration *was* indeed employed by the Nazis in the thirties as a means of ridding the Reich of Jews. From 1933 until 1939 the Nazis vigorously pushed the Jews to emigrate, and more than three hundred thousand, or approximately 50 percent of the German Jewish population, did so. While deniers use this data to portray the Nazis as benignly engaged in a population transfer, the Nazis' true intentions during the 1930s were to brutally destroy the German Jewish community and simultaneously sow seeds of antisemitism abroad. During the prewar period this was their means of creating a Germany that was *Judenrein*. The chaos of the war allowed them or, some would argue, forced them to move from emigration to annihilation.* But even emigration – when employed by the Nazis as a solution to the Reich's Jewish 'problem' – had diabolical intentions. A Foreign Office memorandum of January 25, 1939, delineated the more cynical aspects of the emigration plan: 'The poorer and therefore more burdensome the immigrant Jews to the country absorbing them, the stronger the country will react and the more favorable will the effect be in the interest of German propaganda.'[24] As the Nazis exported penniless and desperate Jews, they also exported antisemitism. This was, in part, the reason why they stripped Jews of their possessions through an increasingly onerous emigration tax. By January 1939 they had been totally excised from the German economy. On occasion Reich leaders simply took groups of Jews and placed them outside Germany's borders, forcing their neighbors to have to accommodate a large group of destitute immigrants. The best known of these incidents took place on the Polish border at the end of October 1938 on the eve

* Scholars debate at what point in 1941 the Nazis decided to murder all the Jews in their sphere of influence. The prospect of having many millions of Jews, including those in the Soviet Union, under their rule when they overran that country led them to conclude that murder was the only 'efficient' means of dealing with the Jewish 'problem.' Intentionalists argue that the Nazis intended from the outset to eventually murder the Jews and that there was a high degree of consistency and orderly sequence in the Final Solution. Functionalists believe that there was no blueprint for the murder of the Jews but that the annihilation program was initially a means for the Nazis to emerge from a blind alley into which they had maneuvered themselves. Functionalists argue that in its first stages the murder program was improvised, and it proceeded in a haphazard fashion.

I do not intend to enter the debate between the intentionalists and the functionalists. Both groups essentially agree that the war and especially the invasion of the Soviet Union made the annihilation process possible – irrespective of when and how the idea originated. Until 1939 the Nazis tried to get rid of the Jews by pressuring them into emigration. After that time they forcibly extruded them. For an excellent summary of this entire debate see Michael R. Marrus, *The Holocaust in History* (New York, 1989 [pbk.]), pp. 34–48.

of Kristallnacht, the anti-Jewish Nazi pogrom of November 1938 during which hundreds of synagogues were destroyed and twenty-six thousand Jews were put into concentration camps.

The emigration myth – the idea that the Nazis stuck to their original aim of getting rid of Jews by emigration – is easily refuted by Nazi documents, newspapers, and journals themselves, which are replete with statements by high-ranking officials and party leaders, attesting to their ultimate objective. The Nazi leader, Dr. Robert Ley, articulated these intentions in 1942 when he said that it was not enough to 'isolate the Jewish enemy of mankind. The Jews have got to be exterminated.'[25] In his testimony at Nuremberg, Victor Brack, who was in charge of the gassing of fifty thousand mentally deficient and chronically ill Germans and Jews under the euthanasia program from 1939 to 1941, acknowledged that by March 1941, it was no secret among higher party circles that the 'Jews were to be exterminated.'[26] In a May 1943 article in the Berlin weekly *Das Reich*, Goebbels announced: 'No prophetic utterance by the Fuhrer is being fulfilled with so gaunt an assurance and inescapable force as that another world war would cause the extinction of the Jewish race.'[27] In October 1943 Heinrich Himmler, the head of the SS, told high-ranking officers in Posen that 'we had a moral duty towards our people, the duty to exterminate this people [the Jews].'[28]

Based on these and a multitude of other statements by Nazi leaders, including Hitler's own January 1939 promise to exterminate the Jews and his wartime repetition of that promise, there is no doubt that while emigration was employed to rid Germany of its Jewish population during the 1930s, once Poland came under Nazi control and portions of the Soviet Union, with its large Jewish populations, were targeted to be conquered, annihilation became German policy.

Antisemitism was such a fundamental aspect of national socialism that even the most creative denier cannot claim it did not exist. Thus what they cannot deny or distort, they rationalize. We have already seen this in the attempts to portray German Jews as spies and partisans who deserved whatever the Nazis meted out. Harwood widened that scope. He interpreted Nazi antisemitism as

Germany's legitimate response to attacks on it by 'international Jewry.' He argued that Zionist leader Chaim Weizmann's statement in 1939, on the outbreak of the war, that the Jews would stand by Great Britain and fight on the side of the democracies, constituted the Jews' declaration of war on Nazi Germany and transformed them into a threat to Germany's security.[29] Actually Weizmann never mentioned Great Britain in his statement but spoke of the democracies in general. Harwood added the reference to Great Britain. Harwood insisted that under the tenets of international law Hitler had the right to declare Jews enemy agents intent on prosecuting a war against the Reich. They could therefore be legitimately subjected to a policy of internment.

Harwood ignored the fact that Nazi antisemitic policies antedated Weizmann's pronouncement by almost seven years. Weizmann's statement was a response to those policies, not the reverse. Since 1933 Germany had excluded Jews from most professions and subjected them to economic boycotts, incarceration, physical violence, and horrendous degradation. This process was followed by the disenfranchisement of German Jews under the 1935 Nuremberg laws and the destruction and brutality of Kristallnacht in 1938. Weizmann was speaking as a leader of a stateless people who were in no position to wage a war of any kind against an independent, well-armed nation.[30] He was, after all, a citizen of Great Britain and Palestine was a British-mandated territory. A declaration of loyalty to the democracies in their war against Germany was the least – and, on some level, the most – he could do.

This ploy to cast Nazi antisemitism as a legitimate response to a threat to Germany's security could be dismissed were it not for the way it has been adopted by prominent historians. The German historian Ernst Nolte, whose books on fascism have become historical classics, espoused the same argument regarding Weizmann's statement in his attempt to lessen Nazi responsibility for the outrages of World War II. Nolte was the historian most prominently associated in the 1980s with what has become known in Germany as the *Historikerstreit*, an effort by some historians, particularly those with conservative political tendencies, to normalize and relativize the history of the Nazi period by arguing that many Nazi policies, including persecution of the Jews, were defensive reactions to foreign threats and were no different from what other countries have done in the past. Chancellor Helmut Kohl's invitation to President Ronald Reagan to join him in a wreath-laying ceremony at Bitburg was a political manifestation of this historical tendency to try to normalize the German past, particularly its National Socialist past. By asking the American president to accompany him to a German military cemetery that included fallen SS soldiers in an act of reconciliation, Kohl was attempting to lessen the historical blot on German nationalism and patriotism. He was not trying to rewrite or deny the past but to cast it in a different light.[31] One of the dangers of Holocaust denial is that it so stretches the parameters of the argument regarding Germany's wartime behavior that it renders Nolte's kind of relativism increasingly respectable. (For a fuller discussion of the relationship between relativism and denial see chapter 11.)

Echoing Harwood, Nolte contended that Weizmann's official declaration at the outbreak of hostilities gave Hitler good reason 'to be convinced of his enemies' determination to annihilate him much earlier than when the first information about Auschwitz came to the knowledge of the world.'[32] What power the Jews had to effect Hitler's annihilation Nolte did not specify. When Nolte was criticized on this point in light of prewar Nazi persecution of Jews, he said that he was only quoting David Irving, the right-wing writer of historical works. How quoting Irving justified using such a historically invalid point remains unexplained, unless one wishes to see it as a reflection of Nolte's personal predilections.[33] As we shall see in subsequent chapters, Irving, who had frequently proposed extremely controversial theories about the Holocaust, including the claim that Hitler had no knowledge of it, has become a Holocaust denier.

These works demonstrate how deniers misstate, misquote, falsify statistics, and falsely attribute conclusions to reliable sources. They rely on books that directly contradict their arguments, quoting in a manner that completely distorts the authors' objectives. Deniers count on the fact that the vast majority of readers will not have access to the documentation or make the effort to determine how they have falsified or misconstrued information.

Harwood attempted to prove that it was statistically impossible for six million Jews to have perished at the hands of the Nazis. The most cursory examination of his sources reveals his spurious methodology. He cited *Chambers Encyclopedia*, which according to Harwood concluded that the total Jewish population of prewar Europe was 6,500,000. 'This would mean that almost the entire number were exterminated.' How then, Harwood asks, was it possible for so many Jews to emigrate to other countries or to receive reparations if almost all had been annihilated?[34]

Chambers does in fact cite a figure of 6,500,000, but not as the size of the Jewish population of prewar Europe:

> On the continent of Europe *apart from Russia*, whose western provinces also suffered terribly, only a handful of numerically unimportant communities in neutral countries escaped and of the 6,500,000 Jews *who lived in the Nazi-dominated lands in* 1939, barely 1,500,000 remained alive when the war ended six years later.[35]

Chambers specifically excluded from its figure of 6,500,000 the Jewish population in the Soviet Union and those countries that were not dominated by the Nazis in 1939.

Harwood also argued that the majority of German Jews left Germany prior to the outbreak of the war. Consequently they were not within reach of the Nazis and were safe from any form of persecution.[36] They could not therefore be counted among the six million. It is correct that more than 50 percent of German Jews emigrated. Though many went to places that in the mid-1930s seemed perfectly safe – for example, the Netherlands, France, and Belgium, they were eventually caught up in the Nazi maelstrom. Given that six million is cited as the death toll of all European Jewry, the percentage of Jews who emigrated is a meaningless statistic unless one notes their destination.

Whatever sources deniers cannot twist they ignore, particularly when they contradict their most basic contentions. Such was the case with the *Chambers Encyclopedia*. After citing the population figures, the encyclopedia discussed the 'systematic campaign of annihilation in a series of death camps' as a result of which one-third of the Jewish population was killed.[37]

Harwood repeatedly used partial information to distort trustworthy sources. He wrote that the *Baseler Nachrichten*, a Swiss newspaper, reported in June 1946 that 'a maximum of only one and a half million Jews could be numbered as casualties.'[38] Harwood neglected to mention a subsequent article in the same paper that acknowledged that the previous figure was incorrect and that the accurate number of victims was 5,800,000.[39]

He similarly twisted the conclusions reached by Margarete Buber in *Under Two Dictators*. According to Harwood she proved that the concentration camps were comfortable institutions with sufficient food and facilities to allow inmates to live in relatively acceptable conditions. He identified the author as a German Jewish woman, who was the only Jew in her group of deportees from Russia who was not immediately allowed by the Gestapo to return to Russia.[40] There is nothing in the book to indicate that Buber was Jewish. More significant is the manner in which Harwood misconstrued her description of Ravensbrück. According to Harwood she found it 'clean, civilized and well-administered.' When she first arrived in 1940 she ate a meal of 'white bread, sausage, leek porridge and dried fruit.'[41] She lived in these comfortable circumstances until 1945, when 'she experienced the progressive decline of camp conditions.' In making this claim, Harwood was voicing a familiar argument. According to the deniers the terrible conditions of the camps were caused by the Allied destruction of the German civilian communication, transportation, and supply systems. The Allies, who wrought havoc on Germany's civilian infrastructure during the latter stages of the war, prevented the Germans from feeding camp inmates. That is why the survivors in the camps were in such an emaciated condition when the camps were opened. Harwood absolved the victimizers and blamed the victors, transforming the Allies into perpetrators responsible for much of the suffering that occurred in Germany. More to the purpose, something that could not be denied – the inmates' skeletal condition – was explained away.

But this version of Buber's account is totally at variance with what she actually says. Buber explicitly describes conditions that had broken down long before 1945. She made specific reference to executions, starvation, and terrible conditions that existed prior to the Allied raids of 1945. In addition to relating how inmates died as a result of being 'beaten, starved, or frozen to death in the punishment cells,' she made specific references to gas chambers and executions. Referring to the crematorium in the camp, she wrote the 'SS men were fond of telling us that the only way we should ever leave Ravensbrück would be "up the chimney."'[42] Harwood ignored these references in Buber's work, transforming a book that explicitly depicted the horror of the camps into one that renders them benign.*

Harwood also used selective quotations to turn Colin Cross's *Adolf Hitler* inside out. He claimed Cross concluded that moving millions of Jews around Europe and 'murdering them in a time of desperate war emergency was useless from any rational point of view.'[43] Harwood implied that Cross, in dismissing the annihilation program as totally irrational, believed it did not exist. Such is not the case; virtually all Holocaust scholars call attention to the fact that the Nazi annihilation of the Jews was irrational. Skilled workers were killed even if their tasks were unfinished. Precious freight cars needed to transport matériel to the front were used to carry Jews to their deaths. The Holocaust must be understood as something inherently lacking in functional reason. Therefore Cross's description of it as irrational cannot be interpreted as indicative of denial tendencies. As he had with Buber's book, Harwood ignored an array of passages that attested to Cross's firm belief that there had been a plan for the annihilation of the Jews: 'It was with the attack on the Soviet Union in 1941 that Hitler's policy switched decisively to mass murder.'[44] Neither was there doubt in Cross's mind about Hitler's role in the Final Solution:

---

* Buber's book contains a variety of historical flaws. I use her work not as a historical source but as an example of how deniers regularly falsify authors' conclusions.

Even the most cursory examination of the facts points to the extreme possibility that Hitler was not only aware of the policy but was its active instigator ... Moreover, Himmler repeatedly and definitely told his officials according to the minutes of meetings, that the extermination programme was based upon the leader's orders. Finally there are statements in Hitler's 'Testament' of 1945 in which are recounted the destruction of European Jewry as his achievement.[45]

Moreover, Cross stressed that the Holocaust was a 'fundamental' aspect of Hitler's policy. 'The number of men, women and children who were herded into gas chambers and murdered simply for being Jews did run into millions.'[46]

Harwood employed this tactic of trying to make a book say what it does not in an even more systematic fashion in his treatment of the three-volume 1948 report of the International Committee of the Red Cross (ICRC) on its attempts to assist those interned in camps. Blatantly misrepresenting the information contained in the report, Harwood tried to make it appear to lend credibility to the deniers' proclamations. He described it as the only survey regarding the Jewish question in Europe during World War II and the conditions of Germany's concentration camps that was not only 'unique in its honesty and objectivity' but strictly politically neutral. According to him it demonstrated that the International Red Cross had found no evidence 'whatever' in camps in Axis-occupied Europe of a 'deliberate policy to exterminate the Jews.'[47] Harwood contended that in all its sixteen hundred pages the report failed to make any mention of 'such a thing as a gas chamber.'* Though the ICRC admitted that Jews had suffered rigors and privations, as had many other wartime nationalities, 'its complete silence on the subject of planned extermination is ample refutation of the Six Million legend.'[48]

Harwood could make this claim only by ignoring key sections of the ICRC report. The Red Cross was absolutely specific about the Jews' fate. It made reference to the Nazi attempt to annihilate them, observing that under Nazi rule Jews had been transformed into

* The American publication *The Myth of the Six Million* made the same claim about the ICRC report (p. 101).

'outcasts condemned by rigid racial legislation to suffer tyranny, persecution and *systematic extermination*.'[49] The ICRC, which was empowered to exercise supervision over other prisoners and POWs, admitted it could not do this for the Jews. 'No kind of protection shielded them; being neither POW nor civilian internees, they formed a separate category without the benefit of any Convention.' Most important, the ICRC specifically delineated how systematic annihilation was carried out: 'They were penned into concentration camps and ghettos, recruited for forced labour, subjected to grave brutalities and sent to *death camps* without anyone being allowed to intervene in those matters.'[50] These were not the ICRC's only references to death camps or systematic annihilation. Among the other references were the following:

> During the period in September 1940, when the 'Iron Guard' [Romania] supported by the Gestapo and the German SS had seized power, the Jews had been subjected to persecution and deportation to *death camps*.[51]
>
> In Germany and her satellite countries, the lot of the civilians belonging to this group was by far the worst. Subjected as they were to a discriminatory regime, which aimed more or less openly at their *extermination*, they were unable to procure the necessities of life.[52]

Harwood contended that the report made 'nonsense' of the allegation that there were 'gas chambers cunningly disguised as shower facilities.' He substantiated this assertion by quoting a passage from the report that depicted how ICRC officials inspected baths and showers in the camps. When they found problems they acted swiftly 'to have fixtures made less primitive and to have them repaired or enlarged.'[53] This, Harwood argued, demonstrated conclusively that showers functioned as showers, however primitive, and not as killing apparatus. The problem with Harwood's choice of this citation, which he quoted correctly, is that the passage had nothing to do with German concentration camps: It referred to *Allied* camps for civilian internees in Egypt.[54]

Harwood repeatedly asserted that from August 1942 the ICRC was allowed to visit and distribute food parcels to major concentration camps in Germany, and that from February 1943 this privilege was extended to all other camps and prisons.[55] Harwood claimed that this information was to be found on page 78 of the report's third volume. The page did refer to 'major concentration camps' in Germany but indicated that they included only Dachau and Oranienburg. The concession that was extended in 1943 included all other camps and prisons *in* Germany.[56] This meant that numerous camps outside Germany were not included. Moreover, the Red Cross acknowledged that it was limited to giving parcels only to deported aliens for whom it had addresses, and that many inmates, among them the vast majority of Jews, were not allowed to receive food parcels at all.

In yet another attempt to misrepresent the ICRC's findings, Harwood contended that the relief organization had documented the fact that a significant proportion of European Jews had not been interned in camps 'but remained, subject to certain restrictions, as part of the free civilian population.' This, he declared, conflicted directly with Jewish claims that the 'extermination programme' was conducted with great 'thoroughness.' In this instance Harwood neglected to quote the opening paragraph of the chapter on which he based these assertions. It completely contradicted his claims regarding the Jews' fate:

> No other section of the population endured such humiliation, privation and suffering. Deprived of all treaty protection, persecuted in accordance with National Socialist doctrine and threatened with extermination, *the Jews were ... generally deported in the most inhuman manner, shut up in concentration camps, subjected to forced labour or put to death.*[57]

Harwood's misuse of the ICRC report is a reflection of how deniers, fairly certain that few people will be able to check the original material, twist information and findings. Rather than misquote, as with other sources, Harwood simply omits those numerous sections of the report which contradict his claims.

Harwood even used other sources to try to misrepresent the ICRC's findings. He claimed that a Swiss paper, *Die Tat*, had surveyed all World War II casualties and concluded, based on ICRC statistics, that the number of victims of political, racial, or religious persecution who died in prisons and concentration camps between 1939 and 1945 amounted to '300,000, not all of whom were Jews.' Harwood argued that this figure was the most accurate assessment of the number of victims.[58] The Swiss paper did cite the 300,000 figure, but only in reference to 'Germans and German Jews,' not nationals of other countries.[59] It did not conduct a survey of all World War II casualties and made no reference to Red Cross figures.

The ICRC, inundated with correspondence about these assertions, has repeatedly attempted to refute the deniers' claims. In 1978 the official *ICRC Bulletin* protested that the rescue agency 'has never published or even compiled statistics' of the kind that were being attributed to it. The work of the ICRC was to 'help war victims not to count them.' Even if it had wished to count victims, it could not have done so because its representatives were permitted to enter only a few concentration camps and 'only in the final days of the war.'[60] This was not the first time the ICRC tried to refute Harwood's charges. In 1975, after Harwood's pamphlet appeared in England and increasing numbers of right-wing groups began to re-iterate the claims about the record of the humanitarian organization, the central office of the ICRC wrote to the Board of Deputies of British Jews in London regarding Harwood's citations: 'The figures cited by the author of the booklet are based upon statistics falsely attributed to us, evidently for the purpose of giving them credibility, despite the fact that we never publish information of this kind.'[61]

Despite the various attempts by the ICRC to set the historical record straight, the deniers have continued to rely on this disinformation. In 1985 at the trial of Ernst Zundel, a German immigrant who was accused by the Canadian government of publishing and distributing Holocaust denial materials, including *Did Six Million Really Die?*, these false claims regarding the ICRC were introduced by the defense as a means of demonstrating that the relief agency thought the Holocaust was a myth.[62]

In a fashion that has become typical of all deniers, Harwood relied on traditional antisemitic stereotypes to make his case. He asserted that Germany's persecution of the Jews was the major reason the

Allies went to war.[63] This claim was intended to buttress the anti-semitic stereotype of the power of the Jews to compel the Allies to accede to their wishes. Harwood conveniently ignored the fact that Germany began the war by attacking Poland on September 1, 1939. The United States, which was well aware of the extent of the suffering of the Jews, did not enter the war in Europe until after Pearl Harbor, when Germany declared war on the United States. All the Allies had carefully tracked Germany's treatment of the Jews since 1933. They had not declared war on Nazi Germany after the Nuremberg laws, Kristallnacht, or any of the numerous indignities meted out to the Jews in the prewar period. The United States, which knew of the massacres of Jews on the Russian front in 1941, did not act to help. Clearly, had it been mistreatment of the Jews that prompted the Allies to act, they should have gone to war long before they did.

Harwood also misconstrued the Nuremberg trials. He claimed that the court accepted three hundred thousand 'written affidavits' containing charges against those accused of war crimes. Harwood insisted that the large number of affidavits was indicative of the extent of the hoax. At the Zundel trial Raul Hilberg, who was called as an expert witness, estimated that in the aggregate approximately forty thousand documents had been submitted by the prosecution. Included in these were copies of German correspondence and Third Reich documentation. Notwithstanding the fact that the assertions regarding three hundred thousand affidavits has no basis in truth, it has become a standard part of Holocaust denial. Harwood's most outlandish assertion regarding the trial was that defense lawyers at Nuremberg were prevented from cross-examining prosecution witnesses.[64] The most cursory examination of the records of the Nuremberg trials indicates that attorneys had the opportunity to conduct cross-examinations.

Harwood also attempted to convince readers that the *Diary of Anne Frank* was a fraud. In a section entitled 'Best-Seller a Hoax,' he asserted that the *Diary* was part of the 'fabrication of a propaganda legend.'[65] Harwood was not the first to try to cast doubt on the authenticity of the *Diary*. He was building on attacks on the *Diary*'s credibility that had begun as early as 1957. (For a more complete discussion of the deniers' campaign against the *Diary* see appendix.)

This theme would be more fully developed by French denier Robert Faurisson and would be at least partially responsible for the 1989 decision of the Netherlands State Institute for War Documentation to issue a critical edition of the *Diary* firmly verifying its authenticity.[66]

Given the vast array of misstatements, misquotes, and outright falsifications in Harwood's pamphlet, questions regarding its impact remain. Until the publication of *The Hoax of the Twentieth Century*, by Arthur Butz of Northwestern University, it remained the most frequently cited work on Holocaust denial. Because it is shorter and more cheaply reproduced than Butz's, it remains in circulation today. It is, of course, impossible to assess the precise degree to which it has entered mainstream literature. But on at least one occasion its arguments were cited virtually verbatim in a major British publication – not as examples of distortions and fallacious findings by a right-wing extremist, but as legitimate historical research.

In 1974 a lengthy two-part review of Joachim Fest's biography of Hitler appeared in the English magazine *books and bookmen*.* The review was written by Colin Wilson, a well-known British novelist and critic, who periodically reviewed books for the magazine. At the end of the second part of his review of Fest's book, the reviewer added what he himself described as 'a curious – but highly relevant – postscript.'[67] Wilson related that a number of years earlier he had received an advertisement from a Dublin publisher for *The Myth of the Six Million*. 'Curious' about this, he sent off for it, only to discover that the publisher had sold out. While he was writing the Fest review he received the pamphlet by Richard Harwood of the University of London. Wilson summarized Harwood's argument:

> What Harwood says, briefly, is that Hitler had no reason to murder Jews when he needed them for forced labour. He goes on to point out that the total number of Jews in Europe before the war was six and a half millions [*sic*], and that one and a half million emigrated abroad. Harwood cites figures from international organizations – all quoted – to demonstrate that there were not more than three million Jews in Nazi Germany.[68]

* Joachim C. Fest, *Hitler* (London, 1974).

Wilson was impressed by Harwood's denial of the existence of extermination camps and accepted as fact his allegation that most of the memoirs about the camps were 'journalistic forgeries, churned out like pornography for an audience that revels in horrors.' He also believed Harwood accurately cited figures from international organizations such as the ICRC. Wilson acknowledged that when he checked Raul Hilberg's 'gigantic, half-million word' book and the fifty-plus other books he had in his library on the topic he found it hard to believe that the Holocaust was 'all an invention.' He conceded that there was plenty of evidence to prove that the Third Reich detested Jews and that Hitler would have 'thought nothing of exterminating' them. Nonetheless, after reading Harwood's volume he found it pertinent to ask whether the Nazis had really exterminated *six million* Jews or whether claims that they had were just another 'emotional historical distortion.' Finally, in his most provocative musing thus far – others would follow – he wondered, if the Final Solution had indeed been a hoax, 'would it not be better to be prepared to face the whole truth, no matter how unpleasant?'[69] Wilson left no doubt that Harwood had convinced him of the unpleasant truth: The Holocaust was a myth.

As was to be expected, Wilson's ruminations launched an avalanche of letters to the magazine, including two from Harwood. Many of the letters cited evidence contradicting Harwood's conclusions. In the face of such information Wilson became even more passionate in his defense of Harwood's views. In response to this barrage of letters he offered a strange prediction that, it could be argued, reflected his own personal biases: 'Some time over the next ten years or so, an Israeli historian is going to write a book called *The Myth of the Six Million*. It will cause a tremendous scandal; he will be violently attacked – and will become a rich man. And no one will be able to accuse him of being anti-Jewish.'[70] Wilson was trying to bolster his case by relying on the same argument made by both Barnes and App: Jews accuse those who question the existence of the Holocaust of being antisemites in order to silence them.

Regarding the books he had collected on the topic, he wrote, 'I would like to know how many of my fifty books on the death camps are forgeries.'[71] His willingness tacitly to accept Harwood's contention that the books were forgeries or 'communist propaganda,' and to ignore the possibility that Harwood might be the forger, is particularly telling. In response to still more letters, he described Harwood's tone as 'reasonable and logical' and 'devoid of hysteria or emotional antisemitism.' He explained that Harwood made sense to him because he quoted figures and listed his sources and his tone was 'generally rather pedantic.' This evaluation by Wilson is further evidence of why the new pseudo-academic style adopted by deniers in recent years is so dangerous. Their packaging, which mimics legitimate scholarly research, confuses consumers. Readers are more susceptible to being influenced by an academic style than by poorly printed extremist and racist publications.[72]

In response to attacks for espousing Harwood's views, Wilson protested almost reflexively that he was not anti-Nazi or anti-Jewish but 'deeply pro "objectivity."' Such protestations are reminiscent of deniers' claims that they are only interested in the truth and harbor no sympathies toward Nazis or antipathies toward Jews.[73]

The controversy continued until June 1975. Eventually even the editors of *books and bookmen* felt compelled to respond to readers who criticized the magazine for assigning Harwood's work for review. The editors assured readers that the pamphlet was 'never sent to Colin Wilson for review by *b&b* nor has it ever been the subject of a review in *b&b*.'[74] Wilson had included it on his own. The penultimate letter the editors published on this controversy was from Harwood himself. In it he reiterated his false claims regarding the *Chambers Encyclopedia*'s estimates of the prewar Jewish population of Europe. It was followed by a letter that can be interpreted as the magazine's final editorial comment on the entire matter. The letter writer wondered if the deniers could explain: 'What happened to my German Jewish parents, grandparents and cousins, since I find it hard to attribute their deaths, attested to by the International Red Cross, either to Nazi benevolence or Russian propaganda.'[75]

In the face of this query there was only silence.

7
Entering the Mainstream

The Case of Arthur Butz

In 1976 a previously unknown professor of electrical engineering at Northwestern University in Evanston, Illinois, initiated a concerted effort to win Holocaust denial scholarly and historical legitimacy. Arthur R. Butz, author of *The Hoax of the Twentieth Century*, garnered considerable attention, and his book was the subject of news stories in some of the nation's major papers. Butz's position as a professor at one of the more prestigious universities in the country enhanced the sense of controversy. It was hard for the public to reconcile Holocaust denial with the pursuit of truth to which universities and their faculty are supposedly dedicated. But there was another draw as well: Taking a different tack than his predecessors, Butz not only revealed a more subtle, sophisticated and, ultimately, devious approach to this material, but he also significantly changed the nature of Holocaust denial.

Relatively little is known of Butz.[1] Born in the mid-1940s in New York of German and Italian ancestry, he graduated from MIT and received his Ph.D. from the University of Minnesota. What distinguishes Butz from virtually all the deniers who preceded him was the veneer of scholarship and the impression of seriousness and objectivity he is able to convey. Tenured at Northwestern University since 1974, he is well versed in academic etiquette. His book's format indicated that he understood the structure and nuances of scholarly debate and would use them to his advantage. In contrast to many of the previous publications, particularly the poorly printed pamphlets that had typified much of denial writing, Butz's book contained the requisite myriad notes and large bibliography that were the hall-marks of scholarly works, quoting many of the prominent historians who worked in this field and thanking a number of legitimate research centers and archives. At first glance there were few reasons to question the book's true import or intent but readers who were aware of the identity of the publishers would have had little trouble discerning either. In England the book was brought out by the His-torical Review Press, which had published Richard Harwood's *Did Six Million Really Die?* In the United States the book was released by Noontide Press.[2]

But it was not just the form of Butz's publication that distin-guished it from its predecessors. His putative willingness to confront a host of issues most deniers had previously ignored gave the book a different tone – one that was clearly designed to disarm innocent readers and enhance Butz's aura of scholarly objectivity. He criti-cized contemporary deniers, describing *The Myth of the Six Million*, the American denial publication on which Richard Harwood based much of his work, as full of 'errors of fact.'[3] Nor did he try to white-wash German wartime behavior. Of equal importance in establishing his scholarly veneer was his willingness to concede that as many as a million Jews may have actually died at the hands of the Nazis. More-over, he acknowledged that the *Einsatzgruppen* may have actually murdered civilians and that Jews were singled out for special perse-cution by the Germans and suffered in concentration camps.

In contrast to Barnes, App, Rassinier, and others, Butz did not justify the German persecution of the Jews by claiming that Jews were disloyal, untrustworthy, or intent on causing Germany's down-fall. He gave the impression of being a serious scholar who was critical of Nazi antisemitism.[4] Closer examination revealed that he harbored precisely the same attitudes and used the same method-ology that had characterized all Holocaust denial literature up to this point. The packaging had changed but the contents remained the same. Anything that disagreed with Butz's foregone conclusion and the thesis of his book – that the story of Jewish extermination in World War II was a propaganda hoax and that the Jews of Europe had not been exterminated[5] – was dismissed as 'obvious lies,' 'ludicrous,' 'breathtakingly absurd,' 'absolutely insane,' 'fishy,' 'obviously spurious,' and 'nonsense.'[6] 'Survivor' literature – the term is always placed in quotes – is dismissed as full of 'endless raving about extermination.' Despite his attempt to project a scholarly aura, however, Butz allows his rhetoric to fall into a very different category: American diplomats engaged in 'hysterical yapping about the six million,'[7] and stories of 'gas chambers' were 'wartime propaganda fantasies,' 'garbage,' and 'tall tales.'[8]

Evincing the same sympathies as previous generations of deniers, Butz declared that the greatest tragedy was that the Germans and Austrians had been the real victims.[9] He also showed the same antipathies as those who had preceded him. Describing Jews as among 'the most powerful groups on earth,' he argued that they possessed formidable powers to manipulate governments, control war crimes trials, govern the media, and determine other nations' foreign policy, all in the name of perpetrating the hoax of the twentieth century.[10] According to Butz, Jews invented this hoax in order to further 'Zionist ends.'[11] Thus one could extrapolate from Butz's argument that whatever antisemitism the Nazis displayed was well justified. This demonology, common to virtually every denier, is an affirmation of Nazi ideology. The Nazis depicted Aryans as the 'master race' – strong and invincible. Jews, in contrast, were not human. Despite their superiority Aryans were considered highly vulnerable to Jewish conspiracies. The Jews' ability to create the hoax had proven the Nazi thesis correct: They were a threat to the world.

In the book and in subsequent articles published in the *Journal of Historical Review*, Butz acknowledged the validity of a number of the criticisms commonly directed at deniers, including that their ranks numbered no historians with any scholarly academic standing. Bemoaning this, Butz attributed it to the fact that respected scholars had been frightened away from questioning something as 'established as the Great Pyramid.' It was because of the 'default' by professional historians that nonhistorians such as himself were left with the responsibility for exposing the 'idiotic nonsense' of the Holocaust.[12]

In order to mainstream Holocaust denial and attain for it scholarly respectability, Butz also had to acknowledge that denial books,

articles, and journals are published by neo-Nazi, extremist, and racist groups, side by side with intensely nationalist or white-supremacist
racial diatribes. Attempting to deflect this criticism, Butz agreed that
in an optimal situation deniers' work would appear in scholarly journals, but the normal channels of scholarly research had been blocked
to those who would reveal the 'truth.' In the interest of exposing the
hoax, those who worked in this field had no option but to turn to
these ideological publications. When he depicted the deniers as martyrs willing to risk their reputations by appearing in these publications
because they had no other option, he ignored the intensive, symbiotic
relationship – far more than a marriage of inconvenience – that
existed between these groups.

Since the publication of the book, Butz, who has assiduously tried
to maintain his image as a disinterested scholar, has been associated
with a variety of extremist and neo-Nazi groups. His books are
promoted and distributed by the Ku Klux Klan and other neo-Nazi
organizations. When his book first appeared it was serialized in the
neo-Nazi German weekly *Deutsche National Zeitung*. In 1985 he
presented his hoax ideas at the Savior's Day meeting of Louis Farrakhan's Nation of Islam.[13]

Despite its veneer of impartial scholarship, Butz's book is replete
with the same expressions of traditional antisemitism, philo-Germanism
and conspiracy theory as the Holocaust denial pamphlets printed by
the most scurrilous neo-Nazi groups. This is particularly evident
when he turns to the hoax itself and the 'culprits' responsible for it.
Although Jews were the instigators, they engineered this effort with
the assistance of other forces. Together they formed a vast conspiratorial network that, despite the broad assortment of groups involved,
managed to keep its existence a secret. According to Butz all these
vastly different forces were coordinated by Zionists, who nurtured
the legend until it achieved the stature of an international, historical
hoax.[14] A complex and convoluted process that involved multitudi-
nous forces, it remained undetected, amazingly, until a professor of
electrical engineering conducted his own brand of historical research.

Butz's list of culpable parties is all-encompassing. He blames the
'Zionist International' and the Communists as well as the U.S.

government's War Refugee Board and Office of Strategic Services.[15] In addition the New York-based research institute YIVO; U.S. government officials; the prosecutors and judges at the war crimes trials; Polish-Jewish 'propagandists'; and Soviet officials all helped perpetrate this fraud, aided and abetted by the media and such international welfare organizations as the Red Cross.[16]

Butz vacillated between holding Jews solely responsible for this 'Jewish hoax' – which was also a 'Zionist hoax'[17] – and presenting it as the result of a cooperative effort in which Washington, London, Moscow, Jerusalem, and Jews everywhere had participated. Using their political power, Jews had amassed a broad array of allies, 'official Washington' among them.[18] It is noteworthy that those Jews who pressured Washington to cooperate in the hoax were the same ones who were unable to convince it during the prewar and war years to liberalize the immigration system, open its doors to the nine hundred Jews on the *St. Louis*, admit German Jewish refugee children, transport refugees on empty transport ships returning from Europe, or permit any more than a token number of Jews to enter the United States during the war itself.[19]* Butz would have us believe that the same Jews whose rescue record was a dismal failure were somehow able to manipulate Washington into participating in this massive hoax.

According to Butz the key to perpetrating the hoax was the forging of massive numbers of documents, an act committed with the complicity of Allied governments. There was no shortage of people to assist in this endeavor: Hundreds of trained staff members were sent to Europe in the immediate aftermath of the war. They were responsible for 'a fabrication constructed of perjury, forgery, distortion of fact and misrepresentation of documents.'[20] Without being discovered by anyone, they created reports by *Einsatzgruppen* commanders listing the precise cities in which massacres had been conducted and the exact numbers of men, women, and children who had been killed. They prepared documents purporting to be official

---

* The *St. Louis* was the German ship that was turned away from Cuba in May 1939 because the Cuban government had invalidated the landing certificates of the refugees on board. When the ship tried to land in Miami government officials denied permission.

communiqués from the highest-ranking offices of the Third Reich. Not only were they able to falsify and fabricate at will, but they even succeeded in planting the documents in the correct places so that those who were not part of the hoax would happen upon them. So complete was their control that they were able to determine whether the war crimes courts received genuine documents, forged documents, or no documents at all.[21] They even created false recordings of speeches by Nazi leaders and inserted them into the materials collected by the liberating forces.[22] Without their scheme being discovered and exposed by anyone, these hundreds of forgers – working in both Western and Eastern zones, and with the acquiescence of American, British, French, and Soviet officials – somehow managed, in an incredibly short space of time, to produce thousands of documents, all of which were designed to prove that the Nazis intended to annihilate the Jews.

The most important question was never addressed by either Butz or any of his compatriots: Why, if the 'propagandists' responsible for the hoax were so successful at producing such a vast array of documents, did they not produce the one piece of paper deniers claim would convince them there had been a Final Solution – that is, an order from Hitler authorizing the destruction of the Jews?

Butz attempted to explain away Nazi references to extermination, including Hitler's repeated use of the phrase '*Vernichtung des Judentums*,' the destruction of Jewry. He acknowledged that while it could be interpreted to mean 'the killing of all Jews,' Hitler had used it to mean the 'destruction of Jewish influence and power.' Recognizing that this stretched the parameters of rational explanation, Butz reluctantly conceded that Hitler 'could have chosen his words more carefully.'[23]

But it was not only Hitler's references to extermination that were problematic. Himmler, in his famous October 1943 Posen speech to the SS, spoke of the 'annihilation' of the Jews:

> I am referring to the evacuation of the Jews, the annihilation of the Jewish people. This is one of those things that are easily said. 'The Jewish people is going to be annihilated,' says every party member.

'Sure, it is our program, elimination of the Jews, annihilation – we'll take care of it.' And then they all come trudging, 80 million worthy Germans, and each one has one decent Jew. Sure, the others are swine, but this one is an A-1 Jew. Of all those who talk this way, not one has seen it happen, not one has been through it. Most of you must know what it means to see a hundred corpses lie side by side, or five hundred, or a thousand. To have stuck this out and – excepting cases of human weakness – to have kept our integrity, that is what has made us hard. In our history, this is an unwritten and never-to-be-written page of glory, for we know how difficult we would have made it for ourselves if today – amid the bombing raids, the hardships and the deprivations of war – we still had the Jews in every city as secret saboteurs, agitators, and demagogues. If the Jews were still ensconced in the body of the German nation, we probably would have reached the 1916–17 stage by now.*

It was critically important for Butz to destroy the credibility of this speech because of its explicit references to the annihilation program.

For those unwilling to dismiss the speech as a forgery, Butz suggested that the corpses to which Himmler referred were actually corpses of Germans killed by Allied air raids[24] – a suggestion rendered preposterous by even the most cursory examination of that portion of Himmler's speech.[25]

Butz even tried to cast doubt on Hitler's last will and testament. In it the Nazi leader, well aware that his entire Reich had crumbled around him, identified the Jews as 'the race that is the real guilty party in this murderous struggle' and observed that he had kept his promise that the real culprits would pay for their guilt. Butz, aware that since the document bore Hitler's signature it would be difficult to dismiss it as a forgery, suggested that it might have been 'tampered with.'[26] However, he offered no evidence to support his contention. Apparently cognizant of the fact that this was not a very convincing argument, he assured readers that even if the will were genuine, it should not be taken seriously because it simply typified the tendency

---

* In 1916 the Germans began to lose World War I. The National Socialists attributed this loss to a 'stab in the back' administered by the Jews.

of all politicians, before terminating their public careers, 'to exaggerate the significance of their work.'[27]

Butz seemed oblivious to the disturbing implications of his attempt to explain away the true meaning of Hitler's statements by casting the will as an exaggeration. Exaggeration has a number of functions: It can serve to amplify one's own merits and positive accomplishments, compensate for one's failings, or consciously agitate one's followers to take certain actions. What function did Butz think Hitler's 'exaggerations' served in this regard? Was he exaggerating in order to compensate for his failure to see this 'murderous' struggle through to the end? Was he exaggerating in order to amplify his own merits, which in this case included the persecution of the Jews? Or was he exaggerating as a form of triumphalism to celebrate acts of oppression terrible enough, according to Butz's estimate, to have resulted in the death of a million Jews? Whatever the particular function Butz had in mind, his suggestion that Hitler would want 'to exaggerate the significance' of this particular aspect of his 'work' bespeaks a very strange notion of National Socialism's 'triumphs;' in fact, his reasoning is reminiscent of App's argument that the fact that some Jews survived is proof that no Jews were killed.

In order to convince his readers that the Holocaust is *the* propaganda hoax of the century, if not of recorded history, Butz had to demonstrate that the testimony of numerous war crimes defendants confirming the existence of an annihilation program was false. First he tried to shed doubt on the credibility of witnesses in general by declaring all testimony inferior to documents. His reasons for making this pronouncement were evident.[28] The extensive testimony that exists, whether it comes from victims, perpetrators, bystanders, or neutral parties, all confirms the existence of an annihilation program. Documents could be discounted as forgeries, declared to have been 'tampered with,' or interpreted in a tangled fashion to satisfy a particular ideological bent. It would have been more difficult – though Butz, like all deniers, tried to do so – to dismiss everyone who spoke of an extermination program as either a liar, dupe, propagandist, or self-incriminator.

Butz's preference for documents notwithstanding, he still had to explain away those defendants who said, 'I was there,' 'I saw the killings,' or 'I heard Hitler and Himmler speak of the extermination of the Jews.' Indeed, Butz's resourcefulness in this regard constitutes the most 'creative' aspect of his book. Breaking ranks with previous deniers, he dismissed the explanation that the only reason Nuremberg defendants confessed was because they had been tortured into admitting their guilt. He argued that they recognized that since the world was convinced that a Holocaust had taken place, they could not possibly deny it and hope to be believed. Though they had done no wrong, the world was intent on finding them guilty. Since protesting their innocence would have been counterproductive, the defendants and their lawyers decided that the best tactic was to plead guilty. This approach provided Butz with a reply to one of the most oft-heard criticisms directed at deniers: If the Holocaust is a hoax why did the Nazi defendants themselves acknowledge that it happened? For Butz it was all quite simple: It was better to admit to the crime of the century and risk losing one's life than to protest against a monstrous fraud. However, in pursuing this theory, Butz ignored a basic problem: If the end result promised to be the same – a death sentence – what purpose was served by falsely pleading guilty to such a vicious act?

Butz still had to try to discredit defendants who not only testified that the annihilation happened but admitted their complicity in it. Why would defendants confess to personal involvement in such a horrendous crime when they knew that they were innocent and the charges a hoax? Their objective, Butz explained, was to do whatever was necessary to survive while a temporary wave of 'post-war hysteria' swept Germany. Thus they deferred setting the record straight to a future time when the truth could emerge.[29]

Because not all the defendants behaved in the same fashion, Butz had to find different ways to demonstrate that their confessions had been duplicitous. Those who admitted that it had occurred – even though they knew it had not – but argued that they had had nothing to do with it, did so in order to shift the blame onto someone else. This made 'it politically possible for the court to be lenient.'[30] Oswald Pohl, the high-ranking SS officer in charge of the concentration camp system who oversaw the transfer back to Germany of all the personal possessions of Jews who had been killed, fell into this category. Essentially responsible for running the camps and for the economic aspect of the Final Solution, Pohl was condemned to death for his role. He testified at the 1947 war crimes trial that he had heard Himmler deliver his famous 1943 speech to the SS leaders in Posen.[31] Butz declared this to have been part of Pohl's legal strategy to exploit the culpability of the SS leadership by engaging in a 'self-serving' attempt to blame those who could not defend themselves.[32]

Butz offered yet another explanation for the defendants' confessions: They had made a mistake. They had not meant to confess to the existence of an annihilation program. They had not comprehended the questions posed to them by their captors. Though their answers made it sound as if they were acknowledging the existence of a death plan, in reality they were not. For example, when Hermann Göring explicitly accepted that there had been mass murders, he was confused. Asked about the mounds of corpses or the high number of deaths, he misunderstood the question. He thought he was being asked about German concentration camps, where many corpses had been found. Had he grasped the question, he would have told the Allies that those corpses were the result of the difficult circumstances that existed toward the end of the war – circumstances that resulted from *Allied* actions.[33] How men who had reached positions of incredible power in the German Reich could have misunderstood such serious questions that would determine their own fate remains a mystery, as does why they did not clarify their answers when they saw how they were being interpreted.

Butz also claimed that defendants' confessions about the Holocaust were the result of their having been subjected since the end of the war to a barrage of 'familiar propaganda': These former leaders of Nazi Germany had themselves become victims of the hoax. One must marvel at the power of those responsible for the hoax. Not only had they won the cooperation of the world's greatest military and political powers, forged thousands of pages of documents in record time without being detected, and created physical evidence attesting to an annihilation program, but among their most impressive achievements was success at convincing the very people they accused of perpetrating the hoax that it had actually happened. According to Butz even this did not exhaust the full extent of Jewish powers. Their most impressive accomplishment was winning the defendants' co-operation in their *own* incrimination! They persuaded Nazi leaders not only to testify to the veracity of the myth but to sign their own names to the forged documents. 'Jewish propagandists' convinced the defendants that this would win them clemency from the prosecutors and the court.[34] That is why some documents have signatures that cannot be dismissed as forgeries. Butz never explained why, long after the war crimes tribunals were concluded, defendants did not come forward and say they had lied in order to win lenient treatment. In fact, many of them continued to acknowledge that the annihilation had happened and that they had played a role in it.

Butz declared that the conspirators not only concocted the proofs to establish the hoax as fact but had won the cooperation of the mass media in disseminating the story. Motivated by both gullibility and culpability, the mass media in Western democracies constituted 'a lie machine of vaster extent than even many of the more independent minded have perceived.'[35] These charges hark back to the work of Rassinier, App, and Barnes and evoke what has become a standard litany of antisemitic charges regarding Jews' control of the banks and the media.

Butz dismissed the media as a 'lie machine' for disseminating the Holocaust legend. At the same time, however, he used the media's wartime failure to highlight news of the annihilation as proof that the story was false[36] (if it were true, the media would have stressed it). This 'explanation' ignored an array of other factors that governed the media's and much of the rest of the world's response to this story.[37]* It also failed to address the fact that all the Allied governments publicly condemned it in December 1942 and a number of papers did consistently feature the story, among them the *New Republic*, *Nation*, *PM*, the Hearst papers, and the Catholic journal *Commonweal*. Butz's 'explanation' had its own internal contradiction: How could

---

* The most significant was its unprecedented nature.

the Jews have had such control over the media after the war but virtually none during it?

Butz favorably contrasted the record of the Nazi press with that of the American media. The refusal of newspapers in the Third Reich to even mention the 'Jewish extermination claim' was evidence that it was on a higher level than the Allied press. Butz credited the German press for ignoring the propaganda about death camps and focusing its attention on 'legitimate' questions such as the 'extent and means of Jewish influence in the Allied press.'[38] Butz's citation of the Nazi press as an example of high-level journalism, when all forms of public information in the Third Reich were under absolute government control, is itself significant. So, too, is his description of the question of Jewish control of the media as a 'legitimate' one. These are reliable indicators of his own worldview.

But references to the annihilation of the Jews were contained not only in German documents and the testimony of war crimes defendants. As we have seen in the discussion of Richard Harwood's work, the ICRC's report specifically mentioned the 'extermination' programs. It is in his treatment of the report that Butz parts company with deniers such as Harwood and his anonymous American counterpart. He did not deny that the ICRC made specific reference to extermination, but he offered a series of explanations as to why these references to 'extermination' did not mean just that. Butz insisted that the ICRC capitulated to external political pressures to inject into the report an 'anti-German bias.'[39] The references to extermination placated the Allies in general and the Russians in particular.[40] Readers who rejected the notion that the ICRC was willing to acquiesce in such tactics were offered another explanation. The ICRC, just like some of the war crimes defendants, was a victim of the hoax. Despite the humanitarian agency's experiences in Europe during the war, its postwar thinking was contorted by the war crimes trials, with their forged documents and spurious testimony.[41]

Finally the reader was warned that the ICRC report which described the aid the relief agency had provided European Jewry was 'self-serving.' Butz argued that it was typical of a charitable organization's publications to exaggerate the efficacy of the help it rendered and that the ICRC may have done less than the report claimed. In probably one of the more revealing observations in the book, he consoled his readers: 'We should not be crushed if it were found that the Hungarian Jewish children or the Jews who walked to Vienna, both of whom were aided by the Red Cross, actually suffered a little bit more than might seem suggested by the *Report*.'[42] His contention that readers might not be 'crushed' to learn that Jewish children suffered more than the report suggested they did offers a frightening insight into Butz's sentiments.

Butz's treatment of the report reflected the flaws in his methodology. He diminished its trustworthiness, accusing the authors of being political pawns, duped by the hoax. However, when it served his purposes, this same report became an authoritative source for determining that the Holocaust had been a hoax. At one point the report mentioned that many of the inhabitants of Theresienstadt had been 'transfer[red] to Auschwitz.' Given the report's repeated references to extermination, there was little doubt as to what that statement meant. But Butz postulated that because there were no 'sinister interpretations' placed on that remark, the Red Cross did not think it meant anything notorious. For everyone but Butz and his cadre of deniers, the words 'transfer to Auschwitz' were sinister enough; no further comment was necessary.

This attempt to give meaning to the absence of a specific statement is reminiscent of an incident that occurred during the trial of Adolf Eichmann when Pastor Heinrich Gruber, a Protestant minister, appeared as a witness. During the war he had repeatedly attempted to persuade Eichmann to ameliorate the treatment of the Jews. He had asked that unleavened bread be sent to Hungarian Jews for Passover and had traveled to Switzerland to urge his Christian friends to obtain immigration visas and entry permits for Jews. He even tried to visit the concentration camp at Gurs in southern France, where Jews were living in horrendous conditions. He was incarcerated in a concentration camp for his efforts. At his trial Eichmann tried to prove that his behavior during the war had been acceptable to the German public, arguing that no one had 'reproached' him for anything in the performance of his duties. 'Not even Pastor Gruber claims to have done so.' Eichmann acknowledged that Gruber had sought alleviation of Jewish suffering but had 'not actually object[ed] to the very performance of my duties as such.'[43]

Eichmann and Butz used the same tangled kind of thinking to try to make a situation appear to be other than it was. Eichmann argued that because the pastor had not specifically said 'Stop the extermination,' he approved of it. So, too, Butz contended that because the ICRC report did not explicitly mention extermination in relation to 'transfer to Auschwitz,' those words meant nothing sinister.

Butz's treatment of the ICRC report was a prime example of how he tried to play both ends against the middle, claiming that the ICRC officials had been duped while at the same time citing their statement to prove that nothing sinister happened at Auschwitz. As with his treatment of the media, such internal contradictions are standard elements of his methodology. In fact, it is possible for a portion of an individual's testimony or a particular document to contain errors while other portions are correct. Witnesses in a court of law often differ on the details surrounding an event but agree on the essential element. It is axiomatic among attorneys, prosecutors, and judges that human memory is notoriously bad on issues of dimensions and precise numbers but very reliable on the central event. Nevertheless, one of the deniers' favorite tactics is to charge that if a defendant errs in one portion of his testimony, then all of it must be dismissed as false.

But Butz engaged in a different tactic in relation to both the media and the ICRC. He was not declaring that they had made occasional errors but that they had to be rejected in their entirety as factual sources because they themselves constituted 'vast lie machine[s]' and political pawns. And then he tried to use both these institutions as reliable judges of what happened. Butz cannot have it both ways: Either they were telling the truth about the essential elements or they were not. It cannot be logically argued that when the ICRC spoke of 'extermination' it was speaking as a political pawn or a victim of the hoax, but when it spoke of 'transfer to Auschwitz' it was indicating that there was no Holocaust.

Butz advanced no independent source of evidence to corroborate his conclusions. Scholars in any field (including electrical engineering) look for data to verify their conclusions. Deniers consistently ignore existing evidence that contradicts their claims. Many years ago Saint Anselm, a prominent figure in the medieval church, spoke of 'faith in search of reason.' Such is the work of the deniers. Their faith that the Holocaust did not happen leads them to shape reason, facts, and history for their own purposes.

Butz could not conclude his attempt to create his hoax theory without addressing the question of the 'missing' Jews. What happened to the Jews whose immediate family say they were killed? He proposed various explanations but offered no proof to support them. First, he scattered these Jews in different places – most, he claimed, throughout the Soviet Union.[44] In addition, at least fifty thousand entered the United States. These phantom Jews settled in New York City, where they were able to avoid detection because there were already millions of Jews. Who 'would have noticed a hundred thousand more?'[45]

What, then, about all the 'survivors' who claimed that their immediate families had been killed? Butz suggested that they may have well been lying and that others may not have been lying but mistaken in thinking their families had been murdered when in fact they were really alive.[46] Where then had they gone? They survived the war but did 'not reestablish contact with [their] prewar relatives.'[47] While some survivors may have been forbidden by the Soviet Union from contacting their families, Butz offered 'a more plausible motivation': Many of these survivors were in marriages that were 'held together by purely social and economic constraints.'[48] Those constraints were dissolved by the war. In the postwar period these 'lonely wives and husbands' found other partners and established relationships that were 'more valuable' than their previous ones.[49] Abandoning their spouses, children, and other relatives, they started a new life, becoming part of the hoax in order to justify their decision. (This casual explanation of why these people deserted their families could be dismissed as amusing were the topic not so serious.)

Obviously aware that this could not account for even a fraction of the people who are missing, Butz expanded on how this part of the hoax operated. One person was reported missing by a spouse, children, parents, siblings, and in-laws. Consequently one Jew was repeatedly counted as a victim. 'The possibilities for accounting for missing Jews in this way are practically boundless.'[50] Assuring readers of the credibility of this thesis, Butz observed that he too had 'lost contact with a great many former friends and acquaintances but I assume that nearly all are still alive.'[51] Even by Butz's own standards of what happened to the Jews – they were forcibly moved from their homes, placed in ghettos, incarcerated in work camps, separated from their families, and forced to live under such difficult circumstances that one million died – such a statement was casual and callous. Given the reality of what did happen, it was far more than that.

Every author aspires to some form of immortality, hoping that his or her work will continue to speak beyond the limits of the years. Butz has achieved that. His conclusions are posted on numerous computer bulletin boards, including both mainstream ones as well as those associated with the Klan and neo-Nazis. Armed vigilante groups cite Butz's conclusions to legitimate their antisemitism.[52] Fascists, racists, and radical extremists all weave his conclusions into their worldview. Together with such other infamous works as the *Protocols of the Elders of Zion*, it will serve as a standard against which other implausible and prejudicial theories will be measured.

8

The Institute for Historical Review

Late in the summer of 1979 on the campus of a private technical school near Los Angeles Airport, a relatively obscure organization, the Institute for Historical Review (IHR), convened the first Revisionist Convention. At that time the IHR, which had been founded the previous year, had garnered little publicity. Most people who were aware of its existence dismissed it as a conglomeration of Holocaust deniers, neo-Nazis, philo-Germans, right-wing extremists, anti-semites, racists, and conspiracy theorists. At the meeting the director of the institute, a man known to those gathered there as Lewis Brandon, announced that the IHR would pay a reward of fifty thousand dollars to anyone who 'could prove that the Nazis operated gas-chambers to exterminate Jews during World War II.' Brandon, whose real name (it would soon be learned) was William David McCalden, subsequently admitted that the offer was never a serious endeavor but was designed as the linchpin of the institute's publicity-seeking campaign: 'The reward was a gimmick to attract publicity.' McCalden boasted to readers of the IHR's journal, the *Journal of Historical Review*, that the plan was a great success. It generated newspaper clippings that could be measured in 'vertical inches.' McCalden's enthusiasm notwithstanding, the stunt actually ended up costing the IHR dearly.[1]

McCalden, who in addition to Lewis Brandon used a series of other pseudonyms, including Sondra Ross, David Berg, Julius Finkelstein, and David Stanford, was born in 1951 in Belfast, Northern Ireland, where he attended grade school and high school.[2] He then received a teaching certificate from the University of London. He was known in England for his neofascist and extremist involvements.

THE INSTITUTE FOR HISTORICAL REVIEW

A former officer of England's right-wing extremist party, the National Front, McCalden edited antisemitic and racist publications in England prior to coming to the United States. An admitted racist, McCalden was denied membership in the English National Union of Journalists because of what was termed his 'racist politics.' When he appealed the union's decision, McCalden acknowledged that he believed in writing that encouraged 'race discrimination' and called himself a 'racialist.'[3] He claimed to have been converted to Holocaust denial by Richard Harwood's *Did Six Million Really Die?* In 1978 he moved to California, where he initially worked for the antisemitic journal the *American Mercury*. According to McCalden, when he saw that the magazine and everything associated with it were moribund, he helped found the IHR to spread the gospel of Holocaust denial.[4] He served as IHR director from 1978 until 1981.*

For the first year after the reward was announced the media ignored it and virtually everything else associated with the IHR. McCalden decided that in order to generate publicity, which was the real aim of the 'contest,' letters should be sent to a number of well-known survivors challenging them to prove that Jews had been gassed in Auschwitz and offering them a reward of fifty thousand dollars if they could do so.[5] The survivors received an application form for the contest and a list of the rules,[6] which stipulated that claimants were to attend the second Revisionist Convention at their own expense to present their evidence. The decision of a tribunal of experts – to be named by the IHR to determine the validity of the testimony and evaluate the evidence presented – would be final. Claimants were asked for their ethnic origins, the dates of their internment in any concentration camp, and the exact date and location of any gassing operations they witnessed. In addition they were to describe fully all the mechanics involved in the gassing process they witnessed, and to provide any 'forensic evidence' that would support their claim, including diaries they kept or photographs they took.[7]

* In the spring of 1981 he left the IHR because of differences with the organization's controlling power, Willis Carto. He spent most of the rest of his life until his death in 1991 engaged in a bitter and vitriolic fight with Carto and the IHR.

One of the challenges was sent to Mel Mermelstein, a survivor of Auschwitz whose mother and sisters had been gassed there and whose father and brother were killed at a subcamp of Auschwitz called Jaworzno. Mermelstein, a resident of Long Beach, California, had come to the IHR's attention because he had written letters to various newspapers, including the *Jerusalem Post*, decrying the institute and its activities. In its bulletin the IHR published an open letter to Mermelstein, accusing him of 'peddling the extermination hoax.' McCalden also sent him a letter challenging him to participate in the contest. The IHR director demanded a speedy response and warned Mermelstein that if none was received the IHR would draw its 'own conclusions' and publicize his refusal to participate in the contest in the media.[8] The implication was clear: Refusal to participate would be interpreted by the IHR as an inability to substantiate the Holocaust as fact.

Mermelstein accepted the challenge.* Within the month he sent the IHR a notarized declaration of his experiences at Auschwitz, along with additional names of other eyewitnesses and scientific witnesses who could be made available to the tribunal judging the matter. In his letter Mermelstein warned that if he received no response by January 20, 1981, he would institute civil proceedings to enforce the contract. On January 26, 1981, Mermelstein's lawyer again asked the IHR for a 'speedy resolution' of the matter. The ultimate resolution of what would become known as the Mermelstein case was anything but speedy.†

McCalden informed Mermelstein that Simon Wiesenthal had also filed a claim and that the IHR would deal with his application first.[9] According to Wiesenthal he had been offered fifty thousand dollars if he could prove that at least one Jew had been gassed in a concentration camp and twenty-five thousand dollars if he could prove that the *Diary of Anne Frank* was authentic. Wiesenthal agreed to

---

* Various Jewish organizations with which Mermelstein consulted, including the ADL and the Simon Wiesenthal Center, suggested that he ignore the IHR's challenge because participating would only give the deniers the attention they craved. He decided to proceed nonetheless.

† In 1990 Mermelstein's story was made into a television movie starring Leonard Nimoy.

participate, which for the IHR constituted a publicity coup. In April 1981, in a letter to subscribers of the *Journal of Historical Review*, McCalden acknowledged that the contest was a trap into which they had hoped some 'naive zealot' would walk. He joyfully proclaimed that, in Wiesenthal, they had attracted the 'most eminently suitable mouse.'[10] What McCalden did not tell subscribers was that the 'mouse' had already extricated himself from the trap.

Wiesenthal had proposed that a judge of the California Supreme Court preside over the case. The IHR rejected this proposal and insisted on its right to designate its own tribunal to judge the proof. On March 4, 1981, Wiesenthal informed 'Brandon' that he was withdrawing because he believed the IHR judges would be biased. In a signed statement Wiesenthal explained that he was declining because he would not participate in an effort in which one party served as both prosecutor and judge.[11] Wiesenthal's suspicions were proved valid when Tom Marcellus, McCalden's successor as IHR director, was deposed by Mermelstein's lawyer. The lawyer asked Marcellus who would be selected to sit on the tribunal the IHR had promised to convene to hear the evidence. He suggested that appropriate members would be Robert Faurisson, Arthur Butz, and Ditlieb Felderer. All three were members of the editorial advisory board of the *Journal of Historical Review*. Butz had already made his mark with his *The Hoax of the Twentieth Century*. At the time of the Mermelstein case, Faurisson had already been convicted, put on probation, fined, and ordered to pay damages by a French court for the libel of denying the fact of the Holocaust. Ditlieb Felderer, an Austrian-born resident of Sweden who claims to be a Jew, published a vitriolic antisemitic publication, *Jewish Information Bulletin*, which, in contrast to the *Journal of Historical Review*, did not even try to camouflage its antisemitic diatribes under a respectable veneer.* In 1983 he was

---

* Among the mailings distributed by his so-called Jewish Information Society is a grossly distorted sexually explicit cartoon depicting a male and female elderly Jew. Both have large hooked noses. The woman, whose breasts droop down to her knees, has stubble on her chin and is smoking a cigarette. The man's penis, which is erect, is supported by a splint, and his scrotum droops to his knees. The caption reads, 'In spite of his feeble condition, Dr. Mengele was able to rejuvenate him and

sentenced to ten months in prison for disseminating hate material. According to the prosecutor in the case, Felderer had sent leaders of the European Jewish community mailings that contained pieces of fat and locks of hair with a letter asking them if they could identify the contents as Hungarian Jews gassed at Auschwitz.[12]

Undeterred by such considerations about the 'judges', on February 19, 1981, Mermelstein filed a lawsuit against the IHR, Carto, and Brandon/McCalden. During pretrial hearings the presiding judge, Thomas T. Johnson, took judicial notice of the fact that Jews had been gassed to death in Auschwitz, ruling that it was not 'subject to dispute' but was 'simply a fact.' After many lengthy delays Mermelstein won his case. In July 1985 the Los Angeles Superior Court ordered the IHR to pay Mermelstein ninety thousand dollars, which included the fifty-thousand-dollar reward plus forty thousand dollars for pain and suffering. The defendants also agreed to sign a letter of apology to Mermelstein for the emotional distress they had caused him and all other Auschwitz survivors. The apology contained a verbatim repetition of the judicial notice regarding Auschwitz.[13] (The Mermelstein case did not end there. On August 7, 1985, in the course of a radio interview, Mermelstein said that the IHR defendants had signed the judicial notice. On August 6, 1986, one day before the statute of limitations expired, Willis Carto and the IHR filed suit against Mermelstein, claiming that he had defamed them in the interview. A year and a half later the defendants voluntarily dismissed the suit. Mermelstein has subsequently filed action against the IHR and Carto for malicious prosecution. That case remains in litigation.[14]) Despite the financial loss and public ridicule the Mermelstein case caused the IHR, there were those in the organization's leadership who continued to maintain that, given the press coverage generated by the contest, it succeeded.

But the Mermelstein case was not the IHR's only public imbroglio during its early years. It rented the University of California's Lake

he is now proudly showing off his fine restoration to his beautiful, most anticipating, and sensuous looking sweetheart.'

Arrowhead Conference Center for its 1981 meeting. Apparently, when the IHR applied for use of the facility, the university official in charge of renting the conference center assumed that the IHR was a legitimate scholarly group. Despite vigorous protests by faculty and students about the inappropriate nature of the use of a University of California building, the administration – with the support of Gov. Jerry Brown – claimed it could not legally break the contract. When the university learned that McCalden had used his Brandon pseudonym to sign the contract, it charged that 'deception was involved' and that this constituted legitimate grounds for cancellation of its agreement with the IHR. At approximately the same time that the university was trying to find a way to break its contract, McCalden had written a letter to IHR supporters acknowledging that the entire gas chamber contest was a public relations maneuver. The university also justified its decision to cancel by citing McCalden's admission that the contest was a 'publicity gimmick.'[15]

In many respects this case represented a detour from the IHR's primary objective. The creation of the IHR had the same objective as Arthur Butz's *The Hoax of the Twentieth Century*: to move denial from the lunatic fringe of racial and antisemitic extremism to the realm of academic respectability. The IHR was designed to win scholarly acceptance for deniers, which is why it was so anxious to use the University of California facility. Although the IHR and its followers proclaim that Holocaust denial is heir to a genuine intellectual legacy,[16] analysis of the institute, its publications and activities, and the people most closely associated with it throws into stark relief the fact that, notwithstanding its claims to intellectual legitimacy, the IHR is part of a continuum of extreme antisemitism and racism. Were its publications and activities not enveloped in the aura of research, they would be dismissed out of hand for what they truly are: fanatical expressions of neo-Nazism. The institute's anti-Israel, racist, and antisemitic attitude is reflected in virtually all its activities. The organizational form the IHR adopted – a research institute – and its outward trappings may have been innovative but its agenda was not: to rehabilitate national socialism, inculcate antisemitism and racism, and oppose democracy.

From the outset the IHR has camouflaged its actual goal by engaging in activities that typify a scholarly institution. It sponsors annual gatherings that are structured as academic convocations and publishes the *Journal of Historical Review*, which imitates the serious and highbrow language of academia. Though virtually all its activities are concerned with Holocaust denial, the institute depicts itself as engaged in a far broader and loftier quest. It claims that its goals are to align twentieth-century history with the facts and expose the historical totems that are manipulated by secret vested interests. Primary among them are myths about previous wars. Like virtually every denier before it, the IHR professed that it was motivated by no animus toward any other group but only by a 'deep dedication to the cause of truth in history.'[17] In response to the accusation that Holocaust deniers are intent on reclaiming national socialism's reputation, the IHR protested that it was not interested in resurrecting any regime. Its interest was 'rehabilitating the *truth*' because, unlike establishment historians, it was willing to confront the 'shadowy suppressors' of historical truth.[18] Only through the exposure of historical myths that have been imposed on the United States could the country be prevented from being 'railroaded' into one conflagration after another, particularly in the Middle East.[19] These remain the IHR's claims; however, the reality is quite different.

Despite its claims to a total revision of all history, the IHR focuses almost exclusively on World War II and the Holocaust. It is, they claim, the 'most distorted period' in history and the event most often used as a 'historical club to bully public opinion.' David McCalden was explicit about precisely what it was public opinion was being bullied into believing. In a letter urging people to subscribe to the *Journal of Historical Review*, McCalden described it as a step that could not only save every American family hundreds of dollars in taxes but deliver the United States from the threat of a disastrous nuclear war. McCalden spelled out how a simple act of subscribing to a journal could accomplish these lofty goals:

Each year a foreign government literally steals millions of dollars from you and other U.S. taxpayers. This thief is the corrupt, bankrupt government of Israel and its army of paid and unpaid agents in the United States – particularly in Washington. And the theft is perpetrated primarily through the clever use of the Greatest Lie in all history – the lie of the 'Holocaust.'[20]

(The Israel connection is a constant refrain in IHR material.)

For the IHR debunking the 'so-called "Holocaust" ' was far more than an act of rewriting the historical record – it had critical policy implications. Until the Holocaust was revealed to be a hoax, the future of the United States would not be secure. According to the IHR, exposing the truth about the Holocaust also exposes the secret group that controls much of America's military and foreign policy. Relying on traditional antisemitic motifs, the IHR accused this 'superwealthy' and 'tiny segment' of the population of being unconcerned about the 'damage and distortion' it caused the culture at large. This group – a thinly veiled reference to Jews – control the media and use it to flaunt the Holocaust as the main rationale for 'America's dog-like devotion to the illegal state of Israel.'[21]

Tom Marcellus, McCalden's successor as IHR director, broadened this line of argument. The Holocaust lie not only served as a 'justification' for the commission of genocide by Israel but also affected the rights of American citizens in their own country. Americans' constitutional guarantee of freedom of speech was suppressed in order to protect the interests of 'Israel-firsters.' But it was not just the United States that was threatened. The 'very existence of Germany and the Western Culture' were also caught in the balance.[22]

Marcellus revealed another of the IHR's true agenda items with his warning that acceptance of the Holocaust myth resulted in a radical degeneration of accepted standards of human behavior and a lowering of the 'self-image of *White people.*' These racist tendencies, which the IHR has increasingly kept away from the public spotlight, are part of the extremist tradition to which it is heir.[23]

The IHR's ideology can be directly linked to its founder and primary supporter, Willis A. Carto, who was also the founder and treasurer of the Liberty Lobby, a well-established ultra-right organization that has a direct connection with other antisemitic publications, including the *American Mercury*, *Washington Observer Newsletter*, and Noontide Press. Only the most superficial attempt has been made by either the IHR or any of these publications to camouflage the connection between them. In fact, at one point the IHR, Noontide Press, and the *American Mercury* all shared the same post-office box.[24] This antisemitic network is known for its anti-Israel publications, many of which contain details of a 'World Zionist conspiracy.' In some of them Israel is referred to as a 'bastard state.'[25]

Carto was born in 1926 in Indiana. After serving in the army he attended college and then moved to San Francisco to work for a finance company as a debt collector. For a short while he was associated with the radical, right-wing John Birch Society, until he had a falling out with its founder, Robert Welch. According to a former editor at the Liberty Lobby, Carto's antisemitic activities were too extreme even for Welch, a known antisemite, who personally fired him.[26] In 1958 he organized a 'pressure group for patriotism,' which eventually emerged as the Liberty Lobby. A former chairman of the Liberty Lobby's Board of Policy acknowledged that by the 1980s its annual income was close to four million dollars. The lobby's antisemitic, anti-Zionist newspaper, *Spotlight*, claims a circulation of more than 330,000. When it reached this goal in 1981 it celebrated by holding a gala reception at the National Press Club in Washington.

The Liberty Lobby has been described as so extreme that it is 'estranged from even the fringes of the far right.'[27] The investigative columnist Drew Pearson described Carto as a Hitler 'fan' and the Liberty Lobby as 'infiltrated by Nazis who revere the memory of Hitler.' The Wall Street Journal is also among those who have identified Carto and the Liberty Lobby as antisemitic.[28]

The Anti-Defamation League (ADL) believes Carto to be the most important and powerful professional antisemite in the United States. According to the ADL, the Liberty Lobby stands at the helm of a major publishing and organizational complex that for more than two decades has propagated antisemitism and racism in the United States.[29] The *Wall Street Journal* and the ADL are not alone in their assessment. When Carto and the Liberty Lobby sued the *Wall Street*

Journal for calling them antisemites, the District Court for the District of Columbia ruled against them and concluded that it would be difficult to imagine a case in which the evidence of antisemitism was 'more compelling.'[30]

Some of the strongest condemnations of Carto and the Liberty Lobby have come from conservative and right-wing political groups in the United States. Scott Stanley, the managing editor of *American Opinion*, the publication of the John Birch Society, believes Willis Carto responsible for preserving antisemitism as a movement in the United States. In 1981 William F. Buckley described the Liberty Lobby as 'a hotbed of antisemitism' centered around the 'mysterious' Carto, who 'regularly poisons the wells of political discourse.'[31] The conservative weekly *Human Events* condemned the Liberty Lobby as an organization that exploited racist and antisemitic sentiments and Carto as someone who has long maintained sympathy for Hitler's Germany. Buckley's *National Review*, which accused Carto of always having 'his eyes on Jewry,' warned that it was not only Carto's antisemitism that was dangerous but his philosophy of pure power, which was alien and fundamentally hostile to the American tradition.[32] The conservative columnist R. Emmett Tyrell, Jr., editor in chief of the *American Spectator*, condemned the lobby as an organization that always attracted a 'colorful collection of bigots and simpletons' who make an art of applying conspiracy theories to every problem that vexed the public.[33] Not surprisingly Carto denied these charges. Examination of what he has written, said, and done, however, reveals otherwise.

Willis Carto's political vision is encapsulated by three things: contempt and revulsion for Jews, a belief in the need for an absolutist government that would protect the 'racial heritage' of the United States, and a conviction that there exists a conspiracy designed to bring dire harm to the Western world. The articles, journals, and books brought out by the Carto nexus of publications consistently focus on predictable themes: the ignoble Allied treatment of Nazi Germany; Jewish responsibility for the ills of the Western world; the grotesque misdeeds of the 'bastard' state of Israel; and the existence of a conspiracy perpetrated by a 'high elite,' consisting mainly of people with Jewish names, to control American foreign and financial policy. Jews besmirch Germany's good name and support the Communists' attempt to impose their system on the Western world. At the heart of every serious problem facing the United States – civil rights, energy, defense, racial integration – are Jews manipulating matters for their own benefit.

Nevertheless, the Jews are not Carto's sole target. Carto believes that at the root of civilization's problems are the 'Jews and Negroes.'[34] In 1955, in a letter to the racist author Earnest Sevier Cox, Carto bemoaned the fact that so few Americans were concerned about the 'inevitable niggerfication of America.'[35] Racial purity is the lens through which much of Carto's view of the world is seen. In 1962 he advocated a racial view of history and argued that racial equality would be easier to accept if there were 'no Negroes around to destroy the concept.'[36] Carto's sentiments are reminiscent of the German right wing's fear of 'foreignization' (*Überfremdung*). In an attempt to protect the United States from what Carto considered the danger posed to it by African Americans, he organized the Joint Council for Repatriation, which was designed to return all blacks to Africa. Shortly before the creation of the Liberty Lobby in 1957 Carto predicted to Judge Tom P. Brady, a member of the Mississippi Supreme Court and founder of the anti-civil-rights White Citizens Council, that the lobby would be a tremendous asset to the repatriation scheme. In a fashion that would become typical of his organizational methodology, Carto was intent on keeping the link between the two secret: 'You can see that there must never be an obvious connection between the two, for if there is, either would kill the other off.'[37] But the Joint Council for Repatriation did not envision just the repatriation of African Americans. It also aimed to deliver the strongest imaginable blow to the power of organized Jewry.[38] During World War II, Carto argued, it had been the Jews' influence on American policy that was responsible for blinding the West to the benefits of an alliance with Hitler. Treacherous Jewish 'propaganda and lies' had led to Hitler's defeat, which for Carto constituted the 'defeat of Europe. And of America.'

But for Carto the danger had not been limited to World War II:

'If Satan himself had tried to create a permanent disintegration and force for the destruction of nations, he could have done no better than to invent the Jews.'[39] In a memo Carto expressed it even more succinctly: The Jews were 'Public Enemy No. 1.'[40]

The essence of Carto's political philosophy and his introduction to Holocaust denial can be traced to *Imperium – The Philosophy of History and Politics*, by Francis Parker Yockey. The book, dedicated to Adolf Hitler, preached that the future greatness of the West would be modeled on the German 'revolution' of 1933. Yockey, who has been described by some researchers as 'America's Hitler,' was born in 1917 in Chicago. After attending five different colleges, he graduated from Notre Dame Law School.[41] He enlisted in the army in 1942 and went AWOL for an extended period shortly thereafter. He was eventually given a medical discharge from the army in 1943 on the grounds that he suffered from 'dementia praecox, paranoid type.' According to the army report, he revealed marked delusions of persecution, had auditory hallucinations, and involved prominent people in his delusional system.[42]

In 1945, after the war, he took a job as a legal researcher for the War Crimes Tribunal in Germany. He left that post in less than a year because of what he claimed was the tribunal's unfair treatment of the Nazi leaders awaiting trial. He subsequently went to Ireland, where he wrote *Imperium*. In 1952 his passport was revoked in absentia by the State Department, and by 1954 he was identified as a U.S. agent for a neo-Nazi, Rudolph Aschenauer.[43] After writing *Imperium* he traveled throughout the United States, Canada, Europe, and Egypt spreading its message. He was arrested in 1960 when he was discovered to be holding three different passports with three different names. (His suitcase had been lost by an airline company. When it was retrieved, airport officials opened it to discover the identity of its owner. Instead they found the passports.) While in prison awaiting trial, Yockey took a cyanide pill and committed suicide. His last visitor, less than a week earlier, was Carto.

In *Imperium* Yockey called for an absolute imperial system, an imperium of Western Aryan nations united by the principles of Hitlerian national socialism. Yockey envisaged a time when power would no longer be held by individuals and all enterprises would be under public control and ownership. The regime Yockey proposed envisioned the death knell of democracy. He called for an age of absolute politics in which elections would become old-fashioned until they ceased altogether.[44]

It is the book's antisemitic ideology that harks back most directly to national socialism. 'The Jew is spiritually worn out,' according to Yockey. 'He can no longer develop. He can produce nothing in the sphere of thought or research. He lives solely with the idea of revenge on the nations of the white European-American race.'[45] Obsessed with the power of the Jews, Yockey warned that they were bound to destroy the West. *Imperium* is filled with descriptions of conspiracies against both the West and the United States. It christened those orchestrating these conspiracies as the 'Culture-Distorters.' Included in their ranks were racial and cultural miscegenists, egalitarians, believers in human rights and participatory democracy, and 'the rear-guard in the West of the fulfilled Arabian Culture, the Church-State-Nation-People-Race of the Jew.'[46]

In 1949 Yockey wrote the 'Proclamation of London,' which, in addition to calling for the reinstatement of national socialism, advocated the expulsion of the Jews by the nations of Europe. (In a sworn deposition in 1979, in a Liberty Lobby lawsuit against the ADL, Carto acknowledged under oath that he agreed with the tenets of Yockey's proclamation.[47])

But Yockey went beyond even this most extreme antisemitic rhetoric. Twenty years prior to the formation of the IHR, Yockey laid out the essential elements of Holocaust denial. He attributed the myth of the Holocaust to the culture-distorters' claim that six million Jews had been killed in European camps. Not only had they made this claim, Yockey charged, but they had woven a web of propaganda that was technically quite complete:

> 'Photographs' were supplied in millions of copies. Thousands of the people who had been killed published accounts of their experiences in these camps. Hundreds of thousands more made fortunes in post-war black markets. 'Gas-chambers' that did not exist were

photographed and a 'gasmobile' was invented to titillate the mechanically minded.[48]

Yockey's book might have had little if any impact if not for the fact that in 1962 Noontide Press reissued it with a thirty-five-page introduction by Carto in which he expressed profound support for Yockey's plans for world rule and contended that in order to obtain the necessary political power 'all else must be temporarily sacrificed.'[49] Noontide has kept the book in circulation since then.

During the late 1960s Carto participated in the creation of a number of political groups to advance his agenda of winning control of America's right wing. The United Republicans for America, which was designed to win control of the Republican party, conducted a direct-mail campaign for G. Gordon Liddy's congressional race in New York. (Liddy would shortly thereafter become infamous for his role in the Watergate break-in.) He also helped found Youth for Wallace, which, after supporting George Wallace's presidential aspirations, became the National Youth Alliance (NYA). Officially the goals of the NYA were to oppose drugs, black power, the left-wing Students for a Democratic Society (SDS), and American involvement in foreign wars. But another item was on the organization's agenda. According to former officials of the organization, who were drummed out by Carto when they protested, the NYA advocated Francis Yockey's philosophy. Paperback copies of *Imperium* were printed for NYA members to sell. An NYA informational letter acknowledged that the organization's political approach was based on the philosophy of Yockey's 'monumental *Imperium*.'[50] At a 1968 meeting of the NYA in Pittsburgh at which Nazi paraphernalia were evident and Nazi songs sung, Carto praised Yockey's ideas and described his own plan to amass as much political power as possible within an array of institutions. Anticipating a national swing to the right, he aimed to capture the leadership of as many conservative groups as possible. A former Liberty Lobby staffer who hosted its radio show testified in court that Carto often indicated that what this country needed was a 'right-wing dictatorship.'[51] Because leaders of the 'legitimate right,' such as William F. Buckley, constituted an obstacle to his plan to win control of the conservative right Carto labeled them with the most extreme term of opprobrium he could conjure up: 'ADL agents.'[52] The publications linked to Carto and his organizational orbit disseminated plans for this right-wing dictatorship and called for active suppression of those who would conspire against it.

Among the publications under Carto's direct control was the *American Mercury*.* Though the journal had begun its descent into antisemitica under its previous owners, under Carto's tutelage, which began in 1966, the pace of that descent quickened. By the time of the creation of the IHR in 1978 the *American Mercury*, which had been under the Carto aegis for thirteen years, was considered one of the leading antisemitic publications in the United States.[53] It functioned as a cheerleader for Holocaust deniers. An editorial in the *American Mercury* lauded the IHR because it would function as an antidote to 'the Anti-Defamation League's campaign to prod public discussion of the "Holocaust." '[54]

But *American Mercury* was not the only publication in the Carto orbit to disseminate these views. The Liberty Lobby's newsletter, *Liberty Letter*, echoed the same themes. It praised *Imperium* as a major work of philosophy and ranted about the 'aggressive minority' that tightly controlled the so-called free press. This 'alien-minded and America-last group,' was the 'ruthless Zionist pressure machine.' The *Liberty Letter* claimed to have uncovered thousands of undercover 'Zionist "fixers," lobbyists and Leftists' prowling the corridors of Congress and converging on the White House.[55]

In 1975 the lobby's *Liberty Letter*, whose circulation was more than one hundred thousand, was subsumed by the *Spotlight*, a tabloid newspaper that regularly featured articles on Bible analysis and the putative efforts of the Council on Foreign Relations and the Trilateral Commission to dominate the nation. It offered its readers tips on avoiding taxes and fighting the IRS. The paper attacked Martin Luther King, Jr., as a Communist and praised members of the Ku Klux Klan. It has memorialized Gordon Kahl, the leader of the

---

* In 1979 Carto turned control of the *American Mercury* over to Ned Touchstone, who had been on the Board of Policy of the Liberty Lobby at the same time as he served as editor of the journal published by the White Citizens Council.

right-wing-extremist group Posse Comitatus, who killed three federal marshals and wounded a number of others before he was killed in 1983 in a shootout with federal agents.

These publications find conspiracies everywhere. In 1976, shortly before the presidential election, the paper charged that Jimmy Carter was directly linked with the international cocaine trade.[56] (The Federal Election Commission fined the Liberty Lobby for publishing this unsubstantiated story so close to the election.) In 1979 Spotlight's lead article described how a global elite planned to topple world governments. The paper claimed that its reporter had attended an international conference in Austria at which such plans were discussed. In truth, no one from the Spotlight attended this legitimate conference, and the reporter who wrote the story admitted to falsifying it.[57]

But the main focus of Spotlight's attention has been exposing what it calls the 'Jew-Zionist' international bankers' conspiracy designed to cause pain and suffering for dedicated, honest, and hardworking Americans. Though the tabloid finds conspiracies in many places, generally they are linked to Israel and its supporters' successful efforts to control Congress and dictate American policy.[58] During the 1979 gas shortage the paper informed readers that as a result of a secret deal between President Carter and Prime Minister Begin 'your gas [was going] to Israel.'[59] According to Spotlight, these Zionists do not work alone; cliques of bankers, Red Chinese, and American politicians, including Sen. Jesse Helms and the late Congressman Larry McDonald, were all part of the pro-Israel conspiracy against the United States.[60]

Since a major aspect of that conspiracy was the Holocaust hoax, Holocaust denial has also become a regular staple of Spotlight. The paper, which has identified Carto as the force behind the IHR, has devoted entire issues to Holocaust denial.[61] The paper has frequently reported on the IHR's annual meetings and on their retrieval of history from the 'memory hole.'[62] A fifteen-page supplement in the December 24, 1979, issue was completely dedicated to denial articles. Reiterating familiar denial themes, Spotlight has claimed that the bodies at Auschwitz were cremated as a hygienic measure to control typhoid, that the so-called gas chambers were actually life-saving delousing showers, that the *Diary of Anne Frank* was a propaganda hoax, that the six-million number was used to entice the United Nations to support the creation of the 'illegal state of Israel,' and that professional Zionist 'survivors' planned to extort five million dollars from America. It also touted the IHR's contest. The front page of the 'Holocaust Supplement' carried the following headlines:

WERE SIX MILLION JEWS EXTERMINATED?
FAMOUS 'GAS CHAMBER VICTIMS' LIVING WELL
NEED $50,000? FIND A HOLOCAUST VICTIM
TORTURE USED TO MAKE GERMANS 'CONFESS'
CHASING THE 'WAR CRIMINALS' FOR PROFIT'.[63]

In 1981 a two-page article bore the following headline:

GATHERING OF 'LIBERATORS' MAY EXPOSE ALLIED WAR
ATROCITIES; BELIEVERS IN THE 'HOLOCAUST' HAVE
INVITED THE 'LIBERATORS' OF THE CONCENTRATION
CAMPS TO GATHER FOR A CONVENTION. BUT TO SHOW
UP WOULD BE TANTAMOUNT TO ADMITTING HAVING
MURDERED INNOCENT GERMAN GUARDS.[64]

The nature of *Spotlight*'s readership can be gauged to some degree by the contents of its classified advertising section. There are ads for poetry, laetrile prescriptions, dating services for patriotic Christians, and devices for dramatically increasing a car's gasoline mileage (these devices have supposedly been kept off the market in a conspiracy against the American consumer). In addition, its classified section regularly offers Nazi paraphernalia, gun silencer parts, bullet-proof vests, clandestine mail drops, and instructions for manufacturing false identification.[65] The Noontide Press has also participated in spreading the message espoused by Yockey, Carto, the Liberty Lobby, and the IHR. Among the books listed in the 1992 Noontide Press catalog was Yockey's *Imperium*. The catalog described Yockey as a brilliant young American who 'saw through the Holocaust propaganda as early as 1948.' Also offered for sale were the standard works on Holocaust denial, many of which were published by Noontide, among them the *Journal of Historical Review*, Butz's *The Hoax of the Twentieth Century*, and Harwood's *Six Million Lost and Found*. The catalog also featured the antisemitic standards – Henry Ford's *The International Jew* and *The Protocols of the Learned Elders of Zion*. Included as well was a listing of books on 'Race and Culture,' many of them described by the catalog as focusing on the inherent dangers of racial integration. *The Testing of Negro Intelligence*, by Travis Osborne and Frank C. J. McGurk, was described as a searching evaluation of black performance on intelligence tests from 1966 to 1980 whose findings 'give little comfort to egalitarians.' *Race and Reason: A Yankee View*, by Carleton Putnam, was touted as the 'intelligent reader's guide to the pitfalls of Black-White integration from the White standpoint.' The sequel, *Race and Reality*, demonstrated how 'egalitarians' have used botched science and faulty scholarship to obscure 'biological facts about racial differences.'[66] Noontide not only offered these racist publications in its catalog, but it also tried to win subscribers for a tabloid newspaper, the *White Student*. According to Noontide the paper was designed to help students on campus 'fight back.' It was an antidote to being brainwashed by Marxist teachers and debilitated 'by the rigors of survival in our integrated schools.'[67]

In their espousal of antisemitism, racism, and extremism, these publications are no different from a variety of similar offerings worldwide. In fact, the articles in all of them are mind-numbingly similar. However, what is particularly disturbing about this group of publications is their interlocking network and growing source of funds.[68] In 1989 the director of the IHR protested that neither he nor any other member of the staff could offer advice as to the merits of other 'patriotic movements' or right-wing groups. The IHR, he claimed, 'pleads agnosticism' concerning the goals or methods of any group whose objective was not the 'revision of history.'[69] This was an attempt by the IHR to maintain its facade as an independent research entity dedicated to the exposure of historical falsehoods. Despite its pronouncement, the connection between the Institute for Historical Review, the *American Mercury*, and Noontide Press had already been officially established. In 1980 Carto's wife, Elisabeth, acting on behalf of the Legion for the Survival of Freedom, filed an application in Torrance, California, for a business license for the IHR. The institute, according to the papers filed, was to operate as the Noontide Press/Institute for Historical Review. The mailing address listed on the application for the IHR was identical with those of the *American Mercury* and Noontide Press. Some of the members of the management of the *American Mercury* were also officers of the Noontide Press/Institute for Historical Review. Former staffers, including David McCalden, have testified under oath that Carto had 'ultimate authority' over all decisions made by the IHR.[70]

The courts have also found the IHR, Noontide Press, *Spotlight*, the Liberty Lobby, and Willis Carto intimately connected. In 1988 the United States Court of Appeals rejected the attempt of the IHR, Noontide Press, and the Legion for the Survival of Freedom to present themselves as unrelated entities. Justice Robert Bork, in his decision dismissing Carto's attempt to sue the *Wall Street Journal* for labeling him an antisemite, stated that Carto had 'specifically designed the Liberty Lobby/Legion/Noontide/IHR network so as to divorce Liberty Lobby's name from those of its less reputable affiliates.'[71] One of the main tactics the Carto network uses to keep critics at bay has been the lawsuit. It has filed numerous lawsuits throughout the United States charging defamation. The Court of Appeals noted that Carto and his nexus of organizations have consistently used the libel complaint as a 'weapon to harass.'[72]

The IHR's early loss in the Mermelstein case did not stop it from proceeding with its objectives of spreading denial, antisemitism, and racism. One of the ways it has tried to give credence to its claim that it is a research institute with a broad historical agenda is by publishing articles in the *Journal of Historical Review* on topics that have no connection with World War II or the Final Solution. David McCalden, in a letter sent to students on various campuses, argued that history had long been orchestrated by those who were 'willing to parrot . . . just what the establishment wants them to,' and that the IHR was dedicated to ending this.[73] The spring 1982 edition of the *Journal of Historical Review* contained an article by Harry Elmer Barnes entitled 'Revisionism and the Promotion of Peace,' in which Barnes argued that revisionism was dedicated to the 'honest search for historical truth and the discrediting of misleading myths that are a barrier to peace and goodwill among nations.' Revisionists, as Barnes described them, were engaged in an effort to correct the historical record through the collection of more complete historical facts in 'a more calm political atmosphere and [with] a more object-ive attitude.'[74]

The *Journal* enumerated a series of instances other than the Holo-caust in which the historical record had also been manipulated. In need of a 'revisionist' analysis were the American Revolution (the policies of the British had not been that harsh), the War of 1812 (Mad-ison was not pushed into war but made the decision based on his own convictions), the German invasion of Belgium in World War I (the British would have done the same thing if Germany had not done it first), and Theodore Roosevelt's role in the Spanish-American war (he ordered an attack on the Spanish fleet as part of his Ameri-can imperialist and expansionist philosophy).[75] As was often the case with revisionist arguments, the issues raised had a kernel of truth to them. But the deniers proceeded not only to distort that kernel but ascribed to it a conspiratorial nature – premeditated distortions introduced for political ends. By offering alternative conclusions in each of these cases the *Journal* apparently believed it could lull its readers into accepting that revisions were also needed in relation to the Holocaust.

This was the objective of an article on Civil War prisoner-of-war camps. The author, Mark Weber, claimed that false reports about Union prisoners' suffering in Southern camps prompted the North to order similar abuse for prisoners in its 'concentration camps.' Weber's reliance on *Sonderbehandlung* (special treatment), the euphemistic term the Nazis used for what was to happen to the Jews once they were taken to the death camps in the East, was designed to make a link in the reader's mind with the Holocaust. Exaggerations about conditions in the South multiplied with the passage of time, as former prisoners wrote books they claimed documented their experiences. Henry Wirz, the commander of Andersonville, the most notorious camp in the South, was executed by the United States because the inmates imagined him 'the cruel and inhuman author of all their sufferings.' Weber described a proposal that Andersonville be maintained as a permanent reminder of the war as 'shades of Dachau' and maintained (correctly) that many prisoners on both sides had died but prisoners had not been deliberately killed. It was 'bad management,' particularly in the South, which caused such extensive death and misery. In the main, Weber's article followed fairly well-established historical grounds; only his conclusion revealed his true agenda. He drew a direct parallel between the Civil War and World War II – in both wars the victors 'hysterically distorted' the conditions in the camps and branded the defeated adversary as 'intrinsically evil.' In Weber's view: 'All the suffering and death in the camps of the side that lost the war was ascribed to a deliberate policy on the part of an inherently atrocious power. The victorious powers demanded "unconditional surrender" and arrested the defeated government leaders as "criminals."'[76]

There was one major difference, Weber insisted: 'The Civil War rendition of "Sonderbehandlung" never achieved the sinister notoriety of its Second World War counterpart.' Nonetheless, Weber continued, in both wars the political system of the vanquished was considered to be not 'merely different but morally depraved,' and the ethics of the side that lost the war were judged 'in terms of [the losers'] readiness to atone for past sins and embrace the social system of the conquerors.'[77] This argument harked back to a basic tenet of Holocaust denial: War is evil; no side can claim the moral upper hand, and defeated parties are regularly accused by the victors of having committed terrible misdeeds. Weber's immoral equivalency in terms of treatment of the defeated enemy was part of the deniers' effort to cast the 'myth of the Holocaust' as part of a long-established pattern of the distortion of history for political ends.

According to the deniers the Holocaust is not the only deceptive legacy of World War II. Another issue of prime importance to them is the Japanese attack on Pearl Harbor. Continuing the battle that had been begun by the revisionists after World War II ended, an entire issue of the *Journal of Historical Review* was devoted to this topic.[78] Its explicit objective was to portray Roosevelt as having known that the attack was imminent and having allowed it to take place unhindered so that America would be forced to enter the war.

The deniers' obsession with Pearl Harbor has a dual objective: to demonstrate Roosevelt's and, by association, the American government's duplicity. It is also designed to dispel the Allied and 'court historians'' claim that World War II was a moral as opposed to a power struggle. The revisionists believe that if they can demonstrate that this war was at its heart a conflagration like all others, they can argue that any unique accusations of guilt or special war crimes trials are invalid. In this case the revisionists established a straw man in order to knock him down. The United States entered the war because it was attacked by Japan. Japan's ally, Germany, then declared war on the United States. But proving that the Allies were motivated by the age-old quest for 'power and advantage' is far subtler and less distasteful than creating an immoral equivalence of the gulag versus the death camps or Auschwitz versus the bombing of Dresden.[79]

Despite its attempts to portray itself as a respectable organization, the Institute for Historical Review and its subsidiary publications and associated organizations are in essence nothing but part of a larger effort to further goals remarkably similar to those articulated by national socialism. Just as Holocaust denial must be regarded as not just an attack on a portion of history that is of particular importance to Jews but as a threat to all of history and to reasoned discourse, so too the IHR must not be seen as an entity whose only interest is attacking the historicity of the Holocaust. The tradition to which it is heir and the activities of those who are part of its amorphous orbit indicate that it poses a far greater danger.

9
The Gas Chamber Controversy

In 1984 the Canadian government charged Ernst Zundel, a forty-six-year-old German citizen who had immigrant status in Canada, with stimulating antisemitism through the publication and distribution of material he knew to be false.* The case against Zundel, who was the country's most prolific distributor of Holocaust denial and neo-Nazi publications, resulted in two trials, numerous appeals, and extensive media coverage. The Crown Counsel charged that Zundel instigated social and racial intolerance through the publication of two works, 'The West, War and Islam,' which argued that there existed a Zionist-banker-Communist-Freemason-sponsored conspiracy to control the world, and Richard Harwood's *Did Six Million Really Die?*

Though much of the material he distributed was written by other neo-Nazis, Holocaust deniers, and right-wing extremists, Zundel himself contributed two books to this mélange. *The Hitler We Loved and Why*, which was published by White Power Publications in West Virginia, portrayed Hitler as a saintly man, a messianic figure whose white supremacist ideology had brought salvation to Germany. It concluded with the proclamation that Hitler's spirit 'soars beyond the shores of the White Man's home in Europe. Where we are, he is with us. WE LOVE YOU, ADOLF HITLER!'[1] His book, *UFOs: Nazi Secret Weapons?*, argued that UFOs were Hitler's

* In bringing charges against Zundel the Canadian government joined what had begun as a private complaint. Sabrina Citron, a survivor of the Holocaust and a citizen of Canada, initiated the action against Zundel. Most Canadian Jewish organizations did not support her decision.

secret weapon and are actually still in use at bases in the Antarctic beneath the earth's surface. In addition Zundel wrote and distributed scores of fliers and pamphlets praising Nazism, advocating fascism, and denying the Holocaust.

Zundel created a publishing house, Samisdat Publications, to reprint and distribute the usual array of antisemitic, racist, and Holocaust denial material. It also sold tapes of Hitler's speeches, copies of Nazi-sponsored films, and cassettes of music from the Third Reich, including a selection of Hitler's 'favorites' and storm trooper songs and marches. Zundel did not just wait for customers to order his wares. He sent Canadian members of Parliament a steady stream of Holocaust denial publications. Nor did his reach end at Canada's border. Thousands of Americans received his publications, as did U.S. radio and television stations. (He claims his American mailing list numbers above 29,000.) But it was West Germany that was his main target. In December 1980 government officials informed the Bundestag that during the preceding two years two hundred shipments of neo-Nazi extremist books, periodicals, symbols, films, records, and cassettes had been shipped to the country by Samisdat Publishers in Toronto. In 1981, during a German crackdown on neo-Nazis, West German police discovered in the hundreds of homes they raided weapons, ammunition, and explosives as well as thousands of copies of Zundel-produced material. The German Ministry of the Interior identified Zundel as one of the country's most important suppliers of radical right and neo-Nazi propaganda material. Zundel has also sent his publications to Australia, the Middle East, and a variety of other countries. (He claims to have subscribers in more than forty-five countries.)

But Zundel is not just a prolific disseminator of extremist, denial, and neo-Nazi publications. A showman who is extremely adept at winning media attention – he has been dubbed by Manuel Prutschi the P. T. Barnum of Holocaust denial[2] – Zundel has honed his public antics over many years. When NBC's *Holocaust* was screened in Canada in April 1978 he created an organization, 'Concerned Parents of German Descent,' to protest the screenings. He declared the West German government to be the 'West German Occupation

Regime.' In September 1981 he placed an ad in the classified section of the *Toronto Star* wishing a 'Happy New Year to all our Jewish Friends,' signed by himself and Samisdat Publishers.[3] He has written rabbis and synagogues throughout Canada offering to lecture on topics of common interest to Germans and Jews. When the Canadian Jewish Congress advertised for a director of its Holocaust Documentation Bank Project, Zundel applied for the job. (His application arrived after the official deadline.) He created a German Jewish Historical Commission and announced that it would organize symposia on topics of Jewish interest.

His publicity stunts received the most attention at his trial. Each day he appeared at the courthouse wearing a bullet-proof vest and a hard hat bearing the words 'Freedom of Speech.' (His followers sported similar headgear.) On the day of his sentencing he arrived at court in a Rent-A-Wreck vehicle, emerging with a blackened face to demonstrate that 'whites could not receive justice in Canada,' hefted an eleven-foot cross labeled 'Freedom of Speech' on his shoulders, and carried it up the steps to the courthouse door.[4]

Born in Germany in 1939, Zundel's childhood memories were of 'hunger, cold, sickness,' and life under occupation. He came to Canada in 1958 to learn to be a photo retoucher. While in Canada he was greatly influenced by the country's leading antisemite and neo-Nazi, Adrien Arcand, who introduced him to a group of ardent antisemites including Paul Rassinier. Zundel recalled that Arcand 'made a German out of me.' Zundel built a professional reputation as an accomplished photo retoucher. Most of his clients, which included Canada's leading magazines, did not know that he was one of the country's most active distributors of neo-Nazi material. One customer who inadvertently came into his shop discovered a huge swastika on the wall surrounded by pictures of Hitler and other Nazis.[5]

During his trial the prosecution stressed Zundel's ardent devotion to Hitler, allegiance to the Nazis, advocacy of revolution in the Federal Republic of Germany, and his belief that the white race's position in the world had deteriorated because of the success of an international Zionist conspiracy. Israel was a 'terrorist state,' which was 'financially and morally bankrupt,' and Zionists controlled the 'moguls' in Bonn.[6]

Found guilty in 1985 and sentenced to fifteen months in prison, Zundel was given a temporary reprieve when the ruling was overturned on appeal because of procedural errors.* The second trial, which began in 1988, was memorable because it served to set off the deniers' most important salvo – fired by a newcomer to the movement who was guided into Holocaust denial by Zundel's team of advisers – in their assault on the truth since the publication of Arthur Butz's book. Zundel's lawyer, Douglas Christie, the main legal defender of Holocaust deniers, antisemites, Nazi war criminals, and neo-Nazis in Canada, came to Zundel's attention when he defended Jim Keegstra, a schoolteacher in Red Deer, Alberta. Keegstra, who denied the Holocaust, taught his students that a group of Jews called the 'Illuminati' was behind all the revolutions and debts in the world since the 1700s and that Judaism was an evil religion. He believed it his Christian duty to fight the evil conspiracy controlled by Jews (John D. Rockefeller was declared to be a Jew) through their money system.[7] The worst Jews were Talmudic Jews, though such 'atheistical' Jews as Leon Trotsky were also a danger.[8] Zionism was a Jewish fraud, and the Holocaust was a hoax.[9] (The most disturbing aspect of the Keegstra case was that he taught this array of material for fourteen years before anyone complained.)

Christie's tactics during the first Zundel trial were the subject of great controversy. He tried to have all potential jurors who were Jewish or who had Jewish friends or relatives screened out. Treating Holocaust survivors in a brutal fashion, calling one a liar and insisting that another give him the full names of at least twenty family members who had been killed in the camps,[10] he exhibited what *Ontario Lawyers Weekly* described as 'sheer nastiness.' In the midst of cross-examining Raul Hilberg, Christie asked him if he recognized a certain historical tract and then declared, 'I thought you might – you're a historian of sorts.'[11] He managed to structure his

---

* The jury found him guilty of spreading false information about the Holocaust but acquitted him on charges connected with 'The West, War, and Islam.'

defense so that it seemed to some observers that the Holocaust, not Zundel, was on trial.[12] For Christie the chief issue in the trial was the Zionist 'power' to curtail freedom of speech. He declared the belief that the Nazis killed six million Jews during the Holocaust to be the result of brainwashing, and told the jury that they were being prevented from asking questions about the Holocaust.[13]

In addition, Robert Faurisson came to Canada to advise Zundel and his lawyers. One of the world's leading deniers, he was a proponent of the notion that it was technically and physically impossible for the gas chambers at Auschwitz to have functioned as extermination facilities. Faurisson argued that compared to American execution chambers the German facilities were too small and primitive to have been killing chambers.[14] Faurisson, who testified as an expert witness for the defense during the first trial, was asked by the Crown to explain the missing six million Jewish victims of the Holocaust. Faurisson acknowledged that he did not know what happened to them but urged surviving Jews to give him the names of family members they had lost so he could try to locate them.[15]

At the second trial Christie and Faurisson were joined by David Irving, who flew to Toronto in January 1988 to assist in the preparation of Zundel's second defense and to testify on his behalf. Scholars have described Irving as a 'Hitler partisan wearing blinkers' and have accused him of distorting evidence and manipulating documents to serve his own purposes.[16] He is best known for his thesis that Hitler did not know about the Final Solution, an idea that scholars have dismissed.[17] The prominent British historian Hugh Trevor-Roper depicted Irving as a man who 'seizes on a small and dubious particle of "evidence,"' using it to dismiss far-more-substantial evidence that may not support his thesis. His work has been described as 'closer to theology or mythology than to history,' and he has been accused of skewing documents and misrepresenting data in order to reach historically untenable conclusions, particularly those that exonerate Hitler.[18] An ardent admirer of the Nazi leader, Irving placed a self-portrait of Hitler over his desk, described his visit to Hitler's mountaintop retreat as a spiritual experience,[19] and declared that Hitler repeatedly reached out to help the Jews.[20] In 1981 Irving, a self-described 'moderate fascist,' established his own right-wing political party, founded on his belief that he was meant to be a future leader of Britain.[21] He is an ultranationalist who believes that Britain has been on a steady path of decline accelerated by its misguided decision to launch a war against Nazi Germany. He has advocated that Rudolf Hess should have received the Nobel Peace prize for his efforts to try to stop war between Britain and Germany.[22] On some level Irving seems to conceive of himself as carrying on Hitler's legacy. In an interview with the *Daily Telegraph* in June 1992, he related that his one mistake in life was getting married: 'Marriage is a detour.' This was, Irving observed, something Hitler understood. Irving related that Hitler's naval adjutant once told him how Hitler decided he could not marry because Germany 'was his pride.' Irving asked when the German leader had informed the naval adjutant of this decision. When told the date was March 24, 1938, Irving responded, 'Herr Admiral, at that moment I was being born.'[23]

Irving had long equated the actions of Hitler and Allied leaders, an equivalence that was made easier by his claims that the Final Solution took place without Hitler's knowledge. Prior to participating in Zundel's trial, Irving had appeared at IHR conferences – at one he declared Hitler the 'biggest friend the Jews had in the Third Reich' – but he had never denied the annihilation of the Jews.[24] That changed in 1988 as a result of the events in Toronto.

Both Irving and Faurisson advocated inviting an American prison warden who had performed gas executions to testify in Zundel's defense, arguing that this would be the best tactic for proving that the gas chambers were a fraud and too primitive to operate safely. They solicited help from Bill Armontrout, warden of the Missouri State Penitentiary, who agreed to testify and suggested they also contact Fred A. Leuchter, an 'engineer' residing in Boston who specialized in constructing and installing execution apparatus. Irving and Faurisson immediately flew off to meet Leuchter. Irving, who had long hovered at the edge of Holocaust denial, believed that Leuchter's testimony could provide the documentation he needed to prove the Holocaust a myth.[25] According to Faurisson, when he first met Leuchter, the Bostonian accepted the 'standard notion of the

"Holocaust." '²⁶ After spending two days with him, Faurisson declared that Leuchter was convinced that it was chemically and physically impossible for the Germans to have conducted gassings.²⁷ Having agreed to serve as an expert witness for the defense, Leuchter then went to Toronto to meet with Zundel and Christie and to examine the materials they had gathered for the trial.

Within a few days Leuchter left for a week in Poland. Accompanied by his wife, a cinematographer supplied by Zundel, a draftsman, and an interpreter, the group toured Auschwitz/Birkenau and Majdanek. In light of the fact that Zundel paid Leuchter approximately $35,000 to make the trip,²⁸ one cannot help but wonder what would have been the reaction if Leuchter had returned to confirm the existence of gas chambers. However, Leuchter's leanings were revealed by his observation that although Zundel and Faurisson could not accompany the group, they were ex-officio members of the team, whose spirit was with them 'every step of the way.'²⁹

The group spent three days in Auschwitz/Birkenau and one in Majdanek surreptitiously and illegally collecting bricks and cement fragments – Leuchter called them 'forensic samples' – from a number of buildings, including those associated with the killing process. On returning to Massachusetts, Leuchter had the samples chemically analyzed. (He told the laboratory that the samples had to do with a workmen's compensation case.) He summarized his findings in *The Leuchter Report: An Engineering Report on the Alleged Execution Gas Chambers at Auschwitz, Birkenau, and Majdanek, Poland*, which was published by Zundel's Samisdat Publications and David Irving's publishing house, Focal Point Publications in London.* In it he concluded that there had never been homicidal gassings at any of these sites. Leuchter claimed that his findings were based on his 'expert knowledge' of the design criteria for gas chamber operation, and his visual inspections of both the remains of the chambers and

---

* The London edition was entitled *Auschwitz: The End of the Line: The Leuchter Report – The First Forensic Examination of Auschwitz*. It contained a foreword by Irving.

of 'original drawings and blueprints of some of the facilities.' The latter, he asserted, had been given to him by officials of the Auschwitz museum.[30]

According to Leuchter the design and fabrication of these facilities made it impossible for them to have served as execution chambers.[31] Moreover, Leuchter argued, given the size and usage rate of the alleged facilities at Auschwitz and Majdanek, it would have required sixty-eight years to execute the 'alleged number of six millions of persons.'[32] (This typifies the deniers' methods of obfuscation: No one had claimed that the gas chambers at Auschwitz or Majdanek were used to kill six million people. Millions of people died at the hands of the *Einsatzgruppen* and at other death camps.)

Deniers consider Leuchter's testimony at the trial a 'historical event.' It marked, Faurisson claimed expansively, the end of the 'myth of the gas chambers.'[33] Emotions were intense as Leuchter tore away the 'veil of the great swindle.' Faurisson described his own feelings as a mixture of 'relief and melancholy: relief because a thesis that I had defended for so many years was at last fully confirmed, and melancholy because I had fathered the idea in the first place.'[34] The record reveals that something quite different occurred. If any veil was lifted it was that of Leuchter's expertise. On the stand Leuchter was shown to have little technical training to equip him to reach his conclusions. The judge derided aspects of his methodology as 'gross speculation' and dismissed his opinion as being of no greater value than that of an ordinary tourist.[35]

Perhaps Faurisson's relief was also rooted in the fact that he knew that despite the revelations about Leuchter's lack of credentials and his fallacious scientific and historical methodology, the *Leuchter Report* would have a life of its own, as has been the case with the *Protocols of the Elders of Zion*, which has repeatedly been demonstrated to be a forgery. In fact, when it was originally published in France in the mid-nineteenth century, Jews did not appear in the book at all. Only at the beginning of this century was it rewritten with Jews as the primary culprits. This easily documented information has not stopped the *Protocols* from being accepted by people in different parts of the world as a factual rendition of 'international

Jewry's' nefarious goal to rule the world. So, too, Faurisson may have recognized that Leuchter's so-called scientific report would make Holocaust denial plausible despite its having been shown to be rooted in spurious scientific principles.

With the jury out of the room, the court began to determine Leuchter's qualifications as an expert witness. When the Crown Counsel questioned him about his training in math, chemistry, physics, and toxicology, he acknowledged that his only training in chemistry was 'basic . . . on the college level.' The only physics he had studied likewise consisted of two courses taken when he was studying for a bachelor of arts (not sciences) degree at Boston University. Admitting that he was not a toxicologist and had no degree in engineering, he rather cavalierly dismissed the need for it.[36] To this the judge responded sharply:

> THE COURT: How do you function as an engineer if you don't have an engineering degree?
>
> THE WITNESS: Well, I would question, Your Honour, what an engineering degree is. I have a Bachelor of Arts degree and I have the required background training both on the college level and in the field to perform my function as an engineer.
>
> THE COURT: Who determines that? You?[37]

Throughout the trial Judge Ronald Thomas made it clear that he was appalled by Leuchter's lack of training as an engineer as well as his deprecation of the need for such training. The judge was particularly taken aback by Leuchter's repeated assertions that anyone who went to college had 'the necessary math and science' to be an electrical engineer and to conduct the tests he conducted at Auschwitz.[38] The judge ruled that Leuchter could not serve as an expert witness on the construction and functioning of the gas chambers. The judge's findings as to Leuchter's suitability to comment on questions of engineering was unequivocal:

> THE COURT: I'm not going to have him get into the question of what's in a brick, what's in iron, what is in – he has no

expertise in this area. *He is an engineer because he has made himself an engineer in a very limited area.*[39]

Unknown to the court, Leuchter, who admitted under oath that he had only a bachelor of arts degree, was not being entirely candid regarding his education. Implying that an engineering degree had been unavailable to him, he told the court that when he was a student at Boston University, the school did not offer a degree in engineering. In fact it did, three different kinds.[40] Later in the trial, when the jury returned to the room, Zundel's lawyer and Leuchter obfuscated the paucity of his training:

q. And you are, I understand, a graduate of Boston University, with a B.A. in a field that entitles you to function as an engineer. Is that right?

a. Yes, sir.[41]

That field was history.

Leuchter was also less than candid about his methodology. He repeatedly asserted that he obtained the 'bulk' of his research material on the camps – including maps, floor plans and 'original blueprints' for the crematoria – from the official archives at Auschwitz/Birkenau and Majdanek. He testified that these drawings and blueprints played a far more important role in shaping his conclusions than the samples he collected at the camp.[42] After the trial Kazimierz Smolen, the director of the Auschwitz museum, unequivocally denied that Leuchter had received any plans or blueprints from the museum.[43] He may have procured tourist materials sold in the official souvenir kiosks in the camps. (It may have been the same material thousands of visitors, myself included, have bought during visits to these sites.)

Irrespective of who gave him the materials, he acknowledged that he 'didn't see any necessity' to reveal to camp officials that he was asking questions in order to gather material for a scientific report or legal action.[44] Anyone who had visited a heavily frequented tourist site, which – for better or for worse – Auschwitz/Birkenau has become, knows that the caliber of the answers one receives from officials varies markedly. If they believe that they are speaking to someone who has a professional expertise pertaining to the site they tend to be more precise. Nor, for that matter, did he see any necessity to ask permission to violate the Polish law against defacing national monuments and memorials.[45]

As citations from Leuchter's report were read, the judge's impatience intensified. He characterized Leuchter's methodology as 'ridiculous' and 'preposterous.'[46] Ruling that 'this report is not going to be filed,' the judge dismissed many of his conclusions as based on 'second-hand information.' He refused to allow Leuchter to testify about the impact of Zyklon-B on humans because he was neither a toxicologist nor a chemist and had never worked with the gas.[47] Again and again the judge kept coming back to Leuchter's capabilities and credibility:

> THE COURT: His opinion on this report is that there were never any gassings or there was never any exterminations carried on in this facility. *As far as I am concerned, from what I've heard, he is not capable of giving that opinion* . . . He is not in a position to say, as he said so sweepingly in this report, what could not have been carried on in these facilities.[48]

On the question of the functioning of the crematoria, despite the defense attorney's opposition, the judge's decision was unequivocal. He could not testify on this topic for a simple reason.

> THE COURT: He hasn't any expertise.[49]

The judge might have been even more irritated had he known that Leuchter misrepresented the extent of his familiarity with the operation of hydrogen cyanide. He told the court that he had discussed matters relating to the gas with the largest U.S. manufacturer of sodium cyanide and hydrogen cyanide, Du Pont, and that such consultation was 'an on-going thing.' Leuchter was again being less than accurate. He may have obtained Du Pont's published guidelines about the care needed in using hydrogen cyanide or any other of the myriad of substances the company manufactured. But Du Pont, denying Leuchter's claims of ongoing consultations, stated that it had 'never provided any information on cyanides to persons representing themselves as Holocaust deniers, including Fred Leuchter. Specifically, Du Pont has never provided any information regarding the use of cyanide at Auschwitz, Birkenau, or Majdanek.'[50]

But it was not only Leuchter's scientific expertise, or lack thereof, which was questioned by the court. The judge also expressed serious doubts about Leuchter's historical knowledge, which, as it emerged at the trial, was limited and often flawed. Leuchter was unaware of a host of documents pertaining to the installation and construction of the gas chambers and crematoria. He did not know of a report filed in June 1943 by the Waffen-SS commandant of construction at Auschwitz on the completion of the crematoria. The report indicated that the five crematoria had a total twenty-four-hour capacity of 4,756 bodies.[51] Leuchter had stated that the crematoria had a total capacity of 156 bodies in the same period of time.[52] Even if the SS's calculation was overly 'optimistic,' the difference between it and Leuchter's was staggering. He also had to admit that he did not know that there existed correspondence and documentation regarding powerful ventilators installed in the gas chambers to extract the gas that remained after the killings. After hearing these and other admissions by Leuchter, Judge Thomas expressed his dismay that Leuchter had reached his conclusions despite the fact that he had only a 'nodding acquaintance' with the history of the gas chambers. To suggest that he had any more than that, the judge declared, would be an insult.[53]

Leuchter told the court that his findings regarding Auschwitz were based on the supposition that the physical plant at the camps was the same today as it had been throughout the war.[54] He did not seem to know or take into account the fact that certain areas at Auschwitz had been rebuilt after the war. At Majdanek, Leuchter reached his conclusions knowing that he was looking at something that had been completely reconstructed. Hearing this, the judge dismissed the credibility of Leuchter's analysis of the Majdanek facility.

THE COURT: We have no plans; we have a reconstruction. This witness is in no better position than I will be to give evidence on this point. He went to Majdanek; he has seen something and it is really just speculation. This is creating a tourist attraction. I'm not going to have evidence in this court about tourist attractions.[55]

Leuchter claimed that his scientific conclusions were based, in great measure, on the residue left by Zyklon-B. In addition to being used by the Nazis to murder people, the gas was used to delouse clothing and combat insects and rodents.[56] The samples Leuchter took from the delousing chambers contained a far higher residue of hydrogen cyanide than those from the homicidal gas chambers. The bricks of the delousing chambers generally showed far more of the blue coloration often left by hydrocyanic acid than did those in the homicidal gas chambers. Leuchter argued that this lower-level residue and stain were conclusive proof that the structures presented to visitors as homicidal facilities could not have been used for that purpose.

But both Faurisson and Leuchter either ignored or did not know a number of critically important facts. Lice, which were destroyed in the delousing chambers, have a far higher resistance to hydrogen cyanide than do humans. It takes a more concentrated exposure to cyanide gas over a longer period of time to kill lice than to kill humans, hence the more intense blue stain. When the Crown Counsel asked Leuchter about this, he declined to answer because it was an area about which he was not qualified to testify.[57] Yet he used the delousing chamber as a 'control' for his findings.

Furthermore, the amount of hydrogen cyanide used in the homicidal gas chambers was lethal to humans forty to seventy times over. Because of the intensity of the gas, only a limited amount of it was inhaled by the victims. The remainder was quickly extracted from the chamber by the powerful ventilation system. Consequently the gas was in contact with the walls of the gas chamber for a very brief time each day it was in operation.

In the delousing chambers the situation was quite different. According to both technical manuals and the accounts of former prisoners, the cyanide gas was in contact with the walls for between twelve to eighteen hours a day. One would, therefore, logically expect a higher residue of cyanide in the delousing chambers, and the blue stain that indicated presence of the cyanide was more likely to be found on the bricks of a delousing chamber than those of a homicidal gas chamber.

Both Leuchter and Faurisson argued that 'it would be insanity' to operate a gas chamber in close proximity to crematoriums because of the danger of explosion. But records show that the amount of gas used by the SS was well below the threshold of explosion.[58] The Crown Counsel also pointed out that the manufacturer's manual stated that three times as much of the substance was required to kill rats than to kill humans, and twenty times as much to kill beetles as to kill rats.[59] The Crown argued that if it had been safe to use these much larger amounts for beetles without the threat of explosion then it would certainly have been safe to use the far smaller amount for humans.[60]

There was also a basic contradiction inherent in Faurisson and Leuchter's argument that the crude construction of the gas chambers proved that they could not have served as homidicial units without causing serious harm to the SS personnel operating them. The delousing chambers were constructed in the same fashion as the homicidal gas chambers. Irrespective of whether people or clothing would be contained therein, if one facility posed a threat of leakage the other would as well. Theoretically the delousing chamber would have been even more dangerous because it needed a higher concentration of hydrogen cyanide for a longer period of time.

In a certain gas chamber no cyanide traces were found.[61] Leuchter cited this as proof that this facility was never used as a gas chamber. But this particular gas chamber had been dynamited in January 1945. Its ruins were inundated with thirty centimeters of water in the summer and up to one meter of water in spring. The exposure to the elements lessened the presence of hydrogen cyanide.[62] Moreover, documents in the archives indicate that tests done on the grilles of the crematorium by Polish authorities shortly after the war showed residue of hydrocyanide compounds. Three of these grilles are in the Auschwitz museum. Had Leuchter asked museum officials, with whom he claimed to have consulted, they might have shown him the test results.[63]

This was not the only time that Leuchter was tripped up by history. In one crematorium some samples were negative and some were positive. Logically all should have been either positive or negative. (In fact, they should probably have been negative, since this gas chamber had hardly been used.) Had he asked the authorities in the Auschwitz museum, they could have told him that this crematorium, which had been destroyed in the wake of the abortive inmate uprising of October 1944, had been rebuilt with both original bricks as well as bricks from other buildings. Consequently, Leuchter's test was conducted on some bricks that did not even come from that particular crematorium. Nor did Leuchter seem to consider that the building had been exposed to the elements for more than forty years so that cyanide gas residue could have been obliterated.[64] He also took samples from a floor that had been washed regularly by the museum staff.[65]

In a move apparently calculated to enhance the drama of Leuchter's escapade, a cameraman had videotaped the collection of samples. On the tape Leuchter stressed that he had used protective gloves in order to collect his samples. Since the tests he was conducting were chemical and not bacteriological the gloves served relatively little purpose other than a theatrical one. He and his associates also wore protective masks. But the masks were dust masks, which do not prevent chemical contamination (a closed-respirator system would be needed for that). Moreover, Leuchter and his associate were not consistent. The videotape of this sample-collecting enterprise reveals that sometimes they had the masks on and sometimes they did not. This haphazard approach suggests that the masks were primarily for show, not protective purposes.[66]

By the end of his testimony in the Toronto courtroom on April 20 and 21, 1988,* Leuchter had been exposed as having virtually no

---

* Zundel was found guilty a second time and sentenced to nine months in jail. In 1992 the law under which Zundel had been charged was declared unconstitutional by the Canadian Supreme Court.

educational training as an engineer, and his historical knowledge had been shown to be even more limited. His historical knowledge was based on two hundred pages of Raul Hilberg's book, *The Destruction of the European Jews*; articles by deniers; conversations with Faurisson, Irving, Zundel, and Christie; and documents Leuchter claimed, but the director of the Auschwitz museum categorically denied, had been given to him at the site by museum authorities. Judge Thomas ruled that Leuchter could testify before the jury about what he saw on his trip and compare it 'within his area of expertise' to what he 'normally worked with.'[67] Although it did not emerge until after the trial, what Leuchter 'normally worked with' was not only far more limited than what the court assumed but likewise the subject of significant controversy.

On July 20, 1990, Alabama Assistant Attorney General Ed Carnes sent a memo to all capital-punishment states questioning Leuchter's credentials and credibility. Carnes stated not only that Leuchter's views on the gas-chamber process were 'unorthodox' but that he was running a death-row shakedown scheme. If a state refused to use his services, Leuchter would testify at the last minute on behalf of the inmate, claiming that the state's death chamber might malfunction.[68] According to Carnes, Leuchter made 'money on both sides of the fence.'[69] Describing Leuchter's behavior in Virginia, Florida, and Alabama, Carnes observed that in less than thirty days Leuchter had testified in three states that their electric-chair execution technology was too old and unreliable to be used. In Florida and Virginia the federal courts had rejected Leuchter's testimony because it was unreliable. In Florida the court had found that Leuchter had 'misquoted the statements' contained in an important affidavit and had 'inaccurately surmised' a crucial premise of his conclusion.[70] In Virginia, Leuchter provided a death-row inmate's attorney with an affidavit claiming that the electric chair would fail. The Virginia court decided that the credibility of Leuchter's affidavit was limited because Leuchter was 'the refused contractor who bid to replace the electrodes in the Virginia chair.'[71]

After the dissemination of Leuchter's report, yet another blow was delivered to his reputation as America's leading expert on gas execution chambers. Despite his claims to the contrary, it appears that he had no actual experience with their building or installation. His claims to have advised states on this execution methodology were denied by officials from the very states with which he said he had worked. According to Leuchter's testimony at the Zundel trial, the Department of Correction in North Carolina, a state that permits gas chamber executions, consulted with him regarding the functioning of its gas chamber. In the *Leuchter Report* he reiterated his claim to have been a consultant to North Carolina.[72] Gary Dixon, the warden of the Central Prison in Raleigh, North Carolina, where the gas chamber is located, contradicted Leuchter's claims. According to Dixon the former warden 'vaguely recalled' that he had received a telephone call from Leuchter trying to sell the prison a lethal injection machine. Dixon denied Leuchter's contention that he had consulted with North Carolina prison officials on gas-chamber matters: 'Our records do not support that Mr. Leuchter performed either consultation or any service during the installation of our execution chamber.'[73]

There were, in fact, six states in the United States at the time of the publication of Leuchter's report that permitted executions by gas chambers: Arizona, California, Maryland, Mississippi, North Carolina, and Missouri used to permit executions by gas, but recently switched to lethal injection. Representatives of each of these states provided crucial information on Leuchter's connections with them. Despite Leuchter's claim to the contrary, according to these officials, he had not advised them on executions. A spokesman for Mississippi, Ken Jones, stated that while Leuchter had visited Mississippi's execution facility and commented on it, the visit had been initiated at Leuchter's request. Moreover, the state had not entered into 'any financial agreement' with him. According to Shelly Z. Shapiro, the head of a Holocaust education center in Albany, New York, who coordinated an investigation into Leuchter's background, he has not worked for either Arizona or Maryland. Maryland used Eaton Ironworks to check its chamber prior to an execution. State officials reported that Leuchter had 'never worked or consulted' with the Maryland Penitentiary.[74] An official of the Arizona Corrections

Office also stated that they had 'never used' Fred Leuchter's services.[75] In fact, the official observed, Arizona does not even maintain its gas chamber in working order, and any maintenance done in the past was performed by the state's service personnel.

Leuchter may have misrepresented his technical expertise in areas other than gas chambers. At the Zundel trial he claimed to have consulted with Warden Daniel B. Vasquez of California's San Quentin prison about a heart-monitoring system that would replace the older-type mechanical stethoscope then being used. Subsequently Vasquez denied that San Quentin had ever contracted with Leuchter for either the 'installation of a heart monitoring system or for any other work.'[76]

The credibility of Leuchter's report was founded on his expertise in building gas chambers. Missouri was the only state Leuchter actually advised on gas execution chambers. The closest his company had apparently come to building one was a proposed blueprint it prepared for refurbishing the state penitentiary. He submitted a plan that was never used because the state switched to lethal injection for executions.[77]

But it was not only his educational record, historical knowledge, business integrity, and professional experience that were subjects of controversy. According to an affidavit by Dr. Edward A. Brunner, chair of the Department of Anesthesia at Northwestern University Medical School, Leuchter's lethal injection system caused excruciating pain but rendered victims incapable of screaming to communicate their distress.[78] Based on Brunner's findings, some death penalty opponents argue that Leuchter's lethal injection system constituted cruel and unusual punishment. Others, particularly those who support capital punishment, dismiss this point as moot because pain and suffering are part of capital punishment. Ironically, Leuchter is not one of the latter. He believes that no execution system should be a cause of pain and says he slept well at night because his work resulted in fewer people being 'tortured.'[79]

In 1989 Leuchter formed an engineering firm and incorporated in the Commonwealth of Massachusetts. The firm's purpose was to 'engage in the practice of engineering' and consult in all areas of engineering.[80] The company provided electrocution hardware, charging $35,000 for an electrocution system, $30,000 for a lethal injection system, and $85,000 for a gallows. (The gallows is disproportionately expensive because it is infrequently requested.) Gas chambers were listed at $200,000. For states without an existing execution facility, Leuchter designed a self-contained 'execution trailer' that cost $100,000 and came complete with a lethal-injection machine, a steel holding cell for the inmate, and areas for the witnesses, medical personnel, and prison officials.[81]

In April 1990 Shelly Shapiro, director of a Holocaust education center – Holocaust Survivors and Friends in Pursuit of Justice – and Beate Klarsfeld filed a letter of complaint with the Massachusetts Board of Registration of Engineers in Boston about Leuchter's erroneous claim to be an engineer and his use of this designation to 'mislead the public' about gas chambers.[82] The commonwealth investigated and found sufficient grounds to charge him with 'illegally' practicing or 'offer[ing]' to practice engineering.[83] In June 1991, two weeks before he was to go on trial for practicing without a licence, Leuchter signed a consent agreement with the commonwealth admitting that he was 'not and never had been' a professional engineer and had fraudulently presented himself to Massachusetts, New Jersey, Alabama, and other states as an engineer with the ability to consult on matters concerning 'execution technology.' In addition he acknowledged that although he was not an engineer and had never taken an engineering licensing test, he had produced reports, including the ' "Alleged Execution Gas Chambers at Auschwitz, Birkenau, and Majdanek," containing my engineering opinions.' He agreed to 'cease and desist' presenting himself as an engineer and issuing any reports, including the one on Auschwitz, in which he provided engineering opinions.[84]

While this constituted a major blow to Leuchter's credibility, an even greater one was delivered from a completely different source. A Frenchman who at one time had been intrigued by Faurisson's contentions regarding gas chambers rendered a devastating assault on the deniers' claims. Born in 1944 in France, Jean-Claude Pressac, a trained pharmacist, first visited Poland and the remains of the death camps in 1966. Sometime thereafter he decided to write a novel depicting life as it would have been had the Germans won. His research for this proposed book included another visit to Auschwitz in October 1979. This marked the beginning of an incredible personal and scientific journey that would have dire consequences for the claim that the homicidal gas chambers were a hoax. It was a journey that entailed years of study, more than fifteen trips to Auschwitz, and groundbreaking research in archives in the former Soviet Union.

During his research trip to Auschwitz in 1979 he examined photographs, documents, and work orders pertaining to the design and construction of the gas chambers. Perplexed by what appeared as contradictions in the plans, Pressac questioned museum officials and archivists about the construction of the gas chambers. Officials allayed some of his doubts by showing him an array of plans and documents relating to the camps and the execution chambers.* Though Pressac acknowledged the power of their arguments, he remained troubled by the fact that he could not find on the drawings the specific designation 'gas chamber.' Pressac's confusion was, in fact, justified because, as he learned, a number of the gas chambers were not originally built as homicidal units but were transformed to serve that purpose.[85] When he subsequently examined the documentation on this transformation, he found an abundance of evidence attesting to the specific purposes of the gas chamber. But before he reached that point he engaged in a potentially dangerous but illuminating detour; he almost became a denier.

During his visit to the Auschwitz archives, Pressac learned of a French professor who had made a very brief visit to the archives in 1976 but after two days took ill and left. Shortly thereafter this professor published a series of articles asserting that hydrocyanic-acid homicidal gas chambers were an impossibility and that therefore the annihilation of the Jews at such places as Auschwitz was only a legend, the result of historical fakery if not purposeful deceit.[86] On

---

* They showed him documentation regarding the design and fabrication of sophisticated ventilation systems that had been installed in the gas chambers. What purpose, they asked, would such a system have served in a morgue or crematorium?

his return to France, Pressac sought out Robert Faurisson. Impressed by Faurisson's seemingly vast array of knowledge and 'serious and unimpeachable references,' Pressac began to meet with him on a regular basis.[87] The meetings lasted for approximately nine months, during which time, Faurisson, anxious to co-opt the pharmacist into the ranks of Holocaust deniers, opened his files to him.[88] Initially Pressac found himself greatly attracted to Faurisson's arguments. After a number of months of intensive contact, the meetings became less frequent. Pressac broke off all contact in April 1981, when he discovered that for Faurisson 'dogma [was] paramount' to truth. Pressac's own reading of the documents convinced him that Faurisson's arguments were fatally flawed.

After Pressac broke with Faurisson he recognized that it was not Faurisson's theories that attracted him but the professor's seeming ability to explain away something that was inherently unbelievable. This is the deniers' ultimate trump card. They have the only rational explanation for something that remains, despite massive research, essentially irrational: It could not happen. When Pressac subjected deniers' theories to documentary analysis he understood that they were not just scientifically flawed. They ignored reams of evidence that proved precisely what Faurisson and his cohorts wished to deny.

Pressac's doubts about Faurisson's methodology first surfaced when together they reviewed weekly reports on the prisoners killed at the concentration camp near Strasbourg, Natzweiler-Struthof. In August 1943 a gas chamber was put into operation there in order to provide August Hirt, a professor at the Strasbourg University Institute of Anatomy, with skeletons for his collection. Another professor, Otto Bickenbach, availed himself of the gas chamber to conduct medical experiments on prisoners. Approximately 130 people, primarily Jews and Gypsies, were killed in it. When Pressac and Faurisson reviewed the documents from the camp, Pressac saw the 'honest and meticulous professor in a more worrying light.'[89] The camp administrators had prepared weekly reports on the number of prisoners in the camp. Two reports from August 1943, the month the gas chamber started operating, contained important evidence. The report of August 14 indicated that there had been 90 Jews present at the outset of the week of whom 30 had 'left' the camp deceased. The report for the next week indicated that of the 60 remaining at the beginning of that week, 57 had died. This extremely high death rate, two weeks in a row at precisely the time the gas chamber commenced working, aroused Pressac's suspicions. He soon discovered additional evidence. On all the other reports some cause of death was entered on the reverse side. In these two cases the reports were left blank. All other deaths were recorded in the Natzweiler town hall. In the case of these deaths no record was kept.[90] Pressac considered the two reports 'damning evidence' that these Jews had been killed en masse. However, Faurisson had a ready 'explanation.' The forms used for the week of the fourteenth and twenty-first of August differed slightly from previous ones. (They were printed in Gothic script while previous ones had been printed in Roman script.) Faurisson explained to his doubting disciple that the change in script confused the SS. Instead of listing the Jews on the line for 'liberation,' the SS mistakenly listed them on the line for 'deaths.' And somehow the SS made precisely the same mistake two weeks in a row. This convenient explanation, which ignored an array of contradictory evidence, constituted a 'warning bell' for Pressac. Faurisson's explanations no longer seemed as precise and logical as they had; they certainly bore little relationship to the evidence.

(It is ironic that Pressac's doubts should have been aroused by Faurisson's treatment of the Natzweiler reports. Apparently at the time Pressac did not know that the Waffen-SS unit that supervised the building of the gas chamber left behind a document that explicitly described the facility's purpose. They submitted a bill to Strasbourg University's Institute of Anatomy for the 'construction of a gas chamber.'[91])

Faurisson's description of his meeting with Auschwitz museum officials sounded yet another alarm for Pressac:

I made one of the Auschwitz Museum officials, Mr. Jan Machlek, come to the place (Crematorium I). I showed him the furnaces. I asked him 'Are they authentic?' He replied 'Of course!' I then passed my finger across the mouth of one of the furnaces. I showed him there was no soot. With an embarrassed air, he told me that these furnaces were a 'reconstitution.'[92]

Faurisson made it appear as if he had caught this official in a lie and forced him to tell the truth.* But it was Faurisson, not the museum representative, who engaged in obfuscation. Faurisson's contention that, if the furnaces were authentic, soot should have been present, more than thirty-five years after they had been used, made as much sense as his claim that SS officers could not decipher a form printed in Gothic script. Equally manipulative was his claim that it was *his* revelation that there was no soot present that forced the 'embarrassed' official reluctantly to admit that the facility was a 'reconstruction.' Why should the official have been embarrassed? The museum's own photographs demonstrate that the structure was rebuilt after the war.[93]

This kind of tactic is typical of deniers, Faurisson in particular. In 1987 he appeared on a radio interview show in France. Another guest on the show was a Holocaust survivor who – the host told Faurisson prior to the show – had been interned in Auschwitz from April 11, 1943, until April 11, 1945. Faurisson immediately told the host that this was impossible because most prisoners at Auschwitz were evacuated in January 1945. According to Faurisson, when the host reported these objections to the survivor, 'the latter, not without some embarrassment, then had to confess that he had been transferred from Auschwitz to Buchenwald in the last months of the war.'[94] Relying on what has become a mainstay of deniers' reasoning, Faurisson contended that if one item was false much if not all else was false. The survivor, Faurisson wrote to the host of the show, 'lied to you on this point. I fear he lied to you and to the listeners on many other points.'[95]

Once again, as in the case of the Auschwitz museum official, one wonders why the man should have been embarrassed. It is common knowledge that Auschwitz was evacuated in January 1945 and that the Soviet Army entered the camp shortly thereafter. (By April they had reached Berlin.) Why would this former prisoner have lied about

* He did the same thing with Otto Frank, Anne Frank's father (see Appendix).

something so widely known? His 'lie' did not make his experience sound more severe. If anything, his 'admission' that he was evacuated in the final months of the war intensified his saga of suffering. This was a time when the Nazis marched survivors of the death camps west to Germany to keep them from falling into the liberators' hands. Thousands died as a result. The host may have assumed that when the survivor said he was interned for two years, the entire time was spent in Auschwitz. Faurisson transformed what in all likelihood was a misunderstanding into a deliberate lie that was part of a nexus of conspiratorial falsehoods.

Given the exposure of Leuchter's historical and technical deficiencies at the Zundel trial, the publication of Pressac's findings, and his encounter with the Massachusetts legal system one might assume that his report would have been totally discredited. But, in an amazing display of incompetence and culpability, a number of powerful and respected media outlets have enhanced Leuchter's credibility and enabled deniers to use his pseudoscientific work to assault the truth. In February 1990 an article appeared in the *Atlantic Monthly*, 'Justice: A Matter of Engineering, Capital Punishment as a Technical Problem,' intended – according to the editorial staff of the magazine – to depict Fred Leuchter as the eccentric but legitimate headsman of the execution industry.[96] The author, Susan Lehman, described Leuchter as a 'trained and accomplished engineer' who was more conversant with electric chair technology than anyone else: He keeps a chair in his basement. Despite the article's contempt for Leuchter's specialization – killing people – it cast him as an expert who was 'distressed' to find that much of this nation's execution equipment was defective. Leuchter's apparatus, Lehman wrote, was designed not to torture its victims.[97]

While the story was apparently intended to present Leuchter as a ghoulish grim reaper who 'likes what he does,' deniers began to cite it as validation of Leuchter's expertise.[98] The *IHR Newsletter* identified Leuchter as the man 'certified by the *Atlantic* as America's leading expert on gas chambers and other execution systems.' As soon as the article appeared the *Atlantic*, one of America's most prestigious magazines, was deluged with phone calls.[99] The editors acknowledged that they had not known about Leuchter's lack of training, false claims to be an engineer, involvement in Holocaust denial, appearance as an expert witness for Zundel, or his denier-sponsored investigative trip to Poland. The editors defended themselves by claiming that his participation in the deniers' efforts had 'no direct bearing' on the subject of the article. The publisher of the magazine protested that neither he nor his staff could be expected to know about Leuchter's 'hobby.'

As an expression of its contrition – a simple computer search in a media data base would have revealed Leuchter's involvement in the Zundel trial – the magazine agreed to publish one letter on Leuchter's background.

If the *Atlantic* was guilty of incompetence, the same cannot be said of 'Prime Time Live,' the ABC television show starring Diane Sawyer and Sam Donaldson, which aired a segment on Leuchter in May 1990. Entitled 'Dr. Death,' the piece profiled Leuchter as 'the country's foremost expert at creating, designing and maintaining execution equipment. His business . . . is death.' Weeks before this segment aired, Beate Klarsfeld and Shelly Shapiro found out about it. They alerted ABC executives to the fact that Leuchter had been a witness at the Zundel trial, where the presiding judge had ruled that his report could not be used as evidence because he was not a toxicologist, chemist, or engineer. They told the television executives that Leuchter had become a regular participant in IHR and other extremist gatherings and that the *Leuchter Report*, which had been condemned by the British House of Commons as a 'fascist publication' and 'pernicious' effort, is distributed by white supremacist and extremist groups.[100] They also screened Leuchter's video of his trip to Auschwitz-Birkenau.

The 'Prime Time' producers were cautioned that airing the segment would enhance both Holocaust denial and the reputation of a thoroughly discredited man. Bob Currie, the ABC 'Prime Time' producer in charge of the segment on Leuchter, informed Shapiro and Klarsfeld that Leuchter's reputation and activities, which were already known to him, were not germane.[101] 'Prime Time' ignored letters from scholars in this field urging them not to proceed with this segment. (A personal letter I sent to the executive producer of the show explaining why this was a dangerous move was never acknowledged.) After the segment aired Currie justified his failure to include any reference to Leuchter's activities as a Holocaust denier by arguing that it simply 'wasn't relevant to what the story was about.'* He blamed the 'sanitization' of Leuchter's background – that is, the elimination of references to his Holocaust denial activity – on decisions by 'high-ups' including Ira Rosen, senior producer, and Rick Kaplan, executive producer.[102]

In October 1990 the New York Times entered the fray. A front-page news story on the methodology of capital punishment left no doubt that Leuchter had become a controversial if not discredited figure in the execution business. It identified him as someone whom opponents of capital punishment consider a 'metaphor for much that is wrong with the death penalty.' The article made a passing reference to his involvement in denial activities.[103] An editorial the following week again referred to Leuchter, condemning capital punishment and observing that Leuchter had become persona non grata in the execution business because of his unorthodox and controversial methods. While it acknowledged that Leuchter 'once told a Canadian court that he regarded the killing of Jews in Hitler's gas chambers as a myth,' it dismissed this as of little significance to 'the culture of executioners,' in which such views do not 'disqualify' him. 'Leuchter, after all, only designs death machines; others create the market for them.' Portraying Leuchter as an innocent cog in a perverse system, the editorial declared that the problem was not 'with the headsman [but] with the system.' Despite its shortcomings, the editorial together with the previous article destroyed whatever remained of Leuchter's 'technical credibility.'[104]

But it was another major media institution, London's Sunday Times, that eventually gave the Leuchter Report and its proponents another

---

* In the segment Leuchter took the film crew on a tour of the North Carolina chamber. The impression given viewers was that he had worked on this facility when, in fact, he had not. Prime Time Live (ABC-TV), May 10, 1990.

lease on life. David Irving, who during the Zundel trial declared himself converted by Leuchter's work to Holocaust denial and to the idea that the gas chambers were a myth, described himself as conducting a 'one-man intifada' against the official history of the Holocaust.[105]

In his foreword to his publication of the *Leuchter Report*, Irving wrote that there was no doubt as to Leuchter's 'integrity' and 'scrupulous methods.' He made no mention of Leuchter's lack of technical expertise or of the many holes that had been poked in his findings. Most important, Irving wrote, 'Nobody likes to be swindled, still less where considerable sums of money are involved.' Irving identified Israel as the swindler, claiming that West Germany had given it more than ninety billion deutsche marks in voluntary reparations, 'essentially in atonement for the "gas chambers of Auschwitz."' According to Irving the problem was that the latter was a myth that would 'not die easily.'[106] He subsequently set off to promulgate Holocaust denial notions in various countries. Fined for doing so in Germany, in his courtroom appeal against the fine he called on the court to 'fight a battle for the German people and put an end to the blood lie of the Holocaust which has been told against this country for fifty years.' He dismissed the memorial to the dead at Auschwitz as a 'tourist attraction.'[107] He traced the origins of the myth to an 'ingenious plan' of the British Psychological Warfare Executive, which decided in 1942 to spread the propaganda story that Germans were 'using "gas chambers" to kill millions of Jews and other "undesirables."'[108]

Branding Irving and Leuchter 'Hitler's heirs,' the British House of Commons denounced the former as a 'Nazi propagandist and longtime Hitler apologist' and the latter's report as a 'fascist publication.'[109] One might have assumed that would have marked the end of Irving's reputation in England, but it did not. Condemned in the *Times* of London in 1989 as a 'man for whom Hitler is something of a hero and almost everything of an innocent and for whom Auschwitz is a Jewish deception,' Irving may have had his reputation revived in 1992 by the London *Sunday Times*.[110] The paper hired Irving to translate the Goebbels diaries, which had been discovered in a Russian archive and, it was assumed, would shed light on the conduct of the Final Solution. The paper paid Irving a significant sum plus a percentage of the syndication fees.*

Journalists and scholars alike were shocked that the *Times* chose such a discredited figure to do this work. Showered with criticism, the editor of the *Sunday Times*, Andrew Neil, denounced Irving's views as 'reprehensible' but defended engaging Irving because he was only being used as a 'transcribing technician.' Peter Pulzer, a professor of politics at Oxford and an expert on the Third Reich, observed that it was ludicrous for Neil to refer to Irving as a 'mere technician,' arguing that when you hired someone to edit a 'set of documents others had not seen, you took on the whole man.'[111]

However the matter is ultimately resolved, the *Sunday Times* has rescued Irving's reputation from the ignominy to which it had been consigned by the House of Commons. In the interest of a journalistic scoop, this British paper was willing to throw its task as a gatekeeper of the truth and of journalistic ethics to the winds. By resuscitating Irving's reputation, it also gave new life to the *Leuchter Report*.

Leuchter has also had his reputation resurrected by a recent book and documentary film about America's capital punishment industry. *The Execution Protocol*, by Stephen Trombley, examines the steps between the imposition of the death sentence and the actual execution.[112] A major focus of both Trombley's book and film is Fred Leuchter. Trombley draws a sympathetic portrait of Leuchter, depicting him as a slightly bizarre and unconventional, myopic craftsman and entrepreneur who filled a need in the execution industry in a creative fashion. Trombley does address Leuchter's denial activities

---

* The Russian archives granted Irving permission to copy two microfiche plates, each of which held about forty-five pages of the diaries. Irving immediately violated his agreement, took many plates, transported them abroad, and had them copied without archival permission. There is serious concern in archival circles that he may have significantly damaged the plates when he did so, rendering them of limited use to subsequent researchers.

Irving believes Jews are 'very foolish not to abandon the gas chamber theory while they still have time.' He 'foresees [a] new wave of antisemitism' due to Jews' exploitation of the Holocaust 'myth.' C. C. Aronsfeld, 'Holocaust "Revisionists" Are Busy in Britain,' *Midstream*, Jan. 1993, p. 29.

but represents them as simply *another* aspect of this iconoclastic man. In contrast to his portrayal of Leuchter, he presents the ADL, Shapiro, Klarsfeld, and others who protested Leuchter's denial activities as unfairly harassing this committed craftsman who may harbor some bizarre notions but, in truth, only wants to make killing more humane.

As a result of Trombley's book and film Leuchter has once again been invited to appear on various talk shows as an expert on gas chambers. He has been interviewed on German, French, and British television. Most of these segments fail to mention his association with the Holocaust deniers. A similar attitude is evident in the media reviews of David Irving's books: Most rarely address his neofascist or denial connections.[113]

Irving is one of the most dangerous spokespersons for Holocaust denial. Familiar with historical evidence, he bends it until it conforms with his ideological leanings and political agenda. A man who is convinced that Britain's great decline was accelerated by its decision to go to war with Germany, he is most facile at taking accurate information and shaping it to confirm his conclusions. A review of his recent book, *Churchill's War*, which appeared in *New York Review of Books*, accurately analyzed his practice of applying a double standard to evidence. He demands 'absolute documentary proof' when it comes to proving the Germans guilty, but he relies on highly circumstantial evidence to condemn the Allies.[114] This is an accurate description not only of Irving's tactics, but of those of deniers in general.

The impact of Leuchter's work is difficult to assess. Rationally one would like to assume that, since Leuchter has been exposed as a man without the qualifications necessary to perform this analysis, and since his work has been demonstrated to be scientifically and methodologically fallacious, the destiny of the *Leuchter Report* would be the dustbin of history. But the Holocaust and, to only a slightly lesser degree, Holocaust denial itself remind us that the irrational has a fatal attraction even to people of goodwill. It can overwhelm masses of evidence and persuade people to regard the most outrageous and untenable notions as fact. This is easier to accomplish when the public does not have the historical and technical knowledge necessary to refute these irrational and inherently fantastic claims. Ultimately the deniers' ability to keep repeating Leuchter's conclusions even though they have been discredited is another indication that truth is far more fragile than fiction and that reason alone cannot protect it.

10

The Battle for the Campus

This is not a public stagecoach that has to take everyone who buys a ticket.

– *Benjamin Franklin*[1]

In the early 1990s American college campuses became loci of intensive activity by a small group of Holocaust deniers. Relying on creative tactics and assisted by a fuzzy kind of reasoning often evident in academic circles, the deniers achieved millions of dollars of free publicity and significantly furthered their cause. Their strategy was profoundly simple. Bradley Smith, a Californian who has been involved in a variety of Holocaust denial activities since the early 1980s, attempted to place a full-page ad claiming that the Holocaust was a hoax in college newspapers throughout the United States. The ad was published by papers at some of the more prestigious institutions of higher learning in the United States.

Entitled 'The Holocaust Story: How Much Is False? The Case for Open Debate,' the ad provoked a fierce debate on many of the campuses approached by Smith. His strategy was quite straightforward: He generally called a paper's advertising department to ascertain the charge for publication of a full-page ad and then submitted camera-ready copy and a certified check in the proper amount. On occasion he inquired in advance whether a paper would be willing to run this particular ad.*

---

* Among the papers that accepted it, either as an ad or an op-ed column, were those of the University of Arizona, Cornell, Duke, the University of Georgia, Howard, the University of Illinois at Urbana-Champaign, Louisiana State, the University of

Even when he was rejected, the attempt to place the ad won him significant media attention.[2] Campus newspapers began to use his name in headlines without identifying him, assuming readers would know who he was. Articles, letters, and op-ed pieces defended Holocaust denial's right to make its 'views' known. But not all the results were necessarily what Smith would have wanted. On some campuses there was a backlash against him and Holocaust denial. Courses on the Holocaust that had languished on the back burner for an extended period materialized in the next semester's offerings. Campus administrators admitted that the ad constituted the final push necessary to move these courses from the planning stage to the schedule books.[3] Professors from a wide variety of disciplines included discussion of the Holocaust in their courses. Movies, speakers, photographic exhibits, and other presentations relating to the Holocaust were brought to campus. Students participated in rallies, teach-ins, and protests.

This response prompted some observers to argue that the controversy had a positive impact. Students had become increasingly aware not only of the Holocaust but of the contemporary attempt to subvert history and spread antisemitism. While this may be a relatively accurate analysis of the immediate outcome of Smith's endeavor, there is another more sobering and pessimistic aspect to the matter. Analysis of the students', faculty's, and administration's responses reveals both a susceptibility to the worst form of historical revisionism and a failure to fully understand the implications of Holocaust denial, even among those who vigorously condemned it.

This was not Smith's first use of college newspapers to spread Holocaust denial. For a number of years Smith, along with other deniers, had been placing small ads containing the phone number

---

Michigan, the University of Montana, Northwestern, Ohio State, Rutgers, Vanderbilt, Washington University, and the University of Washington.

Among those colleges rejecting the ad were Berkeley, Brown, the University of California at Santa Barbara, the University of Chicago, Dartmouth, Emory, Georgetown, Harvard, the University of Minnesota, the University of North Carolina, the University of Pennsylvania, Purdue, Rice, the University of Southern California, the University of Tennessee, the University of Texas (Austin), UCLA, the University of Virginia, the University of Wisconsin (Madison), and Yale.

and address of the Committee on Open Debate on the Holocaust (CODOH), an organization Smith had created with fellow denier Mark Weber in 1987. According to the ADL, CODOH was initially funded by the late William Curry, a Nebraska businessman known for his antisemitic activities. In 1986, he first attempted to place an ad denying the Holocaust in a campus newspaper. He sent one thousand dollars to the *Daily Nebraskan* for a full-page ad claiming the Holocaust was a hoax.[4] The paper rejected the ad. Shortly thereafter Curry died, and Smith continued his work.

Smith claims that he has no connection to any other denial group and his only association is with CODOH. He has had a long-standing association with the IHR, serving as a contributing editor of its newsletter since June 1985. At the time he was placing the ads he still maintained a relationship with it.[5] In 1986 he launched the IHR radio project, writing a regular column on the project for the IHR's newsletter, in which he touted his success in getting Holocaust denial onto the radio. Under the auspices of the IHR he planned to tour colleges and universities to speak about 'Holocaust fraud and falsehood.'[6] Smith's objective was not to 'plant seeds' for coming generations but to 'take revisionist scholarship directly into our universities NOW!' In a letter to his followers he announced that the IHR had guaranteed to pay a portion of both his 'start-up costs' and his 'on-going expenses.'[7]

Before becoming involved with the IHR's radio project, Smith published *Prima Facie*, which he dedicated to 'monitoring Holocaust Cultism, Censorship and Suppression of Free Inquiry.' In it he attacked Mel Mermelstein, who had successfully challenged the IHR's demand for 'proof' that the Holocaust happened. Smith's description of Mermelstein – as a 'yokel' who had sued the institute because it refused to believe that 'a hank of hair and a jar full of ashes proves' that Jews were 'exterminated' in gas chambers – typified the tone of the newsletter. Mermelstein had developed a 'tongue so twisted he could drill his own teeth.'[8]

Articles from *Prima Facie* have been reprinted in *Spearhead*, the publication of the right-wing extremist British National party. One such article referred to a wire service report of how a Gestapo officer watched with a smile as his German shepherd dog killed an elderly Jew in Poland in 1942. Smith's use of sarcasm in his attempt to cast doubt on the story was a hallmark of his style.

> Let's say the dog was an 80-pounder – hell let's say it was a 100-pounder! Now let's say the elderly Jew was frail and small, perhaps only a 100-pounder himself. Hell, let's say he was an 80-pounder! I do want to be fair about this. So one question to get straight about the German dog and the elderly Jew is this: How much of the one could the other really eat?[9]

Smith's accomplice was Mark Weber, co-director of CODOH,[10] one of the more active spokesmen for Holocaust denial, and a former member of the National Alliance, a neo-Nazi organization. *Spotlight* described Weber as the 'shining star' of defense witnesses at the Zundel trial.[11] At the trial and in denial publications Weber has argued that the Jews who died were the 'unfortunate victims' not of an extermination program but of 'disease and malnutrition brought on by the complete collapse of Germany in the final months of the war.' Repeating a denial argument that had first been voiced by Austin App, Weber contended that if the extermination program had actually existed, the Jews found alive by the Allied forces at the war's end 'would have long since been killed.'[12]

Born in 1951, he was educated in a Jesuit high school in Portland, Oregon. In an interview in November 1989 with the *University of Nebraska Sower* he expressed his concern about the future of the white 'race' in the United States and about the future of the country. Weber contended that the country was heading in one of two possible directions. Either it would become 'a sort of Mexicanized, Puerto Ricanized country,' a result of the failure of 'white Americans' to reproduce themselves, or it would break up because of long-standing racial problems. He rejected the possibility of a unified American heritage or culture based on a multiplicity of races and groups. He did not think it desirable or feasible for 'black Americans to be assimilated into white society.' He seemed to yearn for a time when the United States was defined as a 'white country' and nonwhites were 'second-class citizens.' This gave the country a 'mooring, an anchor.' He bemoaned the fact that 'today we don't even have that.'[13] As the newspaper controversy became more public and Weber became more publicly involved in denial activities, his ideas on race were increasingly left unarticulated.

One of the first papers approached by CODOH, which for all intents and purposes consisted of Smith and Weber, was Pennsylvania State University's *Daily Collegian*. After running the small ad that contained CODOH's number for a few weeks it dropped it in response to campus criticism. Smith immediately sent a series of letters to local newspapers accusing the *Daily Collegian* of trying to 'suppress and even censor radical scholarship.'[14] It may have been the '*Sturm und Drang*' he created with this small ad that persuaded him to expand his efforts.

Shortly after his failed attempt at Penn State he experienced the same problem with the *Stanford Daily*, which had been running a similar ad for a period of seven weeks. The editor cancelled it due to student protests. Smith, implying that Hillel, the Jewish student organization, controlled the *Daily*'s coverage of other issues, including American politics in the Middle East, urged the editor to take a stand for 'free inquiry and open debate' by running the ad.[15] He told Hillel students that it was in Jews' best interests to know the truth about the Holocaust.[16]

In his publication *Revisionist Letters*, Smith tried to differentiate between antisemites who used Holocaust denial to attack Jews and his putative objective of uncovering the truth. He asserted that his editorial policy objective was to encourage 'exposés of bigotry and antisemitism' in Holocaust 'revisionism.' An article in the magazine argued that the participation of 'Nazi apologists' in Holocaust denial circles precluded the participation of other supporters, particularly the radical left.[17] The author, Laird Wilcox, wondered how 'revisionists' could argue that their speech was suppressed when there was a 'substantial element in [their] own ranks that doesn't believe in it [free speech], except for themselves.'[18] Smith reiterated this idea in a column in his local newspaper, admitting that although the 'search for truth' about the Holocaust was not antisemitic, there were 'bigots' in the movement who were 'self-avowedly anti-Jewish and who used revisionist scholarship as an attack on Jews.'[19] Smith seemed to be aware that any linkage of his efforts with extremist and racist groups would be a liability, particularly on campus.

His effort to distance himself from these overtly antisemitic groups was reflective of a shift by deniers to sever their overt ties to an array of neo-Nazi and extremist groups. Leonard Zeskind, the research director of the Center for Democratic Renewal in Kansas City, Missouri, and a respected specialist on extremism in America, categorized Smith's efforts as reflective of a general shift among 'white supremacists' and extremists away from the political margins into the mainstream by avoiding any overt association with swastika-bedecked or white-sheeted fascist groups. David Duke's re-creation of his past during the presidential campaign was an example of this strategy,[20] which confuses many people who can easily identify the objectives of the Klan, White Aryan Nation, and Posse Comitatus but who find it more difficult to recognize extremism when it is cloaked in a seemingly rational and familiar garb.

The ad Smith began to circulate in the spring of 1991 contained the deniers' familiar litany of claims. It declared the gas chambers a fraud, photographs doctored, eyewitness reports 'ludicrously unreliable,' the Nuremberg trials a sham, and camp internees well fed until Allied bombings destroyed the German infrastructure in the most 'barbarous form of warfare in Europe since the Mongol invasions,' preventing food from being delivered and causing the inmates to starve. According to Smith the notion of a Nazi attempt to destroy the Jews was the product of Allied efforts to produce 'anti-German hate propaganda.' Today that same propaganda was used by powerful forces to 'scape-goat old enemies,' 'seek vengeance rather than reconciliation,' and pursue a 'not-so-secret political agenda.'[21]

He repeated the familiar protest that his sole objective was to uncover the truth through an open debate on the Holocaust – debate that had been suppressed by a powerful but secret group on campus as part of their larger political agenda. 'Let's ask these people – what makes such behavior a social good? Who benefits?'

The ad contended that denial was forcing 'mainline Holocaust historians' to admit the 'more blatant examples' of Holocaust falsehoods.

It was the deniers who had forced them to revise the 'orthodox' Holocaust story. They had had to admit that the number of Jews killed at Auschwitz was far smaller than originally claimed, and had been made to confess that the Nazis did not use Jewish cadavers for the production of soap. It is correct that in recent years newly revealed documentation has allowed scholars to assess more precisely the number of Jews thought to have been murdered at Auschwitz.[22]* It is also accurate that scholars have long written that despite wartime rumors to the contrary, the Nazis apparently did not use Jewish cadavers for soap. There has been a wide array of other 'revelations' by Holocaust historians, all part of the attempt to uncover the full details of one of the most horrifying acts of human destruction. Smith suggested to his readers that scholars and others who work in this field, all of whom vigorously repudiate Holocaust denial, have been compelled to admit the truth of deniers' claims: 'We are told that it is "anti-Jewish" to question orthodox assertions about German criminality. Yet we find that it is Jews themselves like Mayer, Bauer, Hier, Hilberg, Lipstadt and others who beginning [sic] to challenge the establishment Holocaust story.'[23] This notion – that deniers have exposed the truth and mainline historians are scrambling to admit it – remains a linchpin of the deniers' strategy. It has two objectives: to make it appear that Jewish scholars are responding to the pressure of the deniers' findings and to create the impression that Holocaust deniers' 'questions' are themselves part of a continuum of respectable scholarship. If establishment scholars, particularly those who are Jews, can question previously accepted truths, why is it wrong when Bradley Smith does the same?

Though much of the ad consisted of familiar rhetoric, Smith added a new twist that had a particular resonance on American college campuses. Since the 1980s the concept of 'political correctness' has been a source of academic conflict. Conservative political groups have

---

* The memorial stone at Auschwitz lists the number of victims of the camp as 4 million. Research now indicates that the number of people who died in the Auschwitz/ Birkenau gas chambers was between 1.5 and 2 million, of whom 85 to 90 percent were Jews.

accused the 'liberal establishment' of labeling certain topics politically incorrect and therefore ineligible for inclusion in the curriculum. Smith framed his well-worn denial arguments within this rhetoric, arguing that Holocaust revisionism could not be addressed on campus because 'America's thought police' had declared it out of bounds. 'The politically correct line on the Holocaust story is, simply, it happened. You don't debate "it."' Unlike all other topics students were free to explore, the Holocaust story was off limits. The consequences, he charged, were antithetical to everything for which the university stood. 'Ideology replaces free inquiry, intimidation represses open debate, and . . . the ideals of the university itself are exchanged for intellectual taboos.'[24] While most students who had to decide whether the ad should be published did not overtly succumb to CODOH's use of the political correctness argument, many proved prone to it, sometimes less than consciously – a susceptibility evident in their justifications for running the ad. Among the first universities to accept the ad were Northwestern, the University of Michigan, Duke, Cornell, Ohio State, and Washington University.[25]*

At the University of Michigan the saga of the ad had a strange twist. Smith mailed camera-ready copy directly to the *Michigan Daily*. According to the paper's business manager, the ad 'slipped through without being read.' When it appeared the business staff was appalled to learn what they had allowed to happen. On the following day they placed a six-column ad in the paper apologizing for running Smith's ad and acknowledging that its publication had been a mistake. They declared it a 'sorrowful learning experience for the staff.'[26] The manager told the *Detroit Free Press*, 'We make mistakes like any organization.'[27]

The story might well have ended here – an example of faulty monitoring by a segment of the staff of the *Michigan Daily* – but the

---

* The papers discussed in this chapter function as private newspapers. The courts have broadly defined their editorial discretion to accept or reject ads. In situations of 'state action,' where a state university administration controls the newspaper's content, the courts may prohibit content-based rejection of the ads. *Discretion of Student Editors to Accept or Reject Holocaust Revisionist Advertisements* (ADL Legal Affairs Dept., Feb. 1992).

issue became more complicated when, despite the fact that those responsible for running the ad acknowledged doing so as a mistake, the editorial board attempted to transform a blunder into a matter of principle. They recast a snafu as an expression of freedom of speech. On the same day that the advertising staff published its apology, the front page carried an editorial explaining that, though the editors found the ad 'offensive and inaccurate,' they could not condone the censorship of 'unpopular views from our pages merely because they are offensive or because we disagree with them.'[28] Editor in chief Andrew Gottesman acknowledged that had the decision been in his hands, he would have printed the ad. He argued that rejecting it constituted censorship, which the editorial board found unacceptable.[29]

The following day a campus rally attacked both Holocaust denial and the paper's editorial policies. Stung by student and faculty condemnations and afraid that its editorial was being interpreted as an endorsement of CODOH, the editorial board devoted the next issue's lead editorial to the topic. Condemning Holocaust denial as 'absurd' and 'founded on historical fiction and anti-Jewish bigotry,' they dismissed it as irrational, illogical, and ahistorical propaganda. The editors accurately assessed the ad as lacking intellectual merit. Nonetheless, they continued to support its publication. Their powerful condemnation of Holocaust denial in general and Smith's ad in particular appeared under a banner quoting Supreme Court Justice Hugo Black's opinion on free speech: 'My view is, without deviation, without exception, without any ifs, buts, or whereases, that freedom of speech means that you shall not do something to people either for the views they have or the views they express or the words they speak or write.'[30]

The strange set of circumstances at Michigan – snatching a constitutional principle from the jaws of a mistake – was further complicated by the entry of the university's president, James Duderstadt, into the debate. In a letter to the *Daily* he declared the ad the work of 'a warped crank' and proclaimed that denying the Holocaust was to 'deny our human potential for evil and to invite its resurgence.' But he, too, defended the paper's decision, which was more of a nondecision, to run the ad. The president asserted that the *Daily* had a long history of editorial freedom that had to be protected even when 'we disagree either with particular opinions, decisions, or actions.' Most disturbing was Duderstadt's elevation of Smith's prejudices to the level of opinions.

There was no doubt about the message the editors and the president were trying to convey: As absurd, illogical, and bigoted as the ad may be, First Amendment guarantees were paramount. The dictates of the American Constitution compelled the *Daily* to publish. None of those involved seemed to have considered precisely what the First Amendment said: 'Congress shall make no law ... abridging the freedom of speech or of the press.' Those who argued that free speech guarantees acceptance of the ad ignored the fact that the First Amendment prevents *government* from interfering in any fashion with an individual's or group's right to publish the most outlandish argument.[31] The *New York Times* made this point in an editorial when it adamantly repudiated the notion that this was a First Amendment question: 'Government may not censor Mr. Smith and his fellow "Holocaust revisionists," no matter how intellectually barren their claims.'[32]

To call rejection of the ad censorship was to ignore the fact that, unlike the government, whose actions are limited by the First Amendment, these papers do not have a monopoly of force.[33] If the government denies someone the right to publish, they have no other option to publish in this country. But if a paper rejects someone's column, ad, or letter, there are always other publications. The First Amendment does not guarantee access to a private publication. It is designed to serve as a shield to protect individuals and institutions from government interference in their affairs. It is not a sword by which every person who makes an outlandish statement or notorious claim can invoke a Constitutional right to be published.* Nor did the *Michigan Daily* seem to notice how Justice Black, whom they

---

* In 1931, in *Near v. Minnesota*, the Supreme Court struck down a state attempt to gag a paper's freedom to publish 'malicious, scandalous or defamatory' material. Fred W. Friendly, *Minnesota Rag* (New York, 1981).

quoted, framed it: 'you shall not do something to people . . .' No one was advocating 'doing' anything to Smith.

One of the most ardent advocates of the free-speech argument was the *Duke Chronicle*. In an editorial column the editor in chief, Ann Heimberger, justified the paper's decision by acknowledging that while the paper knew it could reject the ad, it 'chose' to accept it as an expression of the paper's desire to 'support the advertiser's rights.' The editorial board believed that it was not the paper's responsibility to protect 'readers from disturbing ideas,' but to 'disseminate them.'[34]

Echoing his Michigan colleague, Duke University president Keith Brodie repeated the free-speech defense in a statement that, though it contained a strong refutation of the ad, was more vigorous in its support of the *Chronicle*'s publication of the ad. To have 'suppressed' the ad, he argued, would have violated the university's commitment to free speech and contradicted its 'long tradition of supporting First Amendment rights.'[35]

When the *Cornell Daily Sun* ran the ad, the editors justified the decision in an editorial statement warning that 'page twenty will shock most readers' but proclaimed that it was not the paper's role to 'unjustly censor advertisers' viewpoints.' Echoing their colleagues on many of the other campuses that printed the ad, the editors declared that they decided to print it because the 'First Amendment right to free expression must be extended to those with unpopular or offensive ideas.'[36] Neeraj Khemlani, the editor in chief of the *Daily Sun*, said his role was not to 'protect' readers.[37] Cornell president Frank H. T. Rhodes joined his colleagues at Duke and Michigan in defending the paper's decision.[38]

The University of Montana's paper, the *Montana Kaimin*, also used the First Amendment to defend its publication of the ad. The editor contended that it was not the paper's place to 'decide for the campus community what they should see.'[39] The University of Georgia's paper, the *Red and Black*, expressed the hope that publishing the ad would affirm America's unique commitment to 'allowing every opinion to be heard, no matter how objectionable, how outright offensive, how clearly wrong that opinion may be.' After the ad appeared the paper's editor defended the decision by describing it as 'a business decision,' arguing that 'if the business department is set up to take ads, they darn well better take ads.' Given the juxtaposition of these two explanations, there was, as Mark Silk, an editorial writer for the *Atlanta Constitution*, pointed out, something dubious about 'this high-minded claim.'[40]

After an extensive debate Washington University's *Student Life* decided to run the ad. When the ad appeared in the paper, Sam Moyn, the opinion editor, was responsible for conveying to the university community the reasoning behind the staff's 'controversial action.' The editors, he wrote, conceived of this as a free-speech issue: 'The abridgement of Mr. Smith's rights endangers our own.'[41] The *St. Louis Post Dispatch* defended the students' actions. Declaring the ad 'offensive, provocative and wrong,' it praised the student newspaper's courage to print it and stated that its actions strengthened the cause of freedom of speech.[42] The University of Arizona also depicted its actions as protecting the First Amendment. The editor in chief, Beth Silver, proclaimed that the mission of student newspapers is 'to uphold the First Amendment and run things that are obviously going to be controversial and take the heat for it.'[43] This attitude – we have to do what is right irrrespective of the costs – was voiced by a number of papers. Ironically, it echoed a theme frequently voiced by the deniers themselves: We will tell the truth, the consequences notwithstanding.

At Ohio State University the decision-making process was complex. The *Lantern*'s advertising policy is in the hands of a publications committee comprising faculty, students, editorial board members, and the paper's business manager.[44] University policy requires committee approval before acceptance of an ad designating a religious group. The committee voiced five to four to reject CODOH's submission.[45] But the story did not end there. Enjoined by the committee's decision from running the ad, the *Lantern*'s editor, Samantha G. Haney, used her editorial powers to run it as an op-ed piece, explaining that the paper had an 'obligation' to do so.[46] This decision gave Smith added legitimacy and saved him the $1,134 it would have cost to place a full-page ad in the paper.[47]

A lengthy editorial explaining the *Lantern*'s decision condemned Bradley Smith and his cohorts as 'racists, pure and simple' and the ad as 'little more than a commercial for hatred.' Nonetheless the newspaper had to publish it because it could not only 'run things that were harmless to everyone.'[48] Haney and her staff rejected the suggestion that they turn to the Ohio State History Department to 'pick apart' the ad fact by fact. That, they explained, might suggest that the ad had some 'relevancy' and some 'substance,' which they were convinced it did not. Given that one of the rationales the *Lantern* offered for publishing the article was that 'truth will always outshine any lie,' its refusal to ask professional historians to elucidate how the ad convoluted historical fact seemed self-defeating.[49] It seemed to reflect an understandable reluctance to accord denial legitimacy. There is no better example of the fragility of reason than the conclusion by these editorial boards that it was their obligation to run an ad or an op-ed column that, according to their *own* evaluation, was totally lacking in relevance or substance.

In contrast to the position adopted by James Duderstadt at the University of Michigan, Ohio State's president, Gordon Gee, attacked the decision to give Smith space in the newspaper, declaring the deniers' arguments 'pernicious' and 'cleverly disguised' propaganda that enhanced prejudice and distorted history.[50]

When this issue was being debated at Ohio State, a CBS reporter came to that campus to film a segment on Holocaust denial for a network show on hatred and extremism in the United States. Alerted in advance to the pending controversy, the cameras were conveniently present when the editor received a call from Smith congratulating her for running the ad and standing up for the principles of free speech and free press. When Haney hung up, the television reporter, who was standing nearby, asked how she felt. She turned and somewhat plaintively observed that she thought she had been had.

Not all the papers subscribed to the First Amendment argument; indeed, some explicitly rejected it. The University of Tennessee's *Daily Beacon* dismissed the idea that not running the ad harmed the deniers' interests: It was not 'censorship or even damaging.'[51] Pennsylvania State University's *Daily Collegian*, which had been one of the first to receive an ad from Smith, denied that the issue was one of free speech. After seeing student leaders and numerous individuals on campus inundated with material by deniers, the paper reasoned that those behind the ad had sufficient funds to propagate their conspiracy theory of Jewish control without being granted space in the paper.[52]

In an eloquent editorial the *Harvard Crimson* repudiated Smith's claim to a free-speech right to publish his ad. To give CODOH a forum so that it could 'promulgate malicious falsehoods' under the guise of open debate constituted an 'abdication' of the paper's editorial responsibility.[53] The University of Chicago *Maroon* agreed that while the deniers 'may express their views,' it had 'no obligation at anytime to print their offensive hatred.'[54]

The argument that not publishing the ad constituted censorship was not only a misinterpretation of the First Amendment but disingenuous. The editorial boards that reached this decision ignored the fact that they all had policies that prevented them from running racist, sexist, prejudicial, or religiously offensive ads. (Some of the papers in question even refuse cigarette ads.) How could they square their 'principled' stand for absolute freedom of speech with policies that prevented them from publishing a range of ads and articles? Why was Bradley Smith entitled to constitutional protection while an ad for an X-rated movie, *Playboy*, the KKK, or Marlboros was not? Recognizing this inconsistency, some of the boards tried to reconcile these two seemingly contradictory positions by adopting a stance that drew them even further into the deniers' trap. They argued that Holocaust denial was not antisemitic and therefore not offensive. The *Cornell Daily Sun* editorial board determined that the 'ad does not directly contain racist statements about Jewish people.'[55] Valerie Nicolette, the *Sun*'s managing editor, told the *Chronicle of Higher Education* that the editors had evaluated the ad based on their standards of 'obscenity and racism' and decided that it passed.[56] When a group of Jewish students at Duke met with the editorial board of the *Duke Chronicle* to protest the running of the ad, they were told that the paper's policy was not to run any ad that was 'racist or contained ethnic slurs' but that this ad did not fall into that category.[57]

Andrew Gottesman, who vigorously argued that he could not condone 'censorship' of Smith's advertisement and whose *Michigan Daily* published its ringing denunciation of Holocaust denial under Justice Hugo Black's interpretation of the First Amendment, admitted that there were ads he would not run in the paper. This ad, however, did not deserve to be 'banned from the marketplace of ideas, like others might be.' Among those he would ban were a Ku Klux Klan announcement of lynching or a beer ad with a woman holding a beer bottle between her breasts.[58] For Gottesman keeping such sexist and racist ads out of the paper would not constitute censorship; keeping Smith's out would. When Washington University's *Student Life* published the ad, an editorial explained that it did so in the interest of preventing 'freedom of ideas from disappearing from its newspapers.'[59] Yet the same paper includes the following policy statement on its advertising rate card: '*Student Life* reserves the right to edit or reject any advertisement which does not comply with the policies or judgment of the newspaper.'[60]

The claim that the rejection of the ad constituted censorship also revealed the failure of editorial staffs and, in certain cases, university presidents to think carefully about what their papers did regularly: pick and choose between subjects they covered and those they did not, columns they ran and those they rejected, and ads that met their standards and those that did not. The *Daily Tar Heel*, the paper of the University of North Carolina, proclaimed that as soon as an editor 'takes the first dangerous step and decides that an ad should not run because of its content, that editor begins the plunge down a slippery slope toward the abolition of free speech.'[61] What the *Tar Heel* failed to note was that newspapers continuously make such choices. As Tom Teepen, the editor of the *Atlanta Constitution*'s editorial page, observed, 'Running a newspaper is mainly about making decisions, not about ducking them.'[62] In fact the *Duke Chronicle*, whose editor had wondered how newspapers founded on the principles of free speech and free press could 'deny those rights to anyone,' had earlier rejected an insert for *Playboy* and an ad attacking a fraternity.[63]

While some papers justified their decision by arguing that the ad was not antisemitic and others leaned on the censorship argument, an even more disconcerting rationale was offered by many papers. They argued that however ugly or repellent Smith's 'ideas,' they had a certain intellectual legitimacy. Consequently it was the papers' responsibility to present these views to readers for their consideration. Those editors who made this argument fell prey to denial's attempt to present itself as part of the normal range of historical interpretation.[64] That they had been deceived was evident in the way they described the contents of the ad. The editor in chief of the *Cornell Daily Sun* described the ad as containing 'offensive *ideas.*'[65] The *Sun* argued that it was not the paper's role to 'unjustly censor advertisers' *viewpoints*' however 'unpopular or offensive.'[66] In a similar vein the *University of Washington Daily* defended giving Smith op-ed space because the paper must constitute a 'forum for diverse *opinions* and *ideas.*'[67] Ironically, six weeks earlier, when it rejected the ad, it had described Smith's assertions as 'so obviously false as to be unworthy of serious debate.'[68] The paper insisted that the op-ed column it eventually published was different because it was Smith's 'opinion' and did not contain the 'blatant falsehoods' of the ad. In the column Smith asserted that for more than twelve years he has been unable to find 'one bit of hard evidence' to prove that there was a plan to 'exterminate' the Jews, and that the gas-chamber 'stories' were 'allegations' unsupported by 'documentation or physical evidence.'[69]

The *Michigan Daily* engaged in the same reasoning. It would not censor 'unpopular *views*' simply because readers might disagree with them.[70] In a show of consistency, two weeks after Smith's ad appeared, the *Daily* supported the decision by Prodigy, the computer bulletin board, to allow subscribers to post Holocaust denial material. Prodigy, they contended, was similar to a newspaper, and like a newspaper it must be a '*forum for ideas.*'[71] In another suggestion that Smith's views were worthy of debate, the editor in chief of the *Montana Kaimin* argued that 'this man's *opinions*, no matter how ridiculous they may be, need to be heard out there.'[72] According to the editor in chief of Washington University's *Student Life*, the board voted to run the ad because 'we didn't feel comfortable censoring offensive *ideas.*'[73]

The *Ohio State Lantern*'s explanation of why it let Smith have his 'public say' despite the fact that it condemned Smith and CODOH as 'racist, pure and simple,' was more disturbing than the decision itself. The *Lantern* argued that it was 'repulsive to think that the quality, or total lack thereof, of any idea or opinion has any bearing on whether it should be heard.'[74] It is breathtaking that students at a major university could declare repulsive the making of a decision based on the 'quality' of ideas. One assumes that their entire education is geared toward the exploration of ideas with a certain lasting quality. This kind of reasoning essentially contravenes all that an institution of higher learning is supposed to profess.

The editors of Washington University's *Student Life* demonstrated a similar disturbing inconsistency. They dismissed Smith's claim to be engaged in a quest for the truth, describing him as someone who 'cloaks hate in the garb of intellectual detachment.' They believed that Smith was posing as a 'truth seeker crushed by a conspiratorial society.'[75] Given their evaluation of Smith, his tactics, and the way conspiracy theorists have captured the imagination of much of American society, what followed was particularly disconcerting. Notwithstanding all their misgivings, the editors decided that they must give 'Mr. Smith the benefit of the doubt if we mean to preserve our own rights.' In an assertion typical of the confused reasoning that student papers nationwide displayed on this issue, the *Student Life* editors acknowledged that they could have suppressed Smith's views 'if we attributed motives to him that contradict his statements. But we cannot in good conscience tell Mr. Smith that we "know" him and his true intentions.' Was not the fact that he was denying a historical fact about whose existence there is no debate among any reputable scholars indicative of something significant? The editorial board had concluded that 'if we refused Mr. Smith's advertisement, we could censor anyone based on ulterior motives that we perceive them to harbor.'[76] At what point would the board feel it was appropriate to make a decision based on the objective merits of the information contained in the ad?

In this instance what the paper considered to be ulterior motives is what scholars call coming to a conclusion based on a wide variety of facts, including historical data. In giving Smith the 'benefit of the doubt,' the editors fell prey to the notion that this was a rational debate. They ignored the fact that the ad contained claims that completely contravened a massive body of fact. They transformed what the *Harvard Crimson* described as 'vicious propaganda' into iconoclasm.

The most controversial interpretation about precisely what this ad represented was expressed by the *Duke Chronicle*. In a column justifying the paper's decision to run the ad, Ann Heimberger contended that 'Revisionists are ... reinterpreting history, a practice that occurs constantly, especially on a college campus.'[77] In a private meeting with Jewish student leaders on the Duke campus, the editors reiterated this argument. The students were told that the ad was neither racist nor antisemitic but was part of an ongoing 'scholarly debate.'[78] The Duke editorial board viewed the advertisement more as 'a political argument than as an ethnic attack.'[79] In editorials, articles, and interviews, those at helm of the *Duke Chronicle* repeatedly referred to Holocaust denial as 'radical, unpopular *views*,' and 'disturbing *ideas*' and argued that the ad was not a 'slur' but an '*opinion*.'[80] By doing so they not only clung to their First Amendment defense, they gave the ad historical and intellectual legitimacy.

The *Chronicle*'s acceptance of the ad and the editor's defense of having done so elicited two reactions. Bradley Smith, quite predictably, praised Heimberger's column as 'fantastic' and an example of sound reasoning.[81] A less laudatory response came from the Duke History Department, which, in a unanimously adopted statement, asserted that the ad aimed to 'hurt Jews and to demean and demonize them.' It was particularly vehement about Heimberger's contention that the ad was nothing more than a reinterpretation of history. The department observed that the 'scholarly pretensions' of the ad were effective enough to deceive Heimberger so that she believed the ad's claims were part of the 'range of normal historical inquiry.' The statement continued:

> That historians are constantly engaged in historical revision is certainly correct; however, what historians do is very different from this advertisement. Historical revision of major events is not concerned

with the actuality of these events; rather it concerns their historical *interpretation* – their causes and consequences generally.[82]

If the ad convinced Heimberger, one can only imagine its impact on individuals who have had less exposure to history and critical thinking.

There were, of course, those college newspapers that had no problem evaluating the ad's intellectual value. The *Harvard Crimson* repudiated the idea that the ad was a 'controversial argument based on questionable facts.' In one of the most unequivocal evaluations of the ad, the *Crimson* declared it 'vicious propaganda based on utter bullshit that has been discredited time and time again.' More than 'moronic and false,' it was an attempt to 'propagate hatred against Jews.'[83] The editorial board of the University of Pennsylvania's *Daily Pennsylvanian* argued that 'running an ad with factual errors that fostered hate' was not in the best interests of the paper.[84]

The *MIT Tech* simply decided that it would not accept an ad that it knew 'did not tell the truth.'[85] For the *Brown Daily Herald* the ad was 'a pack of vicious, antisemitic lies' parading as 'history and scholarship.'[86] The *Daily Nexus*, the publication of the University of California at Santa Barbara, refused the ad because of its 'blatant distortions of truth and its offensive nature.' The paper described receiving the ad itself and the more than one thousand dollars to print it as 'chilling.'[87] The *Dartmouth Review*, no stranger to controversy, also rejected the ad. It acknowledged that by so doing it was denying 'someone a forum through which to speak to the paper's readership' but explained that it had a 'bond of trust' with the public, which expected it to abide by 'standards of accuracy and decency.' Accepting an ad 'motivated by hatred and informed by total disregard to the truth' would be to violate that trust.[88] The *Chicago Maroon* saw no reason why it should run an ad whose 'only objective is to offend and incite hatred.'[89] The *Yale Daily News* 'simply' let Smith know that it found the ad 'offensive.'[90]

Some of the papers that ran the ad did so on the basis of what may be called the light-of-day defense, a corollary of the free-speech argument: In the light of day, truth always prevails over lies. Neeraj

Khemlani of the *Cornell Sun* believed that by running the ad he had done the Jewish people a favor – reminding them that there were a 'lot of people out to get [them],' which was something they needed to know.[91] This attitude is reminiscent of the concept of 'saving the Jews (or women, African Americans, or any other potentially vulnerable group) despite themselves. Michael Gaviser, business manager of the *Daily Pennsylvanian*, decided to run the ad because of his belief that Smith was a 'dangerous neo-Nazi' of whom the public had to be aware. (His decision was reversed by the editorial board.)[92]

A number of the nation's most prominent national papers echoed the light-of-day position. A *Washington Post* editorial rejected the freedom-of-the-press argument but accepted the light-of-day rationale. Acknowledging that college newspapers had no obligation to accept the ads, it argued that it was 'bad strategy' automatically to 'suppress' them. What the ad needed was the 'bracing blast of refutation.' The *Post* did not seem to consider the possibility that an article fully analyzing the ad would have served the same purpose.[93] In an archetypal deniers' move Smith cited the *Post*'s editorial as proof that the paper believed it both 'ethical and permissible' to debate the 'Holocaust story.'[94] He made the same claim about a *New York Times* editorial that left it up to each newspaper to decide whether to publish Smith's 'pseudo-scholarly' and 'intellectualy barren' tract.[95]

The Rutgers *Daily Targum* contended that publication of the ad constituted a means of defeating Smith. The editors argued that 'you cannot fight the devil you cannot see.'[96] Exposing Smith's views through publication of his ad could thwart his objectives.[97] The *Targum* correctly understood that the First Amendment did not apply – ('CODOH has wrapped itself so tightly in the First Amendment it borders on suffocation') – and the claim to be engaged in historical investigation was dismissed as 'a sham.' Nonetheless it chose to reprint Smith's ad in full on the editorial page, surrounding it with three op-ed pieces and an editorial, all of which attacked the ad's contents. In addition, an editors' note introducing the column noted that the ad had originally been rejected by the paper's business section because of 'its false content and antisemitic nature.' The editorial board argued that despite all this it was necessary to print the advertisement in full because, 'more than anything else, [it] makes it painfully obvious that a clear and present danger exists.'[98] Reiterating this point in a letter to the *New York Times*, *Targum* editor Joshua Rolnick argued that publishing the ad in its entirety was the best way of 'mobilizing the community in opposition to its hateful ideas.'[99]

The *Targum*'s decision to print the ad as a column and surround it with dissenting opinion won it the editorial praise of the *New York Times*: 'The editors thus transformed revulsion into education.'[100] Nevertheless there is reason to question that decision. First of all it saved Smith the approximately five hundred dollars it would have cost to purvey his extremist arguments. The paper proudly proclaimed that it had 'not accepted any payment' from him, as if the acceptance of money made them accomplices. In fact it was Smith, Rolnick acknowledged, who had 'encouraged' him to run it as an op-ed piece. Smith may well have recognized that, the dissenting articles notwithstanding, the full text of his ad was likely to win converts to his cause even as it mobilized some people against him. Given the space the *Daily Targum* devoted to the topic, a lengthy analytical piece quoting heavily from the ad and demolishing it point by point would have served the same purpose and given Smith less of a chance to lay out his 'argument.' Some wonder what was the danger of allowing Smith his say, particularly when surrounded by articles that firmly and swiftly refuted him. But the *Daily Targum* had given Smith just what he wanted: They made him the other side of a debate. Although it may not have been evenly balanced, although more room may have been given to the articles that surrounded his, and although editorials may have condemned him, he had nonetheless been rendered a point of view.[101] Smith seems to be acutely cognizant of the efficacy of even bad publicity. That may well be why, when a rally at Rutgers denounced Holocaust revisionism and his ad, he declared himself 'grateful and delighted' that the rally was held.[102]

In the spring of 1992 Smith began to circulate a second ad that was essentially a reprint of an article from the *Journal of Historical Review* by Mark Weber. The article, entitled 'Jewish Soap,' blamed the postwar spread of the rumor that the Nazis made Jews into soap on Simon Wiesenthal and Stephen Wise – a claim that has no relationship to reality. Echoing the first ad, it charged that historians of the Holocaust have 'officially abandon[ed] the soap story' in order to 'save what's left of the sinking Holocaust ship by throwing overboard the most obvious falsehoods.'[103] The point of this second effort, Smith acknowledged, was to submit a piece that was thoroughly 'referenced.'[104] The ad was submitted with a cover letter that claimed that the original ad had been rejected by a number of papers because it was not 'sourced.' In contrast, every 'significant claim' in the second ad was backed up by sources.[105] Entitled 'Falsus in Uno, Falsus in Omnibus [False in one thing, false in all] . . . The "Human Soap" Holocaust Myth,' the essay on soap was preceded by a statement citing Roman law: If a witness could not be 'believed in one thing, he should not be believed in anything.'[106]

Most universities that received the second ad, including those who had accepted the first, rejected it out of hand. When it was submitted to the *Ohio State Lantern*, the editor immediately refused it, observing that 'the only news value in this is that Bradley Smith is approaching schools again.' Having been burned once, the editor seemed far more cognizant of Smith's motives. 'The fact that it is Holocaust Remembrance Week indicates that he's in to ruffle some feathers and stir up trouble again.'[107] The arguments about the First Amendment and censorship no longer seemed to apply.*

At the University of Texas the deliberations about the second ad were directly linked to what had occurred with the first ad. The editor of the *Daily Texan*, Matthew Connally, had wanted to run the first.[108] However, after familiarizing himself with the 'group behind

---

* The *Tufts Daily* was the only paper that decided to run portions of the ad. Its editors voiced the opinion that it was necessary to run the ad so that readers could 'fully comprehend' the deniers' arguments and then make 'informed judgments' and engage in 'active dialogue' about 'complex issues.' They reached that conclusion despite their conviction that Smith's views had little if any 'legitimacy' and were filled with 'hateful sentiments and ideas that defile the memories' of the millions killed in World War II. To have rejected it would have 'unilaterally censored' the campus community from the issue. Tufts joined other campuses in falling prey to the light-of-day argument: In search of a principled stand, they gave Smith exactly the exposure he sought.

the ad,' he reversed his decision. 'They were not only showing a disregard for the truth but they were doing it with malicious intent.'[109] The Texas Student Publication Board (TSPB), which has ultimate authority over the paper's advertising and financial affairs, supported Connally and voted to reject the ad. After hearing Connally's arguments, TSPB member Professor John Murphy, who initially voted in favor of running the ad, decided to oppose it.

But that was not the end of the story at Texas. In April the paper received Smith's second ad. Though the *Daily Texan*'s editorial board was firmly against running it, they quickly discovered that the decision was not in their hands: They were told by the TSPB that they must run it. 'We do not want to do this. But we're being told we must follow orders,' a member of the editorial board told me sadly.[110] This time Professor Murphy emerged as the ad's most vociferous supporter. According to the *Houston Chronicle*, Murphy, supported by a number of other UT faculty members, argued that the paper needed to publish 'divergent and unpopular opinion.'[111] Facing a situation in which it would be forced to publish something it 'detested,' the editoral board considered leaving all the pages blank except for the ad. (They were told that since this would affect advertising revenues, they did not have the authority to do so.)

The ad was scheduled to run on Holocaust Memorial Day, Yom HaShoah, 1992. Students opposed to the ad discovered that the internal regulations of the TSPB prohibited the newspaper from printing opinion ads unless all persons cited in those ads had granted permission to be quoted. I was among the scholars quoted in the ad. Fortuitously, I was scheduled to visit the campus to deliver a lecture on Holocaust denial the day before the ad's scheduled publication. When I indicated my opposition to being cited in the ad, an emergency meeting of the TSPB board was called to discuss the matter. I informed the board that I had not given my permission to be quoted in the ad and was opposed to being associated with it. I pointed out that the ad specifically violated their own regulations.* Despite my objections and

---

* At the meeting one of the editors of the paper, an African American, stood up and said that while he could not personally know what it felt like to lose so many of one's coreligionists in the Holocaust, he 'knew' the pain of slavery. He would fight

my announcement that I would explore the possibility of legal remedies should the ad be published, the TSPB voted to run it, postponing publication for a few days so that my name could be dropped and a rebuttal prepared. Two days later the university's legal counsel suggested that because individuals quoted in the ad had protested – by this time other professors mentioned in the ad had joined the protest – the ad should be dropped.[112] The TSPB then voted to reject the ad. But the story did not end here. In February 1993 the TSPB compelled the paper to accept an ad promoting a video exposé of the gas chambers by a CODOH member claiming to be a Jew. Based on advertisements and articles by this young man, the video apparently contains the same recycled arguments deniers have been making for years. Though the editorial board and the university president opposed the ad because it was 'deceptively rigged,' the TSPB ran the ad. Five of the six students on the TSPB and one of its faculty members voted for the ad. Both working professionals voted against it.

During this period students were not the deniers' only campus targets. For more than two years – not for the first time – deniers had tried to insinuate themselves into the scholarly arena by finding ways to place Holocaust denial on the agenda of organizations of professional historians. They sought to force these groups to treat denial as a legitimate enterprise. In the spring of 1980 all members of the Organization of American Historians (OAH) received a complimentary copy of the first issue of the *Journal of Historical Review*. It was quickly revealed that the IHR had purchased the OAH's twelve thousand member mailing list. Some OAH members protested the sale of the list to this neo-Nazi group. Others argued that to deny anyone the right to purchase the list would be to abridge intellectual freedom. The executive secretary of the OAH proposed to resolve the issue by inviting a panel of 'well-qualified historians' to analyze the

---

anyone's attempt to deny that. Consequently he felt obligated to fight this attempt at denial.

He also turned to Murphy and said that he understood that one of Murphy's objections was that it was infantilizing to prevent the students from deciding on the contents of the ad themselves. He wondered if it was not equally infantilizing to tell an entire editorial board to publish something whose publication it uniformly opposed.

Journal and evaluate it based on the 'credentials of the contributors and the use of evidence.' He would then transmit this evaluation to the OAH executive board so it could decide how to treat the matter.

Lucy Dawidowicz, a fierce critic of the OAH response, wondered what those historians would evaluate: 'Perhaps that the neo-Nazis did not have proper academic credentials or that they failed to use primary sources?'[113] Carl Degler, a past president of the OAH, defended the suggestion that the OAH should sponsor an analysis of the *Journal*. He argued that once historians begin to consider the 'motives' behind historical research and writing, 'we endanger the whole enterprise in which the historians are engaged.' Following the same pattern as the student editors who described the contents of the denial ad as opinions, views, and ideas, he described the articles contained in the *Journal* as 'bad historical writing.' Given the *Journal*'s contents and its publisher's identity, Degler's categorization of it as bad history was described by Dawidowicz as a 'travesty.'[114]

A far-less-ambiguous position was adopted by the editors of the *Journal of Modern History*, when the Liberty Lobby bought its subscription list and sent out antisemitic material. The journal's editors sent a letter of apology to its subscribers acknowledging that an 'antisemitic hate organization' had obtained its mailing list. It 'repudiate[d] and condemn[ed] the propaganda' that readers had received and apologized that both the readers and the academic discipline had been 'abused in this thoroughly scurrilous manner.'[115]

Another attempt to force professional historians to treat Holocaust denial as a legitimate enterprise began in 1990, when members of various university history departments began to receive letters soliciting support for 'Holocaust revisionism.' That same year the American Historical Association's (AHA) annual meeting was disrupted by pickets calling for recognition of a book charging Gen. Dwight Eisenhower with consciously causing the death of a million German POWs at the end of the war.* The AHA issued a statement noting that 1995 marked the fiftieth anniversary of the defeat of

---

* The deniers have cited these contentions, which have been subjected to serious historical and methodological critiques, to support their claims that whatever atrocities the Nazis committed, those committed by the Allies were worse.

Nazism and calling on scholars to 'initiate plans now to encourage study of the significance of the Holocaust.'[116]

The AHA statement referred to the Holocaust but did not explicitly say that the Holocaust was a fact of history. According to the then-president of the AHA, William Leuchtenburg, it did not want to 'get into the business of certifying what is and is not history.'* Moreover, he believed that for a group of historians to say there had been a Holocaust was tantamount to 'an organization of astronomers saying there is a moon.'[117] The press, he believed, would simply ignore such a statement. In December 1991 the AHA unanimously adopted a statement deploring the 'attempts to deny the fact of the Holocaust' and noting that 'no serious historian questions that the Holocaust took place.'[118] Leuchtenburg opposed allowing deniers a table at the convention because the AHA was a professional organization and they were not professionals. It would be the equivalent of the AMA allowing quacks to hawk miracle cures at its meetings.

The OAH was also a target of the deniers. In November 1991 the OAH's executive committee agreed to allow its newsletter to publish a call by the IHR's *Journal of Historical Review* for 'revisionist' papers. This action was taken after David Thelen, the editor of the OAH's scholarly journal, the *Journal of American History*, refused to list articles by deniers because it was the responsibility of an academic publication to 'make judgments on the quality of scholarship.'[119] He felt it was harder to refuse them space in the association's newsletter because it contained both scholarly and nonscholarly information. Joyce Appleby, OAH president, protested the executive committee's decision to accept the announcement in the *OAH Newsletter*. 'This is not a question of respecting different points of view but rather of recognizing a group which repudiates the very values which bring us together,' Appleby wrote. It was the responsibility of a professional organization to make 'professional judgments' and,

---

* The full text of the resolution read 'As we approach the fiftieth anniversary of the downfall of the Nazi regime in 1995, the American Historical Association calls attention to the need to initiate plans now to encourage study of the significance of the Holocaust. To that end the association will make available the names of experts on the history of the event.' *Chronicle of Higher Education*, January 8, 1992.

Appleby asserted, 'these people are not professionals and to allow them to advertise is to legitimate them.'[120]

Mary Frances Berry, a former president of the OAH and a history professor at the University of Pennsylvania, disagreed with Appleby. She compared the debate within the OAH to campus codes against 'hate speech,' to which she objected. Her primary concern was 'guaranteeing civil liberties for everyone.' She argued that since the OAH did not have a general policy regarding advertisements it would accept or reject, it was obligated to accept everything it received.[121] The next issue of the OAH Newsletter contained a series of letters regarding the decision to include the ad and Appleby's dissent. A group of prominent historians, including Thelen and Berry, wrote in support of the inclusion of denial announcements.[122] They argued that however 'abhorrent' the goals of the Journal of Historical Review, the constitutional principle of free speech as well as the OAH's commitments to freedom of expression and the search for historical truth demanded that the ad be printed. In an apparent attempt to 'balance' their support of the ad, they suggested a variety of strategies for dealing with the future efforts by the Journal of Historical Review and other deniers to place ads in OAH publications. One idea was that the OAH 'pressure' the deniers' journal to abide by international standards of scholarship, including that experts in appropriate fields evaluate articles submitted to the journal. Given the way they handle documents and data, it is clear that deniers have no interest in scholarship or reason. Most are antisemites and bigots. Engaging them in reasoned discussion would be the same as engaging a wizard of the Ku Klux Klan in a balanced and reasoned discussion of African Americans' place in society. But on some level Carl Degler was right: Their motives are irrelevant. Some may truly believe the Holocaust a hoax – just as hundreds of antisemites believed the Protocols genuine. This does not give the contents of their pronouncements any more validity or intellectual standing. No matter how sincerely one believes it, two plus two will never equal five. Among the historians' other suggestions was that a 'truth-in-advertising' group be created to unmask the misleading claims in denial notices and announcements and that this group insist that their exposure be published along with the deniers' claims. But such a suggestion would imply that a debate was being conducted by mainline historians and 'revisionists.'[123] The historians' ideas, offered in the name of an attempt to resolve a situation that confounds many academics, played directly into the deniers' hands. Given the response of such eminent teachers of history, it is not surprising that the *Daily Northwestern*, Northwestern University's student newspaper, writing in support of inviting Arthur Butz to debate his 'unorthodox view' of the Holocaust, declared that 'even outrageous and repugnant theories sometimes deserve a forum.'[124] Students emulated exactly what these professors had done. They had elevated what the *Harvard Crimson* had properly characterized as 'utter bullshit' to the level of a theory deserving of a forum. After the IHR's announcement appeared, the executive board voted to establish a policy henceforth to exclude such advertisements and announcements from the newsletter. There was significant debate within the OAH's leadership on this matter, and the decision to exclude denial ads in the future passed by one vote.[125]

Writing in support of Appleby, the *Los Angeles Times* provided an interesting slant to the argument. It pointed out that the First Amendment guaranteed freedom of association as well as freedom of speech. As a result the OAH had the right to 'exclude fake historians from its ranks.'[126] It was probably the most appropriate and possibly the most creative citation of the First Amendment during this entire debate.

The responses to Holocaust denial by both students and faculty graphically demonstrate the susceptibility of an educated and privileged segment of the American population to the kind of reasoning that creates a hospitable climate for the rewriting of history. There were a variety of failures here. All of them are sobering indicators of the ability of Holocaust denial to gain legitimacy. There was a failure to understand the true implications of the First Amendment. There was also a failure by student editors to recognize that their high-minded claims about censorship were duplicitous, given their papers' policies of rejecting a broad range of ads and articles. In fact, campus policies are often more restrictive than those of the commercial press.

There was a failure to look at the deniers' own history and to understand what they represented. The observation of the *Ohio State Lantern* rings hauntingly in my ears: 'It is repulsive to think that the quality, or total lack thereof, of any idea or opinion has any bearing on whether it should be heard.'[127] It is a response likely to make professors nationwide cringe. But, as we have seen, professors also showed their confusion on this matter.

Most disturbing was the contention voiced by students, faculty members, and university presidents that however ugly, the ad constituted an idea, opinion, or viewpoint – part of the broad range of scholarly ideas. However much they disassociated themselves from the content of the ad, the minute they categorized it as a 'view,' they advanced the cause of Holocaust denial. That students failed to grasp that the ad contravened all canons of evidence and scholarship was distressing. But those at the helm sometimes also failed to grasp that the ad was not advocating a radical moral position but a patent untruth. Writing in the *Cornell Daily Sun*, President Frank Rhodes couched the discussion in terms of freedom of the press, arguing, 'Free and open debate on a wide range of ideas, however outrageous or offensive some of them may be, lies at the heart of a university community.' Rhodes was positing that Holocaust denial should be considered an idea worthy of inclusion in the arena of open debate.[128]

This assault on the ivory tower of academe illustrated how Holocaust denial can permeate that segment of the population that should be most immune to it. It was naive to believe that the 'light of day' can dispel lies, especially when they play on familiar stereotypes. Victims of racism, sexism, antisemitism, and a host of other prejudices know of light's limited ability to discredit falsehood. Light is barely an antidote when people are unable, as was often the case in this investigation, to differentiate between reasoned arguments and blatant falsehoods. Most sobering was the failure of many of these student leaders and opinion makers to recognize Holocaust denial for what it was. This was particularly evident among those who argued that the ad contained ideas, however odious, worthy of discussion. This failure suggests that correctly cast and properly camouflaged, Holocaust denial has a good chance of finding a foothold among coming generations.

This chapter ends where it began. Given the fact that even the papers that printed the ad dismissed Smith's claims in the most derogatory of terms – absurd, irrational, racist, and a commercial for hatred – one might argue that the entire affair had a positive outcome. Rarely did the ad appear without an editorial or article castigating Holocaust denial. Students were alerted to a clear and present danger that can easily take root in their midst. Courses on the Holocaust increased in number. One could argue that all this is proof that CODOH's attempt to make Holocaust denial credible backfired.

My assessment is far more pessimistic. It is probably the one issue about which I find myself in agreement with Bradley Smith. Many students read both the ad and the editorials condemning it. Some, including those who read neither but knew of the issue, may have walked away from the controversy convinced that there are two sides to this debate: the 'revisionists' and the 'establishment historians.' They may know that there is tremendous controversy about the former. They may not be convinced that the two sides are of equal validity. They may even know that the deniers keep questionable company. But nonetheless they assume there *is* an 'other side.' That is the most frightening aspect of this entire matter.

Watching on the Rhine

The Future Course of Holocaust Denial

Although the instances of outright denial explored in this book are a cause for concern, the deniers may have an impact on truth and memory in another, less tangible but potentially more insidious way. Extremists of any kind pull the center of a debate to a more radical position. They can create – and, in the case of the Holocaust, have already created – a situation whereby added latitude may be given to ideas that would once have been summarily dismissed as historically fallacious.

The recent 'historians' debate' in Germany, in which conservative German historians attempted to restructure German history, offers evidence of this phenomenon. Though these historians are not deniers, they helped to create a gray area where their highly questionable interpretations of history became enmeshed with the pseudohistory of the deniers; and they do indeed share some of the same objectives. Intent on rewriting the annals of Germany's recent past, both groups wish to lift the burden of guilt they claim has been imposed on Germans. Both believe that the Allies should bear a greater share of responsibility for the wrongs committed during the war. Both argue that the Holocaust has been unjustifiably singled out as a unique atrocity.

This debate was foreshadowed in the late 1970s by the publication of Hellmut Diwald's *History of the Germans*. Diwald, a prominent German historian, believed that since 1945 Germany's past had been 'devalued, destroyed and taken away' from the German people. He sought to rectify this by demonstrating how Germans themselves had been victimized: His book devoted significant space to the expulsion of the German population from Eastern Europe at the end of World War II, but only two pages to Nazi crimes against humanity, including the Holocaust.[1] Although Diwald's book was vigorously criticized by German historians of all political persuasions – one called it 'confused and stupid' – it was a harbinger of things to come. (Not surprisingly, the deniers were quick to adopt Diwald's work as an extension of their own. In a letter to the *New Statesman*, Richard Verrall, editor of the extremist *Spearhead* and the author of *Did Six Million Really Die?*, grouped Diwald's research with that of Butz and Faurisson, arguing that together they were all 'carrying on the work initiated by Rassinier.'[2] Diwald had unwittingly given the deniers the scholarly respectability they so craved. His successors in the debate would inadvertently do the same.)

Germany's intensive rewriting of its past from a politico-historical perspective continued in earnest in the mid-1980s, when Chancellor Kohl, initiating what would become the Bitburg debacle, invited President Reagan to participate in a wreath-laying ceremony at a German military cemetery, in a 'spirit of reconciliation.' Reagan agreed and, with a remark that can be described as thoughtless at best, informed the press that he would not go to a concentration camp because the Germans 'have a guilt feeling that's been imposed on them and I just think it's unnecessary.' In many ways Reagan was an innocent pawn in a debate whose nuances he may not fully have grasped.[3] Kohl's invitation to the American president, issued in the wake of Germany's exclusion from the fortieth anniversary commemoration of the Allied landing at Normandy, was designed to blur Germany's historical image as the aggressor. Conservative politicians and journalists had already begun to urge Germans, in the words of Bavarian Minister-President Franz Josef Strauss, to get off their knees and once again learn to 'walk tall.'[4] (The juxtaposition of this image with that of the late former Chancellor Willy Brandt falling to his knees at the Warsaw Ghetto monument is telling.)

Kohl, Strauss, and other politicians on the right were joined in this struggle by a group of historians. In 1986 Andreas Hillgruber, an internationally respected specialist in German diplomatic, military, and political history, published *Two Kinds of Downfall: The Shattering of the German Reich and the End of European Jewry*. It consisted of two essays, one on the postwar Soviet expulsion of Germans from Eastern Europe, and the other on the genocide of the Jews.[5] According to Hillgruber these two catastrophes 'belong[ed] together.' He argued that the Allies, who had long intended to cripple Germany so that it could never again subjugate Europe, emasculated Germany by usurping its territories for Poland and installing the Russian army as an occupying force. By claiming that they emanated from the same policies of population transfer and extermination, Hillgruber essentially equated Allied treatment of Germany and the Nazi genocide.[6] He responded to historians who had criticized the Wehrmacht's decisions to continue fighting the Soviets well after their colleagues in Berlin had attempted to end the war by assassinating Hitler. This, Hillgruber asserted, was an honorable decision even though it greatly prolonged the horrors of the death camps.[7] It was basically an act of self-defense, preventing the Russian forces from laying waste Germany and its people. Other historians in this struggle would take a far more extreme stand than Hillgruber, but his insistence that the reader see the latter stages of the war from the perspective of the German soldier, and his grouping together of these two different 'downfalls,' opened the door to much of the apologia and distortion that followed.[8]

The conservative historian Michael Stürmer, Chancellor Kohl's historical adviser, believed that the Germans' 'obsession with their guilt' had deleteriously affected their national pride.[9] Contending that too much emphasis had been placed on the Third Reich, Stürmer, who advised Kohl on the Bitburg affair, called for a rewriting of history that would help Germans develop a greater sense of nationalism.

The most prominent member of this effort was Ernst Nolte, the German historian renowned for his study of fascism.[10] Along with Hillgruber and other conservative historians, he compared the Holocaust to a variety of twentieth-century outrages, including the Armenian massacres that began in 1915, Stalin's gulags, U.S. policies in Vietnam, the Soviet occupation of Afghanistan, and the Pol Pot atrocities in the former Kampuchea. According to them the

Holocaust was simply one among many evils. Therefore it was historically and morally incorrect to single out the Germans for doing precisely what had been done by an array of other nations. Joachim Fest, the editor in chief of the prestigious Germany daily, the *Frankfurter Allgemeine Zeitung*, published a detailed defense of Nolte, illustrated with a photo of a mound of skulls of Pol Pot's victims.[11] As Oxford historian Peter Pulzer observed, the message was clear: Germans may have sinned but they did so 'in good company.'[12] Fest had already engaged in his own form of revisionism when he directed a documentary film, *Hitler: A Career*. Intended to show the fascination that Hitler had aroused among most Germans, the film relied on clips from Nazi propaganda films, synchronizing them with such stereo sound effects as clicking bootheels and exploding bombs. The commentator argued from Hitler's perspective. Nazi suppression of human rights, oppression, and war crimes were ignored. (Since these had not been filmed by the Nazis, the filmmakers treated them as nonexistent.) The film presents Nazi-produced propaganda as an authentic documentation of the period, showing Hitler as he wanted to be seen.[13]

The historians' attempt to create such immoral equivalencies ignored the dramatic differences between these events and the Holocaust. The brutal Armenian tragedy, which the perpetrators still refuse to acknowledge adequately, was conducted within the context of a ruthless Turkish policy of expulsion and resettlement. It was terrible and caused horrendous suffering but it was not part of a process of total annihilation of an entire people. The Khmer Rouge's massacre of a million of their fellow Cambodians, to which the Western world turned a blind eye, was carried out, as Richard Evans observes, as a means of subduing and eliminating those whom Pol Pot imagined had collaborated with the Americans during the previous hostilities. The ruthless policy was conducted as part of a brutalizing war that had destroyed much of Cambodia's moral, social, and physical infrastructure. This is not intended in any way as a justification of what happened in Cambodia. The Khmer Rouge's treatment of their countrymen was barbaric. But what they did was quite different from the Nazis' annihilation of the Jews, which was 'a gratuitous act carried out by a prosperous, advanced, industrial nation at the height of its power.'[14]

These historians also seem intent on obscuring the crucial contrasts between Stalinism and Nazism.[15] Whereas Stalin's terror was arbitrary, Hitler's was targeted at a particular group. As the German historian Eberhard Jäckel observed in an attack on Nolte and his compatriots, never before in history was a particular human group – its men, women, children, old, young, healthy, and infirm – singled out to be killed as rapidly as possible using 'every possible means of state power' to do so.[16] The fate of every Jew who came under German rule was essentially sealed. In contrast, no citizen of the Soviet Union assumed that deportation and death were inevitable consequences of his or her ethnic origins.[17] People in the USSR did not know who might be next on Stalin's list. This uncertainty terrorized them. By contrast, during the Nazi assault on the Jews *every single one* of millions of targeted Jews was to be murdered. Eradication was to be total.'[18] The Nazis did not borrow these methods from the Soviets. They were *sui generis*, and the refusal of these historians to acknowledge that fact reflects the same triumph of ideology over truth that we have seen throughout this study.

This is not a matter of comparative pain or competitive suffering. It is misguided to attempt to gauge which group endured more. For the victims in all these tragedies the oppressors' motives were and remain irrelevant. Nor is this a matter of a head count of victims or a question of whose loss was larger. In fact, Stalin killed more people than did the Nazis.[19] But that is not the issue. The equivalences offered by these historians are not analogous to the Holocaust. To attempt to say that all are the same is to engage in historical distortion. To suggest that the disastrous U.S. policies in Vietnam or the former Soviet Union's illegal occupation of Afghanistan were the equivalent of genocide barely demands a response. These invalid historical comparisons are designed to help Germans embrace their past by telling them that their country's actions were no different than those of countless others – an effort that at times disturbingly parallels much of what we have seen in this book.

But this is not the only way these historians tried to reshape the past. Unlike the deniers, who seek to exonerate Hitler, some of these German historians tend to blame the worst excesses of Nazis, including the Holocaust, on him alone. Thus Nazism becomes 'Hitlerism,' and the German populace is absolved. They also depict the Holocaust as a German response to external threats. As we have seen above, Nolte, echoing David Irving, argues that the Nazi 'internment' of Jews was justified because of Chaim Weizmann's September 1939 declaration that the Jews of the world would fight Nazism. This, Nolte argues, convinced Hitler of his 'enemies' determination to annihilate him.' Klaus Hildebrand, a Nolte defender, praised Nolte's essay as 'trailblazing.'[20] As I noted in chapter 6, this comparison lacks all internal logic. First of all Weizmann had no army, government, or allies with which to wage this war. World Jewry was not a national entity capable of mounting an offensive against the Nazis. Moreover, Hitler did not initiate his oppression of the Jews in September 1939 when Weizmann made his statement. Weizmann's statement was a reaction to six years of brutal Nazi oppression. In another attempt at immoral equivalence, Nolte contends that just as the American internment of Japanese Americans was justified by the attack on Pearl Harbor, so too was the Nazi 'internment' of European Jews. In making this comparison Nolte ignores the fact that, however wrong, racist, and unconstitutional the U.S. internment of the Japanese, the Jews had not bombed Nazi cities or attacked German forces in 1939. Even his use of the term *internment* to describe what the Germans did to the Jews whitewashes historical reality.

In his most recent work, *The European Civil War, 1917–1945,* Ernst Nolte comes dangerously close to validating the deniers. Without offering any proof, he claims that more 'Aryans' than Jews were murdered at Auschwitz. According to Nolte this fact has been ignored because the research on the Final Solution comes to an 'overwhelming degree from Jewish authors.' He described the deniers' arguments as not 'without foundation' and their motives as 'often honorable.' The fact that among the core deniers were non-Germans and some former inmates of concentration camps was evidence, according to Nolte, of their honorable intentions. Nolte even advanced the untenable notion that the 1942 Wannsee Conference, at which Heydrich and a group of prominent Nazis worked out the implementation of the Final Solution, may never have happened. He disregards the fact that participants in that meeting have subsequently attested to it and that a full set of minutes survived. This suggestion implies that if Wannsee was a hoax, many other Holocaust-related events that we have been led to believe actually happened may also be hoaxes. He suggests, in an argument evocative of Butz's analysis, that the *Einsatzgruppen* killed numerous Jews on the Eastern Front because 'preventive security' demanded it since a significant number of the partisans were Jews. While he acknowledges that the action may have been carried to an extreme, it remains essentially justified.[21] Another of his unsubstantiated charges was that the documentary film *Shoah* demonstrates that the SS units in the death camps 'were victims in their way too.'[22]

Coming from a denier these arguments would have been utterly predictable. Coming from Nolte they are especially disturbing and revealing. Nolte cannot be ignorant of the vast body of research on this topic that has been conducted by scholars of every religious persuasion and nationality, including his fellow German non-Jews. Nor, since he tries to defend them, can he be ignorant of the deniers' explicit antisemitism. In his writings he has too often referred to the reality of the Final Solution to be accused of espousing Holocaust denial. Yet his recent writings make him so palatable to the deniers that the IHR is seriously attempting to convince Nolte to participate in its meetings and address its conventions. Whether he will do so is not known. (Even if he came and told them that the Holocaust is a fact, he would be welcomed as David Irving was during his predenial days, and as the author of popular, demi-historical works, John Toland, is today. They offer a legitimacy the deniers can currently find nowhere else.)

This attempt to resurrect German history was intensely criticized both within Germany and abroad. The historians' debate harmed the reputations of the scholars most prominently involved in it, and even the president of Germany eventually spoke out against this trend. Why, then, should it be a matter of concern? Despite widespread criticism, the debate gave the German media and general public the imprimatur to conduct the kind of discussion about contemporary Germany's relationship to its past that would never have been heard before. Calls for a 'sanitized version' of German history appeared in Germany's most prominent newspapers.[23] Those involved in the current antiforeigner campaign in Germany find this perspective on history particularly inviting. If Germany was also a victim of a 'downfall,' and if the Holocaust was no different from a mélange of other tragedies, Germany's moral obligation to welcome all who seek refuge within its borders is lessened.

These historians are not crypto-deniers, but the results of their work are the same: the blurring of boundaries between fact and fiction and between persecuted and persecutor. Ultimately the relativists contribute to the fostering of what I call the 'yes, but' syndrome.[24] Yes, there was a Holocaust, but the Nazis were only trying to defend themselves against their enemies. Yes, there was a Holocaust, but most Jews died of starvation and disease (as is the case in every war) or were killed as partisans and spies. Yes, there was a Holocaust, but the Jews' behavior brought it on them. Yes, there was a Holocaust, but it was essentially no different than an array of other conflagrations in which innocents were massacred. The question that logically follows from this is, Why, then, do we 'only' hear about the Holocaust? For the deniers and many others who are 'not yet' deniers, the answer to this final question is obvious: because of the power of the Jews. 'Yes, but' is a response that falls into the gray area between outright denial and relativism. In certain respects it is more insidious than outright denial because it nurtures a form of pseudohistory whose motives are difficult to identify. It is the equivalent of David Duke without his robes.

Relativism, however convoluted, sounds far more legitimate than outright denial. These German historians have created a prototype that may prove useful for the deniers. In the future, deniers may adopt and adapt a form of relativism as they attempt to move from well outside the parameters of rational discourse to the fringes of historical legitimacy. Rather than engage in outright denial they will espouse more opaque quasi-historical arguments that confuse well-meaning and historically ignorant people about their motives.*

* Countries such as the United States, where the degree of ignorance about historical matters is legendary, are particularly susceptible to this kind of rewriting of history. In 1990 only 45 percent of Alabama high school seniors knew that the

Denial aims to reshape history in order to rehabilitate the persecutors and demonize the victims. What relativism seeks to do is not that different. It, too, attempts to rehabilitate the perpetrators, and if in the course of that rehabilitation a certain re-evaluation of the victims occurs, so be it.* In the years to come, as relativism increasingly becomes the deniers' protective veneer, distinguishing between these two groups may grow more difficult.

If Holocaust denial has demonstrated anything, it is the fragility of memory, truth, reason, and history. The deniers' campaign has been carefully designed to take advantage of those vulnerabilities. While there is no precise means of gauging their success, there are enough signs on the horizon – many of which I have examined in the previous pages – to offer some assessment. Right-wing nationalist groups in Germany, Italy, Austria, France, Norway, Hungary, Brazil, Slovakia, and a broad array of other countries, including the United States, have adopted Holocaust denial as a standard facet of their propaganda.[25] Whereas these groups once justified Nazi murder of the

---

Holocaust was the Nazi attempt to exterminate the Jews. It is telling that many of those who gave the wrong answer thought that the United States had committed the Holocaust against the Japanese with the bombing of Hiroshima and Nagasaki (*Birmingham, Alabama, News*, Aug. 12, 1990).

* The same kind of rehabilitation is evident in France among the highest reaches of the political and judicial establishment. President François Mitterrand recently had a wreath placed on the grave of the Vichy leader, Marshal Philippe Pétain, who collaborated with Nazi Germany and was directly responsible for the deportation of thousands of Jews. Pétain, who in World War I was commander in chief of the French forces, was convicted of treason by a French court in 1945. Mitterrand insisted in a radio interview that present-day France should not be held responsible for the crimes of the Vichy regime. While the contemporary French government does not bear 'guilt' for Vichy's actions, honoring one of the perpetrators with a presidential wreath sends a revisionist message to the population at large. It revises the historical perception of France's role in the Holocaust. It can, and already has, become part of a historical whitewash.

Another form of French historical revisionism has been the refusal of French courts to try Vichy war criminals for their actions. The courts have thrown out these indictments, though the Supreme Court recently reinstated one of them. Thus far no citizen of France has been tried for crimes against humanity (*Jewish Telegraphic Agency*, Nov. 23, Dec. 2, 1992).

Jews, now they deny it. Once they argued that something quite beneficial to the world happened at Auschwitz. Now they insist that nothing did. Their antisemitism is often so virulent that the logical conclusion of their argument is that though Hitler did not murder the Jews, he should have. Since they are intent on weakening liberal democratic institutions, Holocaust denial constitutes a seminal weapon in their arsenal. Though they have fomented social upheaval and in certain instances caused significant physical harm, the threat posed by these groups is limited because they are so easily identified. Their dress, behavior, and tactics leave no doubt as to who they are. We know them by their shaved heads, leather jackets, tattoos, terror tactics (including murder), swastikas, cries of *sieg Heil*, and Nazi paraphernalia–laden rallies. They are as identifiable as a group of Ku Klux Klan members fully bedecked in white-sheeted regalia, chanting racist slogans, and carrying a fiery cross through a black neighborhood. They cause havoc and strike justifiable fear into the hearts of their potential victims. But their outward demeanor is like a flashing yellow light warning the innocent passerby of the danger. No one can mistake them for anything but exactly what they are: neofascists, racists, antisemites, and opponents of all the values a democratic society holds dear. The chance of their attracting a wide following from the general public is slim.

The deniers also sport an outward veneer, but rather than expose who they are, it camouflages them. The stripping away of the deniers' cloak of respectability – which was one of the main objectives of this book – reveals that at their core they are no different from these neofascist groups. They hate the same things – Jews, racial minorities, and democracy – and have the same objectives, the destruction of truth and memory. But the deniers have adopted the demeanor of the rationalist and increasingly avoided the easily identifiable one of the extremist. They attempt to project the appearance of being committed to the very values that they in truth adamantly oppose: reason, critical rules of evidence, and historical distinction. It is this that makes Holocaust denial such a threat. The average person who is uninformed will find it difficult to discern their true objectives. (That may be one of the reasons why Canadian high school teacher James

Keegstra was able to espouse Holocaust denial and virulent antisemitic theories for more than a decade without any protest being mounted against him. He made them sound like rational history.)

The deniers will, to be sure, cultivate this external guise of a reasoned approach all the more forcefully in years to come. They will refine this image in an attempt to confuse the public about who they really are. Any public contact with white-power and radical right-wing groups will be curtailed. People without identifiable racist or extremist pasts will be drafted for leadership positions. The Willis Cartos, who have spoken of the need to prevent the 'niggerfication' of America, will increasingly recede into the background as their public roles are diminished. Young men and possibly even women (at the moment there are no prominent women deniers) with pseudotraining in history will be sought out to become the symbolic vanguard of the movement. Overt expressions of antisemitism will be restrained so that those who fail to understand that Holocaust denial is nothing but antisemitism may be fooled into thinking it is not.

We have already seen frightening manifestations of the success of this approach on the various campuses where students, faculty, and administrators declared Bradley Smith's ad not to be antisemitic. If Smith succeeded so easily on campus, imagine the success he might have among groups who are even less accomplished at critical reasoning! This tactic has been particularly successful in Australia and New Zealand, where, under the guise of defending free speech, the Leagues for Rights – which in essence are nothing but Holocaust-denial organizations – have successfully attracted individuals who would normally have eschewed antisemitic activities. This strategy is behind some deniers' calls for a change in the IHR's methodology. They argue that it should place less emphasis on the Holocaust and instead make it only one among the many 'hoaxes' they address. This call does not stem from a genuine broadening of their interests or a lessening of their obsession with Jews. It is rooted in their desire to achieve some academic legitimacy. As long as they appear to be consumed with this single issue, that respectability and acceptance will elude them. What they project as a widening of their interests is merely a tactic designed to gain access to the mainstream.

A strategic change will also mark the activities of the racist, neo-Nazi, ultranationalist groups. So easily identifiable by their outer trappings, they will adopt the deniers' tactics, cast off the external attributes that mark them as extremists, and eschew whatever pigeonholes them as neofascists. They will cloak themselves and their arguments in a veneer of reason and in arguments that sound rational to the American people.* The physical terror they perpetrate may cease, but the number of people beguiled by their arguments will grow. They will begin to espouse a form of denial that hovers between the relativism of the German historians' debate and the outright lies seen so often in these pages – a metamorphosis that will make it easier for them to attract new adherents. This pseudorespectability will render them more appealing to a younger, economically disenfranchised segment of the lower middle class, who see themselves living on the brink of failure in the midst of a prosperous society whose benefits are not available to them. This is as true for the United States as it is for Germany, France, and Austria.†

What, then, are the most efficacious strategies for countering these attacks? Much of the onus is on academe, portions of which have already miserably failed the test. Educators, historians, sociologists, and political scientists hold one of the keys to a defense of the truth. What those who cannot be beguiled by diversionary arguments and soft reasoning know to be fact must be made accessible to the general public.

The establishment of Holocaust museums may play an important role in this effort. These institutions, and all who teach about the Holocaust, must be scrupulously careful about the information they impart so as not inadvertently to provide the deniers with room to

---

* This tactic was evident in the 1992 attempt of the Cincinnati Ku Klux Klan to erect a cross on city property during the Christmas season. They claimed it was part of their campaign to remind Cincinnatians of the religious significance of the holiday. It was a way for the Klan to present itself as more than just a racist organization.

† It will prove particularly true for those beset by what my colleague David Blumenthal has termed 'alterphobia' – the fear of the other. The other may be homosexuals, women, foreigners, Jews, people of color, or all of the above.

maneuver. They must also be careful about 'invoking' the Holocaust as a means of justifying certain policies and actions.

This is particularly true for the Jewish community. The purveyors of popular culture – television and radio talk-show hosts prominent among them – must understand that by giving denial a forum they become pawns in a dangerous war.* As individuals who help shape public opinion, they must recognize that this struggle is not about ignorance but about hate.

There are those who believe that the courtroom is the place to fight the deniers. This is where Austria, Germany, France, and Canada have mounted their efforts. The legislation that has been adopted takes different forms. Some bills criminalize incitement to hatred; discrimination; or violence on racial, ethnic, or religious grounds. Others ban the dissemination of views based on racial superiority for one sector of the population and expression of contempt toward a group implying its racial inferiority.[26]

The problem with such legal maneuvers is that they are often difficult to sustain or carry through. In August 1992 the Canadian Supreme Court threw out Zundel's conviction when they ruled that the prohibition against spreading false news likely to harm a recognizable group was too vague and possibly restricted legitimate forms of speech.[27]† An even greater difficulty arises when the court is asked to render a decision not on a point of law, as happened in the Mermelstein case, but on a point of history, as happened in the Zundel trial, in which the judge took historical notice of the Holocaust. It transforms the legal arena into a historical forum, something the courtroom was never designed to be. When historical disputes become lawsuits, the outcome is unpredictable.

The main shortcoming of legal restraints is that they transform the deniers into martyrs on the altar of freedom of speech. This, to some measure, has happened to Faurisson, who in March 1991 was

* Having written this book in the shadow of the 'industry' that produces these shows, I recognize that of all my calls for action, this one has the least possibility of realization.

† Charges may again be brought against Zundel on the basis of his having incited hatred against Jews.

convicted of proclaiming the Holocaust a 'lie of history.' The same court that found him guilty denounced the law under which he was tried and convicted.[28] The free-speech controversy can obscure the deniers' antisemitism and turn the hate monger into a victim.[29] A recent National Public Radio report on controlling neofascist activities in Europe took exactly this approach toward Faurisson's conviction. Rather than dwell on what he has said and done, it focused on his loss of freedom of speech.[30] When the publisher of the Austrian magazine *Halt* was convicted of 'neo-Nazi activities' for his Holocaust-denial statements, *Spotlight* published the news under a headline that read, NO FREE SPEECH.[31] A disturbing reversal of the free-speech argument has recently been used by deniers to penalize those who oppose them. In 1984 David McCalden, the former director of the IHR, contracted to rent exhibit space at the California Library Association's annual conference. The subject of his exhibit was the Holocaust 'hoax.' The Simon Wiesenthal Center and the American Jewish Committee (AJC) protested to both city and association officials. The Wiesenthal Center rented a room near McCalden's exhibit space to set up its own exhibit, and the AJC threatened to conduct demonstrations outside the hotel in which the meeting was to be held. When the association cancelled McCalden's contract he sued the Wiesenthal Center and the AJC, arguing that they had conspired to deprive him of his constitutional rights to free speech. Though the court dismissed his complaint, the U.S. Circuit Court of Appeals reversed that decision in 1992. The case constitutes the first time that the First Amendment has been used to attempt to still the voices of those who oppose Nazi bigotry.[32]

Another legal maneuver has been adopted by a growing number of countries. They have barred entry rights to known deniers. David Irving, for example, has been barred from Germany, Austria, Italy, and Canada. Australia is apparently also considering barring him.[33]

Others have argued that the best tactic is just to ignore the deniers because what they crave is publicity, and attacks on them provide it. I have encountered this view repeatedly while writing this book. I have been asked if I am giving them what they want and enhancing their credibility by deigning to respond to them. Deny them what they so desperately desire and need, and, critics claim, they will wither on the vine. It is true that publicity is what the deniers need to survive, hence their media-sensitive tactics – such as ads in college papers, challenges to debate 'exterminationists,' pseudoscientific reports, and truth tours of death-camp sites. I once was an ardent advocate of ignoring them. In fact, when I first began this book I was beset by the fear that I would inadvertently enhance their credibility by responding to their fantasies. But having immersed myself in their activities for too long a time, I am now convinced that ignoring them is no longer an option. The time to hope that of their own accord they will blow away like the dust is gone. Too many of my students have come to me and asked, 'How do we know there really were gas chambers?' 'Was the *Diary of Anne Frank* a hoax?' 'Are there actual documents attesting to a Nazi plan to annihilate the Jews?' Some of these students are aware that their questions have been informed by deniers. Others are not; they just know that they have heard these charges and are troubled by them.

Not ignoring the deniers does not mean engaging them in discussion or debate. In fact, it means *not* doing that. We cannot debate them for two reasons, one strategic and the other tactical. As we have repeatedly seen, the deniers long to be considered the 'other' side. Engaging them in discussion makes them exactly that. Second, they are contemptuous of the very tools that shape any honest debate: truth and reason. Debating them would be like trying to nail a glob of jelly to the wall.

Though we cannot directly engage them, there is something we can do. Those who care not just about Jewish history or the history of the Holocaust but about truth in all its forms, must function as canaries in the mine once did, to guard against the spread of noxious fumes. We must vigilantly stand watch against an increasingly nimble enemy. But unlike the canary, we must not sit silently by waiting to expire so that others will be warned of the danger. When we witness assaults on truth, our response must be strong, though neither polemical nor emotional. We must educate the broader public and academe about this threat and its historical and ideological roots. We must expose these people for what they are.

The effort will not be pleasant. Those who take on this task will sometimes feel – as I often did in the course of writing this work – as if they are being forced to *prove* what they know to be fact. Those of us who make scholarship our vocation and avocation dream of spending our time charting new paths, opening new vistas, and offering new perspectives on some aspect of the truth. We seek to discover, not to defend. We did not train in our respective fields in order to stand like watchmen and women on the Rhine. Yet this is what we must do. We do so in order to expose falsehood and hate. We will remain ever vigilant so that the most precious tools of our trade and our society – truth and reason – can prevail. The still, small voices of millions cry out to us from the ground demanding that we do no less.

APPENDIX
Twisting the Truth

Zyklon-B, the Gas Chambers, and the Diary
of Anne Frank

Some may find that I have already accorded antisemitic slander parading as a scientific theory far too much space – that I have taken people like Butz, Faurisson, Leuchter, and their associates too seriously. Nonetheless, after a number of years of working in this field, I am aware of how these pseudoscientific attacks on history obfuscate and obscure the truth. Most people do not believe the deniers' claims but are at a loss as to how to address their charges. Some, fearful that the deniers' findings have a measure of legitimacy, respond by seeking alternative explanations.

Consequently I devote this section to three of the charges most frequently made by Holocaust deniers, citing a variety of documentary and technical proofs that demolish any semblance of credibility they might be accorded. I do so with some reluctance, lest it appear that I believe that serious consideration must be given these people's claims. I do, however, believe that even a cursory perusal of the relevant sections of these documents will demonstrate the deceitful quality of the deniers' claims. I hope it will also demonstrate, as much of this book is intended to do, that it is Goebbels's theory of the 'big lie' that the deniers are emulating.

ZYKLON-B: A FIRE-BREATHING DRAGON

Deniers, led by Faurisson, argue that Zyklon-B (prussic acid) was totally inappropriate for use as a homicidal agent. As proof they cite a document prepared for the war crimes trials summarizing the manufacturer's instructions for the safe use of Zyklon-B as a fumigant.[1] The guidelines stipulated that a room in which prussic acid had been used to destroy vermin had to be ventilated for twenty hours before reentry. Deniers argue that this demolishes all the 'testimonies' on the use of Zyklon-B to kill human beings, asking how bodies could have been removed from the gas chambers shortly after execution if the room could not be safely entered for twenty hours? Not surprisingly the deniers ignored significant and well-known facts that demonstrate the fallacy of their claims.

The instructions cited were for use in a room or a private home – not gas-tight areas such as those in the death camps – full of furniture, household goods, bedding, carpeting, and the like. They stipulated how windows were to be sealed, keyholes taped, and chimneys covered. After fumigation, gas would be trapped in all sorts of nooks and crannies. Consequently mattresses, pillows, upholstered furniture, and similar items had to be shaken or beaten for at least an hour in the open air. The homicidal gas chambers were of an entirely different nature. They were empty of any items except a small number of phony shower heads and dead bodies. The floors and ceilings were made of bare concrete. A powerful ventilation system especially designed for the gas chambers had been installed. In this open and unencumbered setting it served as an extremely efficient means of extracting the gas. Each of the crematoria was equipped with such a system, something the normal home or business area would never have.[2] Moreover, according to both former prisoners and SS personnel, the Sonderkommandos, the inmates who carried out the bodies, wore gas masks.[3]

This argument about the extreme toxicity of Zyklon-B is designed to foster the conclusion that the gas posed too great a danger to SS personnel to be safely used. However, Faurisson and Leuchter also assert that it was used in the delousing chambers on clothes. (It is unclear how they could have concluded that it could be safely used in the delousing chambers but was too toxic to be used in homicidal gas chambers.)

Leuchter found traces of cyanide in rooms that Auschwitz officials described as killing chambers but that deniers claim were morgues. In an attempt to explain why residues of the gas would have been found in a room that supposedly served as a morgue, Faurisson and Leuchter explained that the morgues were disinfected with Zyklon-B, hence the residue.[4] This thesis is illogical: Disinfection is carried out with a bactericide, not an insecticide, particularly one so powerful as Zyklon-B.

Moreover, there is an internal contradiction in the deniers' own argument. They have asserted that Zyklon-B could be safely used under only the strictest of conditions and that twenty hours had to elapse before a facility in which it had been used could be entered. Yet they would have us believe that in order to clean a morgue, something that needed to be done on a regular basis, the SS would, instead of employing something as common and effective as bleach, choose this highly toxic substance that needed, according to the deniers' own calculations, stringent arrangements for safe use.[5]

Pressac observed that Faurisson presented prussic acid as 'dragon breathing fire, scarcely to be approached and with clawed feet clinging strongly to the ground even when dead.' The apocalyptic picture bore little relationship to actual practice. If hydrogen cyanide were as Faurisson would have us believe it was, the staff of Degesch, the German company that produced it, 'would long have been unemployed.'[6]

THE GAS CHAMBERS: 'ONE PROOF – JUST ONE PROOF'

Deniers, led by Faurisson, repeatedly call for 'one proof . . . one single proof' of the existence of homicidal gas chambers.[7] They dismiss the reliability of *all* human testimony, whether it came from the SS, surviving inmates, or Sonderkommando members. They do so

despite the fact that regarding the general details of gassings, the testimony of all the parties tends to corroborate each other.[8] Pressac's
monumental study of the gas chambers is, in essence, a response to
this demand for documentary proof. Pressac's sensitivity to Faurisson's demand for documents may be rooted in the fact that he almost
was lured into denial and it was his own archival investigation which
proved to him that Faurisson was consciously ignoring unequivocal
evidence of homicidal gas chambers. On a trip to Auschwitz shortly
after he met Faurisson, he was shown a series of documents that
constituted far more than 'the one single proof' upon which deniers
insisted. On subsequent visits he discovered additional documents,
some of which were previously unpublished. Since the publication of
his book in 1989, he has spent time in former Soviet archives and has
uncovered additional documents that demonstrate the absolute falsehood of the deniers' claims that there is no material or documentary
proof of gas chambers.

The next few pages contain a brief summary of Pressac's extensive findings. Those who have found the deniers' claims about gas
chambers the least bit troubling should have their doubts set aside.
Those who have never been persuaded in the least by this assault on
the truth will find the documents overwhelming proof of the degree
to which the deniers distort history and lie about the evidence. These
documents include work orders, supply requisitions, time sheets,
engineering instructions, invoices, and completion reports. All clearly
indicate that the gas chambers were to be used for nothing but homicidal gassings. The company contracted to design and install the
execution chambers was Topf and Sons. Much of the documentation
comes from reports they, their subcontractors, and civilian employees submitted to the SS. They generally made it appear as if they
were building morgues. But they slipped up often enough to provide
us with detailed documentation of the construction and installation
of homicidal killing units.

- An inventory of equipment installed in Crematorium III
  called for the installation of one gas door and fourteen
  showers. These two items were absolutely incompatible one

with the other. A gas-tight door could only be used for a gas chamber. Why would a room that functioned as a shower room need a gas-tight door?[9]

- Pressac, not content with this simple proof that this was not a shower room, calculated the area covered by a single shower head. He used the genuine shower installations in the reception building as a guideline. On the basis of this calculation, Crematorium III, which had a floor space of 210 square meters, should have had at least 115 shower heads, not fourteen.[10]

- On the inventory drawings, the water pipes are not connected to the showers themselves. Were these genuine showers the water pipes would have been connected.

- In certain gas chambers the wooden bases to which the shower heads were attached are still visible in the ruins of the building.[11] A functioning shower head would not have been connected to a wooden base.

- In a letter of January 29, 1943, SS Captain Bischoff, head of the Auschwitz Waffen-SS and Police Central Construction Management, wrote to an SS major general in Berlin regarding the progress of work on Crematorium II. In his letter he referred to *Vergasungskeller* (gassing cellar).[12] Butz and Faurisson tried to reinterpret the term *Vergasung*.[13] Butz's explanation was that it meant gas generation. Faurisson argued that it meant carburetion and that *Vergasungskeller* designated the room in the basement 'where the "gaseous" mixture to fuel the crematorium furnace was prepared.'[14] There are fundamental problems with this explanation. Not only is there a significant amount of documentation which refers to gassing but, more importantly, the cremation furnaces were coke fired and did not use gas generation.[15]

- Pressac found a time sheet in which a civilian worker had written that a room in the western part of Crematorium IV was a 'Gasskammer' (gas chamber). Faurisson, in need of proof that this was something other than what it said, suggested that these were 'disinfection gas chambers.' How he reached this conclusion, especially when he had determined that *Vergasungskeller* meant 'gas generation,' was left unexplained.[16]

- On February 13, 1943, an order was placed by the Waffen-SS and Police Central Construction Management for twelve *gasdichten Türen* (gastight doors) for Crematoria IV and V.[17]* According to the files in the Auschwitz Museum the work on this order was completed on the 25th of February. On February 28, according to the daily time sheets submitted by the civilian contractors, the gastight shutters were fitted (*Gasdichtefenster versetzten*) and installed.[18] A time sheet of March 2, 1943, submitted by the same firm for work conducted on Crematorium IV, contained the following entry: 'concrete floor in gas chamber.' The information on this work order and these two time sheets, when analyzed as a whole, indicate that on March 2, 1943, civilian employees of a German firm officially designated a room in Crematorium IV as a 'gas chamber.'[19] It made absolute sense for them to do so because two days earlier they had installed 'gastight shutters' in the same room.[20]

- A telegram of February 26, 1943, sent by an SS second lieutenant to one of the firms involved in the construction of the gas chambers, requested the immediate dispatch of 'ten gas detectors.' The detectors were to be used to check the efficiency of the ventilation system in the gas chamber.[21]

- In a book containing the record of work carried out by the metal workshops for the construction and the maintenance of Birkenau Crematorium II, there is an order dated March 5, 1943, requesting the making of 'one handle for a gas[tight] door.'[22]

- In a letter of March 6, 1943, a civilian employee working on the construction of Crematorium II referred to modifying

---

* Because the dimensions of the 'doors' were thirty by forty centimeters, Pressac hypothesizes that they were probably shutters rather than doors.

the air extraction system of 'Auskleidekeller [undressing cellar] II'. A normal morgue would have no use for such a facility.[23] During March 1943 there were at least four additional references to 'Auskleidekeller.' It is telling that civilians who, according to the deniers, had been brought to Birkenau in January 1943 to work on 'underground morgues' repeatedly referred not to morgues but to the ventilation of the 'undressing cellars.'[24]

- In the same letter the employee asked about the possibility of preheating the areas that would be used as the gas chamber. But a morgue should not be preheated. It should be kept cool. However, if the room were to function as a gas chamber, then the warmer the temperature the faster the Zyklon-B pellets would vaporize.[25]

- A letter dated March 31, 1943, signed by SS Major Bischoff, contained a reference to an order of March 6, 1943, for a 'gas[tight] door' for Crematorium II. It was to be fitted with a rubberized sealing strip and a peephole for inspection. Why would a morgue or a disinfection chamber need a peephole? It certainly was not necessary in order to watch cadavers or lice. There were also references in the Crematorium III work orders for gastight doors and for iron bars and fittings for gastight doors. The deniers, still clinging to their 'morgue' theory, claimed that morgues needed gastight doors to prevent odors and infectious germs from spreading. They also claimed the doors were necessary because the morgues were disinfected with Zyklon-B. This is a charge that, as indicated above, contradicts basic science, since Zyklon-B is an insecticide and not a disinfectant. This argument still leaves them scrambling for an explanation of why fourteen shower heads, none of which were connected to a plumbing system, were necessary for a morgue.[26]

- The inventory of Crematorium II, prepared when the civil firm had completed the conversions on it, contained references to it being fitted with a *Gastür* and a *Gasdichtetür* (gastight door).

- A letter of March 31, 1943, regarding Crematorium III spoke of it having a *Gastür*, a gas door. Deniers are quick to argue that this could mean many things. But the inventory attached to the hand-over documents for the crematorium makes short shrift of this argument. The list states that it had a *Gasdichtetür*, a 'gastight door.' One could possibly argue about the meaning of *Gastür*, but it is hard to squabble over a gas*tight* door.[27]

The deniers also contended that Birkenau was designed to serve as a quarantine and hospital camp, not a death camp. They based their argument on architectural drawings of April 1943, which contained plans for a barracks for sick prisoners, a prisoners' hospital, and a quarantine section. Why, they ask, would the Nazis build a health camp but a few hundred yards from gas chambers where people were being annihilated on a massive scale? All this, they assert, indicates that Birkenau was not built as a place of homicide and annihilation.[28]* But there exists another official drawing of an overall plan of Birkenau, completed approximately a year later. It reveals that Birkenau was anything but a benign hospital unit. The first set of plans, completed in April 1943, described a camp that would house 16,600 prisoners. The drawings a year later show a camp that housed 60,000 prisoners and contained less than half of the planned barracks from the preceding year's plans. The existing barracks housed four times as many people as indicated by the original drawings. Any suggestion of this being a place of healing is contradicted by these conditions.[29]

These references to gas chambers and this plan of the camp constitute the kind of proof the deniers claim to be seeking. There is, of course, a myriad of additional documentation regarding deportations, murders, supplies of Zyklon-B, and other aspects of the Final

---

* The traditional notation of who had actually done the drawing and who had signed off on it is chilling in both its ordinariness and extraordinariness. The drawing was completed by prisoner 63003 (whose name remains unknown) on March 23, 1944. We know that it was reviewed by a civilian worker named Techmann and approved the next day by SS Lieutenant Werner Jothan.

Solution. I mention them not as proof of the Nazi annihilation of the Jews but as proof of the degree to which the deniers distort and deceive.

THE *DIARY OF ANNE FRANK*

Anne Frank's diary has become one of the deniers' most popular targets. For more than thirty years they have tried to prove that it was written after the war. It would seem to be a dubious allocation of the deniers' energies that they try to prove that a small book by a young girl full of musings about her life, relationship with her parents, emerging sexuality, and movie stars was not really written by her. But they have chosen their target purposefully.

Since its publication shortly after the war, the diary has sold more than twenty million copies in more than forty countries. For many readers it is their introduction to the Holocaust. Countless grade school and high school classes use it as a required text. The diary's popularity and impact, particularly on the young, make discrediting it as important a goal for the deniers as their attack on the gas chambers. By instilling doubts in the minds of young people about this powerful book, they hope also to instill doubts about the Holocaust itself.

On what do these deniers and neo-Nazis build their case? A brief history of the publication of the diary, and of some of the subsequent events surrounding its production as a play and film, demonstrates how the deniers twist the truth to fit their ideological agenda.

Anne Frank began her diary on June 12, 1942. In the subsequent twenty-six months she filled a series of albums, loose sheets of paper, and exercise and account books. In addition she wrote a set of stories called *Tales from the Secret Annex.** Anne, who frequently referred to her desire to be a writer, took her diary very seriously. Approximately five months before the family's arrest, listening to a clandestine radio she heard the Dutch minister of education request

---

* The Secret Annex was the name Anne gave to the family's hiding place.

in a broadcast from London that people save 'ordinary documents – a diary, letters from a Dutch forced laborer in Germany, a collection of sermons given by a parson or a priest.' This would help future generations understand what the nation had endured during those terrible years. The next day Anne noted, 'Of course they all made a rush at my diary immediately.'[30] Anxious to publish her recollections in book form after the war, she rewrote the first volumes of the diary on loose copy paper. In it she changed some of the names of the principal characters, including her own (Anne Frank became Anne Robin.[31])

When Otto Frank was liberated from Auschwitz and returned from the war, he learned that his daughters were dead. He prepared a typed edition of the diary for relatives and friends, making certain grammatical corrections, incorporating items from the different versions, and omitting details that might offend living people or that concerned private family matters, such as Anne's stormy relationship with her mother. He gave his typed manuscript to a friend and asked him to edit it.[32] (Other people apparently also made editorial alterations to it.) The friend's wife prepared a typed version of the edited manuscript. Frank approached a number of publishers with this version, which was repeatedly rejected.* When it was accepted the publishers suggested that references to sex, menstruation, and two girls touching each other's breasts be deleted because they lacked the proper degree of 'propriety' for a Dutch audience. When the diary was published in England, Germany, France, and the United States, additional changes were made. The deniers cite these different versions and different copies of the typescript to buttress their claim that it is all a fabrication and that there was no original diary. They also point to the fact that two different types of handwriting – printing and cursive writing – were used in the diary. They claim that the paper and the ink used were not produced until the 1950s and would have been unavailable to a girl hiding in an attic in Amsterdam in 1942.

But it is the Meyer Levin affair on which the deniers have most

---

* Even after the diary was published to wide acclaim in Europe, American publishers were wary. Ten rejected it before Doubleday published it in 1951. It was an immediate success.

often relied to make their spurious charges. Levin, who had first read the diary while he was living in France, wrote a laudatory review of it when Doubleday published it. Levin's review, which appeared in the *New York Times Book Review*, was followed by other articles by him on the diary in which he urged that it be made into a play and film.[33] In 1952 Otto Frank appointed Levin his literary agent in the United States to explore the possibility of producing a play. Levin wrote a script that was turned down by a series of producers. Frustrated by Levin's failures and convinced that this script would not be accepted, Frank awarded the production rights to Kermit Bloomgarden, who turned, at the suggestion of American author Lillian Hellman, to two accomplished MGM screenwriters. Their version of the play was a success and won the 1955 Pulitzer Prize.

Levin, deeply embittered, sued, charging that the playwrights had plagiarized his material and ideas. In January 1958 a jury ruled that Levin should be awarded fifty thousand dollars in damages. However, the New York State Supreme Court set aside the jury's verdict, explaining that since Levin and the MGM playwrights had both relied on the same original source – Anne's diary – there were bound to be similarities between the two.[34]

Since it appeared that another lawsuit would be filed, the court refused to lift the freeze that Levin had placed on the royalties. After two years of an impasse, Frank and Levin reached an out-of-court settlement. Frank agreed to pay fifteen thousand dollars to Levin, who dropped all his claims to royalties and rights to the dramatization of the play. Levin remained obsessed by his desire to dramatize the diary.* In 1966 he attempted to stage a production in Israel, though he did not have the right to do so, and Frank's lawyers insisted that it be terminated.[35]

It is against this background that the deniers built their assault on the diary. The first documented attack appeared in Sweden in 1957. A Danish literary critic claimed that the diary had actually been produced by Levin, citing as one of his 'proofs' that names such as Peter

---

* In fact, in 1973 he wrote a book, *The Obsession*, about the entire episode.

and Anne were not Jewish names.[36] His charges were repeated in Norway, Austria, and West Germany. In 1958 a German high school teacher who had been a member of the SA and a Hitler Youth leader charged that Anne Frank's diary was a forgery that had earned 'millions for the profiteers from Germany's defeat.'[37] His allegations were reiterated by the chairman of a right-wing German political party. Otto Frank and the diary's publishers sued them for libel, slander, defamation of the memory of a dead person, and antisemitic utterances. The case was settled out of court when the defendants declared that they were convinced the diary was not a forgery and apologized for unverified statements they had made.[38]

In 1967 *American Mercury* published an article by Teressa Hendry, entitled 'Was Anne Frank's Diary a Hoax?' in which she suggested that the diary might be the work of Meyer Levin and that if it was, a massive fraud had been perpetrated.[39] In a fashion that will by now have become familiar to readers of this book, Hendry's allegations were repeated by other deniers as established fact. This is their typical pattern of cross-fertilization as they create a merry-go-round of allegations. In *Did Six Million Really Die? The Truth at Last*, Harwood repeated these charges, unequivocally declaring the diary to be a hoax.[40] In one short paragraph in his book, Arthur Butz likewise stated that he had 'looked it over' and determined that the diary was a hoax.[41]

In his 1975 attack on the diary, David Irving relied on the familiar charge that an American court had 'proved' that a New York script-writer had written it 'in collaboration with the girl's father.' In 1978 Ditlieb Felderer, publisher of the sexually explicit cartoons of Holocaust survivors, produced a book devoted to certifying the diary as a hoax. He repeated the Levin charge but then went on to label Anne a sex fiend and the book 'the first child porno.'[42] (Some of his chapter titles are indicative of his approach: 'Sexual Extravaganza' and 'Anne's Character – Not Even a Nice Girl.' Felderer's charges are designed to build on what is often part of the inventory of antisemitic stereotypes: Jews, unnaturally concerned about sex, are also produc-ers of pornography designed to corrupt young children.)

In 1975 Heinz Roth, a West German publisher of neo-Nazi

brochures, began to circulate pamphlets calling the diary a forgery actually written by a New York playwright. He cited Irving's and Harwood's findings as 'proof' of his charges. When asked to desist by Otto Frank, he refused, claiming, in the familiar defense used by deniers, that he was only interested in 'pure historical truth.' At this point Frank took him to court in West Germany. Roth defended himself by citing statements by Harwood and Butz declaring the diary to be fraudulent. In addition, Roth's lawyers produced an 'expert opinion' by Robert Faurisson, among whose charges to prove the diary fictitious was that the annex's inhabitants had made too much noise. Anne wrote of vacuum cleaners being used, 'resounding' laughter, and noise that was 'enough to wake the dead.'[43] How, Faurisson asked, could people in hiding, knowing that the slightest noise would be their undoing, have behaved in this fashion and not been discovered?[44] But Faurisson quoted the diary selectively, distorting its contents to build his case. When Anne wrote of the use of the vacuum cleaner, she preceded it by noting that the 'warehouse men have gone home now.'[45] The scene in which she described resounding laughter among the inhabitants of the annex took place the preceding evening – a Sunday night – when the warehouse would have been empty.[46] When she wrote that a sack of beans broke open and the noise was enough to 'wake the dead,' Faurisson neglected to quote the next sentence in the diary: 'Thank God there were no strangers in the house.'[47]

In his description of his visit to Otto Frank, Faurisson engaged in the same tactics he used in relation to his encounter with the official from the Auschwitz museum. He tried to make it appear as if he had caught Frank in a monstrous lie: 'The interview turned out to be grueling for Anne Frank's father.'[48] Not surprisingly Frank's description of the interchange differs markedly, and he challenged the veracity of much of what Faurisson claimed he said. Faurisson also claimed to have found a witness who was 'well informed and of good faith' but who refused to allow his name to be made public. Faurisson assured readers that the name and address of this secret witness had been placed in a 'sealed envelope.' As proof of this evidence he included a photograph of the sealed envelope as an appendix to his 'investigation.'[49] In 1980 the court, unconvinced by Faurisson's claims, found that Roth had not proved the diary false.

In 1977 charges were again brought against two men in the West German courts for distributing pamphlets charging that the diary was a hoax. The Bundeskriminalamt (the BKA, or Federal Criminal Investigation Bureau) was asked to prepare a report as to whether the paper and writing material used in the diary were available between 1941 and 1944. The BKA report, which ran to just four pages in length, did not deal with the authenticity of the diary itself. It found that the materials had all been manufactured prior to 1950–51 and consequently could have been used by Anne. It also observed, almost parenthetically, that *emendations* had been made in ballpoint pen on loose pages found with the diary. The ink used to make them had only been on the market since 1951.[50] (The BKA did not address itself to the substance of the emendations, nor did it publish any data explaining how it had reached this conclusion. When the editors of the critical edition of the diary asked for the data they were told by the BKA that they had none.[51])

Given the history of the editing of the diary it is not surprising that these kinds of corrections were made. This did not prevent *Der Spiegel* from publishing a sensationalist article on the diary which began with the following boldface paragraph: ' "The Diary of Anne Frank" was edited at a later date. Further doubt is therefore cast on the authenticity of that document.' The author of the article did not question whether these corrections had been substantive or grammatical, whether they had been incorporated into the printed text, or when they had been made. Nor did he refer to them as corrections as the BKA had. He referred to the possibility of an imposter at work and charged that the diary had been subjected to countless 'manipulations.'

These sensationalist observations notwithstanding, *Der Spiegel* dismissed the charge made by David Irving and other deniers that Levin wrote the diary as an 'oft-repeated legend.' It also stressed that those who wished to shed doubt 'on the diary were the same types who wished to end 'gas chamber fraud.'[52]

On Otto Frank's death in 1980, the diary was given to the Netherlands State Institute for War Documentation. By that time the attacks on it had become so frequent and vehement – though the charges that were made were all essentially the same – that the institute felt obliged to subject the diary, as well as the paper on which it was written, glue that bound it together, and ink to a myriad of scientific tests in order to determine whether they were authentic. They also tested postage stamps, postmarks, and censorship stamps on postcards, letters, and greeting cards sent by Anne and her family during this period (in addition to the diary the institute examined twenty-two different documents containing writings by Anne and her family). Forensic science experts analyzed Anne's handwriting, paying particular attention to the two different scripts, and produced a 250-page highly technical report of their findings.

The reports found that the paper, glue, fibers in the binding, and ink were all in use in the 1940s. The ink contained iron, which was standard for inks used prior to 1950. (After that date ink with no, or a much lower, iron content was used.) The conclusions of the forensic experts were unequivocal: The diaries were written by one person during the period in question. The emendations were of a limited nature and varied from a single letter to three words. They did not in any way alter the meaning of the text when compared to the earlier version.[53] The institute determined that the different handwriting styles were indicative of normal development in a child and left no doubt that it was convinced that it had all been written in the same hand that wrote the letters and cards Anne had sent to classmates in previous years.

The final result of the institute's investigation was a 712 page critical edition of the diary containing the original version, Anne's edited copy, and the published version as well as the experts' findings. While some may argue that the Netherlands State Institute for War Documentation used an elephant to swat a fly, once again it becomes clear that the deniers' claims have no relationship to the most basic rules of truth and evidence.

Notes

1. CANARIES IN THE MINE

1. Dumas Malone, *The Sage of Monticello: Jefferson and His Time*, vol. 6 (Boston, 1981), pp. 417–18.
2. Marvin Perry, 'Denying the Holocaust: History as Myth and Delusion,' *Encore American and Worldwide News*, Sept. 1981, pp. 28–33.
3. For an example of this see how the deniers have treated Anne Frank's diary. David Barnouw and Gerrold van der Stroom, eds., *The Diary of Anne Frank: The Critical Edition* (New York, 1989), pp. 91–101.
4. The incident occurred at Indiana University–Purdue University at Indianapolis on February 9, 1990. It was subsequently revealed that the teacher had been arrested for stealing war memorabilia from a local museum (*Indianapolis News*, Feb. 16, 1990).
5. *Indianapolis Star*, Feb. 22 and 23, 1990.
6. *The Sagamore*, Feb. 26, 1990.
7. 'Like your uncle from Peoria,' was how actress Whoopi Goldberg described the neo-Nazi Tom Metzger, whom she hosted on her television show in September 1992. Metzger, an ardent racist and antisemite, advocates the forced racial segregation of blacks. Goldberg acknowledged that he was particularly dangerous because he appeared so civil. Howard Rosenberg, the television critic of the *Los Angeles Times*, wondered why, if Goldberg recognized this, it was necessary for her to host him on her show. Obviously she had fallen prey to the same syndrome afflicting those who invite the deniers to appear (*Los Angeles Times*, Sept. 21, 1992).
8. *New Orleans Times-Picayune*, Aug. 26, 1990.
9. From a letter signed by David Duke accompanying the *Crusader*, February 1980, as cited in *David Duke: In His Own Words* (New York, n.d.).

10. Interview with David Duke conducted by *Hustler* magazine, reprinted in the *National Association for the Advancement of White People News*, Aug. 1982.

11. Jason Berry, 'Duke's Disguise,' *New York Times*, Oct. 16, 1991. See also Letters to the Editor, *New York Times*, Oct. 19, 1991.

12. Jason Berry, 'The Hazards of Duke,' *Washington Post*, May 14, 1989. He also tried to appear as if he had modulated his views on other topics. No longer did he speak of sterilizing welfare mothers; now it was 'birth control incentives' (*Los Angeles Times*, June 10, 1990). See also Lawrence N. Powell, 'Read my Liposuction: The Makeover of David Duke,' *New Republic*, Oct. 15, 1990.

13. Jacob Weisberg, 'The Heresies of Pat Buchanan,' *New Republic*, Oct. 22, 1990, pp. 26–27.

14. Ibid., p. 26.

15. Report of the Anti-Defamation League on Pat Buchanan, *Los Angeles Jewish Journal*, Sept. 28, 1991.

16. *New York Times*, Feb. 14, 1992.

17. David Warshofsky (pseud.), interview with author, December 1992. 'Warshofsky' is a regular participant in the institute's meetings and is in constant communication with various deniers both in the United States and in Europe.

18. Robert D. Kaplan, 'Croatianism: The Latest Balkan Ugliness,' *New Republic*, Nov. 25, 1991, p. 16.

19. 'Croatia,' *Encyclopedia of the Holocaust* (New York, 1990), Israel Gutman, ed., p. 326.

20. Some of the key Slovakian separatists have engaged in actual denial. *Jewish Telegraphic Agency*, Mar. 17, 1992.

21. *Jewish Telegraphic Agency*, Nov. 6, 1992; *The Times*, Mar. 6, 1988.

22. *Daily Telegraph*, July 10, 1992.

23. *Sunday Telegraph*, Jan. 12, 1992.

24. *Daily Telegraph*, July 10, 1992.

25. *Independent on Sunday*, May 10, 1992.

26. Frederick Brown, 'French Amnesia,' *Harper's*, Dec. 1981, p. 70.

27. Nadine Fresco, 'The Denial of the Dead: On the Faurisson Affair,' *Dissent*, Fall 1981, p. 467.

28. Pierre Vidal-Naquet, *Assassins of Memory: Essays on the Denial of the Holocaust* (New York, 1993), pp. 40–41; Serge Thion, ed., *Vérité historique or vérité politique?* (Paris, 1980), pp. 187, 190, 211.

29. Vidal-Naquet, *Assassins of Memory*, p. 115.

30. Ibid.

31. *Guardian*, July 3, 1986; *Le Monde*, July 4, 1986.

32. *New Statesman*, Apr. 10, 1981, p. 4.

33. *Annales d'Histoire Revisionniste*, vol. 1, Spring 1987; Judith Miller, *One by One by One: Facing the Holocaust* (New York, 1990), p. 134.

34. Miller, *One by One by One*, p. 137; *Jewish Telegraphic Agency*, Oct. 23, 1987.

35. *Time*, May 28, 1990; *U.S. News & World Report*, May 28, 1990, p. 42; *Los Angeles Times*, May 29, 1990, pp. H1, H7. In the following parliamentary election Le Pen's party was routed but this resulted from a change in the voting system and not a loss of support. Miller, *One by One by One*, p. 138.

36. *Jewish Telegraphic Agency*, Oct. 23, 1987; Alain Finkielkraut, *Remembering in Vain: The Klaus Barbie Trial and Crimes Against Humanity* (New York, 1989), pp. 35–44.

37. *L'Express*, Oct. 28–Nov. 4, 1978; Gill Seidel, *The Holocaust Denial* (Leeds, England, 1986).

38. *New Statesman*, Sept. 7, 1979, p. 332.

39. *The Times*, May 11, 1990; *Jewish Week*, Sept. 15, 1989.

40. *Dokumentationszentrum*, 1988 Annual Report, Vienna, Austria.

41. *Austrian News*, Embassy of Austria, Press and Information Dept., Washington, Oct., 1989.

42. *Spotlight*, June 1, 1992.

43. In 1991, the Gallup organization conducted a poll of Austrian attitudes toward Jews commissioned by the American Jewish Committee. Fifty-three percent of the people surveyed thought it was time to 'put the memory of the Holocaust behind us' and 39 percent believed that 'Jews have caused much harm in the course of history.' An almost identical proportion believed that Jews had 'too much influence' over world affairs; close to 20 percent wanted them out of the country. These statistics indicate a country 'ripe' for an antisemitic ideology such as Holocaust denial. Fritz Karmasin, *Austrian Attitudes Towards Jews, Israel and the Holocaust* (New York, 1992).

44. *Jewish Telegraphic Agency*, Aug. 18, 1992, p. 4; Nov. 11, 1992.

45. *Jewish Telegraphic Agency*, Nov. 2, 4, 1992.

46. *Arab News*, May 8, 1988.

47. *New York Times*, Dec. 10, 1989.

48. *New Statesman*, Sept. 7, 1979; *Searchlight*, Nov. 1988, p. 15.

49. *Jewish Telegraphic Agency*, Dec. 22, 1992. Outside of the Union, some Australians have been able to voice Holocaust denial charges with impunity. Dr. Anice Morsey, a prominent member of the

Australian Arab community, has accused Zionists of fabricating the story of the Holocaust. He maintained that the Jews who were killed were fifth columnists or spies. Morsey asserted that Israel was the financial beneficiary of this hoax and Germany the victim. Morsey's views do not seem to have hampered his career. Subsequent to making that statement he was appointed ethnic affairs commissioner by the Victorian government. *An Nahar*, Nov. 8, 1982, quoted in Jeremy Jones, 'Holocaust Revisionism in Australia,' in *Without Prejudice* (Australian Institute of Jewish Affairs), Dec. 4, 1991, p. 53. Kenneth Stern's *Holocaust Denial* contains a useful survey of recent Holocaust denial activities throughout the world (New York: American Jewish Committee, 1993), chap. 2.

50. *New York Times*, Mar. 12, 1987; Jennifer Golub, *Japanese Attitudes Toward Jews* (New York: American Jewish Committee, 1992), p. 6.

51. *The Weekend Australian*, Aug. 19–20, 1989; *New York Times*, Dec. 25, 1988; *Time*, Oct. 7, 1991.

52. Yehuda Bauer, ' "Revisionism" – The Repudiation of the Holocaust and Its Historical Significance,' in *The Historiography of the Holocaust Period*, Yisrael Gutman and Gideon Greif, eds. (Jerusalem, 1988), p. 702.

53. *Los Angeles Times*, Dec. 18, 1990.

54. *Near East Report*, Apr. 16, 1990, p. 72.

55. Interview with Robert Faurisson, Vichy, France, June 1989.

56. *Jewish Telegraphic Agency*, Nov. 26, 1992.

57. *Esquire*, Feb. 1983.

58. *The Progressive*, Apr. 1986, p. 4.

59. Peter Hayes, 'A Historian Confronts Denial,' in *The Netherlands and Nazi Genocide*, G. Jan Colijn and Marcia S. Littell, eds. (Lewiston, 1992), p. 522.

60. Safet M. Sarich to Winnetka educators, May 1991.

61. *New York Times*, Jan. 1, 1981.

62. Gitta Sereny, 'The Judgment of History,' *New Statesman*, July 17, 1981, p. 16; Noam Chomsky, 'The Commissars of Literature,' *New Statesman*, Aug. 14, 1981, p. 13.

63. Noam Chomsky, 'Chomsky: Freedom of Expression? Absolutely,' *Village Voice*, July 1–7, 1981, p. 12. See also Noam Chomsky, 'The Faurisson Affair: His Right to Say It,' *Nation*, Feb. 28, 1981, p. 231. Gitta Sereny, 'Let History Judge,' *New Statesman*, Sept. 11, 1981, p. 12.

64. Alfred Kazin, 'Americans Right, Left and Indifferent: Responses to the Holocaust,' *Dimensions*, vol. 4, no. 1 (1988), p. 12.

65. He was particularly distressed by the University of Lyons's decision not to let Faurisson teach because it could not guarantee his safety.

66. Statement by President H. Keith H. Brodie, Duke University, Nov. 6, 1991.

67. Fish argued that he was not in the business of 'recovering' texts but 'in the business of *making* texts and of teaching others to make them.' He found this a liberating approach because it relieved him of 'the obligation to be right . . . and demands only that I be interesting.' Peter Novick, *That Noble Dream: The Objectivity Question and the American Historical Profession* (Cambridge, 1988), p. 544.

68. Nelson Goodman, *Ways of Worldmaking* (Indianapolis, 1978), cited in Novick, *That Noble Dream*, p. 539.

69. Richard Rorty, 'Pragmatism, Relativism, and Irrationalism,' in his *Consequences of Pragmatism* (Minneapolis, 1982), p. 166. See also Novick, *That Noble Dream*, p. 540.

70. Hilary Putnam, *Truth and History* (Cambridge, 1981), p. 54.

71. *Time*, Aug. 26, 1991, p. 19.

72. *Newsweek*, Sept. 18, 1991, p. 47.

73. Charles Maier, *The Unmasterable Past: History, Holocaust and German National Identity* (Cambridge, 1988), p. 64.

74. Novick, *That Noble Dream*, pp. 448ff.

75. Mark Lane, letter to the editor, *Los Angeles Daily Journal*, Nov. 13, 1991.

76. Conversations with Robert Faurisson, Vichy, France, June 1989.

77. Harry Elmer Barnes, 'Revisionism: A Key to Peace,' *Rampart Journal* (Spring 1966), p. 3.

78. Austin J. App, *History's Most Terrifying Peace*, p. 106, cited in 'Prevent World War III,' n.d., p. 7.

79. Harry Elmer Barnes, *Revisionism and Brainwashing: A Survey of the War-Guilt Question in Germany After Two World Wars* (n.p., 1962) (hereafter referred to as *Brainwashing*), p. 33.

80. Canadian papers covering the trial regularly carried headlines such as: 'Nazi Camp had Pool, Ballroom' (*Toronto Sun*, Feb. 13, 1985); 'Prisoners at Auschwitz dined, danced to band, Zundel Witness Testifies' (*Toronto Star*, Feb. 13, 1985).

81. Conversations with Robert Faurisson, Vichy, France, June 1989.

82. Maier, *The Unmasterable Past*, p. 64.

83. Colin Holmes, 'Historical Revisionism in Britain: The Politics of History,' in *Trends in Historical Revisionism: History as a Political Device* (London, 1985), p. 8.
84. Dumas Malone, *The Sage of Monticello*, pp. 417–18.
85. Novick, *That Noble Dream*, p. 2.
86. Institute for Historical Review, *Newsletter* (Apr. 1987), p. 1.
87. *New York Review of Books*, Mar. 22, 1979, p. 47. See also Pierre Vidal-Naquet, *Assassins of Memory*, pp. 3–7.
88. *Democracy*, vol. 1–2 (Apr. 1981), pp. 73ff.
89. Justus D. Doenecke, 'Harry Elmer Barnes: Prophet of a Usable Past,' *History Teacher* (Feb. 1975), p. 273.
90. Geoffrey Hartman, 'Blindness and Insight,' *New Republic*, Mar. 7, 1988, pp. 26–31.
91. Donald Cameron Watt, 'The Political Misuse of History,' in *Trends in Historical Revisionism: History as a Political Device* (London, 1985), p. 11.

2. THE ANTECEDENTS

1. Sidney B. Fay, 'New Light on the Origins of the World War,' *American Historical Review*, vol. 25 (1920), pp. 616–39; vol. 26, (1920), pp. 37–53; vol. 26 (1921), pp. 225–54.
2. Sidney B. Fay, *The Origins of the World War*, vol. 2 (New York, 1966), pp. 552–54.
3. Novick, *That Noble Dream*, pp. 210ff.
4. Ibid., p. 212.
5. Charles Beard, 'Heroes and Villains of the World War,' *Current History*, vol. 24 (1926), p. 733.
6. Fay, *Origins of the World War*, vol. 1, p. 8.
7. Harry Elmer Barnes, *The Genesis of the World War: An Introduction to the Problem of War Guilt* (New York, 1929), p. 641.
8. For analysis of the evidence placed before the Commission on Responsibility for the War at the Paris Peace Conference and the conclusions based on it see A. von Wegerer, 'Die Widerlegung der Versailles Kriegsschuldthese' (Refutation of the Versailles war guilt theory), in *Die Kriegsschuldfrage* (The war guilt question), vol. 6 (Jan. 1928), pp. 1–77; see also his article and the replies to it in *Current History* (Aug. 1928), pp. 810–28, cited in Fay, *Origins of the World War*, vol. 2, p. 549.

9.   Barnes, *Genesis*, pp. 641–42.

10. Ibid., p. 647.

11. For a discussion of British propaganda, see C. Hartley Grattan, *Why We Fought* (1929), and Walter Millis, *Road to War* (1935), cited in John E. Wiltz, *From Isolationism to War, 1931–1941* (New York, 1968), p. 8.

12. Wiltz, *From Isolationism to War*, p. 7.

13. Charles A. Beard, *President Roosevelt and the Coming of the War* (New Haven, 1948), p. 5.

14. Barnes, *Genesis*, p. 648.

15. Fay, *Origins of the World War*, p. 558.

16. Wiltz, *From Isolationism to War*, p. 17.

17. Wayne S. Cole, *Roosevelt and the Isolationists, 1932–1945* (Lincoln, Nebr., 1983), p. 6.

18. For background on the isolationists-revisionists and a sympathetic portrayal of their efforts, see Justus D. Doenecke, *Not to the Swift: The Old Isolationists in the Cold War Era* (London, 1982); see also Wayne S. Cole, *Charles A. Lindbergh and the Battle Against American Intervention in World War II* (New York, 1974), pp. 379–81.

19. Tom Connally, *My Name Is Tom Connally* (New York, 1954), pp. 211–14, cited in Cole, *Roosevelt and the Isolationists*, p. 161.

20. Cordell Hull, *Memoirs of Cordell Hull*, vol. 1 (New York, 1948), p. 404.

21. Cole, *Roosevelt and the Isolationists*, p. 161; Dexter Perkins, *The New Age of Franklin Roosevelt*, cited in Wiltz, *From Isolationism to War*, p. 50.

22. Wiltz, *From Isolationism to War*, p. 7.

23. Johnson to Hiram W. Johnson, Jr., Feb. 11, 19, 1939, Johnson to Frank P. Doherty, Feb. 11, 1939; Johnson Papers, cited in Cole, *Roosevelt and the Isolationists*, pp. 308, 607.

24. Edward S. Shapiro, 'Antisemitism Mississippi Style,' in *Antisemitism in American History*, ed. David Gerber (Urbana/Chicago, 1986), pp. 129–47. Rankin also opposed the repeal of the Chinese Exclusion Act because 'Japs' would flood America in the postwar period (Doenecke, *Not to the Swift*, p. 21).

25. *Congressional Record*, 77th Congress, 1st sess., 1941, 87:6565; Cole, pp. 475–76.

26. Cole, *Roosevelt and the Isolationists*, p. 465. On antisemitism in America First see James C. Schneider, *Should America Go to War?*

The Debate over Foreign Policy in Chicago, 1939–1941 (Chapel Hill, N.C., 1989), p. 210.

27. Charles Beard, 'We're Blundering Into War,' *American Mercury* (Apr. 1939), pp. 388–90.

28. *The International Jew: The World's Foremost Problem* (Hawthorne, Calif., n.d.). For an analysis of antisemitic conspiracy theories in the United States see Seymour Martin Lipset and Earl Raab, *The Politics of Unreason: Right-Wing Extremism in America, 1790–1977*, 2d ed. (Chicago, 1978), chaps. 4, 5, and 6. For the impact of the belief in the *Protocols* see Norman Cohn, *Warrant for Genocide* (New York, 1966), pp. 156–64. For a compelling overview of the role of conspiracy theories in America see George Johnson, *Architects of Fear: Conspiracy Theories and Paranoia in American Politics* (Boston, 1983). For a discussion of Henry Ford see ibid., pp. 111–14. For information on contemporary uses of the *Protocols* see *Patterns of Prejudice*, Nov./Dec. 1977.

29. Lipset and Raab, *Politics of Unreason*, p. 135.

30. Johnson, *Architects of Fear*, pp. 78–80.

31. Henri Zukier, 'The Conspiratorial Imperative: Medieval Jewry in Western Europe,' in *Changing Conceptions of Conspiracy*, Carl F. Graumann and Serge Moscovici, eds. (New York, 1987), pp. 93–101.

32. *Chicago Tribune*, editorial, Nov. 9, 1945. John T. Flynn, *The Roosevelt Myth* (New York, 1948). Other books that made similar arguments included William Henry Chamberlin, *America's Second Crusade* (Chicago, 1950), and Frederic R. Sanborn, *Design for War* (New York, 1951).

33. Beard, *President Roosevelt*, p. 577.

34. *Time*, June 16, 1947, p. 29, quoted in Doenecke, *Not to the Swift*, p. 101.

35. Charles C. Tansill, *Back Door to War: The Roosevelt Foreign Policy, 1933–1941* (Chicago, 1952), p. 9.

36. Tansill, *Back Door to War*, p. 510.

37. For Tansill's views on Hitler see Charles C. Tansill to Harry Elmer Barnes, November 10, 1950, Barnes Papers, Univ. of Wyoming. For background on Tansill's conservative and segregationist views see Doenecke, *Not to the Swift*, pp. 101–2, 112.

38. Tansill, *Back Door to War*, pp. 554–55.

39. Austin App, *A Straight Look at the Third Reich: Hitler and National Socialism, How Right? How Wrong?* (Tacoma Park, Md., 1974), p. 40.

40. William Henry Chamberlin, 'Shifting American Alignments,' *Human Events* (May 22, 1946).
41. Freda Utley, *The High Cost of Vengeance* (Chicago, 1949), p. 14.
42. George Morgenstern, *Pearl Harbor: The Story of the Secret War* (New York, 1947), pp. 4, 7, 283, cited in Doenecke, *Not to the Swift*, p. 97.
43. William Neumann to H. E. Barnes, Jan. 30, 1946, Barnes Papers, cited in Doenecke, *Not to the Swift*, p. 141.
44. Frederick Libby, *Peace Action*, vol. 9 (July 1945), pp. 3–4.
45. Leonard Dinnerstein, *America and the Survivors of the Holocaust* (New York, 1982), pp. 162–83.
46. Doenecke, *Not to the Swift*, p. 133.
47. Ibid., p. 145.
48. In a far milder and more rational defense of the German people, Philip La Follette, former governor of Wisconsin, described the German people as the first victims of Nazi brutalities.
49. *Congressional Record*, Mar. 29, 1946, p. 2801, and Apr. 18, 1946, p. 3962.
50. Extreme concern about the conditions of the German population did not always *ipso facto* indicate a lack of concern about what Jews had experienced. Langer was one of the outspoken supporters in the Senate of the activist Jewish leader Peter Bergson, who called for a strong American rescue program for European Jewry. In 1943 on the floor of the Senate, Langer had publicly criticized the Bermuda Conference as a ploy sponsored by the British and American governments to give the illusion that plans for rescue were under serious consideration. He warned that '2,000,000 Jews in Europe have been killed off already and another 5,000,000 Jews are awaiting the same fate unless they are saved immediately. Every day, every hour, every minute that passes thousands of them are being exterminated.' Langer's positions both during the war and after it are attributable in great measure to his opposition to the Democrats' foreign policy (David Wyman, *The Abandonment of the Jews: America and the Holocaust, 1941–1945* (New York, 1984), p. 143.
51. Doenecke, *Not to the Swift*, p. 215.
52. Utley, *High Cost of Vengeance*, p. 14 (italics added).
53. Ibid., pp. 14, 15.
54. She included in these crimes 'the obliteration bombing; the mass expropriation and expulsion from their homes of twelve million Germans on account of their race; the starving of the Germans during

the first years of the occupation; the use of prisoners as slave laborers; the Russian concentration camps, and the looting perpetrated by Americans as well as Russians (Utley, *High Cost of Vengeance*, p. 183).

55. 'Slaveholders Always Defend Slavery,' *Chicago Tribune*, December 10, 1946.

56. Karl Brandt, 'Germany Is Our Problem,' pamphlet (Hinsdale, Ill., 1946).

57. *Chicago Tribune*, July 26, 1945; Charles A. Beard to Oswald Garrison Villard, November 8, 1946, Villard Papers, cited in Doenecke, *Not to the Swift*, pp. 140, 141, 149 n. 43.

58. 'The Nazi Trials,' editorial, *Chicago Tribune*, July 24, 1945.

59. *Congressional Record*, 82nd Cong., 2nd Sess., Mar. 11, 1952, pp. 2106, 2110, cited in Shapiro, 'Antisemitism Mississippi Style,' p. 136.

60. Frank C. Waldrop, *McCormick of Chicago* (Englewood, N.J., 1966), p. 263. For additional background information on the foreign policy of the *Chicago Tribune* in the interwar period see Jerome Edwards, *The Foreign Policy of Colonel McCormick's Tribune, 1921–1941* (Reno, 1971).

61. *New York Daily News*, October 6, 1945.

62. *Nation*, May 19, 1945, p. 579.

63. *Progressive*, May 14, 1945, cited in Robert Abzug, *Inside the Vicious Heart* (New York, 1985), pp. 136–37.

64. General doubts about the reports of mass murder and other atrocities committed by the Germans had persisted as late as the liberation of the camps. In April 1945 the BBC had chosen not to broadcast its own reporter's account of the liberation of Buchenwald because it feared the public would not believe him. It waited a number of days until it received Edward R. Murrow's account. Because Murrow was held in such high esteem by the British, the BBC was convinced that his description of the horrors perpetrated by the Germans would be more likely to be accepted as accurate. Even Murrow worried that his report would be dismissed as exaggerated, and in his famous broadcast he asked his listeners, 'I pray you to believe what I have said.'

65. William Hesseltine, 'Atrocities Then and Now,' *Progressive*, May 9, 1945, p. 4.

66. App, *A Straight Look*, p. 5.

67. Mark Weber, 'Civil War Concentration Camps,' *Journal of Historical Review* (Summer 1981), pp. 144, 150–52.

68. C. C. Aronsfeld, *The Text of the Holocaust* (Marblehead, Mass., 1985), p. 52.

69. Ibid., p. 55. Grabert published David Hoggan's *The Forced War*, which would play a seminal role in the evolution of Holocaust denial in the United States and Germany.

70. *Welt der Arbeit*, May 26, 1961, cited in Aronsfeld, *Text of the Holocaust*, p. 56.

71. *Deutsche Hochschullehrer-Zeitung* (Tübingen), no. 4 (1963), quoted in Aronsfeld, *Text of the Holocaust*, p. 56.

72. Nadine Fresco, 'The Denial of the Dead: On the Faurisson Affair,' *Dissent* (Fall 1981), pp. 473–74.

3. IN THE SHADOW OF WORLD WAR II

1. Maurice Bardèche, *Nuremberg ou la Terre Promise* (Paris, 1948), cited in Gill Seidel, *The Holocaust Denial: Antisemitism, Racism and the New Right* (Leeds, England, 1986), p. 95.

2. Ian Barnes, 'Revisionism and the Right,' *A Contemporary Affairs Briefing of the Centre for Contemporary Studies* (reprinted in the Glasgow *Jewish Echo*, Jan. 8, 1982, p. 6).

3. Pierre Hofstetter, Introduction to Paul Rassinier, *Debunking the Genocide Myth: A Study of the Nazi Concentration Camps and the Alleged Extermination of European Jewry* (Torrance, Calif., 1978) (hereafter cited as *Debunking*), p. x.

4. Ibid.

5. *Debunking*, p. 164.

6. Ibid., p. 35.

7. Ibid.

8. Ibid., p. 37.

9. Ibid., p. 36.

10. Ibid., p. 185.

11. Ibid., pp. 53, 55.

12. Ibid., p. 216.

13. Ibid.

14. Ibid., pp. 218–19.

15. Ibid., p. 219.

16. Ibid., p. 214.

17. Paul Rassinier, *The Real Eichmann Trial, or The Incorrigible Victors* (Silver Spring, Md., n.d.), p. 47.

18. *Debunking*, p. 214.

19. Ibid.

20. Ministry of Foreign Affairs, Israel, *Documents Relating to the Agreement Between the Government of Israel and the Government of the Federal Republic of Germany* (Jerusalem, 1953), pp. 9–91. On March 14, 1951, Foreign Minister Moshe Sharett declared in a statement to the Knesset that 'the demand for reparation has been calculated according to the burden that the people in Israel and Jewish organizations throughout the world have taken upon themselves in financing the rehabilitation and the absorption of a half a million survivors of the Holocaust who have settled or will settle in Israel.' Nana Sagi, *German Reparations: A History of the Negotiations* (Jerusalem, 1980), p. 55.

21. *Debunking*, p. 219.

22. Raul Hilberg, *The Destruction of the European Jews* (New York, 1967), p. 311; *Debunking*, p. 219.

23. Hannah Arendt, 'A Reporter at Large: Eichmann in Jerusalem – II,' *The New Yorker*, Feb. 23, 1963, p. 66.

24. *Debunking*, p. 220.

25. Hilberg, *The Destruction of the European Jews*, p. 670.

26. *Debunking*, p. 219.

27. Archival collections in the former USSR, which had previously been unavailable to historians, were recently opened for inspection. It is likely that the information they contain may result in a change in the estimate of the number of victims.

28. Hilberg, *The Destruction of the European Jews*, p. 257.

29. Ibid., p. 266.

30. *Debunking*, p. 224.

31. Ibid., p. 288.

32. 'Raphael Lemkin,' *Encyclopedia of the Holocaust* (New York, 1990), p. 860.

33. *Debunking*, p. 289.

34. Ibid., p. 309.

35. Ibid., p. 306.

36. The *American Mercury* was founded and edited for many years by H. L. Mencken. Under Mencken it was recognized as one of the literary lights of the American scene, publishing the works of Sinclair Lewis, Eugene O'Neill, Carl Sandburg, and Robert Frost. Mencken sold it in 1935. It then became an increasingly conservative publication. In 1955 *Time* magazine reported that most of its top

editors had quit because they were convinced that 'attempts were being made to introduce antisemitic material' into the magazine.
37. *Debunking*, p. 309.

4. THE FIRST STIRRINGS OF DENIAL IN AMERICA

1. Arnold Forster, 'The Ultimate Cruelty,' *ADL Bulletin* (June 1959), pp. 1ff.
2. Ibid., p. 2.
3. Ibid.
4. Benjamin H. Freedman, 'Six Million Jew Hoax,' *Common Sense* (May 1, 1959).
5. Forster, 'The Ultimate Cruelty,' p. 2.
6. Arthur Butz, 'The International "Holocaust" Controversy,' *Journal of Historical Review* (Spring 1980), p. 6.
7. *Our Sunday Visitor*, June 14, 1959; Forster, 'The Ultimate Cruelty,' p. 7.
8. Forster, 'The Ultimate Cruelty,' p. 7.
9. Peter Baldwin, 'The *Historikerstreit* in Context,' in *Reworking the Past: Hitler, the Holocaust and the Historians' Debate*, ed. Peter Baldwin (Boston, 1990), p. 24.
10. Paul L. Berman, 'Gas Chamber Games: Crackpot History and the Right to Lie,' *Village Voice*, June 10–16, 1981, p. 40; Harry Elmer Barnes, *The Court Historians Versus Revisionism* (n.p., n.d.), p. 3.
11. Novick, *That Noble Dream*, p. 208.
12. Charles A. Beard to Harry Elmer Barnes, June 28, 1924, Barnes Papers, Box 79, cited in Novick, *That Noble Dream*, p. 212.
13. His trip to Germany to expound on the Versailles treaty had a major impact on his subsequent historical views, *Brainwashing*, p. 24.
14. *Brainwashing*, pp. 13, 18.
15. Harry Elmer Barnes, 'Revisionism and the Promotion of Peace,' *Journal of Historical Review* (Spring 1982), p. 61. This article originally appeared in *Liberation* (Summer 1958) and was subsequently republished as a pamphlet.
16. H. E. Barnes to C. C. Tansill, Nov. 7, 1950, cited in Doenecke, *Not to the Swift*, p. 105.
17. Barnes, 'Revisionism and the Promotion of Peace,' p. 65.
18. Ibid., pp. 67–68.

19. H. E. Barnes to W. L. Neumann, Feb. 8, 1952, cited in Doenecke, *Not to the Swift*, p. 104.

20. Barnes, 'Revisionism and the Promotion of Peace,' p. 68.

21. Harry Elmer Barnes, *The Struggle Against the Historical Blackout* (n.p., 1952), p. 11.

22. Barnes, 'Revisionism and the Promotion of Peace,' p. 72.

23. *Brainwashing*, p. 3.

24. Harry Elmer Barnes to Oswald Garrison Villard, October 28, 1948, Harvard University.

25. Harry Elmer Barnes to Oswald Garrison Villard, March 5, 1949, Harvard University.

26. *Brainwashing*, p. 5.

27. Ibid.

28. Lucy Dawidowicz, 'Lies About the Holocaust,' *Commentary*, Dec. 1980, p. 32.

29. David Leslie Hoggan, *The Forced War: When Peaceful Revision Failed* (Torrance, Calif., 1989).

30. Hoggan, *The Forced War*, p. 156.

31. Hilberg, *The Destruction of the European Jews*, p. 92.

32. Hoggan, *The Forced War*, p. 101.

33. U.S. Department of State, *Foreign Relations of the United States, 1938*, vol. 2 (Washington, D.C., 1938), pp. 391–92.

34. Hoggan, *The Forced War*, p. 101.

35. U.S. Department of State, *Foreign Relations of the United States, 1938*, vol. 2, p. 361.

36. Helmut Krausnick, then director of the Institute for Contemporary History in Munich, charged that Hoggan had actually engaged in forgery in the preparation of the book. See Krausnick's foreword to Hermann Graml's critique of Hoggan, *Geschichte in Wissenschaft und Unterricht*, August 1963, cited in Dawidowicz, 'Lies About the Holocaust,' p. 32.

37. See Gerhard L. Weinberg's review in *American Historical Review*, vol. 68, no. 1 (October 1962), pp. 104–5.

38. *Brainwashing*, p. 42.

39. Ibid. Barnes translated some of Rassinier's works into English. See Lewis Brandon, 'Introduction,' *The Barnes Trilogy: Three Revisionist Booklets by Harry Elmer Barnes, Historian, Criminologist, Sociologist, Economist* (Torrance, Calif., 1979). Brandon was the alias used by David McCalden, the first director of the Institute for Historical Review.

40. Harry Elmer Barnes, 'Zionist Fraud,' *American Mercury*, Fall 1968, reprinted in an appendix to *The Myth of the Six Million* (Los Angeles, 1969), p. 117.

41. *Brainwashing*, p. 32.

42. Ibid., p. 33.

43. Ibid.

44. Ibid., p. 37 (italics added).

45. Harry Elmer Barnes, 'Revisionism: A Key to Peace,' *Rampart Journal* (Spring 1966), quoted in Dawidowicz, 'Lies About the Holocaust,' p. 33 (italics added).

46. Harry Elmer Barnes, 'The Public Stake in Revisionism,' *Rampart Journal* (Summer 1967), pp. 19–41, republished in *Journal of Historical Review* (Fall 1980) (hereafter referred to as 'The Public Stake'), p. 217 (italics added).

47. 'The Public Stake,' p. 218 (italics added).

48. He specifically referred to *Look*, Mar. 21, 1967; *Saturday Evening Post*, Oct. 22, 1965, and Feb. 25, 1967. 'The Public Stake,' pp. 205–30.

49. 'The Public Stake,' p. 219 (italics added).

50. Ibid., p. 225 (italics added).

51. Ibid., p. 223 (italics added). Barnes apparently thought Brzezinka and Birkenau were two separate camps. Birkenau is the German translation of Brzezinka. Jonowska is Janówska.

52. Ibid., p. 222.

53. Gitta Sereny, 'The Men Who Whitewash Hitler,' *New Statesman*, Nov. 1979, p. 670.

54. Even the former East Germany, which until 1990 did not accept responsibility for the Holocaust, acknowledged that it had occurred. It blamed the fascists, who persecuted the Communists.

55. 'The Public Stake,' p. 228; *Brainwashing*, p. 2.

56. *Brainwashing*, p. 34.

57. Ibid., pp. 2, 25.

58. Ibid., p. 39.

59. Ibid., p. 42.

60. Ibid., p. 43.

61. Harry Elmer Barnes to Oswald Garrison Villard, November 11, 1945; Oswald Garrison Villard to Harry Elmer Barnes, November 14, 1945, in the collection of Harvard University. Barnes originally met Villard in 1926 when Villard had come to lecture in Barnes's classes at Smith College. They both shared revisionist views

regarding World War I and World War II, though Barnes was far more extreme about the latter.

62. Novick, *That Noble Dream*, p. 218.
63. 'The Public Stake,' p. 219.
64. Memo from Barry Youngerman to Jerry Bakst, June 27, 1967, archives of the Anti-Defamation League, New York.
65. Berman, 'Gas Chamber Games', pp. 38–40.
66. Justus Doenecke, 'Harry Elmer Barnes: Prophet of a "Usable" Past,' *History Teacher*, vol. 8 (Feb. 1975).

5. AUSTIN J. APP: THE WORLD OF IMMORAL EQUIVALENCIES

1. Arnold Forster, 'The Ultimate Cruelty,' *ADL Bulletin* (June 1959), pp. 7–8.
2. *New Yorker Staats-Zeitung und Herold*, September 7, 1948; Leonard Dinnerstein, *America and the Survivors of the Holocaust* (New York, 1982), p. 222.
3. Thomas R. O'Donnell to Deborah E. Lipstadt, April 18, 1991; Thomas R. O'Donnell, telephone interview with author, Oct. 1992.
4. Austin App, 'Foreword,' *Morgenthau Era Letters*, 2nd printing (Tacoma Park, Md., 1975).
5. App, *A Straight Look*, p. 40.
6. App, *Morgenthau Era Letters*, pp. 13–14.
7. Ibid., p. 21.
8. Ibid., p. 33.
9. S. F. Berton, 'Das Attentat auf Reinhard Heydrich vom 27 Mai 1942: Ein Bericht des Kriminalrats Heinz Pannwitz,' *Vierteljahrshefte für Zeitgeschichte* (July 1985), pp. 668–706. See also J. Bradley, *Lidice: Sacrificial Village* (New York, 1972); T. Wittlin, *Time Stopped at 6:30* (Indianapolis, 1965); and 'Lidice,' *Encyclopedia of the Holocaust*.
10. App, *Morgenthau Era Letters*, p. 49.
11. Ibid., p. 51.
12. Ibid., p. 59.
13. Ibid., p. 66.
14. At the end of 1946 the official American total of Jewish survivors in the western zones of Germany, Austria, and Italy was 207,788. The Joint Distribution Committee, which assisted the survivors, esti-

mated that there were 231,500. Many of these were refugees who had spent the war years in Central Asia. Dinnerstein, *America and the Survivors*, p. 278. See also Malcolm Proudfoot, *European Refugees: 1939–1952* (Evanston, Ill., 1956), pp. 339, 341.

15. App, *Morgenthau Era Letters*, pp. 66–67. Judge Simon H. Rifkind was the army's adviser on Jewish affairs in Germany in 1945–46.

16. 'Repatriation of Displaced Persons, March 1946' (U.S. Zone), *Monthly Report of Military Governor, U.S. Zone, April 20, 1946*, cited in Dinnerstein, *America and the Survivors*, p. 275.

17. Austin App, *The Six Million Swindle: Blackmailing the German People for Hard Marks with Fabricated Corpses* (Tacoma Park, Md., 1973), p. 8.

18. App, *Morgenthau Era Letters*, p. 79.

19. Peter Kleist, *Auch Du Warst Dabei!* (You too were involved!) (Heidelberg, 1952), cited in Aronsfeld, *The Text of the Holocaust*, p. 53.

20. App, *The Six Million Swindle*, pp. 7–8.

21. App, *Morgenthau Era Letters*, p. 101 (italics added). He reiterated this argument in *The Six Million Swindle*, pp. 7–8.

22. App, *The Six Million Swindle*, p. 8.

23. Richard L. Rubenstein, *The Cunning of History: The Holocaust and the American Future* (New York, 1975), p. 22.

24. Max Weber, 'Bureaucracy,' in H. H. Gerth and C. Wright Mills, eds., *From Max Weber*, pp. 215–16. See also Talcott Parsons, 'Introduction to Max Weber,' *The Sociology of Religion* (Boston, 1963), cited in Rubenstein, *The Cunning of History*, pp. 22–23.

25. App, *Morgenthau Era Letters*, p. 95.

26. App, *The Six Million Swindle*, p. 4.

27. App, 'The Elusive "Six Million,"' *American Mercury*, Summer 1966, reprinted in *The Myth of the Six Million* (Torrance, Calif., 1978), p. 112.

28. App, *The Six Million Swindle*, p. 2.

29. 'Reparations and Restitution,' *Encyclopedia of the Holocaust*, pp. 1255–59.

30. App, *The Six Million Swindle*, p. 29.

31. App, *A Straight Look*, p. 18 (italics added).

32. Ibid., pp. 5, 19, 39.

33. Robert Wistrich, *Antisemitism: The Longest Hatred* (New York, 1991), p. 53.

34. App, *A Straight Look*, pp. 19–20.

35. Henry Morgenthau, *Germany Is Our Problem* (New York, 1945).

36. App, *A Straight Look*, pp. 28–29.

37. Ibid., p. 30.

38. Ibid., p. 48.

39. Ibid.

40. App, *The Six Million Swindle*, pp. 18–19.

41. Ibid., pp. 23–24.

42. Yisrael Gutman makes a similar argument in response to Arthur Butz's claim that Yad Vashem's inability to gather six million names is proof that such a number is a hoax. Yisrael Gutman, *Denying the Holocaust* (Jerusalem, 1985), p. 20.

43. *Jerusalem Post*, Aug. 17, 1986; *IHR Newsletter* (Oct.–Nov. 1987), p. 4.

44. Hilberg, *The Destruction of the European Jews*, p. 631.

45. App, *The Six Million Swindle*, p. 9.

46. Ibid., p. 16.

6. DENIAL: A TOOL OF THE RADICAL RIGHT

1. *Sunday Times*, Feb. 23, 1975; it was also published under the title *Six Million Lost and Found*.

2. *New Statesman*, Nov. 2, 1979, p. 670.

3. *Sunday Times*, Feb. 23, 1975.

4. *books and bookmen* (May 1975), p. 5. For background on the ideology of the National Front see Richard C. Thurlow, 'The Witches' Brew,' in *Patterns of Prejudice*, vol. 5–6 (1978), pp. 1–9.

5. Seidel, *The Holocaust Denial*, p. 113.

6. *New Statesman*, Nov. 2, 1979, p. 670.

7. Holmes, 'Historical Revisionism in Britain,' p. 6.

8. *Daily Express*, June 17, 1974.

9. C. H. Simonds, 'The Strange Story of Willis Carto,' *National Review*, Sept. 10, 1971, p. 981.

10. After a number of years of continued litigation he withdrew his complaint; Dawidowicz, 'Lies About the Holocaust,' p. 33.

11. *The Myth of the Six Million*, pp. 1–3.

12. Holmes, 'Historical Revisionism in Britain,' p. 6.

13. Richard Harwood, *Did Six Million Really Die? The Truth at Last* (London, n.d.), p. 28.

14. Ibid., p. 2.

15. Ibid., pp. 2, 3.
16. Martin Webster, 'Why Zionism Opposes British Nationalism,' *Spearhead* (February 1977), p. 12.
17. Harwood, *Did Six Million Really Die?*, p. 3.
18. Ibid.
19. *The Myth of the Six Million*, pp. 2–3 (italics added).
20. For background on the Madagascar Plan see Leni Yahil, *The Holocaust: The Fate of European Jewry* (New York, 1990), pp. 253–55; Philip Friedman, 'The Lublin Reservation and the Madagascar Plan: Two Aspects of Nazi Jewish Policy during the Second World War,' *YIVO Annual of Jewish Social Studies* (1953), pp. 151–77; Christopher R. Browning, *The Final Solution and the German Foreign Office: A Study of Referat D3 of Abteilung Deutschland, 1940–1943* (New York, 1978).
21. Aronsfeld, *The Text of the Holocaust*, p. 1.
22. Joseph Goebbels, *Der Nazi-Sozi* (Munich, 1929), p. 8, cited in Aronsfeld, *The Text of the Holocaust*, p. 12.
23. Eberhard Jäckel and Axel Kuhn, eds., *Hitler, Sämtliche Aufzeichnungen 1905–1924* (Stuttgart, 1980), p. 368; Aronsfeld, *The Text of the Holocaust*, p. 12.
24. Nuremberg Document PS 3358, cited in Aronsfeld, *The Text of the Holocaust*, p. 13.
25. In a speech at Karlsruhe as reported in the *Strassburger Neueste Nachrichten*, May 2, 1942, cited in Aronsfeld, *The Text of the Holocaust*, p. 13.
26. Robert Wistrich, 'Letters,' *books and bookmen*, Apr. 1975, p. 7.
27. *Das Reich*, May 9, 1943, cited in Aronsfeld, *The Text of the Holocaust*, p. 14.
28. International Military Tribunal, *Trials of the Major War Criminals Before the International Military Tribunal: Official Text*, vol. 29, pp. 110–73. See also Lucy Dawidowicz, *A Holocaust Reader* (New York, 1976), pp. 130–40.
29. Harwood, *Did Six Million Really Die?*, p. 4.
30. Maier, *The Unmasterable Past*, pp. 67–68.
31. Ilya Levkov, 'Introduction,' *Bitburg and Beyond: Encounters in American, German and Jewish History* (New York, 1987), p. 27.
32. Ernst Nolte, 'Between Myth and Revisionism? The Third Reich in the Perspective of the 1980s,' in *Aspects of the Third Reich*, ed. H. W. Koch (London, 1985), pp. 36–37. Maier, *The Unmasterable Past*, p. 29.

33. Maier, *The Unmasterable Past*, p. 179, n. 34.

34. Harwood, *Did Six Million Really Die?*, p. 5.

35. 'Jewish History,' *Chambers Encyclopedia*, p. 99 (italics added).

36. Harwood, *Did Six Million Really Die?*, p. 5.

37. 'Jewish History,' *Chambers Encyclopedia*, p. 99.

38. Harwood, *Did Six Million Really Die?*, p. 14.

39. *Baseler Nachrichten*, October 7, 1952; Aronsfeld, *The Text of the Holocaust*, p. 14.

40. Harwood, *Did Six Million Really Die?*, p. 20.

41. Ibid.

42. Margarete Buber, *Under Two Dictators* (London, 1950), pp. 208, 242–43, 304.

43. Colin Cross, *Adolf Hitler* (London, 1973), p. 307, cited in Harwood, *Did Six Million Really Die?*, p. 20.

44. Cross, *Adolf Hitler*, p. 365.

45. Ibid., p. 366.

46. Ibid., p. 369.

47. Harwood, *Did Six Million Really Die?*, p. 24. For analysis of his use of the ICRC report, see Arthur Suzman and Denis Diamond, *Six Million Did Die: The Truth Shall Prevail* (Johannesburg, 1977), pp. 10–13.

48. Harwood, *Did Six Million Really Die?*, p. 25.

49. *The Report of the International Committee of the Red Cross (ICRC) on its Activities during the Second World War* (Geneva, 1948), vol. 1, p. 641 (italics added). The report is replete with numerous quotes that demonstrate that Harwood totally misconstrued its findings. For additional examples see Suzman and Diamond, *Six Million Did Die*, p. 12.

50. *Report of the ICRC*, vol. 1, p. 641 (italics added).

51. Ibid. (italics added).

52. Ibid., vol. 2, p. 514 (italics added).

53. Harwood, *Did Six Million Really Die?*, p. 25.

54. *Report of the ICRC*, vol. 1, p. 594. Harwood incorrectly cited this passage as coming from vol. 3.

55. Harwood, *Did Six Million Really Die?*, p. 25.

56. *Report of the ICRC*, vol. 3, p. 77.

57. *Report of the ICRC*, vol. 3, chap. 3, cited in 'Harwood's Distortions of Holocaust Facts,' *Patterns of Prejudice* (May–June, 1975), p. 26 (italics added).

58. Harwood, *Did Six Million Really Die?*, p. 28.

59. *Die Tat*, Jan. 19, 1955.
60. *ICRC Bulletin No. 25*, Feb. 1, 1978, cited in *Patterns of Prejudice* (March–April 1978), p. 11.
61. Françoise Perret, Comité International de la Croix-Rouge, to Jacob Gewirtz, Board of Deputies of British Jews, August 22, 1975.
62. *Her Majesty the Queen vs. Ernst Zundel*, District Court of Ontario, 1988 (hereafter referred to as Zundel), vol. 9, pp. 1970ff.
63. Harwood, *Did Six Million Really Die?*, p. 12.
64. Ibid., p. 10.
65. Ibid., p. 19.
66. David Barnouw and Gerrold van der Stroom, eds., *The Diary of Anne Frank*.
67. Colin Wilson, 'The Führer in Perspective: 2,' *books and bookmen* (Nov. 1974), p. 31.
68. Ibid.
69. Ibid.
70. *books and bookmen* (Jan. 1975), p. 5.
71. Ibid., p. 6.
72. Ibid. (Feb. 1975), p. 6.
73. Ibid.
74. Ibid. (Apr. 1975), p. 10.
75. Ibid. (June 1975), p. 6.

7. ENTERING THE MAINSTREAM

1. Butz refused my request for an interview, Oct. 1992.
2. For additional information on the Liberty Lobby, see chapter 8.
3. Arthur R. Butz, *The Hoax of the Twentieth Century* (Torrance, Calif., 1976) (hereafter referred to as *Hoax*), p. 12.
4. Arthur Butz, 'The International Holocaust Controversy,' *Journal of Historical Review*, vol. 1:1 (Spring 1980), pp. 5–22; 'Holocaust "Revisionism": A Denial of History,' *ADL Facts*, vol. 26:2 (June 1980); 'Revisionism and the Right,' reprinted in *Jewish Echo of Glasgow*, January 8, 1982, p. 6; Aronsfeld, 'Hoax of the Century,' *Patterns of Prejudice*, Nov.–Dec. 1976, pp. 13ff.
5. *Hoax*, pp. 68, 239.
6. Ibid., pp. 107, 131, 171, 195, 223.
7. Ibid., p. 249.
8. Ibid., pp. 240, 287.

9. Ibid., p. 240.
10. Ibid., pp. 33, 89.
11. Ibid., p. 87.
12. Ibid., pp. 247–48.
13. At the same meeting Libyan President Muammar Qaddafi addressed the group via television hookup. In addition to announcing a five million dollar gift to the group, he urged the 'destruction of white America' and the formation of a black army in America that would create a separate state. David Moberg, 'The Naysayer,' *North Shore*, Sept. 1985, pp. 38ff. *Youngstown Jewish Times*, Mar. 29, 1985.
14. *Hoax*, pp. 239, 287.
15. Ibid., pp. 93, 94, 100.
16. Ibid., pp. 29, 30, 45, 199, 287.
17. Ibid., p. 87.
18. Ibid.
19. The Jews were taken to Fort Ontario in Oswego, New York.
20. Ibid., p. 173.
21. Ibid., p. 215.
22. Ibid., pp. 128, 150, 158, 195, 200.
23. Ibid., p. 73.
24. Ibid., p. 195.
25. The section immediately before this section of the speech reads as follows: 'I also want to make reference before you here, in complete frankness, to a really grave matter. Among ourselves, this once it shall be uttered quite frankly; but in public we will never speak of it. Just as we did not hesitate on June 30, 1934, to do our duty as ordered, to stand up against the wall comrades who had transgressed and shoot them, so we have never talked about this and never will. It was the tact which I am glad to say is a matter of course to us that made us never discuss it among ourselves, never talk about it. Each of us shuddered, and yet each one knew that he would do it again if it were ordered and if it were necessary.' Dawidowicz, *A Holocaust Reader*, pp. 132–33.
26. *Hoax*, p. 193.
27. Ibid.
28. Ibid., p. 19.
29. Ibid., p. 179.
30. Ibid., p. 181.
31. Ibid., p. 195.
32. Ibid.

33. Ibid., p. 177.
34. Ibid., p. 158.
35. Ibid., p. 249.
36. Ibid., p. 87.
37. See Deborah Lipstadt, *Beyond Belief: The American Press and the Coming of the Holocaust, 1933–1945* (New York, 1986).
38. *Hoax*, p. 89.
39. Ibid., p. 145.
40. Ibid., p. 142.
41. Ibid.
42. Ibid., p. 145.
43. Hannah Arendt, *Eichmann in Jerusalem* (New York, 1963), p. 116.
44. *Hoax*, p. 217.
45. Ibid., p. 237.
46. Ibid., p. 242.
47. Ibid.
48. Ibid.
49. Ibid., pp. 242–43.
50. Ibid., p. 243.
51. Ibid.
52. Moberg, 'The Naysayer,' p. 43.

8. THE INSTITUTE FOR
HISTORICAL REVIEW

1. Lewis Brandon to Subscribers, Supplement to *Journal of Historical Review*, Apr. 16, 1981.
2. *Deposition of William David McCalden, aka Lewis Brandon, Mel Mermelstein v. Institute for Historical Review, et al.,* Superior Court of the State of California, No. C 356542 (hereafter cited as *McCalden Deposition*), vol. 1, Jan. 16, 1984, pp. 8, 37.
3. *Los Angeles Times*, May 3, 1981, part I, p. 3.
4. David McCalden, 'A Few Facts About the Institute for Historical Review [which they'd rather you didn't know]' (Manhattan Beach, Calif., n.d.).
5. *McCalden Deposition*, vol. 2, Feb. 8, 1984, pp. 272ff.
6. *Letter of IHR to All Interested Parties Intending to Claim $50,000 Reward*, Institute for Historical Review, Torrance, Calif., n.d.
7. *Questionnaire and Claim for $50,000 Reward*, Institute for Historical Review, Torrance, Calif., n.d.

8. Lewis Brandon to Mel Mermelstein, November 20, 1980, cited in *Declaration of William Cox regarding the Urgency of Proceedings in Mel Mermelstein v. Institute for Historical Review, et al.*, Superior Court of California, Case No. C 356542 (hereafter cited as *Declaration of William Cox*), Aug. 10, 1981, p. 16.

9. *Declaration of William Cox*, p. 18.

10. Brandon to Subscribers; *Los Angeles Times*, May 3, 1981.

11. Signed statement by Simon Wiesenthal, May 4, 1981.

12. *Jewish Telegraphic Agency Weekly News Digest*, May 13, 1983.

13. *Statement of Record and Letter of Apology to Mel Mermelstein*, signed by G. G. Baumen, Attorney for Legion for Survival of Freedom, Institute for Historical Review, Noontide Press, and Elisabeth Carto, and Mark F. Von Esch, Attorney for Liberty Lobby and Willis Carto, July 24, 1985.

14. *Appellant's Opening Brief, Mel Mermelstein v. Legion for the Survival of Freedom, etc., et al.*, May 4, 1992 (hereafter cited as *Appellant's Opening Brief, Mel Mermelstein v. Legion*), pp. 6ff.

15. *Declaration of William Cox*, p. 20.

16. Paul L. Berman, 'Gas Chamber Games: Crackpot History and the Right to Lie,' *Village Voice*, June 10–16, 1981, pp. 1, 37–43.

17. *IHR Newsletter* (Oct. 1988), p. 7.

18. *IHR Newsletter* (Apr. 1989), p. 1 (italics added).

19. Letter to students from Lewis Brandon on IHR letterhead, n.d.

20. Lewis Brandon, Director of IHR, to Friends of IHR, n.d. (apparently from winter 1980). 'Brandon' was so obsessed with the power of the 'Zionists' that he claimed that the symbols on grocery products denoting that they were kosher indicated that the company had 'paid a Zionist to "bless" the product.' *IHR Newsletter* (Feb. 15, 1981), p. 3.

21. *Declaration of William Cox*, p. 3; *IHR Newsletter* (Feb. 1989), p. 7.

22. *IHR Newsletter* (Feb. 1989), p. 7.

23. Tom Marcellus, Director IHR, to Revisionist Friends, July 1982, n.p. (italics added).

24. 'Holocaust "Revisionism": A Denial of History,' *ADL Facts*, vol. 26:2 (June 1980), p. 4.

25. For background on *Spotlight* and the way certain members of Congress have chosen to cooperate with it, see Mark Hosenball, 'Spotlight on the Hill,' *New Republic*, Sept. 9, 1981, pp. 13–14.

26. Joseph Trento and Joseph Spear, 'How Nazi Nut Power Has Invaded Capitol Hill,' *True*, Nov. 1969, p. 39.

27. Hosenball, 'Spotlight on the Hill,' p. 13.

28. Jason Berry, 'Carto's Day in Court,' *Cleveland Plain Dealer*, Sept. 14, 1991, pp. 1-D, 4-D.

29. 'Liberty Lobby and the Carto Network of Hate,' *ADL Facts*, vol. 27:2 (Winter 1982), p. 7.

30. *Liberty Lobby, Inc., v. Dow Jones & Co., Inc.*, 638 F. Supp. 1149, 1152 n. 5 (D.D.C. 1986), aff'd., 838 F. 2d 1287 (D.C. Cir. 1988) *cert. denied*, 488 U.S. 825 (1988), cited in *Appellant's Opening Brief, Mel Mermelstein v. Legion*, p. 5.

31. William F. Buckley, April 30, 1981, cited in 'Liberty Lobby and the Carto Network of Hate,' p. 18.

32. C. H. Simonds, 'The Strange Story of Willis Carto,' *National Review*, Sept. 10, 1971, pp. 984–85.

33. 'Liberty Lobby and the Carto Network of Hate,' p. 19.

34. Trento and Spear, 'How Nazi Nut Power,' p. 36.

35. Simonds, 'The Strange Story,' p. 979.

36. *The Monitor*, Nov. 1986, p. 6.

37. Simonds, 'The Strange Story,' p. 979.

38. Ibid.

39. Drew Pearson, April 17, 1969, cited in Charles Bermant, 'The Private World of Willis Carto,' *The Investigator*, Oct. 1981, p. 25. This memo by Carto was found by a Liberty Lobby staffer who turned it over to the investigative journalist, Drew Pearson. Carto's associates claim that the memoir was a fraud and the boxes in which it and other material was found were broken into by a thief paid by Pearson. What this argument fails to address is why, if the memo was a forgery, Carto was keeping it in his personal files.

40. Simonds, 'The Strange Story,' p. 979.

41. John C. Obert, 'Yockey: Profile of an American Hitler,' *The Investigator*, Oct. 1981, p. 24.

42. Ibid.

43. Ibid., p. 26.

44. Ibid., p. 22.

45. Ibid., p. 20.

46. Ibid., pp. 20, 22; Simonds, 'The Strange Story,' p. 980.

47. 'Liberty Lobby and the Carto Network of Hate,' p. 8.

48. Obert, 'Yockey: Profile,' p. 22.

49. Simonds, 'The Strange Story,' p. 981.

50. Obert, 'Yockey: Profile,' p. 73.

51. Berry, 'Carto's Day in Court,' p. 4-D.

52. Simonds, 'The Strange Story,' p. 986; Berry, 'Carto's Day in Court,' p. 4-D.

53. 'Holocaust "Revisionism,"' p. 4.

54. *American Mercury*, Summer 1979.

55. *Liberty Letter*, May 1969, July 1970, Sept. 1970; Simonds, 'The Strange Story,' p. 988.

56. *Spotlight*, Sept. 6, 1976.

57. Ibid., May 21, 1979; Bermant, 'The Private World,' p. 41.

58. *Spotlight*, Jan. 19, Jan. 26, Aug. 9, 1976.

59. Ibid., May 28, 1979.

60. Ibid., Feb. 5, 1979; Hosenball, 'Spotlight on the Hill,' p. 13.

61. *Spotlight*, Sept. 24, 1979, as cited in *ADL Facts*, vol. 26:2 (June 1980). See also 'The Spotlight: Liberty Lobby's Voice of Hate,' *ADL Facts*, vol. 26:1 (June 1980), and 'Liberty Lobby and the Carto Network of Hate.'

62. *Spotlight*, Mar. 11, 1985; Hosenball, 'Spotlight on the Hill,' p. 13.

63. *Spotlight*, Dec. 24, 1979.

64. Ibid., Mar. 23, 1981.

65. Kevin Flynn and Gary Gerhardt, *The Silent Brotherhood* (New York, 1989), p. 85.

66. *Noontide Press 1992 Catalog of Books, Audiotapes, Videotapes* (Costa Mesa, Calif., 1992).

67. *Plaintiff's Exhibit 22 (A-B), Mel Mermelstein v. Institute for Historical Review, et al., Defendants*, Feb. 8, 1984, Case No. C 356542.

68. The Liberty Lobby was recently left a bequest of seventy-five million dollars by the granddaughter of Thomas Alva Edison.

69. *IHR Newsletter* (Jan. 1989), p. 6.

70. *McCalden Deposition*, vol. 2, Feb. 8, 1984, p. 210.

71. *Liberty Lobby, Inc., v. Dow Jones & Co., Inc.*, 838 F. 2d 1287, 1296 (D.C. Cir. 1988), cited in *Appellant's Opening Brief, Mel Mermelstein v. Legion*, p. 5.

72. Ibid.

73. Letter to students by Lewis Brandon.

74. Barnes, 'Revisionism and the Promotion of Peace,' p. 52.

75. Ibid., pp. 53–56.

76. Mark Weber, 'Civil War Concentration Camps,' *Journal of Historical Review*, vol. 2, no. 2 (Summer 1981), p. 152.

77. Ibid., pp. 144, 152.

78. *Journal of Historical Review*, vol. 4, no. 4 (Winter 1983–84).

79. This was one of the unspoken objectives of the contemporary German historians' debate. Ernst Nolte has written that all the great

powers have had 'their own Hitler periods.' Josef Joffe, 'The Battle of the Historians,' *Encounter* (June 1987), p. 73. For further information on Nolte's and other German historians' relativism and its connection with denial see chapter 11.

9. THE GAS CHAMBER CONTROVERSY

1. Christof Friedrich and Eric Thomson, *The Hitler We Loved and Why* (Reedy, W.V., 1977), pp. 72, 78, 116.

2. Manuel Prutschi, 'The Zundel Affair,' in *Antisemitism in Canada*, ed. Alan Davies (Ontario, 1992), p. 264.

3. Zundel flyer addressed to 'Comrades,' cited in Prutschi, 'The Zundel Affair,' p. 258.

4. Alan Davies, 'A Tale of Two Trials: Antisemitism in Canada,' *Holocaust and Genocide Studies*, vol. 4 (1989), p. 77; *Toronto Globe*, Mar. 26, 1985; Prutschi, 'The Zundel Affair,' p. 267.

5. Mark Bonokoski, 'Neo Nazi Leads Protest,' *Toronto Sun*, April 19, 1978, cited in Prutschi, 'The Zundel Affair,' p. 273.

6. Leonidas E. Hill, 'The Trial of Ernst Zundel: Revisionism and the Law in Canada,' *Simon Wiesenthal Annual, 1989*, pp. 179, 192, 200.

7. *Calgary Herald*, Apr. 10, 1985, p. 1; *Toronto Globe and Mail*, Apr. 12, 1985, p. 3.

8. Alan T. Davies, 'The Queen Versus James Keegstra: Reflections on Christian Antisemitism in Canada,' *American Journal of Theology and Philosophy*, vol. 9, nos. 1, 2 (January–May 1988), p. 112.

9. *Red Deer Advocate*, June 4, 1984; *Toronto Globe and Mail*, Apr. 8, 11, and 12, 1985.

10. Claude Adams, 'Through the Fingers,' *Canadian Lawyer* (Apr. 1985), p. 18.

11. Kirk Makin, 'Douglas Christie, Counsel for the Defence,' *Ontario Lawyers Weekly*, Mar. 29, 1985, pp. 12, 13.

12. Stanley R. Barrett, *Is God a Racist? The Right Wing in Canada* (Toronto, 1988), p. 161. For analysis of how the trial was covered by the Canadian press see Gabriel Weimann and Conrad Winn, *Hate on Trial: The Zundel Affair, the Media, and Public Opinion in Canada* (New York, 1986).

13. *Calgary Herald*, March 24, 1985, p. E8.

14. Robert Faurisson, 'The Problem of the Gas Chambers,' *Journal of Historical Review* (Summer 1980), reprinted by the Institute for Historical Review in leaflet form.

15. Adams, 'Through the Fingers,' p. 18.
16. Martin Broszat, *Vierteljahrshefte für Zeitgeschichte* (October 1977), pp. 742, 769, cited in *Patterns of Prejudice*, no. 3–4 (1978), p. 8.
17. *Sunday Times*, July 10, 1977.
18. Ibid., June 12, 1977; July 10, 1977.
19. Robert Harris, *Selling Hitler* (New York, 1986), p. 189.
20. *Canadian Jewish News*, Mar. 16, 1989.
21. Ibid., *London Jewish Chronicle*, May 27, 1983.
22. *Spotlight*, June 1989.
23. *Daily Telegraph*, July 10, 1992.
24. 'David Irving,' Clipping Collection, Calgary Jewish Community Council, Alberta, Canada.
25. *Toronto Star*, April 20, 1988; Stephen Trombley, *The Execution Protocol: Inside America's Capital Punishment Industry* (New York, 1992), p. 85.
26. Robert Faurisson, 'Foreword,' *The Leuchter Report: The End of a Myth: An Engineering Report on the Alleged Execution Gas Chambers at Auschwitz, Birkenau, and Majdanek, Poland* (U.S.A., 1988) (hereafter cited as *Leuchter Report*), p. 1.
27. Robert Faurisson, 'The Zundel Trials [1985 and 1988],' *Journal of Historical Review* (Winter 1988–89), p. 429.
28. *Her Majesty the Queen vs. Ernst Zundel*, District Court of Ontario, 1988 (hereafter referred to as *Zundel*), p. 9037.
29. Fred Leuchter, 'Inside the Auschwitz "Gas Chambers,"' a paper published by the Institute for Historical Review (reprinted from *Journal of Historical Review*, Summer 1989), p. 3.
30. *Zundel*, pp. 8984, 9223. Shelly Z. Shapiro, transcripts of conversation between Fred Leuchter and Shelly Z. Shapiro, February 2, 1990.
31. *Leuchter Report*, p. 4.
32. Fred Leuchter, 'Inside the Auschwitz "Gas Chambers,"' p. 6.
33. *Leuchter Report*, p. 1.
34. Faurisson, 'The Zundel Trials,' p. 429.
35. *Zundel*, p. 9075.
36. Ibid., pp. 8962, 8969, 8972, 8978.
37. Ibid., p. 8973.
38. See testimony of Raul Hilberg at the first Zundel trial. *Her Majesty the Queen vs. Ernst Zundel*, District Court of Ontario, 1985, p. 1112; *Zundel*, pp. 9010, 9011, 9013.
39. *Zundel*, p. 9048 (italics added).

40. Shelly Shapiro, 'An Investigation,' in *Truth Prevails: Demolishing Holocaust Denial: The End of 'The Leuchter Report'*, ed. Shelly Shapiro (New York, 1990), p. 14; Arthur Goodman, 'Leuchter: Exposed and Discredited by the Court,' in Shapiro, ed., *Truth Prevails*, p. 78.

41. *Zundel*, p. 9056.

42. Ibid., pp. 8984, 9017, 9061, 9097, 9125, 9154, 9210, 9223.

43. Shapiro, ed., *Truth Prevails*, p. 56.

44. *Zundel*, pp. 8894–95.

45. Ibid., p. 8983.

46. Ibid., pp. 9052–53.

47. Ibid., pp. 9034, 9038.

48. Ibid., pp. 9049–50 (italics added).

49. Ibid., pp. 8976, 9052.

50. Ibid., p. 8951; Statement by E. I. Du Pont de Nemours & Company, Oct. 2, 1990, cited in Shapiro, ed., *Truth Prevails*, p. 28.

51. *Zundel*, p. 9009.

52. *Leuchter Report*, p. 10.

53. *Zundel*, pp. 9028, 9034.

54. Q. And that is all based on the assumption that the physical plan presently at that location in Poland is what was there in 1942, '43, '44 and '45? Is that right?
A. That is correct.
Zundel, p. 9018.

55. *Zundel*, p. 9107. Under further cross-examination Leuchter backed down from some of the conclusions he had drawn in the report. Echoing Faurisson he originally argued that the chambers could not have functioned as execution sites because those whose job it was to throw the Zyklon-B down the roof vents and verify that the prisoners inside had died would themselves have died from exposure to the cyanide gas. Under cross-examination the Crown Counsel easily got Leuchter to agree to the fallacy of this conclusion:
Q. So this stuff you told us about people on the roof who dropped the gas down and how they would be committing suicide, it would take a matter of minutes before the gas got to them, wouldn't it?
A. Unquestionably.
Q. So if they closed the vent and got off the roof, there would be nothing to concern them, would there?
A. If they got off the roof. But at some point they have to do an inspection to determine whether the parties are deceased.

Q. They send in the *Sonderkommandos* to do that, sir, and they don't care what happens to them.

A. Right, all right.

Q. So if someone's on the roof with a gas mask, you agree that they've got all kinds of time to get off the roof after they've closed the vent?

A. Perhaps.

Zundel, p. 9254.

56. Jean-Claude Pressac, *Auschwitz: Technique and Operation of the Gas Chambers* (New York, 1989) (hereafter cited as *Technique*), p. 15.

57. *Zundel*, pp. 8991ff.

58. Jean-Claude Pressac, 'The Deficiencies and Inconsistencies of "The Leuchter Report,"' in Shapiro, ed., *Truth Prevails*, p. 45.

59. *Zundel*, pp. 9245ff.

60. Ibid., pp. 9251–52.

61. There were a total of five crematoria in Auschwitz/Birkenau.

62. Pressac, 'Deficiencies,' p. 40.

63. Ibid., p. 41.

64. Ibid., p. 49.

65. Ibid., p. 46.

66. Jean-Claude Pressac, 'Additional Notes: Leuchter's Videotape: A Witness to Fraud,' in Shapiro, ed., *Truth Prevails*, p. 62.

67. *Zundel*, pp. 9044, 9063.

68. Memorandum from Ed Carnes, Alabama Assistant Attorney General, to all Capital Punishment States, July 20, 1990 (hereafter cited as Carnes); Shapiro, ed., *Truth Prevails*, pp. 17, 21; *Newsweek*, Oct. 22, 1990, p. 64; *Swampscott Journal*, Nov. 1, 1990.

69. Associated Press, Oct. 24, 1990.

70. Carnes, p. 2.

71. Shapiro, ed., *Truth Prevails*, p. 22.

72. *Leuchter Report*, p. 7; *Zundel*, p. 9058.

73. Gary T. Dixon to Shelly Z. Shapiro, Sept. 24, 1990, reprinted in Shapiro, ed., *Truth Prevails*, p. 19.

74. Ibid., p. 20.

75. Ibid.

76. Ibid., p. 10.

77. Ibid., pp. 18–20. It was Missouri State Penitentiary Warden Bill Armontrout who, in response to Robert Faurisson's request for an expert on executions, suggested that Leuchter be contacted. Bill Armontrout to Barbara Kulaszka, Jan. 13, 1988, *Leuchter Report*, app. 7.

78. *New York Times*, Oct. 13, 1990, pp. 1, 7; Trombley, *The Execution Protocol*, p. 157.

79. Susan Lehman, 'Justice: A Matter of Engineering: Capital Punishment as a Technical Problem,' *Atlantic Monthly*, Feb. 1990, p. 28.

80. Shapiro, ed., *Truth Prevails*, pp. 14–15.

81. Lehman, 'Justice: A Matter of Engineering,' p. 28.

82. Shelly Z. Shapiro to Daniel Kelley, Apr. 16, 1990; Fred A. Leuchter to Ernst Zundel, May 14, 1988, *Leuchter Report*, app. 6. See also *Leuchter Report*, p. 15.

83. *Washington Post*, June 18, 1991.

84. Consent Agreement, *Commonwealth of Massachusetts v. Fred A. Leuchter, Jr.*, June 11, 1991; *Jewish Telegraphic Agency*, June 13, 1991. Since the agreement Leuchter signed was with Massachusetts, its provisions applied only to that state.

85. *Technique*, p. 545.

86. *Le Matin*, Nov. 16, 1978; *Le Monde*, Dec. 29, 1978, Jan. 16, 1979; *Technique*, p. 546.

87. *Technique*, p. 546.

88. Ibid., p. 548.

89. Ibid.

90. Ibid.

91. 'Natzweiler-Struthof,' *Encyclopedia of the Holocaust*, p. 1039.

92. Serge Thion, *Vérité Historique*, quoted in *Technique*, p. 548.

93. Ibid.

94. Robert Faurisson, 'Talking About Holocaust Revisionism on French Radio,' *Revisionist Letters*, vol. 1, no. 1 (Spring 1989), p. 11.

95. Ibid.

96. Phone conversation with Editorial Offices, *Atlantic Monthly*, Feb. 1990.

97. Lehman, 'Justice: A Matter of Engineering,' pp. 26ff.

98. Bradley R. Smith, 'Commentary,' *Visalia Times-Delta*, Sept. 13, 1990.

99. Phone conversation with Editorial Offices, *Atlantic Monthly*, Feb. 1990.

100. Phone interviews with Shelly Shapiro, Feb. 1990, Apr. 1990.

101. Charles R. Allen, Jr., 'The Role of the Media in the Leuchter Matter: Hyping a Holocaust Denier,' in Shapiro, ed., *Truth Prevails*, pp. 112–13.

102. *Village Voice*, May 22, 30, 1990; Allen, 'The Role of the Media,' pp. 118–19.

103. *New York Times*, Oct. 13, 1990, pp. 1, 7.

104. Allen, 'The Role of the Media,' p. 121; *New York Times*, Oct. 18, 1990, reprinted in *International Herald Tribune*, Oct. 19, 1990.

105. *Searchlight*, Aug. 1989.

106. David Irving, 'Foreword,' *Auschwitz the End of the Line: The Leuchter Report* (London, 1989), p. 6.

107. *Times* (London), May 11, 1992.

108. Irving, 'Foreword,' *Auschwitz: The End of the Line*, p. 6.

109. Early Day Motion no. 99, 'David Irving and Holocaust Denial,' House of Commons, June 20, 1989, Session 1988–1989.

110. *Times* (London), May 14, 1992.

111. *Independent*, July 11, 1992.

112. Trombley, *The Execution Protocol*, pp. 23–43.

113. Ibid., pp. 87–94; *New York Times Book Review*, Nov. 22, 1992, p. 33.

114. *New York Review of Books*, June 15, 1989.

10. THE BATTLE FOR THE CAMPUS

1. Cited in Nat Hentoff, 'An Ad that Offends: Who's On First?' *Progressive*, May 12, 1992, p. 12.

2. Smith was featured on a variety of national television shows and in major newspapers, including the *New York Times*, Dec. 23, 1991.

3. *Louisiana State Daily Reveille*, Apr. 7, 1992.

4. *Holocaust Revisionism: Reinventing the Big Lie* (ADL Research Report), p. 9.

5. ADL memorandum, Feb. 26, 1987.

6. *IHR Newsletter*, Jan., Mar., and Sept. 1987; Jan. and Nov. 1988; Feb. 1989.

7. Undated letter, Bradley Smith to Friends, 5 pp. (1988?).

8. *Prima Facie* (Feb. 1985), p. 1.

9. *Spearhead* (Mar. 1985), p. 20.

10. *Christian News*, Apr. 25, 1987.

11. *Spotlight*, Apr. 11, 1988.

12. *Christian News*, Sept. 14, 1987.

13. *University of Nebraska Sower*, Nov. 17, 1989, p. 10.

14. *Centre Daily Times* (State College, Pa.), Apr. 1, 1989.

15. Bradley Smith to Kathy Lachenauer, editor in chief, *Stanford Daily*, June 16, 1989.

16. Bradley Smith to Rabbi Ari Cartun, June 19, 1989.

17. Laird Wilcox, 'The Spectre Haunting Holocaust Revisionism,' *Revisionist Letters* (Spring 1989), p. 10.

18. Ibid.

19. *Visalia Times-Delta*, Sept. 13, 1990; *Daily Illini*, June 16, 1992.

20. *New York Times*, Dec. 23, 1991.

21. Bradley R. Smith, 'The Holocaust Story: How Much is False? The Case for Open Debate,' *Daily Northwestern*, Apr. 4, 1991.

22. *New York Times*, Nov. 12, 1989.

23. Arno Mayer (Princeton University), Yehuda Bauer (Hebrew University), Marvin Hier (Simon Wiesenthal Center), Raul Hilberg (University of Vermont), and myself (Emory University).

24. Smith, 'The Holocaust Story.'

25. The first paper to run the lengthy ad was the *Daily Northwestern*, April 4, 1991.

26. *Michigan Daily*, Oct. 24, 1991.

27. *Detroit Free Press*, Oct. 25, 1991.

28. *Michigan Daily*, Oct. 25, 1991.

29. *Detroit Free Press*, Oct. 25, 1991.

30. *Michigan Daily*, Oct. 28, 1992.

31. In recent years a series of First Amendment controversies have captured the attention of the American public. The most highly publicized was the debate over the funding by the National Endowment for the Arts of an exhibit of Robert Mapplethorpe photography. Edward de Grazia, *Girls Lean Back Everywhere: The Laws of Obscenity and the Assault on Genius* (New York, 1992); Natalie Robins, *Alien Ink: The FBI's War on Freedom of Expression* (New York, 1992); Rodney A. Smolla, *Free Speech in an Open Society* (New York, 1992).

32. *New York Times*, Jan. 15, 1992.

33. Kathleen M. Sullivan, 'The First Amendment Wars,' *New Republic*, Sept. 28, 1991, p. 39.

34. *Duke Chronicle*, Nov. 5, 1991.

35. Ibid., Nov. 7, 1991.

36. *Cornell Daily Sun*, Nov. 18, 1991; Associated Press newswire, Nov. 19, 1991.

37. *Rutgers Daily Targum*, Nov. 26, 1991, p. 6.

38. *Chronicle of Higher Education*, Nov. 27, 1991.

39. Havre, Mont., *Daily News*, Apr. 29, 1992. One of the defenders of the *Kaimin*'s publication of the ad was the programming adviser of the university's student organization. He had also been instrumental

in arranging for a visit by David Duke to the Missoula campus. He argued that ads such as Smith's and visits such as Duke's challenge 'people to not react emotionally and react rationally.' *Montana Kaimin*, May 5, 1992.

40. *Atlanta Constitution*, Mar. 23, 1992.
41. *Student Life*, Feb. 18, 1992.
42. *St. Louis Post Dispatch*, Feb. 23, 1992.
43. *University of Washington Daily*, Apr. 27, 1992.
44. *Columbus Dispatch*, Jan. 22, 1992.
45. *Ohio Jewish Chronicle*, Jan. 30, 1992, p. 1.
46. Ibid., Jan. 30, 1992.
47. *Columbus Dispatch*, Jan. 22, 1992.
48. *Ohio State Lantern*, Jan. 24, 1992, p. 8.
49. Ibid.
50. Ibid. Tufts's dean of students also strongly dissented from the idea that Smith was protected by the First Amendment: 'Individuals have a right to their own ideas but not to be published on another individual's or group's printing press.' *Tufts Daily*, Apr. 8, 1992.
51. *University of Tennessee Daily Beacon*, Apr. 27, 1992.
52. *Penn State Daily Collegian*, Mar. 31, 1989.
53. *Harvard Crimson*, Dec. 10, 1991, p. 2.
54. *University of Chicago Maroon*, Feb. 28, 1992.
55. *Cornell Daily Sun*, Nov. 20, 1991.
56. *Chronicle of Higher Education*, Nov. 27, 1991.
57. Mark Livingston to Sam Cramer, Nov. 6, 1991.
58. *Michigan Daily*, Oct. 28, 1991.
59. *Student Life*, Feb. 21, 1992.
60. Ibid., Feb. 25, 1992.
61. *Daily Tar Heel*, cited in *Atlanta Constitution*, Nov. 28, 1991, p. H1.
62. Ibid.
63. *Duke Chronicle*, Nov. 5, 1991, p. 9, and Nov. 7, 1991, pp. 1, 3.
64. Resolution adopted by the Duke University History Department, Nov. 8, 1991, and reprinted in *Duke Chronicle*, Nov. 13, 1991.
65. *Rutgers Daily Targum*, Nov. 6, 1991, pp. 1, 6 (italics added).
66. *Cornell Daily Sun*, Nov. 18, 1991 (italics added).
67. *University of Washington Daily*, Apr. 27, 1992 (italics added).
68. Ibid., Mar. 4, 1992.
69. Ibid., Apr. 27, 1992.
70. Ibid., Oct. 18 and 28, 1991.
71. *Michigan Daily*, Nov. 11, 1991.

72. Havre, Mont., *Daily News*, Apr. 29, 1992.
73. *St. Louis Post Dispatch*, Feb. 22, 1992.
74. *Ohio State Lantern*, Jan. 24, 1992.
75. *Student Life*, Feb. 18, 1992.
76. Ibid.
77. *Duke Chronicle*, Nov. 5, 1991, p. 9.
78. Livingston to Cramer, Nov. 6, 1991.
79. *Duke Chronicle*, Nov. 7, 1991, p. 3.
80. Ibid., Nov. 5, 1991, p. 9, and Nov. 7, 1991, pp. 1, 3 (italics added).
81. Ibid., Nov. 21, 1991, p. 3.
82. Ibid., Nov. 13, 1991, p. 7 (italics added).
83. *Harvard Crimson*, Dec. 10, 1991, p. 2.
84. Ibid.
85. *Boston Jewish Advocate*, Mar. 6, 1992.
86. *Brown Daily Herald*, Dec. 11, 1991.
87. *University of California at Santa Barbara Daily Nexus*, Apr. 29, 1992.
88. *Dartmouth Review*, Nov. 6, 1991, p. 9.
89. *University of Chicago Maroon*, Feb. 28, 1992.
90. *Chronicle of Higher Education*, Nov. 27, 1991.
91. *Jewish Voice* (Dec. 1991).
92. *Chronicle of Higher Education*, Nov. 27, 1991.
93. *Washington Post*, Dec. 21, 1991.
94. Smith, 'Falsus in Uno, Falsus in Omnibus ... The "Human Soap" Holocaust Myth,' addendum to Smith, undated letter sent to campus papers.
95. *New York Times*, Jan. 15, 1992.
96. *Rutgers Daily Targum*, Dec. 3, 1991, p. 10.
97. *Michigan Daily*, Dec. 3, 1991, p. 3.
98. *Rutgers Daily Targum*, Dec. 3, 1991, p. 10.
99. *New York Times*, Dec. 30, 1991.
100. Ibid., Jan. 15, 1992.
101. *Rutgers Daily Targum*, Dec. 3, 1991, pp. 10–11.
102. Ibid., Dec. 6, 1991, p. 5.
103. *Tufts Daily*, April 21, 1992.
104. Ibid.
105. Smith, undated letter sent to campus papers with text of second ad.
106. Smith, 'Falsus in Uno, Falsus in Omnibus.'
107. *Ohio State Lantern*, Apr. 29, 1992.
108. *Michigan Daily*, Nov. 26, 1991.

109. *Houston Chronicle*, Dec. 11, 1991.
110. Meeting with members of *Daily Texan* editorial board, Apr. 28, 1992.
111. *Houston Chronicle*, Apr. 24, 1992, pp. 25A, 31A; *Daily Texan*, Apr. 24, 1992, p. 5.
112. Bay City, Tex., *Daily Trubune*, Apr. 30, 1992.
113. 'Journal of Historical Review,' *OAH Newsletter* (July 1980), pp. 14–15; Dawidowicz, 'Lies About the Holocaust,' p. 37.
114. Carl N. Degler, 'Bad History,' *Commentary*, June 1981, p. 17.
115. Ibid.
116. *Chronicle of Higher Education*, Dec. 11, 1991.
117. *Duke Chronicle*, Apr. 27, 1992.
118. *Chronicle of Higher Education*, Jan. 8, 1992.
119. Ibid., Dec. 11, 1991.
120. *OAH Newsletter* (Nov. 1991); *Chronicle of Higher Education*, Dec. 11, 1991, pp. 9–10.
121. *Chronicle of Higher Education*, Dec. 11, 1991, p. 10.
122. Other signatories included Dan Carter, Cullom Davis, Sara Evans, Linda Gordon, Lawrence Levine, and Mary Ryan. *OAH Newsletter* (Feb. 1992), p. 5.
123. Ibid.
124. *Daily Northwestern*, Mar. 5, 1991, p. 6.
125. *OAH Newsletter* (Feb. 1992), p. 4. Conversation with Joyce Appleby, December 1992.
126. *Los Angeles Times*, Dec. 23, 1991.
127. *Ohio State Lantern*, Jan. 24, 1992, p. 8.
128. Carlos C. Huerta, 'Revisionism, Free Speech and the Campus,' *Midstream*, Apr. 1992, p. 10.

11. WATCHING ON THE RHINE

1. Hellmut Diwald, *Geschichte der Deutschen* (Frankfurt, 1978), pp. 15–16.
2. *New Statesman*, Sept. 21, 1979.
3. Geoffrey Hartman, ed., *Bitburg in Moral and Political Perspective* (Bloomington, Ind., 1986); Ilya Levkov, ed., *Bitburg and Beyond: Encounters in American, German, and Jewish History* (New York, 1987); Deborah E. Lipstadt, 'The Bitburg Controversy,' in David Singer, ed., *American Jewish Year Book, 1987* (New York, 1987), pp. 21–38.

4. *Die Welt*, Jan. 19, 1987; *Frankfurter Rundschau*, Jan. 14, 1987, cited in Richard Evans, *In Hitler's Shadow* (New York, 1989), p. 19. See Evans, *In Hitler's Shadow*, p. 147, n. 46, for additional references to Strauss's remarks on this topic.

5. Andreas Hillgruber, *Zweierlei Untergang: Die Zerschlagung des deutschen Reiches und das Ende des europäischen Judentums* (Berlin, 1986). For an evaluation of Hillgruber's contribution to the field see Holger Herwig, 'Andreas Hillgruber, Historian of "Grossmacht-politik," 1871–1945,' *Central European History*, vol. 15 (1982), pp. 186–98.

6. Evans, *In Hitler's Shadow*, pp. 49–54.

7. Maier, *The Unmasterable Past*, p. 20.

8. For various perspectives on Hillgruber's contribution to this imbroglio see Maier, *The Unmasterable Past*, pp. 21–25; Martin Broszat, *Die Zeit*, Oct. 3, 1986; Gordon Craig, 'The War of the German Historians,' *New York Review of Books*, Jan. 15, 1987. One of Hillgruber's most virulent critics was Jürgen Habermas, Germany's most prominent philosopher on the left. He was the one who first called attention to this debate, describing Hillgruber's work as 'scandalous.' *Die Zeit*, July 11, 1986; *Frankfurter Allgemeine Zeitung* (hereafter referred to as *FAZ*), July 8, 1986. For a summary and analysis of Habermas's response see Maier, *The Unmasterable Past*, pp. 39–42.

9. Michael Stürmer, *Dissonanzen des Fortschritts*, pp. 267, 269–70 as cited in Evans, p. 21. See also Evans, *In Hitler's Shadow*, pp. 103, 173, n. 14.

10. Ernst Nolte, *Three Faces of Fascism: Action Française, Italian Fascism, National Socialism* (New York, 1965).

11. Joachim Fest, *FAZ*, Aug. 29, 1986.

12. Peter Pulzer, 'The Nazi Legacy,' *The Listener*, June 25, 1987.

13. Anton Kaes, *From Hitler to Heimat: The Return of History as Film* (Cambridge, 1989), pp. 5–6.

14. Evans, *In Hitler's Shadow*, p. 87.

15. Ernst Nolte, 'Vergangenheit, die nicht vergehen will' (The past that refuses to pass away), *FAZ*, June 6, 1986; Ernst Nolte, *Der europäische Bürgerkrieg, 1917–1945* (The European Civil War, 1917–1945) (Berlin, 1987), pp. 502–4.

16. Eberhard Jäckel, 'Die elende Praxis der Untersteller,' *Die Zeit*, Sept. 12, 1986; Craig, 'The War of the German Historians,' p. 17; Maier, *The Unmasterable Past*, pp. 76–77.

17. Maier, *The Unmasterable Past*, p. 76.
18. Michael Marrus, *The Holocaust in History* (Hanover, N.H., 1987), p. 24. For a more complete discussion of this point see Maier, *The Unmasterable Past*, pp. 66–99, and Evans, *In Hitler's Shadow*, pp. 66–91.
19. Maier, *The Unmasterable Past*, pp. 74–75.
20. Ernst Nolte, 'Between Myth and Revisionism?' in *Aspects of the Third Reich*, ed. H. W. Koch (London, 1985), p. 27; Maier, *The Unmasterable Past*, p. 29.
21. Nolte, *Bürgerkrieg*, pp. 500, 509–13, 592–93, nn. 26, 29; Evans, *In Hitler's Shadow*, p. 168, n. 28.
22. Nolte, *Bürgerkrieg*, pp. 317–18; also Nolte, 'Vergangenheit'; Evans, *In Hitler's Shadow*, p. 152, n. 20.
23. Evans, *In Hitler's Shadow*, p. 123.
24. For discussion of another way the 'yes, but' syndrome manifested itself during the war and prevented many Americans, particularly publishers, editors, and reporters, from grasping the implications of the reports they were receiving, see Lipstadt, *Beyond Belief*, p. 270.
25. *Jewish Telegraphic Agency*, Mar. 17, 1992.
26. According to Stephen J. Roth, only two of the laws, the French and Romanian, make specific reference to antisemitism. Stephen J. Roth, 'Denial of the Holocaust as an Issue of Law' (to be published in *Israel Yearbook of Human Rights*).
27. *U.S. Newswire*, Aug. 27, 1992; *Jewish Telegraphic Agency*, Aug. 28, 1992.
28. It also offered a critique of the Nuremberg trials which 'astounded' those present in the courtroom (*Jewish Telegraphic Agency*, Apr. 19, 1991).
29. *Wall Street Journal*, Apr. 9, 1985.
30. 'Morning Edition,' National Public Radio, December 1992.
31. *Spotlight*, June 1, 1992.
32. Ronald K. L. Collins, 'Tort Case as Gag Device,' *National Law Journal*, June 15, 1992, p. 15.
33. *Toronto Sun*, Oct. 15, 1992; *Jewish Telegraphic Agency*, Nov. 16, 1992.

APPENDIX

1. Document No. NI-9912, cited in *Technique*, p. 18.
2. Ibid., p. 19.

3. Ibid., pp. 16, 165.
4. Robert Faurisson, *Reply to Pierre Vidal-Naquet*, quoted in *Technique*, p. 505.
5. Pressac, 'Deficiencies,' p. 38; *Technique*, p. 16.
6. *Technique*, p. 18.
7. *Le Monde*, Jan 16, 1979, p. 13; *Technique*, p. 429.
8. *Technique*, p. 165.
9. Ibid., p. 429.
10. Ibid.
11. Ibid.
12. Auschwitz State Museum (Panstwowe Muzeum Oswiecim [PMO], file BW 30/40, p. 100; *Technique*, pp. 430–32.
13. *Technique*, p. 503.
14. Ibid., p. 548.
15. Faurisson, *Statement for the Defense*, cited in *Technique*, p. 505.
16. Faurisson, *Reply to Pierre Vidal-Naquet*, p. 78.
17. *Technique*, p. 554.
18. PMO file BW 30/28, p. 73, cited in *Technique*, p. 553.
19. PMO file BW 30/28, p. 68, cited in ibid., p. 555.
20. *Technique*, p. 554. When he discovered this document Pressac confronted Faurisson and told him that because of the many references to gas in the museum archives he no longer believed Faurisson's thesis was valid.
21. *Technique*, p. 367.
22. Ibid., p. 432.
23. PMO file BW 30/25, p. 7, cited in *Technique*, p. 432.
24. Ibid., pp. 434, 438.
25. PMO file BW 30/25, p. 7, cited in *Technique*, pp. 367, 432.
26. BW 30/34, pp. 49, 50, cited in *Technique*, pp. 434, 438–39.
27. *Technique*, pp. 434, 436, 438–39.
28. Bauleitung drawing 252, PMO neg. no. 20943/181, reproduced in *Technique*, p. 512.
29. Bauleitung drawing 3764, PMO file BW 2/38, reproduced in *Technique*, p. 514.
30. March 29, 1944, *Diary of Anne Frank: The Critical Edition* (New York, 1989), p. 578 (hereafter cited as *Diary of Anne Frank*).
31. Gerrold van der Stroom, 'The Diaries, *Het Achterhuis* and the Translations,' in *Diary of Anne Frank*, pp. 59–61.
32. Ibid., p. 63.

33. *New York Times Book Review*, June 15, 1952; *Congress Weekly*, Nov. 13, 1950; *National Jewish Post*, June 30, 1952; David Barnouw, 'The Play,' in *Diary of Anne Frank*, p. 78.

34. *New York Law Journal*, Feb. 27, 1959, cited in Barnouw, 'The Play,' p. 80.

35. *New York Times*, Nov. 27, 1966; Meyer Levin, *The Obsession* (New York, 1973), p. 262.

36. David Barnouw, 'Attacks on the Authenticity of the Diary,' in *Diary of Anne Frank*, p. 84.

37. Ibid.

38. Ibid., pp. 84–89.

39. Teressa Hendry, 'Was Anne Frank's Diary a Hoax?' *American Mercury* (Summer 1967), reprinted in *Myth of the Six Million*, pp. 109–111.

40. Harwood, *Did Six Million Really Die?*, p. 19.

41. *Hoax*, p. 37.

42. Ditlieb Felderer, *Anne Frank's Diary – A Hoax?* (Taby, Sweden, 1978). When the book was reprinted by the IHR the question mark was omitted from the title.

43. Dec. 6, 1943, *Diary of Anne Frank*, pp. 424, 425.

44. Robert Faurisson, *Le Journal d'Anne Frank est-il authentique?* in Serge Thion, ed., *Vérité historique or vérité politique?* (Paris, 1980); Barnouw, 'Attacks on the Authenticity,' pp. 94–95.

45. Aug. 5, 1943, *Diary of Anne Frank*, p. 385.

46. Dec. 6, 1943, ibid., p. 424.

47. Nov. 9, 1943, ibid., p. 301.

48. Robert Faurisson, *Het Dagboek van Anne Frank – een vervalsing* (*The Diary of Anne Frank – a forgery*) (Antwerp, 1985), p. 18, cited in Barnouw, 'Attacks on the Authenticity', p. 95.

49. Barnouw, 'Attacks on the Authenticity,' p. 96.

50. Opinion of Federal Criminal Investigation Bureau, May 28, 1980; Hamburg, Landgericht, Romer/Geiss dossier, cited in Barnouw, 'Attacks on the Authenticity,' pp. 97–98.

51. Barnouw, 'Attacks on the Authenticity,' p. 99.

52. *Der Spiegel*, Oct. 6, 1980, cited in ibid., p. 98.

53. H. J. J. Hardy, 'Document Examination and Handwriting Identification of the Text Known as the Diary of Anne Frank: Summary of Findings,' in *Diary of Anne Frank*, p. 164.

Index